MW01074960

DESERT DAYS

| Praise for *Desert Days*

"*Desert Days* brings to life the field memoirs of the most important figure in Egyptian prehistory since the 1960s. With his captivating narrative style, Fred Wendorf brings us closer to an understanding of his charming, persistent, almost stubborn determination to find hard evidence in his search for signs of peoples who are long gone in Egypt's starkly barren Sahara. Wendorf's uncompromising tenacity over forty years in the desert and along the banks of the Nile has changed almost all of what we knew about Egyptian prehistory."—**Fekri Hassan**, Petri Professor of Archaeology Emeritus, University of London

"Celebrated by his colleagues in the Americas, Europe, and Africa as a brilliant innovator who made significant advances in archaeological method and theory, Fred Wendorf has been a dominant figure in American and North African archaeology in an extremely productive career spanning nearly six decades. His engaging autobiography chronicles his personal and professional lives—warts and all."—**Don D. Fowler**, Mamie Kleberg Distinguished Professor of Anthropology Emeritus, University of Nevada–Reno

"Wendorf's rousing good story of archaeological adventures in harsh desert environments demonstrates that real archaeological adventures are only made possible by good planning, sound organization, scientific discipline, and hard work."—**Raymond H. Thompson**, Riecker Professor of Anthropology Emeritus, and Director Emeritus, Arizona State Museum, University of Arizona

"Fred Wendorf's memoir is unique in the literature of American archaeology. A fascinating read."—**Lewis Binford**, University Distinguished Professor Emeritus, Southern Methodist University

"This is a wonderful story of an archaeologist uncommonly driven to understand the past, a rare inspiring story of a scholar whose intellectual commitment burns bright, reminding us of why we went into archaeology in the first place."—**Stuart Struever**, founding director of the Center for American Archaeology in Kampsville, Illinois, and former president of the Crow Canyon Archaeological Center in Cortez, Colorado

"This is a fabulous and fascinating work. Its publication is a significant contribution to the history of archaeology. It will be a must read for not only archaeologists but for Quaternary geologists, paleontologists, paleoecologists, polynologists, and others. "— **C. Vance Haynes, Jr.**, Regents' Professor Emeritus, University of Arizona

"The academically indifferent teenager who went off to war and, by the grace of just a few inches, came back mauled but alive, was determined to make good his childhood goal of becoming an archaeologist. That Fred Wendorf succeeded beyond measure is clear, though as this unflinching memoir reveals, it was not always a smooth ride—either professionally or personally. But what a ride. At times hair-raising, self-deprecating, funny, humbling, and even painfully self-critical, *Desert Days* is a life honestly appraised. There's almost a Forrest Gump–like quality to Fred's life, in all the exceptional people and seminal events that have been a part of it. He was no mere passive witness to history (or, for that matter, prehistory). As *Desert Days* shows, he helped make it."—**David Meltzer**, Henderson-Morrison Professor of Prehistory, Southern Methodist University, and Director, QUEST Archaeological Research Program

Fred Wendorf in his study in August, 1987, four months after his election to the National Academy of Sciences. *Photo courtesy of SMU Photographic Office.*

DESERT DAYS
My Life as a Field Archaeologist

FRED WENDORF

Introduction by Romuald Schild

•

Published in cooperation with the
William P. Clements Center for Southwest Studies

SOUTHERN METHODIST UNIVERSITY PRESS
Dallas

Copyright © 2008 by Fred Wendorf
Introduction © 2008 by Romuald Schild
First edition, 2008
All rights reserved

Requests for permission to reproduce material from this work should be sent to:
    Rights and Permissions
    Southern Methodist University Press
    PO Box 750415
    Dallas, Texas 75275-0415

Cover photograph: Two Late Paleolithic burials dating 13,700 years ago in the Jebel Sahaba graveyard north of Wadi Halfa. Pencils indicate the numerous projectile "points" embedded in the skeletons. Since these points occur in many skeletons in the graveyard, Jebel Sahaba may represent man's earliest known organized warfare. *Photo by Fred Wendorf.*

Jacket and text design by Tom Dawson

Library of Congress Cataloging-in-Publication Data
Wendorf, Fred.
    Desert days : my life as a field archaeologist / Fred Wendorf ; introduction by Romuald Schild.
    — 1st ed.
        p. cm.
    "Published in cooperation with the William P. Clements Center for Southwest Studies."
    Includes bibliographical references and index.
    ISBN 978-0-87074-524-9 (alk. paper)
    1. Wendorf, Fred. 2. Archaeologists—United States—Biography. 3. Southwest, New—
Antiquities. 4. Indians of North America—Southwest, New—Antiquities. 5. Archaeology
—Southwest, New—Field work. 6. Africa, North—Antiquities. 7. Archaeology—Africa,
North—Field work. I. Title.
    CC115.W39A3 2008
    930.1092—dc22
    [B]

                                                                            2008029886

Printed in the United States of America on acid-free paper

10 9 8 7 6 5 4 3 2 1

To my children, Carl, Mike, Gail, Cindy, Kelly, and Scott,
who suffered my absences and my passion for antiquity
with graceful acceptance, who tolerated my mistakes as a parent
and grew up well despite them, and who continue to be
the most delightful discoveries of my life.

A Partial List of Publications Written, Edited, or Compiled by Fred Wendorf

A Report on the Excavation of a Small Ruin near Point of Pines, East Central Arizona (1950)

Archaeological Studies in the Petrified Forest National Monument (1953)

The Midland Discovery: A Report on the Pleistocene Human Remains from Midland, Texas (1955)
With A. D. Krieger, C. C. Albritton, and T. D. Stewart

Paleoecology of the Llano Estacado (1961)

Contributions to the Prehistory of Nubia (1965)

The Prehistory of Nubia (1968)

A Middle Stone Age Sequence from the Central Rift Valley of Ethiopia (1974)
With R. Schild and C. C. Albritton

The Prehistory of the Nile Valley (1976)
With R. Schild

Prehistory of the Eastern Sahara (1980)
With R. Schild

The Prehistory of Wadi Kubbaniya (1989)
With R. Schild and A. E. Close, assemblers and editors

Egypt during the Last Interglacial: The Middle Paleolithic of Bir Tarfawi and Bir Sahara East (1993)
With R. Schild and others

Holocene Settlement of the Egyptian Sahara, Volume 1: The Archaeology of Nabta Playa (2001)
With R. Schild and Associates

The Fort Burgwin Research Center (2007)
With James E. Brooks

Contents

Chronology of My Life and Career |

July 31, 1924: Born Denver Fred Wendorf, Jr., in Terrell, Texas; only child of Margaret Hall Wendorf and Denver Fred Wendorf.

1932: Parents divorce; beginning interest in archaeology.

August 1936: Meets amateur archaeologist R. King Harris.

1939: Meets first professional archaeologist, William Dutton; visits Dutton's excavations on the Sabine River.

1940: Graduates from high school; attends Texas Military College in Terrell for two years; works for JCPenney.

1941: Attack on Pearl Harbor; United States at war.

1942: Begins classes in anthropology at University of Arizona; meets future wife Nancy Moon. Enlists in the army.

January 1943: Reports for active duty to infantry basic training at Camp Robinson, Arkansas. Is selected for infantry officers' training; is sent for a year to Camp Fannin in Texas, as an instructor.

August 1944: Applies for pilot training to Army Air Corps, but is reassigned to infantry in the Ninety-seventh Division at Fort Leonard Wood, Missouri, and then to Officers' Candidate School at Fort Benning, Georgia.

November 1944: Is commissioned a second lieutenant; volunteers for overseas assignment with 10th Mountain Division; leads the First Platoon, Company G, Eighty-sixth Mountain Infantry Regiment. Departs for Italy.

March 3, 1945: Is severely wounded in Italy; spends next two years in army general hospitals in Texas, Utah, and Michigan.

December 10, 1945: Marries Nancy Moon.

January 1947: Returns to Tucson to finish undergraduate degree at University of Arizona.

June 1947: Attends University of Arizona Archaeology Field School at Point of Pines on the San Carlos Apache Reservation in east-central Arizona; meets Alfred V. Kidder.

August–September 1947: Spends five weeks studying pottery typology with Harold S. Colton, director of the Museum of Northern Arizona.

September 1947–May 1948: Writes report on the pueblo and pit houses excavated at Point of Pines.

January 1948: Applies to graduate school at Harvard and University of Michigan.

May 1948: Receives BA in anthropology from University of Arizona.

June 1948: Becomes assistant to Stanley Stubbs, director of the University of New Mexico Archaeological Field School in Tijeras Canyon.

August 1948: Begins studies at Harvard.

June 1949: Begins dissertation research at Petrified Forest National Monument; receives grants from Wenner-Gren Foundation and Colt Archaeological Institute. Excavates Flattop Site.

April 1950: Passes Harvard General Exam in Anthropology for PhD.

Summer 1950: Receives grant from Colton to excavate Twin Butte Site for dissertation.

August 2, 1950: Is hired by Jess Nusbaum as field director of first archaeological salvage project during construction of a natural gas pipeline.

Spring 1951: Is hired by Stanley Stubbs as assistant at Laboratory of Anthropology of the Museum of New Mexico in Santa Fe.

1952: Son Frederick Carl is born.

October 1952: With Don Lehmer, does pipeline project from Farmington to Gallup, New Mexico.

April 1953: Begins archaeological salvage projects on highways in cooperation with the New Mexico State Highway Department, the New Mexico Bureau of Public Roads, and the Museum of New Mexico.

May 1953: Receives PhD from Harvard.

November 1953: With Alex Krieger, Claude Albritton, and T. Dale Stewart, begins study of Final Pleistocene human burial at Midland, Texas.

1954: Second son Michael Andrew is born.

July 3, 1954: Discovery of the Midland skull is nationally publicized.

Summer 1954: Excavates several pueblos and pit houses on highway construction project near Reserve, New Mexico.

June 1956: Meets Ralph Rounds, finds traces of Cantonment Burgwin. Meets pollen specialist Kathryn Clisby; begins study of environmental changes on the Llano Estacado; writes first proposal to the National Science Foundation (NSF), awarded in May 1957.

Summer 1956: Is named director of Fort Burgwin. In September becomes associate director of the museum at Texas Technological University in Lubbock, Texas, and associate professor of anthropology there.

1957: Daughter Gail Susan is born.

June 1, 1957: Begins Texas Tech Archaeological Field School at Fort Burgwin (later named Fort Burgwin Research Center). Rebuilds enlisted men's quarters.

September 1958: Returns to Santa Fe; becomes director of research and associate director of the Museum of New Mexico.

1959: Daughter Cynthia Ann (Cindy) is born.

July 23, 1960: Death of Ralph Rounds complicates work and funding for Fort Burgwin.

January 1961: NSF awards second grant to continue Llano Estacado research.

Summer 1961: Renovation of Palace of Governors and Hall of Ethnology in Santa Fe.

Fall 1961: Becomes interested in UNESCO efforts to save sites in Nubia threatened by the new Aswan dam; writes two proposals: one to NSF for Sudan, the other to U.S. State Department for Egypt.

June 1962: Requested funds for Egypt and Sudan are awarded.

July and August 1962: Travels to France, England, Egypt, and Sudan to recruit archaeologists with backgrounds in the typology of the Early, Late, and Final Paleolithic. Meets with heads of antiquities in Egypt and Sudan.

September 1962: English, French, and Polish archaeologists begin fieldwork in Sudan; many Lower, Middle, and Late Paleolithic sites are found.

August 1963: Is divorced from Nancy; marries Peta Metcalf.

April 1964: Is fired by Museum of New Mexico.

1964: Daughter Kelly Peta is born.

August 1964: Is hired as full professor at Southern Methodist University in Dallas, Texas.

February 1965: Excavates Jebel Sahaba graveyard.

September 1965: Attends Lake Como conference on prehistory in Aswan Reservoir organized by the NSF; beginning of Combined Prehistoric Expedition (CPE).

1967–1969: CPE surveys and excavates in the Nile Valley north of Aswan; major work at Idfu, Esna, and Fayum basin.

1968: Son Scott is born.

June 30, 1968: Fort Burgwin merges with SMU.

October 1969: Gets pilot's license to commute between Dallas and Taos.

November 1969: Is appointed to Texas Antiquities Committee; is elected chairman.

1969–1973: Claude Albritton and Bill Heroy submit proposals to NSF and the Department of Health, Education, and Welfare requesting funds for new building to house Departments of Anthropology and Geology at SMU. Wendorf drafts proposal for a NSF Science Departmental Development Grant for SMU. All three proposals are successful.

June 1970: Gets scuba diving permit; his group finds looted Spanish treasure ship off Padre Island.

1971–1976: Begins discussions with Bill Clements about developing Fort Burgwin as an educational facility for SMU. Clements supports construction of ten dormitories and dining and kitchen facilities.

January–March 1971: Survey in Ethiopia locates numerous Middle Stone Age sites on the slopes of collapsed volcano.

January–March 1972 and 1973: Excavations at Gademotta and Kulkuletti expose sequence of occupations dating from 149,000 to 235,000 years ago.

May and June 1972: Lower Paleolithic bifaces are found in fossil spring vents at Dakhla; with Issawi and Schild, goes to Bir Sahara East and Bir Tarfawi; finds numerous Middle Paleolithic sites.

January–March 1973–1974: Excavates several rich Middle Paleolithic sites at Bir Sahara East and Bir Tarfawi.

April 1974: Is elected treasurer for the Society for American Archaeology; elected president in April 1978, assumes office in 1979.

January–March 1975–1976: Excavations at Nabta and Kharga Oasis; survey of Gilf Kebir.

April 1976: Is divorced from Peta Metcalf.

Spring 1976 to 1978: Expeditions with Jon Kalb to Middle Awash in Ethiopia. Discovery of Bodo Man.

June 1976: Resigns as director of Fort Burgwin.

August 1976: Marries Angela Close.

January–March 1977: Excavations at Nabta.

January through early March 1978, 1981–1984: Excavations at Wadi Kubbaniya.

January to March 1979 and 1980: Excavations at Bir Kiseiba.

1983–1987: Is appointed to a four-year term to the Secretary of the Interior's Advisory Board for the National Park Service by President Ronald Reagan; serves as chair 1985–1987.

January and February 1985: Survey and excavations at Dagdag Safsaf and Bir Misaha in the far western portion of the Western Desert.

January–March 1986, 1987, 1988: Further excavations at Bir Sahara East and Bir Tarfawi.

April 1987: Elected to United States National Academy of Sciences; inducted into the Academy a year later, in April 1988.

October 1987: Receives Griffon Award from the Historic Preservation League of Dallas.

April 28, 1988: President Ronald Reagan signs Abandoned Shipwreck Act of 1987.

April 1988–1989: Appointed by President Ronald Reagan to Cultural Properties Advisory Committee.

October 1988: Awarded Distinguished Service Medal for Conservation Service by the Department of Interior.

March 1989: Has surgery for prostate cancer.

1990 and 1994: Brief surveys into northern Sudan.

January 1990: Returns to Nabta Playa; numerous carbonized plant remains recovered; first recognition of the megalithic alignments and their implication about Late and Final Neolithic society present at Nabta.

January 1993: Work continues at Nabta.

September 1993: Angela Close files for divorce.

January to March 1994: Continuing excavations at Nabta, discovery of 20,000 charred plant remains.

March 1995: Begins general supervision of a two-year project in eastern Sinai with Romuald Schild, Frank Eddy, Mark Becker, and Kim Banks of an area where many sites would be destroyed by agricultural development.

April 1995 to April 1997: Serves as president of the Society of Professional Archaeologists.

April 27, 1996: Marries Christy Bednar.

September 1996: Receives Lucy Wharton Drexel Medal for Archaeological Achievement from University of Pennsylvania Museum of Anthropology.

March 1997: Receives Egyptian Geological Survey Award for "Thirty years of study of Geology and Prehistory of Egypt."

January through February 1999: Continues excavations at Nabta, studying Nabta's megaliths; retires as director of CPE in April 1999.

January and February 1999: Initiates and teaches in field school in prehistory for Egyptian antiquities inspectors at Nabta.

January and February 2001: Directs second field school in prehistory for Egyptian antiquities inspectors at Nabta; is Wendorf's last field work at Nabta.

September 2001: "Fred Wendorf Collection of Egyptian and Sudanese Prehistory" is housed at the British Museum.

May 2003: Receives honorary doctorate from Southern Methodist University.

July 24, 2004: Governor William P. Clements and Mrs. Rita Clements dedicate "Fred Wendorf Information Commons" at Fort Burgwin.

August 2004: Has several malignant tumors removed from bladder.

October 2004: First lecture is given in the "Fred Wendorf Distinguished Archaeological Lecture Series," endowed by Edward O. (Ned) Boshell.

Main Characters in My Professional Life |

Albritton, Claude, Jr. (1913–1988): Geologist and dean of the Graduate School of Humanities and Sciences at SMU. Hired Fred as a professor and charged him to build an anthropology department. Worked with Fred at the Midland site (1954), Tushka (1965), Fayum (1969), and Lake Ziway (1972).

Banks, Kimball: Anthropology graduate student at SMU; worked five seasons with Fred in the Sahara (1977–1980 and 2000). Fred supervised his dissertation.

Bednar, Christy: Graduate student in SMU's anthropology department in 1981 and 1982; went to Egypt with Fred in 1983. Married Fred on April 27, 1996. Since then, has accompanied him on all his field trips.

Beecher, Henry K. (Lt. Col., later Brigadier General): Assistant surgeon general of the Fifth Army in Italy; in 1945 spent time at the field hospital with Fred after he was wounded. Urged Fred to go to Harvard for his PhD. Was chief of anesthesia at Massachusetts General Hospital and professor of surgery at Harvard Medical School.

Bordes, François (1919 1981): French archaeologist and geologist; created a universal lithic tool typology for the Middle Paleolithic still used today. Emphasized the importance of experimental flint knapping studies and statistical approaches. Sent the Guichards to work with the Sudan section of the Nubia project.

Brandenburg, Jack (1904–2000): Longtime supporter of Fort Burgwin, president of the board of trustees for many years. Helped arrange merger of Fort Burgwin and SMU in 1967.

Brew, J. O. (1906–1988): with Fred Johnson, in 1945–1946, organized the Committee for the Recovery of Archaeological Remains. Fred's dissertation supervisor at Harvard. President of the Society for American Archaeology in 1949; contributed to theory and methodology of archaeology; known for his ideas about artifact typology.

Brooks, James E.: A founder, former president, and chairman of the Foundation of the Institute for the Study of Earth and Man (ISEM) at SMU; chairman of the geology department at SMU when Fred came to SMU; in 1969 became dean of what is now Dedman College; vice president and provost of SMU in 1972; SMU president *ad interim* in 1980–1981. With Said and Issawi did geological research in the Qattara Depression.

Caton-Thompson, Gertrude (1888–1985): From 1924 to 1926, with Elinor Wight Gardner, began the first archaeological survey of the Northern Fayum. With Gardner, wrote *The Desert Fayum* (1934), defining two early Holocene desert cultural traditions. Preceded Fred's interest in the Paleolithic sites at Kharga Oasis by forty years. Her work guided Fred's 1969 study of the Fayum.

Chmielewski, Waldemar: European prehistorian; worked with Fred in the Sudan 1962–1965. Excavated and published data on several early Middle Paleolithic workshops and quarries.

Clisby, Kathryn: Pollen specialist (palynologist) from Oberlin College, Ohio; urged Fred to begin a pollen-based study of Late Pleistocene environments on the Llano Estacado. Her research and collaboration with Paul Sears of Yale University laid the foundation for modern pollen research in the United States.

Close, Angela: Paleolithic archaeologist; Fred's wife from 1976 to 1993. Worked with him from 1977 until their divorce, and produced several single and coauthored publications. Currently professor of anthropology at the University of Washington in Seattle.

Colton, Harold: Founder and director of the Museum of Northern Arizona in Flagstaff; internationally recognized specialist in Southwestern pottery. Sponsored (partly funded) Fred's dissertation research in the Petrified Forest National Monument; published his dissertation as a bulletin of the Museum of Northern Arizona. Recommended Fred to be director of the first pipeline archaeology project.

Courier, Margaret: Librarian at the Peabody Museum Library at Harvard. Guided Fred in the use of "cross-indexing by topic."

Daugherty, Dick: Archaeologist and professor at Washington State University in Pullman. Fred hired him in 1963 as emergency replacement field director in Wadi Halfa.

de Heinzelin, Jean (1920–1988): Belgian Pleistocene geologist at the Universities of Ghent and Brussels; worked mainly in Africa. Senior geologist for Wadi Halfa project 1962–1965; published key stratigraphic data for Wadi Halfa area.

Dutton, William: First professional archaeologist Fred met. Excavated a late archaic camp for the University of Texas, using Works Progress Administration (WPA) labor. Encouraged Fred's interest in archaeology; recommended the University of Arizona for Fred's undergraduate training.

Eddy, Frank: Archaeologist at the Museum of New Mexico; worked on the Egyptian section in Nubia in 1963–1964. Retired in 1995 from the University of Colorado; Fred hired him as field director on a large project in Sinai.

Erwin, C. O. "Pete": Head of the New Mexico Highway Department in the 1950s; with Spike Keller and Fred, jointly established the first statewide highway archaeological salvage program. In 1956, with Keller and Fred, wrote the language inserted into Interstate Highway Act authorizing use of federal funds to conduct excavation and study of threatened archaeological sites. Joined Fred in Egypt in January 1963; went with him by riverboat to Wadi Halfa, where they scouted sites for several weeks.

Gatto, Maria: Italian ceramic specialist; worked two field seasons (2004 and 2005) with the Combined Prehistoric Expedition at Nabta Playa, Egypt.

Gautier, Achilles: Professor of paleontology at the University of Ghent; studied and identified most of the faunal remains found in the Nubian project. In 1968 began working in the field on the Nile Valley project. Joined Fred on most of the field projects in the Sahara in 1970s, 1980s, and early 1990s; contributed to many of the publications resulting from that research. Was the first to suggest the controversial hypothesis that cattle found in the Early Neolithic sites in the Western Desert in Egypt were domesticated.

Griffin, Jimmy (1905–1997): Professor of anthropology and ceramic specialist at the University of Michigan; encouraged Fred's interest in archaeology while he was in the army hospital at Battle Creek, Michigan.

Guichard, Jean and Genevieve: Two of François Bordes's graduate students who worked with Fred on the Sudanese project (1962–1964). In Wadi Halfa, taught Fred the typology and technology of the Lower and Middle Paleolithic in Africa.

Harris, R. King: Amateur archeologist; worked part-time at the Hall of State Museum in Dallas, where Fred met him in 1936. Encouraged Fred to keep records on his artifacts.

Hassan, Fekri: Egyptian student of Rushdi Said's at Cairo University; came to SMU for graduate study, with Fred as his thesis advisor. Received his PhD in 1973. Recently retired as Petri Professor of Archaeology at the University of London.

Haury, Emil (1904–1992): Head of the Department of Archaeology at the University of Arizona. Major research interest in the American Southwest; awarded Viking Fund Medal for Anthropology in 1951 and Alfred Vincent Kidder Award in 1977, and elected to the National Academy of Sciences in 1956. Selected Fred to write the report on Site W:10:51 at Point of Pines.

Haynes, Vance: First geoscientist to systematically investigate the stratigraphy and geochronology of Paleoindian sites. Work at the Hell Gap site, Wyoming, and the Clovis site, New Mexico, provided first Paleoindian chronology for the Southern Great Plains. In 1961 worked with Fred on the Llano project and went with him to Egypt from 1967 into the early 1980s. Recently retired from the Department of Anthropology and Geosciences at the University of Arizona.

Hester, Jim: Staff member at the Museum of New Mexico in 1961 when Fred asked him to be field director for the Llano Estacado project. Joined Fred in Egypt in 1963 and 1964; served as field director of Egyptian section of the Nubian project. Part of the original faculty that moved to SMU with Fred in 1964; left in 1967 to work at the National Institutes of Health; later professor of anthropology at the University of Colorado in Boulder.

Hill, Christopher: As a graduate student in archaeology and sedimentology, worked with Fred for five years at Wadi Kubbaniya and Bir Sahara East/Bir Tarfawi. Received PhD from SMU. Drafted maps, profiles, and cross-sections in *Egypt during the Last Interglacial: The Middle Paleolithic of Bir Tarfawi and Bir Sahara East*. Chairs environmental program at Boise State University.

Hoebler, Phil: Archaeologist on staff of the Museum of New Mexico and on Egyptian section of the Nubian project in 1963 and 1964. Part of the original faculty that moved to SMU with Fred in 1964. In 1967, joined the anthropology faculty at Simon Fraser University in Canada.

Holden, Fran: Curry Holden's wife and a faculty member of the Texas Tech history department.

Holden, W. Curry (1896–1993): Historian and archaeologist; first director of the museum of Texas Tech University in Lubbock. Hired Fred as assistant director of the museum and associate professor of anthropology in 1956; served with Fred on the Texas Antiquities Committee 1969–1983.

Issawi, Bahay: Senior geologist on the staff of the Egyptian Geological Survey; served as camp manager and surveyor for the Combined Prehistoric Expedition during 1962–1973 field seasons. Later vice minister for mining and mineral resources in Egypt.

Kalb, Jon: Geologist and paleontologist; research fellow with Texas Memorial Museum at the University of Texas in Austin. Wrote several publications on early humans in Ethiopia, where he did research for thirty years; asked Fred to join him in the Middle Awash basin.

Keller, Spike: With Erwin and Fred, helped establish statewide highway archaeological salvage project in New Mexico and the national program authorized in the Interstate Highway Act.

Kidder, Alfred Vincent (1885–1963): Foremost archaeologist of the Southwestern United States and Mesoamerica during the first half of the twentieth century. Championed a disciplined system of archaeological methodology; one of the first to create a comprehensive, systematic approach to North American archaeology. In 1929, organized first Pecos Conference. Was instrumental in Fred's acceptance as a graduate student at Harvard.

Kidder II, Alfred (Alfie): Member of the Harvard faculty when Fred was a student there. Taught general course on American archaeology; gave Fred his German and Spanish exams.

Kluckhohn, Clyde: North American ethnologist–social anthropologist; did most of his field work on the Navajo and other Southwestern tribal societies. Member of the Harvard faculty when Fred was a graduate student there; supervised Fred's reading course in ethnology and social anthropology; served on his dissertation committee.

Laury, Bob: Retired geologist at SMU. Worked with Fred at Lake Ziway in 1972 and (with Albritton) published several key papers on Gademotta and Kulkuletti stratigraphy.

Lavender, George: Chairman of the New Mexico State Highway Commission in the mid-1950s; business partner of Ralph Rounds in Pot Creek sawmill. Offered to help fund a field school on the sawmill's land; introduced Fred to Rounds.

Long, Boaz: Director of the Museum of New Mexico in the mid-1950s; Fred's boss 1952–1956. Supported Fred's salvage archaeology on pipelines and highways.

MacNaughton, Lewis (1902–1969): Trustee for the ISEM at Southern Methodist University; member of the board of trustees at Fort Burgwin.

Mariff, Eide: Bedouin who guided the Combined Prehistoric Expedition in the Western Desert of Egypt 1963–1999.

Marks, Anthony E.: Paleolithic archaeologist; worked with Fred in Sudan as a graduate student 1963–1966. After completing his PhD in 1968 at Columbia University, joined anthropology faculty at SMU; part of the original anthropology group Fred brought with him to SMU; now retired as professor emeritus at SMU.

Mosca, Herb: Graduate student at SMU, worked with Fred in Egypt in 1974; with Tom Ryan, surveyed the basin at Nabta Playa. Worked with Fred in 1976 at Kharga Oasis and in Ethiopia, where he surveyed with Jon Kalb in the Middle Awash. Became a geologist, is now a successful independent oilman.

Nelson, Kit: Fred's last PhD student, receiving her degree in 1999. Ceramic specialist with interests in Northeast Africa and South America. Currently assistant professor at Tulane University.

Nusbaum, Jess: Mentor to Fred; senior archaeologist at the Department of the Interior, stationed in Santa Fe, New Mexico. Hired Fred to direct the first pipeline archaeological project in the United States.

Phillips, Jim: Fred's first student to receive PhD (1971); thesis published by the Egyptian Geological Survey in 1973. As graduate student, worked with Fred in Egypt three field seasons (1967, 1968, and 1969). Currently professor emeritus at University of Illinois at Chicago Circle. Focused on understanding modern human behavior and its early development in the Levant.

Radwan, Atiya: Egyptian antiquities inspector, with the CPE in 1980 at Bir Kiseiba, and at Wadi Kubbaniya from 1981 to 1983. Attended three archaeological field schools, two at Fort Burgwin (SMU-in-Taos) and a third sponsored by Washington State University at Pullman, Washington. Has risen through the ranks to become a member of the Supreme Council of Antiquities and director of research.

Rayburn, Sam (1882–1961): A Texan and longtime speaker of the U.S. House of Representatives; in 1945 appointed Fred to West Point. Arranged for Smithsonian to send anthropology publications to Fred while he recovered from his war wounds. Later, persuaded the Department of Transportation to adopt regulations compatible with the goals of the archaeological community.

Rounds, Bill: Older son of Ralph Rounds. Managed Ralph Rounds's property following his death in 1960; served on the Fort Burgwin board of trustees in his father's place. Made several significant gifts to the Fort Burgwin Research Center; helped fund Fred's initial Sudan project.

Rounds, Dwight: Younger son of Ralph Rounds; served on the board of trustees of the Fort Burgwin Research Center.

Rounds, Ralph: Fred's first major benefactor; owner of the site at Fort Burgwin; business partner of George Lavender in the Pot Creek sawmill; interested in archaeology and history; financed the initial development of the Fort Burgwin Research Center.

Said, Rushdi: Graduate student at Harvard with Fred; in 1962 joined Fred as senior geologist on Egyptian section of the Nubia project. Was appointed to the Egyptian Parliament and became chairman of its Finance Committee. Was director of the Egyptian Geological Survey 1967–1979.

Schild, Romuald (Roman): Polish archaeologist. With Waldemar Chmielewski, joined the Sudanese section of the Nubia campaign in 1963 as a new PhD. Worked in Egypt with Fred after the Aswan project; has worked with him every year since. Major interests in stratigraphy, lithic technology, typology in the Nile Valley, the Western Desert, and Ethiopia.

Servello, Frank: Graduate student at SMU; worked with Fred in Ethiopia in 1972 on Middle Stone Age sites at Gademotta and Kulkuletti, and the Acheulean-age spring vents near Dakhla.

Shiner, Joel (1919–1988): Senior archaeologist at the Museum of New Mexico; worked with Fred on highway archaeological salvage projects. Became field director on the Sudanese section of the Nubia project in the fall of 1963; joined Fred at SMU as one of the original faculty members of the anthropology department.

Stubbs, Stanley (1906–1959): Director of University of New Mexico Archaeology Field School; an expert on Rio Grande archaeology. In 1948 hired Fred as summer assistant, Fred's first academic job; taught Fred how to dig an adobe-walled pueblo.

Tallah, Heba: Egyptian antiquities inspector, has worked with the CPE for many years, guiding the expedition through the official bureaucracy. Became a valued full member of the expedition staff. Is completing master's degree in prehistory at the University of Cairo; aspires to be Egypt's much-needed Egyptian prehistorian.

Thompson, Ray: With Fred, attended first field school at Point of Pines in east-central Arizona. A natural historian and a brilliant writer, did his PhD research in Yucatán, Mexico. Replaced Haury as director of the Anthropology Museum at the University of Arizona. Now retired.

Wetherington, Ron: With his BA from Texas Tech, began excavating Pot Creek Pueblo with Fred; continued excavations there as graduate student at Michigan; used data for his PhD in 1963. Joined Fred as assistant professor at SMU, where he's now full professor of anthropology; widely regarded as one of SMU's best teachers.

Introduction |

ROMUALD SCHILD

A careful reader of Fred Wendorf's memoir will notice that I came on the stage in late 1963 in Sudan, during the long second field season of the nascent Combined Prehistoric Expedition. I was then an innocent young man with a brand-new PhD in European prehistory. Fortunately, I am still in Wendorf's life today, crowded as it is with people, places, and achievements. Of course, I am no longer innocent and already I have retired.

I first met Wendorf during the Polish contingent's short visit to the headquarters of the Nubian project in Wadi Halfa. We had come from Arkin, on the east bank of the Nile, where the Poles and Nadia Mustapha were stationed. I would lie if I said that Fred made a striking impression on me. He seemed to me rather arrogant and distant, but I should explain that I didn't speak English, and I was trying to be understood by speaking French words with an English pronunciation. It did not work terribly well; especially since Fred would not speak English words with a French pronunciation. During the 1963–1964 season, I might have seen him perhaps two times, never in my wildest dreams imagining that he would become a brother to me and fill my life, too (Wendorf and Schild 2005).

I saw Fred again a couple of times during the 1965 season in Sudan. One of these occasions was a drinking party with the Scandinavian Joint Expedition in the rugged granite rock country of the Second Cataract. He had no time to spare for me, but our relationship improved during the 1967 season at El Kilh, Deir El Fakhuri, and Thomas Affia Village, near Idfu and Esna in Upper Egypt. This was when I began really to appreciate his scientific competence and management skills. Indeed, I was fascinated by Fred's self-discipline and toughness, two of his character traits that emerge so clearly throughout the pages of his memoir. Obviously, he had been working hard to develop these traits, as I learned much later, perhaps in the 1990s, when he gave me his beloved feather-light wooden drawing board, bought early in his archaeological career. It had the word "Tough" handwritten with a waterproof marker on the back to remind him constantly how to comport himself when needed.

Since the 1967 Nile project, we have spent over forty seasons together in Egypt, Ethiopia, Sinai, Sudan, and Yemen, sharing the thrill of doing archaeology that has never been done before. Doubtless, we were fortunate in that there were almost no footprints of preceding archaeologists in the remote places we explored together with so many friends from so many scientific disciplines.

I write this Introduction because I know Fred very well and feel that I am qualified to comment on Fred's achievements and point them out to a gracious reader of his memoir. Yes, "There's milestones on the Dover Road!" (Charles Dickens, *Mr. F.'s Aunt*); thus, I shall list a few of the milestones on Fred Wendorf's life road.

Wendorf's first archaeological milestones appear quite early in his life, almost sixty years ago in 1950, when he began the first pipeline archaeological salvage project in the world, which, in 1953, led to his statewide highway archaeological salvage programs. In the same year the Midland mission began (1953–1954), resulting in the association of the Midland skull with the extinct fauna that precedes the Folsom archaeological event and making "Midland Minnie" the oldest Early Man remains in the Americas.

Just two years later he began the Fort Burgwin research projects in the mountains of New Mexico, near Taos. This milestone included a beautiful historical archaeology project (1957) that led to the reconstruction of the U.S. First Dragoons' Cantonment Burgwin (1958), the establishment of the Fort Burgwin Research Center, and, eventually, the creation of the western campus of Southern Methodist University. Today, the Fred Wendorf Information Commons, a generous gift of Governor William P. Clements, his wife Rita, and two anonymous donors, stands proudly among the other facilities of the campus. The Fort Burgwin project is one of the best examples of Fred's ability to cooperate closely with many people of varying interests and professions to promote a common idea.

Then came Fred's Llano Estacado project in West Texas (1957–1958, 1960–1962), revealing that a late glacial coniferous forest of pine and spruce once stood in the midst of today's prairie. The Llano Estacado project brought together a number of American and European scientists who came to revolutionary conclusions about paleoenvironments that seem to be a far cry from the landscape of today. No wonder this proposition stirred the blood of several geomorphologists and is still debated, although it is a very plausible hypothesis to my paleoecological nose.

Fred Wendorf's active role in New World archaeology ended in 1970 with his investigation of a Spanish shipwreck off the coast of Texas, near Padre Island. It, and the subsequent negative court decision favoring the treasure hunters, ultimately led to the Abandoned Shipwreck Act of 1987, an extremely important law protecting all historic shipwrecks in U.S. waters. Fred's initiative and the consequent impressive maneuvers that secured the passage and presidential signing of the bill are a clear example of his unusual ability to get things done, told in a fascinating narrative.

His chronicle of the kickoff of his African adventure describes perhaps the major milestone in his career, and more importantly, illustrates his outstanding scientific ability, his drive and managerial skills, and his foresight in predicting that the Nile Valley had a complex and rich Stone Age prehistory. The adventure began in 1961 with the UNESCO-sponsored Nubian Antiquities Salvage Campaign and two proposals: one to the State Department for Egypt and the second to the National Science Foundation for Sudanese Nubia. The subsequent multidisciplinary fieldwork began in 1962 in Sudan, and in Egypt in 1963, in spite of a malevolent letter that was sent to forty-five important persons in England and the United States arguing against Wendorf's plans, written by fellow archaeologists interested in the area. Fred's decision to work in Africa set in motion the Combined Prehistoric Expedition, a multinational research body that still conducts important research in northeastern Africa.

It is difficult to rank the scientific achievements of the CPE under Fred's leadership according to their importance; furthermore, there are too many to list them all. However, at least eight major areas of interest need to be mentioned.

(1) The Nubian salvage work (1962–1966) resulted in the recognition, for the first time, of a number of prehistoric time/space units in the Nile Valley and in their placement in local geological and time sequences, work accomplished in spite of many problems concerning radiochronology. But the early Nubian work cannot be separated from the research done later in Wadi Kubbaniya (1978, 1981–1984), just north of Aswan in Egyptian Nubia. The Nilotic Late Quaternary sequence in the wadi, deciphered from detailed mapping, drilling, excavations, and ^{14}C and thermoluminescence (TL) dating, brought about a new understanding of the behavior of this great river, its local paleoenvironments, and its role in the behavior of its human populations. The recovery of animal bones and immense amounts of the charred remains of plant foodstuffs (the first found in the Late Paleolithic of Africa) opened a window onto the everyday life of people who exploited every possible seasonal niche in their struggle to survive in the overpopulated narrow belt of life bordered by deadly deserts.

(2) Meanwhile, there were projects in Ethiopia and in the Eastern Sahara. I'll begin with Ethiopia and the Central Rift Valley, in the lake region, southeast of Addis Ababa, just west of Lake Ziway. There, a million years ago, a caldera that

once stood on the shore of an ancient Lake Ziway collapsed and awaited the day when the sinking rift valley would slice it in half, opening its inner strata and revealing a long sequence of Middle Stone Age sites. The lowermost of these, slightly above the remains of an older (Late Acheulean) small camp, produced an inventory of tool blanks and tool manufacturing waste made of obsidian. The assemblage was buried in a concave structure, possibly the base of a hut. The inventory was a typical Middle Stone Age one, but with a few technical additions such as the manufacturing of preplanned bladelets that might suggest behavior consistent with modern man *(Homo sapiens sapiens)*. A Potassium/Argon date on the volcanic ash fall above the site gave a surprisingly old date of about 235,000 years, much older than any other dates for a similar development in Africa.

(3) In 1972 the Combined Prehistoric Expedition moved to the southwestern desert of Egypt, a region that has remained its primary area of interest until today. The area was practically unknown to archaeology and Quaternary geology, except for the systematic fieldwork of Gertrude Caton-Thompson at Kharga Oasis in 1930–1932. After a brief episode at Dakhla Oasis in 1972, the expedition concentrated on three major sections of the desert: a cluster of remote, uninhabited desert wells known as Bir Sahara East/Bir Tarfawi, about 300 miles to the west of the Nile Valley (1973–1974, 1986–1988); the Nabta Playa area, some 60 miles west of the Nile (1973–1975, 1977, 1990–1994, 1996–2007); and the Bir Kiseiba area, about 120 miles west of the Nile (1979–1980).

(4) Bir Sahara East and Bir Tarfawi are natural desert wells surrounded by clumps of desert vegetation and located in the middle of the lacustrine deposits of very ancient lakes that have been eroded by desert winds. The lakes are remnants of a once relatively lush savanna sustained by seasonal summer rains that were abundant enough to support permanent lakes with fish and crocodiles as well as megafauna such as rhinoceros, bovids, antelopes, extinct camels, and giraffes. Obviously, these environments were magnets for the people of the Early and Middle Paleolithic. The entire sequence of Middle Paleolithic settlements is represented in the area immediately surrounding the lakes, dating from about 250,000 to 70,000 years ago. The rainy periods coincided with Earth's warm periods (interglacials and interstadials), while the intermediate phases of hyperaridity occurred during cold climates (glaciations). This contrasts sharply with the accepted hypothesis that the pluvials, or wet phases, were coeval with glaciations and that the latest one was only 30,000–20,000 years ago.

(5) The CPE's work on the Middle Paleolithic at Bir Sahara East/Bir Tarfawi revealed that people there used a surprisingly monotonous and stable rep-

ertoire of tool types throughout the entire sequence (almost 200,000 years). Differences occurred only among the frequencies of tool types, i.e., the composition of assemblages, and seemed to be caused by the inhabitants' exploitation of the specific microenvironments as they related to the lakeshores.

(6) Explorations in the Nabta Playa and Bir Kiseiba areas have been almost entirely associated with the Neolithic settlement of the southwestern desert of Egypt and the climatic sequence of the region. Countless radiocarbon dates, stratigraphic studies, and archaeological analyses have reconstructed a complex climatic and archaeological sequence of paleoenvironmental and cultural events. The presence of human groups was tied to wet pulsations interrupted by brief hyperarid episodes, extending from about 10,000 to 3500 years B.C.

(7) From the very beginning of the Holocene settlement of the southeastern Sahara, the communities of early settlers knew how to produce pottery and take care of cattle. Our dating of the appearance of these two important developments was strongly contested by many scholars for a long time. However, many later discoveries have shown that early pottery appears at the southern fringes of the Sahara very early, much earlier than in the Near East; and genetic studies of African cattle have implied early domestication. Furthermore, there are several indications that intentional sowing of small fields with sorghum might have begun in certain areas of the southwestern Sahara as early as 7000 B.C.

(8) In recent years, Nabta Playa has stimulated most of the excitement regarding Fred's work with his collaborators in the Combined Prehistoric Expedition. The long, systematic work in this area has revealed elements of an unusual ceremonial center extending in time from about 7000 to 3500 years B.C. and unique in all of Africa. It is composed of a sacred mountain with dozens of small offering tumuli (7000 B.C.); a Valley of Sacrifices with larger tumuli containing offerings that range from a young cow to pieces of animal carcasses and humans (5500 to 4500 years B.C.); a solar calendar of roughly the same age; four fields of Final Neolithic (4500–3500 B.C.) megalithic structures, each containing many groups of originally upright steles; Final Neolithic alignments of menhirs, or steles, pointing to important stars of our galactic system. The Nabta Playa Ceremonial Center bears witness to the increasing complexity of the Neolithic Saharan societies and to the development of their cosmology, eventually inherited by the ancient Egyptians of the Old Kingdom.

Very successful scientific achievements almost always are accompanied by commitments in professional organizations, advisory boards, and the like. These, too, dot Wendorf's life and range from the Society for American Archaeology, in which he served as treasurer and president, through the Secretary of the Interior's Advisory Board for the National Park Service, to the Cultural Properties Board. Fred Wendorf is certainly not the one of whom St. Matthew says: "A prophet is not without honor, save in his own country, and in his own house" (13:57). The honors bestowed upon Fred are numerous and began as early as 1974 with a medal from the Supreme Council of Antiquities of Egypt. The most precious and cherished one, however, is Fred's election in 1987 to the National Academy of Sciences of the United States of America.

No one can contest the fact that Fred is a giant of African and North American prehistoric archaeology. He, and many other people around him, blazed a wide trail through Northeast African prehistory. As long as twenty years ago, the great J. Desmond Clark announced to the world that "There are few who can match his [Fred's] achievements" (Clark 1987, 1). The places, people, and problems that highlight the recent history of world archaeology make Fred's memoir bustle with scientific information, anecdotes, and lively, often snappy dialogue. Many great archaeological and political figures march through the pages of Wendorf's life story, making it fascinating and important reading.

If only "One crowded hour of glorious life / is worth an age without a name" (Thomas Osbert Mordaunt, *Verses Written during the War, 1756–1763*), how many unnamed ages are worth the thousands of crowded hours of Fred Wendorf?

A Polish prehistorian and director emeritus of the Institute of Archaeology and Ethnology at the Polish Academy of Sciences, Schild was also elected to membership in the United States National Academy of Sciences (as a foreign associate). He recently retired as head of the Combined Prehistoric Expedition, a position he assumed at Fred Wendorf's retirement from the CPE in 1999. He received his PhD from the University of Warsaw, where he did his dissertation on prehistoric stone quarries in Poland. Schild's early work centered on Polish Paleolithic archaeology. His strengths are his knowledge of lithic typology, stratigraphy, and sedimentology, which, along with his skills as a draftsman, he brought to his study of the prehistory of North and East Africa, where he collaborated with Fred Wendorf from 1963 to the present.

·

Everything I've written in this memoir is the truth as I know it.
I regret any inadvertent errors of fact or omission, and I'm sorry if
anything I've written causes anyone pain. As is true in any
autobiographical work, the selection of what to tell and what to
overlook, as well as what I've forgotten, inevitably is my subjective
version of the story of my life and career.

FRED WENDORF

·

"Lieutenant, You're One Lucky | Son of a Bitch"

PROLOGUE

In the Apennine Mountains of northern Italy at 6:30 A.M. on March 3, 1945, it was cold and pitch dark; there were no stars and no moon. Except for an occasional rifle shot or a brief burst of machine-gun fire ahead of me to my right, it was deadly quiet.

I was twenty years old and a new second lieutenant. Three months earlier I had been named commander of the First Platoon of Company G, Eighty-sixth Mountain Infantry. We were about to launch an assault on the German soldiers holding the pass to the north. Now my platoon of forty-one men and I lay head-to-toe in a shallow, man-made ditch waiting to begin our assault on the German position about five hundred yards ahead of us. The ditch was barely deep enough to give more than minimal protection. We were all young, between nineteen and twenty-five years old. Except for a few recent replacements like me, all of the men had received intensive training in mountain warfare, including mountaineering and cross-country skiing. The 10th Mountain Division, of which the Eighty-sixth was a part, was unique in that many of its men had been recruited earlier in the war from those still-fledgling civilian winter sports. Many of the men in the division were, in their former lives, champion cross-country or downhill skiers or members of ski teams from elite colleges like Dartmouth and Yale. But here on the battlefields of Italy, the skis and white camouflage clothing were left behind.

We were on the eastern slope of Mount Della Torraccia, and it was cold, but there was no snow. We were wearing green woolen fatigues and windproof winter jackets. Our light packs held a blanket or sleeping bag, extra socks, and underwear. Most of us carried M-1 Garand rifles and a bandolier or two of ammunition. We were grouped into three rifle squads of twelve men each. Every squad had a leader and an assistant leader, seven riflemen, and a three-man BAR team, one of whom carried a Browning Automatic Rifle (BAR) and a bag containing several clips of ammunition. Each BAR man had two partners who carried two more bags of ammunition clips. The platoon had a bazooka team of two men, one carrying the rocket launcher, the other a bag of rockets. Several carried hand grenades, either in a small canvas sack or clipped to their belts. I was the platoon leader. I carried an M1 Carbine, less powerful but smaller and lighter than the Garand, and five extra clips of ammunition. I also carried a map case. My runner carried an M-1 rifle and a handheld radio.

The ditch was muddy and full of many small, hard lumps of clay. I was aware of a strong sour smell as I pushed my face into the dirt, but I didn't care. I got as close to the floor of the ditch as possible. As the sky brightened and the ground fog lifted, I could see a small, flat pasture around us. I glanced down the line once and thought we were like forty cats trying to stretch out on a warm floor.

From time to time the Germans sent in mortar shells, some of which landed nearby with deafening, terrifying blasts. I knew the enemy shelling would stop at 6:40 A.M. because that was the hour when our artillery was scheduled to open up on their position and pound it hard for twenty minutes. At 7:00 A.M., just after dawn, the artillery was to stop; then my platoon and I were expected to stand up and charge the Germans.

I quivered with fear, knowing that unless the Germans ran away, which was highly unlikely, several of us were going to be hurt that day. I was afraid I wouldn't be able to do what I had to do. I saw the hands on my watch move toward seven o'clock. As shells from our artillery flew overhead right on schedule, I said to myself, "If there's a God, He'll stop this watch and I won't have to get up and attack those Germans."

When my watch read 7:00 A.M., I stood up and yelled, "Let's go!"

The entire platoon started running toward the German position. I was in the lead. Beside me was PFC John Compton, carrying a BAR and a bag containing several clips of ammunition. He was a tall, slim young man, about my size, twenty-two years old, and intelligent. He came from a prominent New York family and had been offered a choice of going to Officers' Candidate School or becoming a general's aide, but he turned down both offers, saying he wanted to stay and fight with his friends. A few steps behind Compton and me was PFC Eugene Goodwin. He was the second member of the BAR team and carried a bag containing several more clips of ammunition. Where the others were I didn't know. They seemed to be well behind the three of us.

As we ran I heard the cracks of several rapid rifle shots ahead of me and slightly to my left. Compton went down, shot in the head. I hit the ground at the same time and found cover between him and a small tree. Later I learned that one of the shots had also killed PFC Goodwin. He was on the ground behind me.

Those damned Germans kept trying to shoot me, firing several rounds at the tree I was lying behind. I was so frightened nothing could have made me move from the shelter of that tree. I knew if I stood up that sniper would kill me, just as he'd killed Compton. I knew Compton was dead and there was nothing I could do to help him. Paralyzed with fear, I hugged the ground, unable to move. I wasn't as brave as I thought I'd be when bullets started flying around me. But frightened as I was, I didn't panic.

In a few minutes the rest of my platoon came up behind me. My platoon sergeant, David Black, crawled up beside me and said, "You've got to get up, lieutenant. We have to keep moving forward." He said it several times. I heard him each time, but I couldn't respond.

Finally, I said, "Okay, sergeant, take that BAR and empty several clips into those trees fifty yards ahead of us. That's where the sniper was who shot Compton." When he'd finished firing into and around the trees, I asked Sergeant Black to help me up. Once I was able to stand I persuaded my legs to move forward. I led my platoon toward what I thought was the first objective: a ditch and a small hill with a house about seventy-five yards ahead. There were no more shots.

A few minutes later Staff Sergeant Wilhart Etelamaki, a farm boy from Michigan, and the leader of my second squad, came by on my right side with thirty German prisoners. He had somehow gotten behind them, killed four of them, and the others surrendered.

Still later we were joined by a group of about twenty men led by Sergeant Torger Tokle, the ranking U.S. ski jumping champion. Earlier that morning Tokle and his section of heavy mortars had lost contact with the unit they were supposed to support. He said he and his men were lost.

"If you want, you can follow us," I said, "and wait until your group catches up to us. No one has passed in front of us."

Tokle decided against my offer, and he and his men took off, heading north. He was killed a few hours later by an artillery or mortar tree-burst.

I gradually got control of myself and thought of what I had to do next. A house about fifty yards ahead was our first objective. The house appeared to be abandoned, which made it a great place for booby traps. To see if the house was empty, I told the man with the bazooka to send a rocket into the front door. The rocket exploded and the door flew open. There was no reaction from inside the house. I started barking orders:

"Sergeant Halstead, take the first squad, keep back from the house, and go around the left side of the house.

"Sergeant Etelamaki, take your squad well to the right side of the house.

"Third squad, set up a base of fire along this fence in case someone is inside the house waiting to shoot at us. When the first and second squads go beyond the house, follow the second squad. Everyone, all three squads, spread out when you get around the house, go to ground, and wait for my orders."

I went around the right side of the house with the second squad, where they were holding a German soldier they had taken prisoner. Since my men were advancing with no fire from the house, I figured I had time to stop and question the prisoner about mines in the vicinity. It was an open area with one badly damaged tree that had two or three scraggly limbs.

I stood there too long, because just as I turned away there was an explosion as a German high-velocity shell (a German 88?) hit a limb over my head and to my right. I immediately felt extreme pain in my right shoulder and arm. The carbine I was carrying in my right hand dropped to the ground. I could not move my right arm. I was lucid and managed to remain standing for a minute or two, but the pain was worse than anything I had ever experienced. It felt as though my arm had been blown off, and I tried to pull it out of my sleeve, but could not.

I fell to the ground. Lying there, I remained aware of the situation around me, at least enough to know I was through fighting. The German prisoner lay next to me, dead from the blast. My runner, however, was unhurt. I gave him my maps and told him to find the platoon sergeant and a medic.

One of the men came by and asked, "Lieutenant, can I have your carbine and ammunition? My rifle is useless. I fired it after I got mud in the barrel."

I could barely move for the pain, but I gave him the carbine and the extra ammunition clips I had strapped to the carbine's stock and those on my belt.

A few minutes later the Germans sent in another shell, a small one that hit the ground but didn't explode. It spun round and round and "fizzed." I knew I had to get away from that shell. I was afraid it might explode at any moment.

The medic assigned to my platoon came up to me, and I moaned, "My right arm is blown off."

The medic assured me my arm was still there. He cut my jacket open over my right shoulder and found a hole in my upper chest. He turned me over and found another hole in my back. He also found a shell fragment embedded in my pack—a jagged piece of metal about three inches long and half an inch in diameter. Holding it up where I could see it, the medic asked, "Would you like to have this?"

"Hell, no," I managed to say. "I've had enough of that damn piece of metal."

"Kick your legs, lieutenant," he said. The shell fragment had come out close to my spine.

When he saw I could move my legs, he said, "You're one lucky son of a bitch, lieutenant, because you're going to live. Your legs aren't paralyzed, and you're going

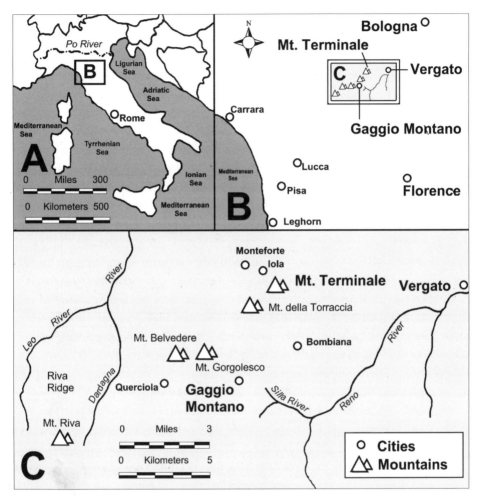

Map 1. Northern Italy, showing (in "C") the areas where the 10th Mountain Division fought the Germans from February 17 to March 3, 1945. Lt. Fred Wendorf was wounded near the base of Mt. Terminale. Drafted by Chris and Cheryl Hill.

home." He gave me a shot of morphine and put bandages on my chest, back, and right arm (where I had been nicked earlier). As he stood up to leave me and rejoin the platoon I asked him to move me away from the unexploded shell near my feet. He took my good arm and pulled me about six feet from the shell.

The rest of the platoon continued their advance toward Mount Terminale, our next objective. I was sure I would never see them again. Minutes passed and I realized I was alone. I didn't see anyone or hear any voices, or even rifle shots. It was quiet, almost deathly quiet. The war had moved on. But my struggle that day had just begun.

During that long morning and afternoon I kept passing out, then returning to consciousness for a few minutes, then passing out again. It's possible that other people or litter teams came by during one of those times when I was out and assumed I was dead.

Those hours were hell. I was alone, afraid I was going to die, and hurting like nothing I had experienced before. All I could think about was the pain in my arm. I didn't think of my girlfriend back in Arizona, or my mother, or my father, only that burning pain. It drove everything else from my mind.

Later in the afternoon, I felt chilled. I could see I was in the shade of the tree and no longer in the sun. With great effort I scooted my body into the sunshine. I did that two or three times as the afternoon wore on and the shadow kept moving. Sometimes the pain was more than I could stand and I lost hope. Then I would fight back, saying to myself, "No, I must keep faith, I must not die. They will find me. They will! They will!"

I remembered the long ride from Texas to Virginia on the troop train, on the first leg of my journey that brought me to this day. I shared a seat with a battalion surgeon of the Eighty-sixth Regiment, a captain, who told me he'd worked as a surgical resident in London during the blitz, and that he'd learned more than he ever wanted to know about treating wounds. We became friends, and a few days later he brought up the subject of going to war again and said, "In your line of work, Fred, as an infantry rifle platoon leader, you may need me before long. If you're wounded and you can get to my battalion aid station, I promise you, I won't let you die."

But now, as I lay wounded on Italian soil, I wasn't so certain I would live. I knew if I wasn't found before dark I wouldn't survive the cold night. Over and over I said to myself, "I must get to the aid station. If I do I'll live. I must live!"

Just as the sun was about to go down, two officers I didn't recognize were within a few yards of me. With great effort I called to them, "Help me! Help me!" They gasped when they saw me.

"How long have you been here?" one asked.

"All day," I said. "Please take me to the battalion aid station."

They refused, saying it would be better if they went ahead to get a litter team to take me there. Fighting back tears I pleaded, "Don't leave me."

They left. I've never known such despair. They've left me to die, I thought. What seemed a long half hour later a litter team arrived and took me to the battalion aid station.

The aid station was a small flat clearing in the bottom of a valley surrounded by trees. Beyond that were two hills that sheltered the valley from the wind and stray bullets.

It was dark and gloomy on the floor of the little valley when I arrived. There were no buildings or tents, just a cleared area with a half dozen wounded men lying on litters. Some of them had a medical aide bending over them. An ambulance was parked beside a tree.

I saw one of the few officers I knew outside my company, the captain in charge of the battalion aid station. When I recognized him I asked, in a shaky voice I didn't recognize, "Do you remember your promise that if I reached your aid station you wouldn't let me die?"

The surgeon put his hand on my head, smiled, and replied, "Don't worry, Fred; you're not going to die." They were the right words because I believed him. He gave me a shot of morphine, and a few minutes later I was placed in an ambulance with several other wounded men and taken to a field hospital about thirty miles away, somewhere near Florence.

The field hospital was like a terrible vision from Dante's *Inferno*. The night was dark, but the receiving and operating theater, a large Quonset hut, was brightly lit. As they carried me in the door, I saw row upon row of litters, each holding a young soldier from the 10th Mountain Division. Some of them were from my own company, and others from other companies in my battalion, which had led the attack. There were more than two hundred seriously wounded men in that Quonset hut, each waiting his turn on one of the operating tables. There had been a major battle after I was wounded.

At some point later that night, a medical officer squatted down by my litter. "Lieutenant," he said, "I need to remove some of the blood from your chest cavity, but I don't want to hurt you, so if you feel pain, tell me and I'll stop."

"Go ahead," I mumbled.

He put a tube in the hole in my chest and began to pump. I immediately passed out. I don't remember any pain; I just passed out. The next thing I knew I was being lifted onto an operating table. I looked at the surgeon and said, "Please don't cut off my arm."

"Don't worry," he said, "you'll keep your arm."

They put the anesthesia mask over my face, and I gratefully pulled in several deep breaths. I had been in such intense pain for so long that I wanted to be unconscious as quickly as possible.

According to my medical records, both the entry wound in my upper chest and the exit wound in the middle of my back were enlarged, and all debris, bits of clothing, and fragments of ribs were removed. The doctors made an effort to clean and rejoin some of the severed nerves, repair my lung, and suture both the front and back wounds. Rejoining the nerves was particularly important, because it would advance the return of feeling and limited function to the arm by several months, perhaps years. Not every surgeon working in a field hospital could do the rejoining and suturing of the ends of severed nerves, particularly the mass of nerves known as the brachial plexus where I had been hit. It was too time-consuming and there were too many others waiting to be operated on. I was lucky to draw a doctor who took the time.

When I woke up the next day the medical officer who had inserted the tube in my chest the day before was sitting by my bed. "I'm Lt. Col. Henry K. Beecher," he said. "I'm an anesthetist, and assistant surgeon general for the Fifth Army. I'm here as a visitor to help out because so many wounded were expected during this advance. You know, young man, you're lucky. The shell fragment that cut the nerves to your arm missed both the adjoining artery to your arm as well as your spine. If that artery had been cut you would have bled out in only a few minutes."

Over the next several days Beecher came to visit with me often. He asked me all sorts of questions about my family background and my goals. "Before I left for the front," I told him, "my mother wrote to tell me that Speaker Sam Rayburn had given me an appointment to West Point."

Beecher asked, "What are you going to do, since you can't pass a physical for West Point now?"

"All my life," I said, "I've thought about being an archaeologist. When I was eight I started going out into the cotton fields around my hometown with my buddies to look for stuff. We found an old Indian camp and collected several arrowheads and a lot of other things. Soon we were going out almost every weekend. I think I'd like to return to the University of Arizona to finish my degree and someday get a PhD in archaeology."

Beecher smiled. "I teach at Harvard, and they have a pretty good archaeology program. You might consider going there. Think about it before you decide."

He handed me his card and said if I got to Harvard to give him a call. His card said he was Chief of Anesthesia at Massachusetts General Hospital in Boston and Professor of Surgery at Harvard Medical School. As Beecher turned to go, I thought, "I really like this man, and I'll hang onto this card. Maybe someday I'll get to Harvard."

I never knew my roommate's name. He told me he was dying. He said he had been shot in the thigh and had gone into a deep shock that caused his kidneys and other organs to stop functioning. Later that day he began to moan softly and seemed to be in great pain. Soon two orderlies came in and moved him and his cot to another room.

A half hour later, one of the orderlies came back to get his things, and I asked, "What happened to the man who was here?"

"He died," he said with no emotion, and left the room. I wished I'd gotten his name and home address. I would've written to his parents.

Later that day, a pretty nurse with brown hair and a sweet smile came in and, noting that my right arm was useless, said, "Could I write a letter home for you, lieutenant, to your mother or your girlfriend?"

"Yes, that would be nice," I said, smiling back at her. "I just don't feel strong enough to write today."

She sat down on the chair at the side of my bed, produced a pad and pen, and I began to dictate a short note to my mother. "Dear Dumpie [that was my nickname for her], I was wounded on March 3rd, and I'm in a hospital in Italy. Everything is okay, except for my right arm; it's paralyzed. I'll soon be home. I love you, Fred."

The next day the pretty nurse came back and found me writing a letter to my girlfriend, using my left hand, which I'd always favored for writing. For shooting a gun and throwing a ball I always used my right arm. Since childhood I've been ambidextrous.

"You deceived me when you told me that you weren't strong enough to write," she said and left before I could explain. I never finished the letter.

As I lay on my bed thinking how fragile life is, I realized I didn't know how seriously I was wounded or what the future would bring. I was still the same young man from Terrell, Texas, in many ways probably typical of boys of that time and place. I had managed to grow up a little, only to be faced with the ugly reality of human warfare.

Later that week I was among a group of patients moved by ambulance to an evacuation hospital near Pistoria. I stayed there for ten days. For the first few minutes I was in an enlisted men's ward where several of the other patients were from my platoon.

My men were pleased to see me alive. A nurse came over and asked if I was an officer, and when I said yes, she shook her head. Speaking softly, she said, "You guys are getting younger all the time. I have to move you to the officers' ward." I protested that I was fine where I was with my men, but she moved me anyway.

A few days later I was up and walking, not far, but far enough to reach the nurses' station on my ward. Later that day my doctor came in holding up a syringe. "Lieutenant," he said, "I'll give it to you straight. You're getting addicted to this morphine, and the only thing I can do to help you is to stop it, cold turkey. This is the last shot you will get. Do you understand?" I nodded yes.

That night was long and hellish, and for many nights after that I don't think I slept at all. One night as I was pacing the hall of the nurses' station, the bandage on my back fell off. There was a mirror on the wall. I had never seen my back where the shell fragment came out, so I backed up to the mirror, and almost fainted when I saw my wound. I saw how close I came to being a paraplegic. I vowed never to complain again. I knew I was lucky; it could have been so much worse. My pledge didn't last long, however.

Among the patients on the officers' ward was a surgeon, a captain who had been wounded when his battalion aid station was hit during an artillery barrage. He could walk around and talk with other patients on our ward and would soon be going back to his post. He was popular because when any of the other officers asked what the long-term effects of his particular wound were, the captain always told them honestly if he thought there'd be permanent damage.

One day I decided to ask him how long he thought my arm would be paralyzed. He looked at where I'd been hit, and where the shell fragment came out, and he stuck a pin in several places in my arm and hand to see if I had feeling. There was none.

"You've had serious damage to the bundle of nerves that controls the function of your arm," he said. "It may take several years, but I think you'll slowly recover some feeling and function in your hand and arm, but lieutenant, your arm is going to be paralyzed for the rest of your life."

I pressed him. "Will I be able to lift my arm?" He looked at my shoulder again and responded, "Some, perhaps, but you won't be able to raise your arm over your head unless you pick it up and put it there."

I knew then I was going to be permanently disabled, a cripple. In spite of my vow only a few days before, I couldn't help being depressed. I spent the next couple days thinking about what he's said, and it hit me hard. Over and over, I asked myself, "How can I ever become an archaeologist with only one functioning arm?"

I didn't know if the wounded doctor told anyone what he'd told me, or if the doctor in charge of my ward noticed I was unusually quiet and no longer flirting with the nurses. He asked one of the nurses to take me for a walk through the amputee and paraplegic wards and then bring me back to my ward. What a shock that was; many of those men were terribly shot up.

Back on the ward I told myself, "I won't be depressed. I know I can't change what happened to me, and I'll be glad to be alive and no more damaged than I am. I'll get on with my life."

A few days later two clerks came by and gave me a Purple Heart for the wound in my chest. They were about to give me a second Purple Heart for the still-bandaged flesh wound in my right arm, but I refused. I couldn't say for sure when or how it happened, and I thought the Purple Heart they gave me for that chest wound was enough.

I had assumed after I was wounded I would never again see any of the men from my platoon. I was wrong. The day after I received the Purple Heart three of my men came into the ward to see me. The 10th Mountain Division was having a break to rest and receive replacements for those who were wounded or killed. We had a good visit. They told me the day I was wounded George Company had ten men killed and thirty wounded. This explained all the men on litters waiting for surgery when I arrived at the field hospital on March 3rd. We talked about those in our platoon who'd died or were wounded. After a half hour or so, they said good-bye and left.

From the evacuation hospital near Pistoria I was moved to a similar hospital not far from the coast, near the port of Leghorn. I arrived in an ambulance, but stood outside for a few minutes to look around. It was cold. I had no coat and was shivering in my shirtsleeves when a black captain, who had also been wounded, came over to me. He took off his field jacket and put it around my shoulders.

He said, "Here, take this." And when I protested, he replied, "Keep it, I can get another." I asked him his name and he told me, and when I asked about his home, he said, "I'm from Chicago, where I have a wife and family."

I said, "I'm from Terrell, Texas, a little town east of Dallas."

We visited a few minutes, and I said, "I don't know how to thank you for the jacket, except to say I'm grateful." I went inside the hospital. Before I had a chance to write to him, I lost the slip of paper on which I'd written his name. I so wanted to write him and tell him how much I appreciated his kindness. I hope he remembers the story and is still alive and reads this. I want him to know that although I was a Southern boy, and steeped in prejudice, I have many good black friends in Terrell and on the cotton farms where I hunted for arrowheads. This captain's generosity has reinforced my long-held feeling that we're all the same people, no matter what our skin color.

I had to wait at the Leghorn hospital about a week for a hospital boat to take me to Naples. Several other officers from the 10th Mountain Division were also waiting. One night the officers tried to organize a game of blackjack, but they were short one so they came to me and urged me to join them for just a few hands. I had a wad of "occupation currency," so I agreed to join them until it was gone. I had never played blackjack before, but they explained the game to me. I had beginner's luck, and in a few hours I had won all their money. I tried to give it back, but they insisted it was mine.

"Wendorf," one of them said, "we wouldn't have returned your money if we'd won. Keep it." I took the money with me to Naples, where an American post office changed the occupation currency I'd won into U.S. dollars. I had slightly over $1,300, and I sent it all to my mother and asked her to put it in the bank.

I was fully ambulatory by the time I arrived in Naples. It was a beautiful April day, and I decided to walk around the hospital grounds. I walked up to the crest of a hill east of the hospital and looked down. The valley below was filled with white crosses, thousands and thousands of them. It was an American military graveyard. I was overwhelmed at the tragedy of it—of the thousands of young men who gave up their lives before they had begun to live. Too recently I was almost in a place like that, and I fell to my knees, weeping uncontrollably. How long I cried there I don't know, but after a while I stood up, wiped my face, turned and went back to the hospital. Part of the reason why I cried may have been a feeling of guilt that I had lived and they had died. I think I was grieving for myself, too.

A couple of days later I decided to go into Naples. I wanted to eat spaghetti and drink red wine. The military police required that soldiers wear a clean, pressed uniform, shined shoes, a tie, and a hat to go into town. I tied my shoes with great difficulty and was struggling with my tie when a young blonde, blue-eyed nurse came over.

"Here, let me help you," she said, smiling. She tied my tie and I thanked her and got on a bus to Naples. Although I was alone, I had such a good time on my first trip to Naples that I decided to go back the next day.

This time I went over to the pretty blonde nurse and asked her to help me with my tie. She said, "Listen, lieutenant, you're going to be a cripple the rest of your life. You may as well start today learning how to tie your own tie."

I was shocked and angry, and I vowed from that moment on I would always tie my own shoelaces and tie. I knew I was crippled for life. Did she need to say it? I tied my tie, even though it took a long time, and left without a glance at the nurse, who no longer looked so pretty.

A day or two later, in mid-April, the Fifth Army went on a general attack meant to end the war in northern Italy. One of the officers in the ward with me was a first lieutenant, an artillery forward observer. When I entered the room he was struggling to put on his dress khakis, even though both of his arms were bandaged.

I asked him why he was getting dressed. He said, "I'm going AWOL from the hospital. I plan to catch a ride on a truck going north and join my unit. I don't want to miss the end of this war." Over his left pocket he wore a Purple Heart ribbon with *four* oak leaf clusters, meaning he had been wounded five times. I helped him put on his shirt and jacket, wished him well, and he left.

In Naples, I was put on the SS *United States*, which had been partially converted to a hospital ship. When it arrived in New York about a week later, several of us were transferred onto a hospital train bound for Texas. I found out from a conductor that we would be going through Fort Worth, so I sent a telegram to my mother and asked her to meet the train.

She did, with my favorite old boyfriend of hers from Terrell. I was overjoyed to see them when I got off the train in a stiff new uniform, my right arm in a sling. My mother got quiet when she saw my arm. Tears ran down her cheeks. I grabbed her and held her close and cried with her. When I had left her five months before to go to Italy, I wasn't sure I'd ever see her again. Standing on the platform with my dear mother crying in my arms, I did my best to reassure her I was okay, despite the paralysis of my right arm. But she knew better. She said her tears were in gratitude to God that I was alive.

She said, "Son, on March 3rd, the day you were wounded, an awful feeling came over me, and I knew that something terrible had happened to you. You were either dead or badly wounded, and I fell to my knees and asked God to spare you and let you come home. If he did, I pledged I'd let you go."

I am not religious and have no faith in extrasensory perception, but it is impossible for me to explain how she sensed that I had been wounded. After our tearful embrace, we had a happy visit, and then I had to get back on the train to go to Temple, Texas, and McClosky General Hospital, where I was to spend the next seven months.

In May, six months after I was commissioned, I was promoted to first lieutenant. It was a routine advancement for second lieutenants wounded in combat.

When I arrived at McClosky, I was in considerable pain. My right hand felt as if it were on a red-hot stove. In Naples I learned I could buy from other officers their beer rations (a case a week), and after three or four beers my pain would be reduced enough that I could sleep at least part of the night. The hospital staff at McClosky frowned on this, but they knew they needed to do more about my pain. They tried various methods with no success. In mid-July they decided to open my chest to cut off the scar tissue growing ever tighter around my brachial plexus. When I woke up after the operation I felt no pain. That day marked the beginning of the partial recovery of my arm.

One of the first things I did on arriving at McClosky was to send a letter to Speaker Sam Rayburn. I thanked him for considering me for an appointment to West Point, and told him that I had been seriously wounded and was no longer able to pass the physical. A few days later I received a letter from Speaker Rayburn telling me that if ever there was anything he could do for me I was to let him know. I wrote back and said I'd decided to study to be an archaeologist. I told him the doctors at McClosky had said I would be hospitalized for about two years, and I asked if he could help me get some archaeological reading material from the Smithsonian Institution. I thought I might receive a packet with three or four pamphlets, but a few weeks later a large wooden crate arrived in my room overflowing with books on archaeology and anthropology published by the Smithsonian. Thus began my library.

In August of 1945, while I was still at McClosky General Hospital, my college sweetheart, Nancy Moon, of Bisbee, Arizona, came for a week's visit. I'd met her in September of 1942 at a student street dance shortly after I arrived in Tucson. Nancy was also eighteen and beautiful. Petite, she had a full figure, and a bright, lovely face framed by naturally wavy dark brown, almost black, hair. She was the only girl I dated while I was at the University of Arizona. We weren't lovers, and we weren't engaged, but I cared a great deal for her. She was always sweet and kind, and I think she liked me, too. When I went into the army, I dated several other girls. I was serious about one of them—a sweet college girl from a ranch near Hays, Kansas. But the army transferred me to Fort Leonard Wood, Missouri, and the romance did not survive the distance.

Nancy and I had written back and forth a few times until I went to Italy, when for some reason I stopped, maybe because I had a premonition that I might not return. I began exchanging letters with her shortly after I got to McClosky. She had received her BA degree from the University of Arizona in May 1945, and would enter graduate training in social work at the University of Washington, in Seattle. With time on her hands she began to write longer letters, and their tone gradually became more affectionate. Although I was worried that the scars on my chest and back and the paralysis of my right arm might repel her, I decided to invite her to visit me.

She never seemed to notice my arm, and when I asked her about it, she said, "What happened to your arm doesn't matter to me. It's your mind I've always loved." We had a great visit, and we learned that we still cared for each other. After she left, we sent many love letters back and forth. Finally, I asked her to marry me, and she said yes.

It took some arranging, but in the first week of December, I went to the Carswell Air Corps Base in Fort Worth and got on a space-available military flight to Seattle. From there I took a taxi to the apartment where Nancy and her mother were staying. Mrs. Gwen Moon, Nancy's mother, was not pleased about the pending nuptials, but when she saw how serious we were, she didn't try to stop us. Just before the wedding, Nancy withdrew from her classes at the university; she told me she wanted to be a housewife, not a social worker. On December 10, 1945, in Seattle, Washington, Nancy and I were married. The only guests present were Nancy's mother, her sister, and her sister's husband, who lived in the Seattle area. My mother was unable to come because she had to work.

We had a brief honeymoon at the Empress Hotel in Victoria, British Columbia.

Then we drove to Bisbee, Arizona, using a car we borrowed from Nancy's mother, and from there to Fort Worth, where a local Plymouth dealer, a friend of my mother's, had offered to sell me one of the first group of postwar cars he would receive from the factory. The new Plymouths arrived, and he sold us a well-built, black, four-door sedan, with no chrome and no bumpers, but a strong engine. I paid nine hundred dollars for the car from the money I'd won at blackjack in Leghorn. We drove to Temple, Texas, and with great luck found an almost new, one-bedroom apartment near the hospital.

After the surgeons had removed the scar tissue around my brachial plexus, the only thing the hospital could do for me was to give me physiotherapy for my arm. I would go to the hospital five days a week to have the arm exercised so the joints would remain flexible. Then, I would have lunch in the officers' dining room and go home. I had a bed at the hospital, but I never slept in it. I slept at home.

There was a military rule that officers with neurological wounds had to be hospitalized for two years after they were wounded because the army paid officers who were retired for physical disability three-quarters of their base salary each month for the rest of their lives. The army wanted to be sure there were no "magical" recoveries.

I spent two years in various army hospitals, ending up at Percy Jones General Hospital in Battle Creek, Michigan. Shortly after the surrender of the Japanese in August 1945, the army began closing down military hospitals as more and more of their patients were discharged. They didn't seem to have a plan for these closures and routinely sent patients to hospitals that were closed three or four months later. Near the end of my stay at Percy Jones I met another lieutenant from the 10th Mountain Division who had suffered a wound similar to mine: Bob Dole, from Kansas. He was a pleasant man, but we never became close friends because I took frequent leaves to take courses at nearby universities and was rarely in the hospital.

At Percy Jones, as I had at the other hospitals where I'd been a patient, I was given a series of ninety-day leaves with one condition: that I would go somewhere every day and have a physiotherapist exercise my arm and hand. It was a small duty, and I was reasonably consistent about getting the treatments. In order to receive the physiotherapy treatments I would go to a medical facility at a military post near a university where I was taking a class. I used these leaves to take courses in anthropology and archaeology at whatever university or college was nearby.

I also had free time between courses, and Nancy and I took trips to meet archaeologists at distant research centers and universities. Among those Nancy and I met were Gordon Willey at the Smithsonian, Duncan Strong at Columbia, and Jimmy Griffin at the University of Michigan in Ann Arbor. I liked all three of these distinguished archaeologists, but most of all I liked Jimmy Griffin. I made several trips to visit him, and we became lifelong friends. He encouraged me to apply to the University of Michigan for graduate training in archaeology with him, after I had finished my undergraduate training at Arizona.

At the beginning of 1947 I knew my required two years in the hospital would be fulfilled in April of that year, and I decided to return to Tucson in January, enroll at the University of Arizona, and return to Percy Jones when my ninety days were up in April. There I would be discharged from the hospital and retired as a first lieutenant.

CHAPTER 1

I was born in Terrell, Texas, a small town thirty miles east of Dallas, on July 31, 1924. My mother and father were divorced eight years later. For two or three years before the divorce there was constant friction between them with many shouting arguments. I never knew the cause of these disagreements, but they disturbed me greatly. I often had nightmares after their fights, and sometimes I walked in my sleep. With no basis in fact, I assumed my father was to blame. My escape was to leave the house and go for long walks with two or three of my friends in the neighborhood. My mother, who from my earliest days always gave me a lot of freedom, let me go on these long walks if I told her where I was going and when I'd be back.

My father, Denver Fred Wendorf, was born in Carmine, Texas, a small town forty miles east of Austin. His father, Henry Lewis Wendorf, had been a leather worker there, who later moved his family to Corsicana, Texas. My father became a merchant. He established an auto supply business in Terrell. Before the divorce he closed that store and opened another auto supply store in Waco, about a hundred miles south of Terrell. He stored the fixtures from the old store in a Terrell warehouse.

My mother, Margaret Hall Wendorf, was born in 1902 in the small community of Elmo, Texas, about ten miles east of Terrell. Before she married my father she taught in a one-room school. Afterward she helped in the store, so she knew a good deal about the business of auto parts. After the divorce my father helped her set up her own store in Terrell, selling her the fixtures he had in storage. I think she got them for a good price, since I don't remember hearing any complaints.

To stock the store she persuaded manufacturers and wholesalers to give her the parts she needed—things like fan belts, oil filters, pistons, rings, and connecting rods—on consignment. She would pay for them as they were sold. It was the depth of the Depression, and the manufacturers and wholesalers were glad to help any retailer who could sell their auto parts.

At first it was hard for her to pay the bills. She had received our home in Terrell in the divorce, but it had a large mortgage. To feed us that first year she sometimes bought a single plate of food for a half-dollar from a restaurant across the street from her store, and we would split it. I don't recall ever being hungry, but my mother probably was.

By 1935–1936 we were eating at a boardinghouse run by Mrs. Hildegard, a Polish lady, who became like a second mother to me. Mrs. Hildegard ran a fine establishment, but it was a boardinghouse: I learned to be on time for meals, to take what I wanted, and to eat rapidly.

I greatly admired my mother. Although it is relatively common today for a woman to establish and manage a retail sales business, I suspect there aren't many who own and operate auto supply stores. I'm almost certain there wasn't another woman anywhere, in 1933, who had the spirit, strength, and determination to begin such a business in the face of what must have been restrictive social conventions. She succeeded by ignoring the gossip about her and by working hard.

Much of the growth of my mother's business came from the mechanics and garages that repaired automobiles in Terrell and the surrounding towns. By 1937 she had become a successful merchant. One afternoon a month, it was my responsibility to go around to all the shops and filling stations, check the inventory of items that had been left there against the items that had been sold or used, prepare a bill for the shop, and collect the money the people owed her. Most of them paid promptly. From the few who didn't, mother had to go around and collect. She was a pretty woman, with wavy, brown hair. I thought some didn't pay me just so she'd come by and talk to them.

My father was a hard and difficult man. His grandfather had immigrated to Texas from Germany and was a strong disciplinarian. Occasionally my father would give me a terrible beating, much more than a spanking, when I did something that provoked him, as he did once when I was three and I put our dog in with the rabbits. Ever afterwards, I tried to avoid his anger. In the mid-1930s he moved to Alexandria, Louisiana, and opened an auto parts store there. Both he and my mother thought I should get to know him, so when I was twelve, mother sent me to spend a month with him in the summer. He had married Mildred Buckner, a sweet Louisiana woman. Eventually she became like another mother to me, and was always kind and loving. I had a great crush on her. They had two girls, my half sisters, Mildred (Millie) DiMaggio and Mary Ann Stripling, of whom I am very fond. Both of my sisters now live in the small East

Texas town of San Augustine, not far from the Louisiana border. Millie's husband owns a drugstore and is a successful merchant. Mary Ann's husband is an architect. Through the years I haven't seen them often, but we still get together occasionally, perhaps once a year, and more often when one of them comes to Dallas on business.

I was never at ease with my father, but we had a few pleasant times when I went to visit him in the summer. The only friction I remember was over my becoming an archaeologist. He offered to cover all of my expenses if I would give up my foolish idea and agree to go to medical school. I turned him down.

About 1935-36 he bought a large block of open rangeland (one-thousand-plus acres) a few miles north of Alexandria. I think he paid ten dollars an acre for it. Soon afterwards the "Big Inch" pipeline was built across his land to carry gas from Louisiana to the Northeast. He received more for the pipeline right-of-way than he had paid for the whole tract. He wanted it as a place to play, a place where he could entertain his friends. He built a big lake on one of the creeks and stocked it with bass. He was a great fisherman, and he and I would sometimes fish together, but my father's greatest thrill came when he and a friend caught some large bass and the local paper ran a picture on the front page of the two fishermen holding up the string of big fish. I tried, but I was never a successful fisherman.

He sometimes took me out to ride around on a couple of horses he kept on the ranch. He also had cattle, including one large, mean Brahma bull he bought to discourage his neighbors from cutting his fences (they were used to running their cattle on his land). It worked, too. With good reason, he warned me never to get off my horse when I was near that bull. I took him seriously.

These rides became part of my business training. He had big dreams about how he would develop the property, but somehow they never materialized. I remember him telling me, "Never sell this land, son. Someday it will be valuable."

In the summers after I started college, I always had a job and I rarely saw him. After I was wounded and was in the army hospital in Temple, Texas, an easy driving distance to Alexandria, Louisiana, Nancy and I made a special effort to see him occasionally. He was always overjoyed when we came and would always give us food to take home. Once his gift was a big crate of eggs, and another time it was a big bag of sweet potatoes he grew on the farm.

He was right about his land, too. When he died in 1979, my sisters assumed responsibility for managing the property. Although they lived less than a hundred miles from the farm, they soon realized it was more than they could handle, and we sold the property at a good price. I gave my share of the money equally to each of my six children. Most of them used the money to pay down their mortgages.

••••

My interest in archaeology began when I was eight. One day my schoolmates, Frank Holman and Paul Moody, and I were walking through a cotton field about a mile east of my home when I saw something sticking up from the soil.

"Paul," I called. "Look, this is an arrowhead!"

We had stumbled on an old Indian camp and spent the rest of the day collecting all kinds of things little boys love. Excited about our loot, the three of us went out almost every weekend after that to collect Indian artifacts, particularly arrowheads.

My interest soon outgrew that of my friends, and before long I was going out alone on collecting expeditions. I began looking for—and finding—additional Indian camps in other fields. As I got older, I expanded my area of exploration, walking through fields near small creeks in the area, sometimes going ten or more miles from my home. The cotton fields of East Texas were prime areas to find artifacts because they were plowed several times a year, and after every rain the artifacts came to the surface.

Black farmers who lived in unpainted shacks owned or sharecropped many of these fields. They were poor, but they always welcomed me, offering me water from their nearby cisterns. I never carried a canteen.

When I was about thirteen I began carrying a shotgun or .22 rifle on my collecting trips. I bought both guns with money my mother paid me for collecting the bills from the garages. In the winter I carried my rifle to look for rabbits; in the fall I would take the shotgun to hunt doves and quail. Very quickly I became an excellent marksman, which later stood me in good stead when I attended Texas Military College, and later still, as an infantryman in the army.

When I was twelve, I attended the 1936 Texas Centennial celebration at Dallas's Fair Park, where I met an amateur archaeologist, R. King Harris. He worked at the Hall of State Museum when he was not driving trains, and he had an exhibit there of some of his artifacts.

King saw me hanging around the exhibit and asked me if I collected arrowheads.

I told him about my growing collection.

"What sort of records do you keep, Fred? Do you plot your sites on a map? You should start right now, and mark the site number on every piece you collect, and not just arrowheads, but scrapers and other tools."

From that time on I began numbering my sites and putting site numbers on the artifacts as I found them. I obtained maps (the county soil maps were particularly helpful) and recorded the site numbers on them.

As a twelve-year-old, I began to tell everyone I was going to be an archaeologist. Most of my family and friends considered archaeology a suitable hobby, but it would never do as a vocation, unless one was rich. My family had such limited financial resources that archaeology seemed an impractical goal for me. I received a little support from my mother, who from time to time bought me a book on archaeology, but even she told me I was being unrealistic and should train to be an engineer or a medical doctor.

I met my first professional archaeologist, William Dutton, when I was fourteen. Sponsored by the University of Texas and using labor supplied by the Works Progress Administration (WPA), he was excavating a large pre-pottery site on the Sabine River sixty miles northeast of Terrell. I got his name and address from the university, and I wrote to see if I could come over for a visit. He encouraged me to come and see his excavations. Probably to quiet my clamoring, a few weeks later my mother took me to meet Dutton.

Dutton's archaeological site was on a low, natural mound in the floodplain of the Sabine River. The surface of the mound was littered with flat sandstone slabs from eight to fourteen inches long and one to three inches thick. One, sometimes both, faces of the slabs were covered with pits about an inch and a half in diameter.

As my mother and I walked around the site with him, Dutton said, "I think these pitted stones were used to process nuts, possibly pecans. There are lots of wild pecan trees between here and the river."

After he had shown us around, I told Dutton I was fourteen, but because I was double-promoted twice while I was in grade school, that next year I would be a senior in high school and I needed to plan for college. Being double-promoted was fairly common then. If the teachers thought you were bright, good in math and reading, and your parents agreed, they would recommend double promotion.

I asked him if he thought I could make a living as an archaeologist and where he thought I might get the best training and a degree in archaeology.

Dutton said, "I recently received my master's degree from the University of Arizona in Tucson, and I got a good education, particularly in archaeology. I was trained by one of the most highly regarded archaeologists in the country, Emil W. Haury. He's head of the Department of Anthropology, and he's directed some of the most important excavations ever done in the Southwest. He's wonderful with his students, helping them at every turn. You couldn't get a better undergraduate education anywhere else."

I decided then to go to the University of Arizona, if I could.

Possibly at the urging of my mother, Dutton added, "Wherever you go, you'll have to study hard and make good grades if you expect to go to graduate school and get an advanced degree, which you'll need if you want to be an archaeologist."

I wasn't a strong student in high school, possibly because of the double promotions in grade school. I was ill-prepared compared to other students in my grade who had moved through the whole sequence and were two years older than I. I was socially immature and my three closest friends were all two years older. Mother managed to persuade them to look after me and keep me out of trouble. We never did anything really wrong; we didn't get involved with drugs or alcohol. Perhaps the most sinful thing we did was to have "petting parties" with local girls.

When I wanted to, I could do as well as anyone at school, but I was reluctant to study hard, despite the admonitions of my mother and teachers. In the summer of 1939, I took a class in trigonometry and got a perfect score on every test and 100 as a course grade. I don't remember why I studied for that course, except that I liked the teacher, who was also the school principal.

Shortly before I graduated from high school in May 1940, my mother said, "Fred, you're too young to go so far away to the University of Arizona. I want you to go to the Texas Military College here in Terrell for two years. And if you live at home, it will save me a lot of money."

It was a small school, about three hundred students, and I got Mother's assurance that she would send me to the University of Arizona if I did two years at the military college. At first I was disappointed, but my disappointment disappeared when I realized that my instructors were good, particularly strong in math and history, two of my best courses. I enjoyed the military training, because I quickly developed competence in parade marching. I also learned how to execute various movements while carrying a rifle. There was never any target practice using our guns, but that didn't matter to me, since I was already a good marksman with both rifle and shotgun.

I began looking for a part-time job to help cover my expenses. When I turned sixteen I got a job at J. C. Penney working for minimum wage—forty cents an hour. At first I worked as a stock boy, later as a floor salesman, and my pay went up slightly. Mostly I sold men's clothing: trousers, shirts, jeans, and overalls. I also sold shoes for men and women. I hated selling women's shoes. My female customers had so much trouble deciding which style they liked the best that I was more than a bit impatient. The staff was helpful, and I worked at Penney's for over two years and grew to like it.

One Sunday afternoon, on December 7th, 1941, I was playing football with my neighborhood team when my mother came running out. "The Japanese have attacked Pearl Harbor in Hawaii," she said. "A lot of people have been killed. We're at war." She looked at me, shook her head to keep from crying, and went back in the house.

The game stopped. We discussed what the Japanese attack would mean for us. One or two of the older boys said they would enlist the next day. We thought it would be a year or two away for the rest of us, and surely our army would quickly defeat the Japanese. On that note, we decided to finish our game.

My mother's health collapsed in the spring of 1942. She was no longer able to take care of the store. She was in her early forties and had gone into early menopause. She was unable to cope with the changes in her body chemistry and became so depressed she couldn't even go to the store. I didn't understand what was happening at the time. She wouldn't tell me, and others just told me she was sick.

I was devastated. I couldn't understand the sudden changes in my always strong, dependable mother. Eventually, Mother was forced to sell her store. Later she recovered enough to take a job as a parts manager at the nearby airport, where a flying school trained young Englishmen who wanted to fly for the Royal Air Force (RAF). The school shut down about a year later, and my mother had to find another job. With her background, that wasn't difficult; she soon found work as a salesperson with the Firestone Auto Parts store in Fort Worth.

Despite the problems with her health, Mother insisted I continue with my plans to attend the University of Arizona. She said she had enough money to cover my tuition, room, and board. In May 1942, I applied for admission to the university and was accepted as a junior, or third-year classman. Two and a half months later, in mid-August, I got on a train in Terrell and traveled two days to Tucson.

Undergraduate Work and Enlisting in the Army
(1943–1944)

CHAPTER 2

M y first semester of undergraduate training at Arizona was uneventful. I gradually got to know Dr. Emil Haury, the head of the Department of Anthropology, but I doubt if I made a favorable initial impression. I was an indifferent student, and my grades were only B's and A-'s. World War II was being fought in earnest. Most of my friends had enlisted or were drafted, and my mind was not on scholarship.

One month after my eighteenth birthday I enlisted in the army. Mother's financial situation was a major factor in my decision. I was afraid she didn't have the resources to pay my expenses for more than my first year in Tucson. I went to an army recruiting office and enlisted. I thought I had an understanding with the army that they would not call me to active duty until May of the following year, but two months later I was ordered to report for active duty on January 10, 1943.

After basic training at Camp Robinson, Arkansas, I was selected to go to Infantry Officers' Candidate School (OCS). I wanted to be an officer because I wanted to lead, and I thought officers had more freedom. The OCS Selection Board, recognizing my youth and inexperience, sent me to Camp Fannin, near Tyler, Texas, for a year, to be an instructor. Most of the time I taught bayonet. After a few months I was bored. One evening I confessed my boredom to the sergeant who shared my two-man hut. He had recently been rotated home from fighting the Japanese at Bougainville in New Guinea.

He asked what I was doing at Camp Fannin. I said I was waiting to go to OCS for infantry officers' training. "Are you crazy?" he asked. "Do you really want to be a rifle platoon leader?"

"Sure," I said. "But I have to wait for six months or a year before I can be sent to Fort Benning."

The sergeant shook his head and said, "Let me show you something." He went to a pile of magazines beside his bed, searched until he found the issue of *The Infantry Journal* he sought. He opened it and said, "Read this," handing it to me. The short article said the average life expectancy of a rifle platoon leader in combat was thirty minutes.

"Why don't you transfer to the Air Corps and take pilot training?" he asked. "They sometimes get killed, but they sleep in beds. As a rifle platoon leader you'll sleep on the ground, and you will almost certainly be wounded or killed. Take it from me, I've been there and I know."

Like all nineteen-year-olds, I noted the word "average" and assured myself that I would make it. As the weeks went on, however, I began to look more favorably on becoming a pilot and sleeping in a bed. So, after a year of bayonet instruction, I decided to apply to the Army Air Corps for flight training and was accepted. I was transferred to the Air Corps and sent to Sheppard Field near Wichita Falls, Texas, for processing, then to school at Fort Hays College, in Hays, Kansas, where I waited for flight instruction to begin. While I was at Hays I took classes in math, physics, and chemistry. I was assigned to a flying instructor for preliminary flight training. One day he decided to do some simple acrobatics, stalls and spins, and the two oranges I had hidden in my coat pocket fell out and floated around in the cockpit. The stalls, spins, and other acrobatics were exhilarating. My instructor let me do a few stalls myself. I was sure I could be a good pilot.

After nine hours of instruction I was scheduled to solo the next day, but it wasn't to be. That evening General Hap Arnold sent a telegram to me (and 36,000 other former ground force soldiers) informing me he was sending me back to the infantry. So many infantry were killed and wounded at Monte Casino, Anzio, and elsewhere, that there was now a surplus of pilots in the Air Corps and not enough soldiers on the ground. I was devastated. I didn't want to return to the infantry because I wanted to become a pilot. It took almost a month, however, before the assignment to the infantry came through, and by then I was reconciled to the idea of being a foot soldier.

I was assigned to the Ninety-seventh Division, then training at Fort Leonard Wood, near Waynesville, Missouri. It was my good fortune that in basic training the army had taught me how to fire a light machine gun. I was rated an "expert." During a live fire training exercise my company commander stood behind me, watching. He asked my sergeant who that soldier was firing that machine gun and said he was impressed with the young man's skill.

Three weeks later I learned fifteen slots were available for OCS. I went to regimental headquarters and got an application. When I handed it to the company commander, he looked at me and asked if I was the soldier who'd been shooting that light machine gun a few weeks ago. I told him I was, and he signed the request without further comment. I was accepted by the evaluation board and two days later sent to Fort Benning, Georgia.

In late November 1944, after almost two years as an enlisted man, I was commissioned a second lieutenant in the infantry. A few minutes before the commissioning ceremony an officer announced that fifteen volunteers were needed for immediate overseas assignment with the 10th Mountain Division, which would soon be fighting in the mountains of northern Italy. I already had my orders to return to Camp Fannin, probably to give more bayonet instruction. Impulsively, I held up my hand and was one of the fifteen selected.

My mother was not pleased that I had volunteered for combat, because like the sergeant at Camp Fannin, she knew there was a high probability that I, as a rifle platoon leader, would be killed or wounded. In an effort to delay my going to war, she asked a great uncle who was closely associated with Sam Rayburn, the longtime speaker of the U.S. House of Representatives, to submit my name as a candidate for West Point, and he agreed. I didn't object to my mother's efforts regarding West Point, because I enjoyed army life.

The 10th Mountain Division | Goes to War in Italy
(1944–1945)

CHAPTER 3

On November 26, 1944, I joined the 10th Mountain Division at Camp Swift, near Austin, Texas. I was assigned to lead the First Platoon, Company G, Eighty-sixth Mountain Infantry Regiment. The day before we were to depart for overseas assignment, my mother and her gentleman friend came to have a meal with me at a local restaurant. Afterwards my mother drove me back to my barracks. She got out of the car with me, we had a long hug, and I kissed her good-bye.

The next day, on November 29, the Eighty-sixth departed by train for Camp Patrick Henry, near Virginia Beach–Newport News, for shipment overseas. The train trip lasted about a week, during which I made friends with the Eighty-sixth's Second Battalion surgeon, whose services I would need before five months passed. We spent another five days at Patrick Henry, waiting to embark. On December 11, 1944, we boarded the former cruise ship the SS *Argentina* and sailed eastward across the Atlantic. We were moving fast in a six- or seven-ship convoy guarded by several destroyers. The seas were rough and most of the people on board were seasick. However, I could eat anything, anytime. When I went down to the officers' dining room that first evening, there was only one other officer present. The steward served us great steaks that evening (my first in a long time), and the food was excellent for the rest of the voyage. Some of my men told me, however, that the enlisted men's food was terrible. When the ship cleared Gibraltar, the stormy seas abated, and more officers began to show up at the dining room.

We arrived in Naples on Christmas Eve, and quickly disembarked. As soon as we checked on our men, Lieutenant Pete Borsuk, the company executive officer, and I went looking for a drink. We found a bottle of brandy in a nearby bar and brought it back to our quarters. It was awful and I got so sick that I've never had another glass of brandy since.

The next morning, Christmas Day, despite one of my first hangovers, the rest of the Eighty-sixth and I were herded onto a broken-down freighter, the SS *Sestriere*, to go to the port city of Leghorn.

The next day we arrived in Leghorn, where we were unloaded and transported in trucks to a bivouac area in the King's Hunting Grounds near Pisa. We stayed there about a week. We were told that just before Christmas the Germans had attacked a division that had serious morale problems and much of the unit had simply pulled back, leaving Leghorn and Pisa undefended. Had the Germans known, they could have attacked and gone all the way to Rome. The Eighty-sixth Regiment was to be put in the gap to stop the Germans if they attacked again.

A few days after the New Year we moved to a camp near the village of Quercianella for tactical training. A railroad track passed along the west side of the camp, and we suffered our first casualties when a soldier walking along the track set off a "bouncing betty" mine. A medic and a litter team went to help him, and one of them set off another mine, killing three more. A chaplain ran to see if he could help and stepped on yet another mine. Eight men were killed that day. Pete Borsuk and I watched the last of this from an embankment above. When Borsuk heard the "snap" of the last mine, he pulled me to the ground with him as the last German S mine detonated.

I tried to express my gratitude for his saving me from injury or death, but Borsuk shrugged his shoulders and said, "It was nothing. Someday you may do the same for me."

On January 9th, 1945, we had been in camp at Quercianella for about a week when we were issued ammunition for machine guns, rifles, and carbines, plus hand grenades, mortar rounds, flares, and a few bazooka launchers and antitank rockets. We were herded onto army trucks and driven into the foothills of the Apennine Mountains. We got out of the trucks and marched for about ten miles up a mountain pass. George Company was assigned to the village of Cutigliano on the east side of the valley, the forward edge of the American lines where each platoon was given a house in the undamaged village. The first platoon got the northernmost house at the edge of the village, closest to the Germans, who were still about five miles distant. The house of the first platoon was a strong stone structure, two stories high with a partial subbasement. Those who had occupied the house before us were leaving as we arrived. They left us some nice foxholes behind the house, toward the Germans. After some argument, they also left us two telephones and enough wire for us to communicate with the foxhole outposts.

We were at Cutigliano about a month, and during that time I led several reconnaissance patrols, often with partisan guides from the village. We never made contact with the Germans who were holed up in houses and a bunker far up and across the valley from us. A 10th Mountain patrol from a company on the other side of the valley did attack an enemy bunker on the west side of the river and killed several German soldiers.

I developed a reputation, not at all justified, as a daredevil among the men of my platoon because on a combat patrol one night, we came across a deep, snow-filled valley that prevented us from reaching an area where I thought some Germans were hiding in a house. I ordered the mortar team to fire a few rounds on the presumed German position to see if we could draw them out. After sending three or four mortar rounds in the general direction of the Germans, we saw no signs of life. I gave up, and we went home without any success, much to the relief of the men on the patrol, but to the disappointment of my battalion commander, who had counted on me to bring back a prisoner.

In early February, another unit relieved us. Late one night, we made our way down to the road, and after we marched a few miles, we boarded trucks and were driven to a small hamlet west of the beautiful medieval walled city of Lucca. My platoon was given a nice two-story farmhouse, and we were told we could bed down on the second floor. The family would continue to live on the first floor.

When we got to the house the farmer and his wife came out to talk with me. In a plaintive voice the man said, "I am afraid that your men may be tempted by my two teenage daughters. Please see that nothing happens to them. Also, please ask your men to stay away from the first floor, where my family is living. And please, do what you can to protect the antique furniture in the house. Some of it is valuable."

I assured the farmer that nothing would happen to either his daughters or his valuable furniture.

We were in the farmer's house about a week when word came that in a few days we were going back into the line and soon would be mounting a major attack.

Our reluctant host heard the news as well, and he came to me and said, "All of you were wonderful soldiers, and my wife and I are so pleased that nothing has been damaged. My family will host a spaghetti and wine party for you the evening before you leave if you can find us some flour and ground meat from your stores."

The supply sergeant provided the flour and ground meat, because I was the company supply officer, and perhaps more important, because we included the supply sergeant in the party. Two mornings later, several long tables were set up on the front lawn, to be covered with long rows of drying spaghetti. By late afternoon all was ready; the owner recruited some of my men to help put chairs and benches along both sides of the long tables. The men sat down and the ladies of the house brought out glasses and bottles of a delightful red wine.

The toasts began, first by the farmer, who said, in broken English, "We are so delighted to have had you here with us, and we wish that your next venture is successful and that all of you return home well and happy."

I responded with a brief, slightly nervous toast, in English: "It has been a great pleasure to be with you these days, and we are grateful to you for sharing your home with us. We will always remember your delightful hospitality and the friendship you have extended to us."

The women brought out plates piled high with pasta covered with tomato and meat sauce. It was a wonderful feast, followed by some fine singing. The Italians sang several romantic ballads, some sad, and we responded. I can't recall what we sang except for two infantry marching songs. The evening ended when the wine ran out.

CHAPTER 4

At noon the day after the feast, on February 17th, we were loaded into army trucks, and in a roundabout way headed toward the mountains. It was well after dark when the trucks stopped to unload us. We were told to march north up the canyon for twenty miles to where there were several bombed-out villages. When we arrived we were to be met by partisan guides who would lead us into a village where we were to take concealment. There were to be no fires and no cigarettes. We were told to keep completely out of sight the next day.

As we marched into one of the destroyed towns that night we saw a high, ice-covered vertical cliff ahead of us, called Riva Ridge. On our right was another mountain, much bigger, known as Monte Belvedere. Over the past year two divisions had tried to take Monte Belvedere, but each had been thrown back after suffering heavy casualties, in part because the Germans controlled Riva Ridge. From there they directed accurate artillery fire onto the slopes of Belvedere. It was now our turn to try to rout them.

The battle plan called for the First Battalion and parts of the Second Battalion of the Eighty-sixth Mountain Infantry to climb Riva Ridge the night of February 18th, kill any Germans present, and hold the ridge against any counterattacks. We believed the ridge was lightly defended, because our senior officer told us that the Germans thought the 1,800-foot-high, ice-covered ridge couldn't be scaled, certainly not at night.

But unknown to the Germans, for several weeks prior to February 18th, the First and Second Battalions had sent out parties of experienced rock climbers. They had marked several trails up the face of Riva Ridge, putting in pitons and ropes where they were needed. Five of these trails had been selected for the assault. At full dark the First

Battalion and parts of the Second Battalion, eight hundred men in all, divided in five companies, began climbing. They reached the crest a little after 1:00 A.M., meeting poorly organized resistance that was quickly suppressed with only a few American casualties (but quite a few German ones). The Germans were caught by surprise.

Heavy fog blanketed the area the next morning. My platoon and I were to take additional ammunition up to the men on Riva Ridge. We loaded our packs, and with the help of a guide, got to the crest of the ridge without trouble. On top, more guides waited to take us to designated ammunition storage sites. The company headquarters was in a small cave dug into the snow at the edge of the scarp. I went into the cave and found that the captain who commanded the company had been shot through the mouth. He'd been hit while he was talking, and the bullet had gone through both cheeks with only minimal damage to his bone and teeth.

I asked if he needed any help.

He said he was okay and thanked me for bringing up the ammunition.

We delivered the ammunition, and our guide led us back down to the base of the ridge. We spent the next night in bombed-out houses.

At 11:30 P.M. on February 19th, the night after Riva Ridge had been taken, the Eighty-fifth and Eighty-seventh Mountain Infantry Regiments began the assault on Monte Belvedere. After much fighting they took and held it, despite heavy casualties. With the capture of Belvedere, the way was open to the Po Valley and beyond. Despite several German counterattacks, U.S. troops successfully secured Belvedere.

The Third Battalion of the Eighty-sixth then launched an attack on Mount Della Torraccia, to the northeast of Belvedere. Heavy fighting over three days left the Third Battalion with many casualties. The Second Battalion, my battalion, moved around on the east flank of Della Torraccia, where there was a strong German counterattack threatening the Third Battalion's position.

After the Della Torraccia counterattack was beaten off, there was a day or two of relative calm. Up to that point no one in my unit had been hurt.

On March 1st, 1945, I was summoned to company headquarters, where Captain Ridgeway Foust, the company commander, met me. Foust was probably in his late twenties. He handed me a contour map of the area north of where my platoon was dug in. Near the center of the map I saw a pencil mark on a small hill with a house on the top.

Pointing to the mark on the map, he said, "Lieutenant Wendorf, that hill is your objective." Then he pointed to another hill about a thousand yards south of my objective. "This is where your platoon is located now. The day after tomorrow morning, on

March 3rd at 6:00 A.M., you are to move your platoon to a position about five hundred yards from the Germans, somewhere here." He pointed to a dot on the map. "You are to begin your assault at 7:00 A.M., and continue attacking until you reach your objective. Our artillery will lay down a heavy barrage on the German position, between 6:40 and 7:00 A.M."

He repeated my orders to be sure I understood. Then he added, "Your platoon will lead the attack. The First and Second Battalions of the Eighty-sixth will make a general assault on Castel d'Aiano, a heavily defended village about two miles to the north and east of your initial objective."

I was in charge of the First Platoon, Company G, Second Battalion, Eighty-sixth Mountain Infantry, 10th Mountain Division, and we were about to go into battle, a serious war now, no more patrolling or raiding. This time we were to make a major assault toward the Po Valley through the heart of the German defense.

I returned to my platoon, dug in on the south face of a large, low hill, just below its crest. We were two hundred yards behind the most forward American units, another company of the Second Battalion. Our position wasn't good for defense against an attack, but it was relatively well protected from German artillery. I asked my platoon sergeant to gather the squad leaders. When the group was assembled I repeated the orders Captain Foust gave me, including the fact that we would be leading the attack.

Late that night the American artillery opened up with a terrific barrage that lasted for a quarter of an hour. The Germans sent back a few rounds, one of which landed close and scattered lumps of dirt on top of my sleeping bag. No one was hit. I was so tired I quickly went back to sleep.

Early the next morning, on March 2, I saw Lieutenant Irving Wall, a friend from Officer Candidate School at Fort Benning, walking toward me. Wall was twenty years old, like me. He was a good-natured, slightly chubby guy. He was in command of the heavy weapons platoon in the Second Battalion.

After a brief greeting, he said, "I'm looking for suitable locations to place my weapons so I can support the attack tomorrow. Do you want to join me?" I told him I did. "My platoon is leading the attack, and I need to look over the area where we'll begin our assault," I said.

We made the short climb to the top of the hill, beyond where my platoon was dug in. We found a gently sloping landscape broken by a deep gully going down toward what I assumed was the German position. The open terrain had a cover of trees that extended for some distance on the west side of the gully. On its east side was a narrow, open flat area. Beyond that limited area the surface was rough, several feet higher, thickly covered by thorn bushes. A trail ran down the middle of the right side to a two-story stone building. I noticed a ditch about two hundred feet long, cutting the gully at right angles near its head. The ditch was about two feet wide and eight inches deep, adequate for my men to lie in while we waited to begin the assault in the morning. The ditch would put us in position to charge down the narrow flat area on the east side of the gully to attack the Germans at the bottom.

As Wall and I continued checking out the terrain, we saw several soldiers in foxholes in the wooded area on the west side of the gully, and we walked over to talk with them. They were the most forward 10th Mountain unit in this action. It was still early in the morning and the light was poor. Although it was eerie and quiet, we could hear the murmur of voices. The men in the foxholes would look at us and glance away, obviously traumatized and turned inward. The previous night must have been hell. Dead German soldiers lay all around their foxholes. I didn't count them, but there seemed to be between thirty and forty bodies. I noticed that many of the dead had their pockets turned inside out. I thought to myself, "Thank God they were killed here and I won't have to face them tomorrow morning."

I saw the platoon leader still in his foxhole and walked over, sat down beside him, and said, "You seem to have had one hell of a fight here last night. What happened?" He heaved a deep, weary sigh. "We were almost overrun. It was a quiet night, but just before midnight we heard metal clanking on that hill over there." He pointed to the west to a small hill about seventy-five yards from where we were sitting. "I sent up some flares, and we saw three Germans trying to set up a machine gun. There were a lot more of them down the slope in front of us, some almost to our outpost foxholes. I had an artillery forward observer with me here, and while the rest of us were shooting at the Germans, he called down an artillery barrage on the Germans in front, almost on top of us. That killed most of them. We killed the rest."

I viewed the somber scene with dread in my heart. I knew for the first time I was in a real war, and I was worried about what I would face the next morning. For a moment, I thought of the battalion surgeon who rode with me on the train to the port of embarkation and his promise that he would keep me alive if I could get to his aid station. Putting those thoughts behind me, and pointing east, I asked, "What's that two-story stone building on the trail over there?"

"That's an old barn," he said. "We're using it as an artillery observation post."

With a last look around, Wall and I walked back to the trail, where we saw two more dead Germans, both young boys. We went down to the stone barn. I knocked on the door, and someone let us in. A few moments later a German shell hit the side of the wall. The observer who let us in chuckled. "That was your welcome, lieutenant. They did that just to let you know they saw you come in."

We decided to leave before the Germans sent us any more welcoming shots. We unlatched the door and scurried back up the hill in silence. We were both shocked by the hill covered with bodies. I was thinking about the next day, and apprehensive. Wall didn't say a word until he turned to go. "Good-bye, Fred, and good luck," he said, shook my hand, and left.

"My God," I exclaimed to Sergeant David Black, as I eased down beside him. "The forward slope of this hill is covered with German bodies. If our artillery hadn't slaughtered them, they would have been all over us last night. Go up there and look at those dead Krauts. And while you're there, look at the ditch at the head of the gully. I want to place the men there tomorrow, before we begin the assault. I need your opinion."

I had volunteered to join the 10th Mountain Division knowing it was about to go to Italy to fight the Germans. I felt it was my duty to serve, and I wanted to be with an elite unit. The next day would bring my first real action, and I thought to myself as I tried to get comfortable on the cold ground, "I'm as ready as I'll ever be."

Back to Tucson
(1947–1948)

CHAPTER 5

I survived March 3rd, although barely. That day was every bit as bad as I feared it would be. I was sure the sniper who killed the two men next to me was going to kill me too, and for a while I didn't think I could stand up, but finally I did, only to be hit by shrapnel from a tree-burst thirty minutes later. Sometimes I still relive that day for a moment or two and wish I had turned left instead of right, but I always remind myself that the next shell might have been worse. Then I go back to work.

With the nightmare of war and two years in army hospitals behind me, I was eager to return to the University of Arizona and continue my undergraduate education. I was a different person from the young boy who left there in January 1943. This time I was a wounded war veteran and a married man. I was determined to be a good student and become an archaeologist. I told myself nothing would stand in my way.

Returning with Nancy to Tucson in January 1947, I soon learned that all of the cheap Quonset hut apartments where most of the married students lived were rented until the end of the spring term. Nancy began looking for a place where we could stay. She found a clean one-bedroom apartment that we could afford not far from the university. Shortly after I enrolled I had to tell my professors that I needed to return to the army hospital to be discharged. I assured them I'd be at the hospital only a few days. I expected the trip would take a week. I left Nancy in Tucson while I went to Michigan. She'd had enough traveling and wanted to stay home while I was away. It took me only three days to get to Battle Creek, to be discharged from the hospital, and retired by the army. It took two more days to drive back to Tucson.

At the university I took the normal load of five advanced undergraduate courses, including Southwestern archaeology and introductory physical anthropology. I discovered I also had to take another three hours of advanced German to complete my foreign language requirement. I had taken two years of German at Texas Military College, but in the intervening years I had forgotten all I'd learned. I knew I couldn't pass an advanced class without preparation. To coach me, I hired an elderly German teacher who lived in Bisbee (where Nancy's mother lived), and I went to him each weekend for an hour-long session. We had a friendly relationship, but my progress was slow, probably because I didn't spend enough time studying German between our review sessions.

Nancy and I were away from Tucson the entire summer of 1947. We spent the first eight weeks at the University of Arizona Archaeology Field School in east-central Arizona at Point of Pines on the San Carlos Apache Indian Reservation. Emil W. Haury, head of the Department of Anthropology at the University of Arizona, was its director. Haury was a delightful man, generous with his knowledge, and open and friendly with the students. He had high standards for himself and his students.

I had been reluctant to sign up for the field school because of my injured arm, and one day Haury stopped me in the hall and asked if I was going. I said, "I don't think so. I'm concerned that I won't be able to dig. How can I use a shovel and a big pick with only one arm? I might just be in the way." He looked me in the eyes for several seconds, and then he said, "Why don't we find out? Go on and sign up for the field school, Fred. I expect you can do more than you think."

So, in June 1947, at the end of that first semester after my discharge from the army hospital, Nancy and I, with nineteen other students from all over the country, went to the University of Arizona Archaeology Field School. Nancy wasn't enrolled as a student, so we had to pay a small fee for her room and board. I wanted her to be with me.

I soon learned that despite my war injuries I *could* dig with a pick and shovel, and I could do it well. I did it in a way that greatly helped my injured arm, too. I couldn't lift with my right arm, but I could use the palm of my hand as a fulcrum. I wore heavy leather gloves and placed the end of the shovel handle firmly in my right palm. With my left hand I held the shovel just above the blade, shoved the blade in the dirt pile with my left foot, lifted the shovel and the dirt with my left hand, and threw the dirt where it needed to go. A little practice and I was almost as good as the other students. I wasn't very good at using the heavy pick, however. I had to swing it with my left hand midway up the pick handle, then put the palm of my right hand at the end of the handle, using it as a fulcrum. I wasn't as effective with the pick as the other students, even the girls, but using the pick rapidly built up the muscles in my left arm.

I admired Haury, or "Doc" as his students called him. He was in his late forties, tall, well built, with a craggy, handsome face. Although he had two assistant supervisors, he managed to get around to talk about the work with each student almost every day. He worked us hard, and we learned a lot about Southwestern archaeology.

At that time Point of Pines was considered one of the best archaeology field schools in the country. In the summer of 1947 we students completed the excavation of a twenty-room, stone-walled pueblo that had been partially dug the previous summer, and twelve, semi-subterranean pit houses. The pueblo rooms were arranged in two long, straight parallel lines, one room in front of the other connected by a doorway. The entrance to the front rooms was through the roof—there were no outside doorways. The walls were made of rough-shaped sandstone blocks laid up as dry masonry. The pueblo had been suddenly abandoned, and everything, including pots, axes, and many other small tools, had been left in place. Against one wall stood a large slab with a painted mask on one surface, probably depicting a spirit or deity. What could have happened to drive the people away so suddenly? No one knew, and today we still don't know.

Most of the students' efforts at Point of Pines went into clearing the rooms and learning how to use trowels to expose a floor. We didn't keep daily journals, but we were expected to complete feature forms recording the details of each room and its contents. Much of the learning occurred in the evening, working in the lab, or listening to lectures on regional archaeology.

We also had volleyball contests almost every evening. The other students urged me to play, and I was soon playing a mean game. My height and the strength in my left (good) arm gave me a real advantage. I think Haury was amused that I, the one who thought he might be in the way, was so aggressive.

Point of Pines was important to me, in part because it was there I met Alfred Vincent Kidder, then the most highly regarded archaeologist in the United States. Kidder was an impressive man, tall and muscular; he was handsome in a rugged sort of way. He frequently came over to the room pit where another student and I were excavating. He'd sit on the ground beside us, and, with his soft, gentle voice, he'd tell stories about his early days in Southwestern archaeology.

Late in the spring of 1947, just before the beginning of the field school, I had written to Harold S. Colton, director of the Museum of Northern Arizona, and asked him if I could study pottery typology with him during the summer after the field school. Colton was widely recognized as the outstanding specialist on Southwestern pottery. He accepted my application and offered Nancy and me the use of museum housing while we were in Flagstaff.

Colton was a short, wiry fellow in his late sixties, with salt-and-pepper hair and a short goatee. Trained as a zoologist, he had given that discipline up for archaeology. His ceramic typologies, however, reflected his background in zoology. As in zoological classifications, he grouped his pottery types into larger units, and these in turn he grouped into still larger units. Pottery types do not breed, as biological species do, yet Colton's typological methodology enabled him to define "keys" that greatly facilitated the identification of the types in a ceramic collection.

Colton taught me about the classification of potsherds using sherds selected from a park service collection of three hundred sites in the Petrified Forest National Monument. He confined my analysis to one hundred sites because of the limited time I had available, and to allow me to focus on the earlier sites in the collection, those dating before A.D. 1200.

He took me to his laboratory where the Petrified Forest collection was stored, got down a box, poured the sherds onto the table, told me to classify them, and left. When he returned about an hour later it must have been obvious that I knew nothing about classifying black-on-white pottery. He sat down and started to show me how to distinguish iron paint from carbon paint, and how to recognize light paste and dark paste. He left me for an hour or so to try again. When he returned he noted a few new mistakes and showed me why I'd made them, then gave me a list of the local pottery types, grouped by paint, paste, and design style, and asked me to record the site number, the types by name and number of each type in the box. Then he got down a second box and I repeated the process, this time with fewer mistakes.

He worked with me for about four weeks, until I'd studied and recorded the entire collection from one hundred sites, and by the end I wasn't making many mistakes. He gave me reprints of articles on the archaeology around the Petrified Forest and west from there to Flagstaff, and asked me to read them. When I told him I had read the reprints he gave me, he had me write a brief description of the pottery I had been studying, which was published in the *Plateau* the next year, 1948, my first publication. What a thrill it was to see my name in print.

My experience with Colton, and all I had learned from studying the pottery, led me to decide to do my dissertation research on the early ceramic sites in the Petrified Forest National Monument. I was fascinated by one of the pottery types, Adamana Brown. It seemed to be the earliest pottery in the collections I studied. During manufacture Adamana Brown was thinned using a paddle and anvil, a technique commonly found in the pottery in southern Arizona, but unknown in northern Arizona except for Adamana Brown. I wondered what the relationship was between the people who made Adamana Brown and those who made the gray-colored and black-on-white pottery, otherwise the earliest pottery in the Petrified Forest. On my last day with Colton, I discussed my plans with him, and he responded enthusiastically. He offered to arrange for the Museum of Northern Arizona to sponsor my project, and even to help me get a grant to cover some of the costs.

This period at the Museum of Northern Arizona has special memories for Nancy and me. The housing the museum offered turned out to be a decrepit A-frame, about six feet high at the ridge, wide enough at the base for two cots with mattresses, with a two-foot space between them. The walls were shingled, but there were a few large holes in them. One evening I was sitting on my cot while Nancy was taking a bath. She was sitting in a washbasin filled with water when a skunk walked in through one of the holes. As it walked around the washbasin, Nancy held her feet up and watched it saunter out through another hole near the front door. She said nothing, but her bath was brief.

At the close of the 1947 field school at Point of Pines, Haury asked me if I'd be interested in writing the report on the small pueblo with underlying pit houses that had been excavated by the 1946 and 1947 field schools. This was an important and unusual opportunity. It told me, and others, that Haury had confidence in me, even though I was an undergraduate with little training in archaeology. It was an opportunity I couldn't refuse, despite the pressure of writing a complex book-length report while continuing my classes.

Haury's instructional technique was not so different from Colton's. When I reported to him that I was ready to start, he took me into a large room with a big table and a few chairs in the center and shelves along an entire wall filled with large cardboard boxes. He waved his hand at the boxes and said, "There it is," and walked out the door, leaving me saying to myself, "What the hell do I do now?"

I decided I would start with "A." That led me to axes, all of which were in one heavy box. I got them out and spent the next several days trying to classify them. There were seventy-one grooved, polished stone axes in this collection, and they all looked alike to me. Haury occasionally walked by and glanced into the lab through the half-glass door. After several days of this, he came into the lab. He said, "You seem to be having difficulty with these axes. Would you like some help?"

"Yes, sir, please," I said in my best army manner.

Haury noted there were only four kinds of axes in this collection, and proceeded to sort out the four groups: Type A, Type B, Type C, and Type D. He showed me how to measure them, their lengths, widths, and thicknesses; the widths and depths of the grooves; and the lengths of the bits. I also recorded the types of stone material used for the axes.

He said, "Let's decide how many and which axes you want to illustrate." He noted that the axes all looked alike, and said, "We don't need to illustrate more than four, maybe a couple from Type A, one from Type B, and one from Type D. First, let's pick out the axes to be illustrated."

He showed me how to draw up a proportional diagonal plot so we could see how many axes it was possible to get on a page and the size they would be when the illustration was reduced for publication. With his guidance and the plot, I drew up two crude dummy sheets, one of which was an outline of the two Type A axes, plus cross-sections of each. Later, the dummy sheets would show me how they would be arranged for publication. He had me put the catalog number of each axe within its outline. Then he put the Type A axes to be illustrated in a cigar box he found under the table, labeled it "figure z," and wrote figure z on the dummy sheet. We did the same for the Type B and D axes. He labeled that box and dummy sheet figure y.

Using the dimension and raw material data I had recorded, he wrote a long paragraph describing the attributes of Type A and noting how many there were, referred to figure z, and moved on to do the same for Types B, C, and D, and figure y. All of this analysis and description took a little over two hours, and when it was done, I was ready to write the descriptions of my artifacts from Point of Pines. I started with B, the numerous *bone* tools in the collection.

Nancy was a great help when we began writing the manuscript and preparing the illustrations for the book. She had real artistic ability, and she drew and inked almost all the artifact illustrations, except for those few pieces that had been photographed. Every night she drew artifacts or typed the text, often for the second, third, or nth time, while I wrote. Neither of us had ever done anything like this before. We had a lot to learn.

Barton Wright, a draftsman at the Arizona State Museum, did all of the individual room drawings. I drafted the charts and two large site maps, one showing the pit houses and their distribution, and the other a map of the pueblo, both at the same scale. The pueblo map showed the position of the artifacts on the floors of the rooms. The two maps were difficult since I had only a beginner's skill as a draftsman. I kept making mistakes that had to be corrected so the maps would be neat and the corrections invisible to the reader. I envisioned that either the two maps would be printed "in register" on the same sheet in two colors, or they would be printed separately and bound together, with the pueblo map printed on translucent paper so the reader could see at a glance the relationship between the two occupations.

After I made many errors on drafting paper and illustration board, someone suggested I use a tracing cloth, where my mistakes sometimes could be corrected with an erasure. I went through a lot of tracing cloth, and never did become a truly competent draftsman. Fortunately, the Veterans Administration reimbursed me for all of my drafting equipment and supplies. I liked the thin, light drafting board that was one of my first purchases. It stayed with me for many, many years.

I was grateful I didn't have to learn artifact photography during this hectic period. Haury asked his assistant, Ted Sayles, to help me with the photos, providing me with a selection of general views of the surrounding area and the excavations, as well as some of the artifacts that were not to be drawn. From time to time Sayles gave me a few prints and told me how to trim and glue them with rubber cement to a mounting board, which I did.

In January 1948, I applied for admission to graduate school in anthropology to two universities, Harvard and the University of Michigan. I asked Haury to write me a letter of recommendation to both institutions. I also asked Alfred V. Kidder to send a letter to Harvard. I was accepted at both universities, but neither offered me a fellowship. Jimmy Griffin had led me to expect that I would receive a fellowship from Michigan, but the departmental faculty decided to give their single fellowship to the promising son of a member of that faculty. I wanted to go to Harvard, in part because it had a strong program in American Southwestern archaeology and that was the area in which I wanted to specialize. By not offering me a fellowship, Michigan made my decision easy. I wrote the school and declined. I wrote to Harvard and accepted. I knew my army pension would cover Nancy's and my living expenses, and the Veterans Administration would pay my tuition and fees, as well as for any supplies I might need.

In the meantime I labored on Haury's project. I didn't show the manuscript to him until I finished it. In late May 1948, nine months after I started the analysis of Site W:10:51, I asked his secretary if I could see him. I went into his office and proudly placed two packages on his desk: a full stationery box containing the manuscript neatly typed and edited; the other, a much larger package wrapped in brown paper, contained the illustrations. Haury glanced at the illustrations first, and then read a few pages of the text. "You may be stubborn," he said, "but you get things done. Thank you, Fred."

The manuscript was published by the University of Arizona Press in 1950 as *A Report on the Excavation of a Small Ruin near Point of Pines, East Central Arizona*. It was my first book.

In late May the University of Arizona awarded me a BA degree with a major in anthropology. I attended the ceremony and Nancy came to observe. Neither my mother nor Nancy's came because I hadn't asked them. To me it was a minor event. I had my eye firmly fixed on one goal, a PhD from Harvard.

Right after graduation, during the summer of 1948, on Haury's recommendation, I was hired as an assistant to Stanley Stubbs, the director of an archaeological field school for the University of New Mexico. Stubbs was head of the Laboratory of Anthropology of the Museum of New Mexico in Santa Fe. He had been loaned to the University of New Mexico to run the archaeology field school. Stubbs was a quiet, easygoing man who taught me a lot about the archaeology of northern New Mexico and the Rio Grande Valley that summer.

With Stubbs's guidance, I learned how to dig an adobe-walled pueblo. In my first trench I cut through four thick adobe walls without knowing they were there. The next day, to my acute embarrassment, Stubbs pointed out each wall to me as we walked down the trench together. His criticism, however, was gentle.

CHAPTER 6

A fter the New Mexico field school was over, Nancy and I drove to Cambridge in our 1945 Plymouth, arriving in late August of 1948. It was a mistake to come in August. Temperatures were high and the humidity made it more uncomfortable than either Tucson or Albuquerque. Not an apartment in the Cambridge area had air-conditioning. We stayed for three nights in a motel on the outskirts of Boston while we looked for a place to live. Everything near Harvard Square was already rented, or far beyond our resources.

After several days, we decided to look in a residential area on the south side of the Charles River, in Boston. There we found a reasonable, almost new one-bedroom apartment in a large multistory building not far from the bridge I would have to cross to attend my classes at Harvard. We moved in and as soon as we unpacked we went back to Cambridge to explore the university, heading first to the Peabody Museum, where the offices of the anthropology department were housed. Only the departmental secretary and the librarian in the Peabody Museum Library were in their offices.

We walked around the beautiful academic quadrangle, admired the student residential halls, and like so many others, fell in love with Harvard. It was everything I'd hoped it would be. Other days we explored the business school, the museums, several classroom buildings, and the magnificent Weidner Library. I scouted out a few places to park my car. I could have used the Metropolitan Transit Authority, but it would have required a trip to downtown Boston, a change of trains, and a trip back to Cambridge—a two-hour commute during rush hour.

Before classes started Nancy found a job in the library in the Boston Athenaeum. She was there only a few months. I don't recall why she left, but I suspect she took the job to keep from being bored or lonely, and she found she was even more bored at the Athenaeum.

On registration day, I reported to the department to find out what courses I should take and to meet some of the faculty. I was delighted to learn that J. O. (John Otis) Brew, the director of the Peabody Museum, was to be my advisor. He was a famous Southwestern archaeologist and the second winner of the Viking Medal for outstanding contributions to American archaeology. He was short and chubby, and had a round, often smiling face.

Brew had me sign up for a course in European prehistory taught by Hugh Hencken, a highly regarded specialist in European prehistory; a course in physical anthropology given by E. A. Hooton, the dean of American physical anthropology; a course on the ethnology of Oceania and Australia given by Douglas Oliver; and a course on Mesoamerican archaeology taught by Alfred M. Tozzer, the recognized master in that subject. They were all good courses, full of data, with lots of discussion and classroom analyses. We spent a great deal of time finding appropriate publications for each topic, and we were expected to read them. This was a professional school, and that first semester this young man from Terrell, Texas, was out of his depth.

Some of the classes were a mix of graduate and undergraduate students. The graduate-only classes were small; there were seven students in Hooton's physical anthropology course, and three in Tozzer's Mesoamerican class. Hooton had a laboratory component where we learned how to measure bones, and, more demanding for me, how to identify small fragments of human bone—not only the name of the bone, but also which side and which end.

Tozzer's class was more alien to me. On the first day we found him writing on the blackboard in small script, listing dozens, perhaps more than a hundred, complete references. Ultimately, he filled one large and two small blackboards. He told us to copy the references and read or at least look at every one. He said he would have a blackboard full of references for us to copy at the beginning of each class. During class he planned to discuss the most useful references and tell us why they were important.

I discovered that each of my four classes required me to write at least two, sometimes three, major papers, between fifty and a hundred pages in length. Soon Nancy was typing them on my little portable typewriter, a gift from my father for passing a typing course in high school. Harvard was a different world from my experience at other universities. After I got the comments and grades from my first papers, I saw that those four courses would require every moment of my time. If I were to succeed, I'd need to put forth more effort than ever before.

The mixed graduate/undergraduate classes were larger, with ten to fifteen students, mostly undergraduates, including a few women from Radcliffe, and three or four graduate students. The same work was required of everyone, and there was considerable competition between the undergraduate and graduate students. The undergraduates were bright, well informed, and highly motivated. Most had attended private preparatory schools; they were the intellectual equals of the graduate students. There were no "gentleman C" students. If Harvard had a few of those, they never turned up in the anthropology courses. I found it frustrating to spend a week working on a paper, one I thought was perfect, or almost so, only to receive a grade in the high 80s, then see a high 90 on my undergraduate neighbor's paper.

The department expected me to make at least half A's and half B's. C's were considered failing. I made three B's and an A- at the end of my first semester. J. O. Brew told me he was disappointed and that I would have to do better next time.

Then there was the problem of German. Before Harvard anthropology students can take the General Exam, they have to pass at least one language exam. In my case it was to be German. I barely passed the three additional hours of advanced German I needed to graduate from Arizona. Whatever German I'd had disappeared while I was in Italy.

Professor Hooton was the senior professor in the anthropology department. He and his wife offered tea and sandwiches every Friday to the graduate students. The new students quickly learned that it was politically expedient to take tea with the Hootons at least once a month. At first I refused to go because I had not been invited. But after I had been at Harvard about two months, Ned Danson, a second-year graduate student, took me aside and told me Mrs. Hooton had asked why I hadn't come for tea on Fridays. Danson said, "Be there at least once a month, Fred. It's important." I went the next Friday.

Hooton was known to be tough, particularly with regard to German. I don't know why I asked him to test my reading ability, but I went to his office and he got down his favorite book, *Das Lehrbuch der Anthropologie*. He opened it, handed it to me, and said, "Start with the first paragraph."

After I'd read a few sentences, he leaned over and closed the book. "You're not ready; come back next year." I was disappointed, but not surprised. I knew my German was poor. I realized I would have to work hard on my German if I expected to stay at Harvard. No more of the casual efforts that had gotten me through before. I knew I had to make an intensive, sustained effort if I was ever going to pass a German exam.

I had a College Outline Series paperback book that provided the essentials of German grammar, so I read it carefully, but the most important thing I did was to buy a box of five thousand German/English vocabulary cards. I took fifteen to twenty of the cards with me everywhere I went. I'd go systematically through the box, over and over again, until I could pick out a card at random and know either the German to English, or English to German. I did this for months, all through my first year at Harvard and the following summer, even in the field.

When I returned to Harvard at the beginning of my second year I asked Kidder's son, Alfred Kidder II, a member of the faculty who specialized in South American prehistory, to give me my German exam, and he agreed. Kidder II (known as Alfie to the students) picked out a book written in German on Peruvian archaeology, opened it somewhere in the middle, and, wonder of wonders, I *was* able to read it fluently. I think I could have passed even with Hooton, but I was not going to take the chance.

Because Harvard required two languages for a PhD, two or three days after I passed my German exam, I went to the student center and bought a box of five thousand Spanish/English vocabulary cards and started learning Spanish, using the same technique that had worked so well for me with the German. I'd had two years of Spanish in high school, and although Spanish was spoken more than German around Terrell and Tucson, I gave it the same intense effort as German. I chose a new set of cards every day, and at the end of the day I would go back to yesterday's cards to be sure I hadn't forgotten any of those. When I took my Spanish exam from Alfie Kidder a year later, I passed with no trouble.

In January 1949, at the beginning of my second semester, Alfred Vincent Kidder, my friend from Point of Pines, and his wife, Madeline, asked Nancy and me if we would stay in their home while they were in Guatemala during the spring semester. Kidder was the director of a large Mesoamerican archaeology project supported by the Carnegie Institution, a science development organization. Kidder and his wife lived in a beautiful old home only three blocks from the Peabody Museum Library. We found it to be a great pleasure to live at the Kidder house that second semester. It was built on a large corner lot with several large trees, and very little traffic on the adjacent streets. The proximity to the Peabody Museum Library saved me a lot of time. When I wasn't in class or sleeping, I lived at that library. We stayed in the Kidder home from mid-January, the beginning of the spring semester, until late May 1949.

When we had come to look at his house in early January, Kidder walked us through the various rooms where we would have free access, including one small bright room lined with bookshelves. He suggested I might like to work there because of the big desk in the room. He called it his "fiction room" because he had a large collection of paperbacks, mostly detective and science fiction works. One caught my eye in the middle of a shelf; its title was *Men out of Asia,* a nonfiction work by Harold Gladwin, once a wealthy supporter of archaeology.

I knew that Kidder and Gladwin had been close friends for years, and that Kidder had been a big help to Gladwin when he built the fabulous Gila Pueblo Archaeological Foundation at Globe, Arizona. In the 1930s and 1940s Gladwin had sponsored and financed many important archaeological projects in the American Southwest. In the mid-1940s he developed an interest in trade across the Pacific to Mexico and Central America that soon became an obsession. He wrote *Men out of Asia* to explain his ideas and got an artist to illustrate his main points. His central character was Professor Phuddy Duddy, modeled after A. V. Kidder, the most vocal opponent of Gladwin's proposed trans-Pacific contacts. The book had won a Whittlesey House Prize as the best book of 1947. Kidder had not been pleased when Gladwin caricatured him in his book. I couldn't help smiling. Filing it with fiction was just the right response.

My dissertation research began during the summer of 1949, after my first year at Harvard, almost a year before my General Exams. I got two grants for my research totaling eight hundred dollars, of which five hundred dollars came from the Wenner-Gren Foundation (then the Viking Fund) and three hundred dollars from the Colt Archaeological Institute. Harold Colton had arranged for both of the grants. He also introduced me to a Ford dealer in Gallup, New Mexico, who allowed me to rent/purchase an old pickup. The terms were that I would insure it and return it in the same condition eight weeks later. He would buy it back for what I'd paid less seventy-five dollars. I would be out only seventy-five dollars, plus the insurance and fuel costs.

I decided I had enough money to feed a crew of seven people for eight weeks: Nancy, five student helpers, and me. The students would get free lodging and food Nancy cooked, but they would have to get to the Petrified Forest on their own and bring their own sheets, pillowcases, and blankets. I soon had my five volunteers, from Harvard and other universities in the Boston area. The student assistants were Alice Dewey, Betty Tooker, Ralph Emerson, and a husband-and-wife team, Clair and Nina Williams.

To work in the remote Petrified Forest it was necessary to have a field camp, so I borrowed seven beds and mattresses; five good sleeping tents; two canvas tarps, one for the kitchen, the other to cover the toilet; a dozen trowels; and six picks and shovels. Most of the equipment came from the Laboratory of Anthropology, the rest from the Museum of Northern Arizona. I borrowed a table on sawhorses for us to eat on and as a place to do our lab work, an ice cooler where we could keep fresh food, a box with kitchen equipment, dishes and tableware, a kerosene stove, about ten army surplus jerry cans for water, and a toilet box. I bought lumber to build frames around the tents and the toilet, and several hundred heavy paper bags to hold the artifacts we expected to recover during the excavations.

Everything was ready when the crew showed up at the post office in Holbrook, Arizona, at noon on the assigned day. Three of them had their own cars, and the others hitched rides with them. We drove the thirty miles to our camping area in the Petrified Forest, and set up our camp, which took us about two days.

We were very proud of the shower we made from a large washtub. We drilled a hole in the center, adding a piece of one-half-inch pipe threaded on both ends, some rubber gaskets and threaded washers, a piece of hose with an attached showerhead, and a clamp to shut off the water. We made a platform so we could stand out of the mud while we showered. We built a frame seven feet high and put the tub on top. Finally, we made a ladder so we could fill the tub with water, and we were ready for our first customer. At first the shower was in much demand, because the days were hot and all of us were working hard. Before long, however, the mud that spread around the shower attracted large red ants. We dug a drainage ditch so the water would drain into a pool about ten feet from the shower, but it didn't help. We had to fight those ants all season.

My research in the Petrified Forest involved the excavation of two villages. We excavated the earlier village in this first season. Known as the Flattop Site, it is on top of the highest mesa in the Petrified Forest National Monument, and has steep sides all around. The pottery and lithic artifacts we found on the surface suggested to me that it had been occupied before A.D. 500, because there was no black-on-white pottery. We excavated eight of the twenty-five small slab-lined houses visible on the surface at the Flattop Site. One house, larger and much deeper than the others, and round in outline, may have been a community ceremonial center, something like the kivas associated with most modern and almost all prehistoric pueblos. All of the other houses were smaller, about 10 to 12 feet in diameter, lined with vertical slabs, with a slab-lined entryway on one side and a slab-lined storage bin beside the entryway. The floors were sandstone bedrock, which the occupants had exposed by removing a few inches of dirt, and then digging around and removing the underlying sandstone slabs to a depth between 6 and 12 inches. Many of the houses had been burned. When we cleared the floors we found numerous pots and other artifacts still in place. The walls and roofs of the houses apparently had been of brush, because there was a lot of charcoal, much of it the size of small poles. The houses contained large quantities of charred corn, but few animal remains, leading me to infer that the people who had once lived here depended on corn for their food.

Archaeologists working in the American Southwest have an annual "rite of passage" each summer when they gather for a two-day meeting known as the Pecos Conference, named after the first meeting A. V. Kidder called in 1929, held at the Pecos

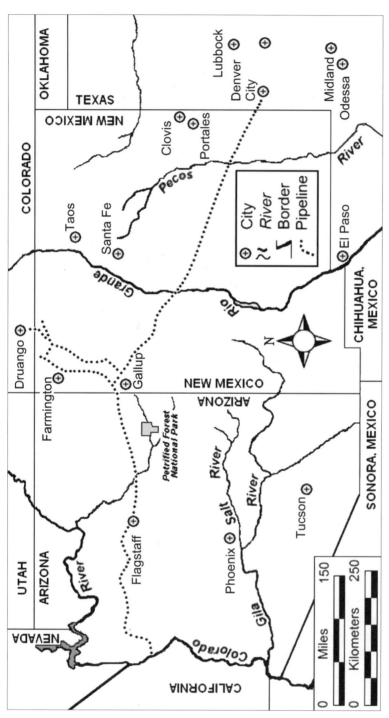

Map 2. Map of Arizona and New Mexico in the American Southwest, where Wendorf excavated two sites in the Petrified Forest National Monument. The dotted lines indicate Wendorf's first three salvage archaeology pipeline projects for the El Paso Natural Gas Company: the first, from near Farmington, New Mexico, south across the Navajo Reservation to near Gallup, New Mexico, and west from there to California (1950–1951); the second, from east of Farmington to a processing plant east of Gallup (1952); the third, from West Texas across New Mexico to Gallup (1953). Drafted by Chris and Cheryl Hill.

Pueblo. Archaeologists working in the area make an effort to be there so they can discuss what they found that summer and what they thought their findings meant. In late August 1949, about 150 archaeologists gathered at the Museum of Northern Arizona for the two-day meeting. I presented the results of my excavations at the Flattop Site, showed a few slides, and displayed one of the pots I had found. Many of those attending seemed pleased to hear what I had learned. Everyone knew I was still a graduate student. All three of my academic advisors, Brew, Colton, and Haury, were there, but they treated me like a colleague. I felt, at last, that I was an archaeologist, although a very junior one.

In the fall of 1949 Nancy and I decided to try to find a place closer to the university. The apartments near Harvard were still too expensive, even the bad ones. We were about to give up when Ray and Molly Thompson, two old friends from the summer at Point of Pines, offered to share an upstairs apartment that had two bedrooms, two baths, a large living room, and kitchen. It was in a run-down section of Cambridge, with a long walk to the Peabody Museum, but a lot closer than the apartment in Boston. We readily accepted their offer.

(Molly Kendall, the daughter of a prominent Arizona ranching family, had recently graduated from the University of Arizona. She had fallen in love with Thompson at Point of Pines, and they had married in the summer of the following year, 1948.)

My grades came up in the third semester. One of my courses in ethnology and theory taught by Clyde Kluckhohn required me to read and be prepared to discuss three to four hundred pages a week, with a tense "acid indigestion luncheon-discussion period" every Tuesday. I soon caught on to the Harvard system—work, work, and more work. I made an A.

Another course I took that third semester was the Archaeology of North America, taught by J. O. Brew. It was similar to Tozzer's course in that it required a lot of reading. Unlike Tozzer, Brew passed out typewritten sheets of references along with several printed bibliographies.

He started in the northeastern United States and covered all of North America, north of Mexico. In each area he discussed the key references. He told us to find each reference, scan it, and determine its major premise. He asked questions about the references, and you were expected to be familiar with them. He could tell instantly if you had not read the piece in question. If you hadn't, he'd frown and go on to someone else.

I got a lot of help from two of my fellow students: Ray Thompson, who helped me with the archaeology of Mexico and Central America, where he planned to do his dissertation research; and Pendleton (Pen) Banks, an ethnology student who tutored me in his field as well as in linguistics, about which I knew nothing. In turn, I helped them with North American and European prehistory.

My final course was on Pleistocene geology, taught by Kirk Bryan. It, too, was challenging. Sitting next to me in the class was an Egyptian named Rushdi Said. He was about three years older than I and had done some graduate work in Switzerland. He knew a lot more geology than I did, and he would explain things to me when I failed to understand something Bryan had said. We soon became good friends, although I never saw him outside Bryan's lectures.

There was no time for a social life, and it must have been boring for Nancy. The exception to our dull existence came because of my association with Henry K. Beecher, the remarkable military surgeon who had spent time with me at the field hospital in Italy after I was wounded. He'd asked me to call him if I came to Harvard, and I did call him a few weeks after classes started. He insisted that I come down to the hospital and have a snack with him and meet his associates. I went and he greeted me like an old friend. He asked me what I'd been doing since 1945.

I said I'd spent two years in various army hospitals, and the rest of the time going to school in Arizona trying to learn how to become an archaeologist. Then he told me that when he visited me at the field hospital he was doing a research project on why some seriously wounded soldiers would go into shock and die, and others with similar wounds would live. "You were one of a thousand wounded soldiers I studied for that project. I expected that those who came from unstable homes, divorced families, and so on would be more sensitive to pain and have a higher frequency of shock. I'm publishing the data in a book that I'm still working on. It is tentatively called *Levels of Pain*. It should be out next year."

I wanted to ask him if he put me in the "low tolerance for pain" group, but I thought maybe it was best that I didn't know. I'm not sure if he would have told me anyway. He wanted me to stay overnight, but I declined because Nancy was alone and I needed to go home to study.

About once a month I went down to Massachusetts General Hospital for a sandwich with Beecher and his staff, stayed an hour or two, and went home. On at least one occasion he had dinner with Nancy and me at our apartment, and once we went to his old colonial house in the country and had dinner with him and his wife.

Early in the third semester I became close friends with Jack Roberts and his family. Jack was a tall man who carried a little too much weight. He had been an army captain, an infantry rifle company commander in France, and he'd won a Silver Star near the end of the Battle of the Bulge for leading an assault when no one else would move. He'd gotten a bad case of trench foot, and as a consequence, had a funny, ducklike walk. Jack was one of three social anthropology assistant professors Harvard hired knowing that only one would be given tenure after five years.

Jack was brilliant. During his career he did such creative things as studying the tourist trade along highways, or the distribution of all the objects found in a Navajo hogan and the relationships between the artifacts and the people who lived there. He looked me up because he thought that as an archaeologist I would be interested in what he was learning, and I was.

I entered the PhD program at Harvard under terms that allowed me to take my General Exams during the fourth semester, and if I passed, I wouldn't have to take the course exams at the end of that term. General Exams were oral. Mine were set for an early afternoon toward the end of April 1950. In February I decided I'd spend all my time preparing for them; I learned for the first time to drink coffee to stay awake.

I studied and studied. My reviewing was systematic, beginning early in the morning and lasting until late at night, seven days a week. The exams were to cover everything in the classes I had taken, plus all four fields of anthropology: archaeology, physical anthropology, ethnology, and linguistics, as well as the anthropology exhibits in the Peabody Museum. In the library were copies of all of the previous exams, some going back for several years. I, and every other graduate student, carefully analyzed these exams to determine if there had been any patterns or changes over the years.

The day of the exam I went to my graduate student mailbox at the Peabody Museum and found a letter from the Smithsonian Institution offering me a job as an archaeologist in the River Basin Archaeological Salvage Program that fall. A few minutes later Brew came by the mail room and I showed him the letter. "Now you can flunk me, J. O. But I'll still eat."

"We're not going to flunk you, Fred. Let's go into the exam." In the room was a large table. I was told to sit at one end, while Brew and Kluckhohn would sit at the other. The rest of the faculty was arranged along both sides of the table. Hooton, as the senior professor, was the first questioner. He asked me the significance of the "rocker ulna." I knew the answer even before he had finished the question, then the next, and the next. They were hard questions, but they had all been asked before, so I was ready. Brew turned to Kirk Bryan, who asked me a general question about Pleistocene climate, which I knew as well. Brew turned to Alfred Kidder II, who had a box of pots hidden under the table, but he was interrupted by Kluckhohn.

"Don't we know enough about this candidate? I'd like to vote now," he said. Brew was flustered. The exam had been going on for less than thirty minutes and was scheduled to last three hours. After a pause, Brew agreed, turned to me, and said, "Please leave the room, but stay close by."

In the outer office the departmental secretary was making tea for the mid-exam break. She saw me and assumed I had failed. She rushed over to offer her condolences. I smiled, held out my hand, and said, "I don't think I failed." The door opened and Brew came out, smiling. "Congratulations, Fred, that was a great exam."

He ushered me back into the room where the other faculty added their congratulations. It was a fluke, of course. Had Brew started with Kidder and his pots, or had Kluckhohn not had an important meeting to go to, it would not have moved so quickly. Afterwards, I looked under the table at Kidder's pots. They were all from Peru, and I was unable to identify a single one.

The next day Brew asked me to join him in his office. He congratulated me again, and then said, "Fred, that was one of the best General Exams in the history of the anthropology department. Your achievements will follow you for many years and lead to many opportunities. I'm proud of you. You've come a long way." The borderline student who had started classes eighteen months before was gone forever.

Before I went back to the Petrified Forest to begin my second season of excavations, I spent two weeks with mineralogist Anna O. Shepard at her home/laboratory in Boulder, Colorado. In the 1930s, A. V. Kidder, then excavating at Pecos Pueblo, a few miles east of Santa Fe, New Mexico, had hired her to study the small bits of rock that potters add to their clay while making a vessel. These grains, known as temper, helped the clay dry evenly, in turn giving the pottery more strength. Shepard's results on the pottery found in the prehistoric pueblos in the Rio Grande area had revolutionized archaeologists' understanding of the role of pottery in the trade between the pueblos in that area. A few years later, in the 1940s, she had done a similar path-breaking study of some pottery in the Maya area.

I hoped Shepard might be able to show me how to identify the temper in the pottery I had collected at the site we were going to excavate again that summer. There were two different wares at this site—one brown, the other gray, and I thought perhaps differences in temper might tell me which ware was locally made and which had been imported. I spent two weeks with Shepard in her lab and learned that the identification of the temper in my pottery was beyond my limited mineralogical skills. I persuaded her to examine a larger sample of the pottery from my site and prepare a short paper that might be published as an appendix in the report on my two field seasons in the Petrified Forest. To my dismay, the sand temper used in both the black-on-white and brown pottery at my sites was not distinctive, and the sources could not be identified.

Colton gave me a grant of twelve hundred dollars for the 1950 season. He told me he had a grant from an unnamed foundation no one had ever heard of. There was never any paper on which the foundation's name was printed. Colton was wealthy, and we had great affection for each other. I'm not sure if he was bankrolling me or if he actually had searched out a small foundation and managed to obtain a small grant for me.

With the twelve hundred dollars I increased the size of my group of student workers to eight and hired a cook to give Nancy a break. I needed her skills as an artifact illustrator. The eight student assistants came from several schools, including Harvard and the University of Arizona. They were Bill Bullard, Jane Goodale, Charles Kellogg, Donald Maynard, Lynn Pease, Connie Peck, Robert Tanner, and Pat Wheat, the wife of archaeologist Joe Ben Wheat. This year I borrowed the tents and other camping gear from the Museum of Northern Arizona, and we rent/purchased another old pickup from our friendly Ford dealer in Gallup. The archaeology, however, was different.

We dug from mid-June to mid-August 1950. Located on an alluvial flat adjacent to a low scarp, the site was near an exposure of several colorful, large, but broken petrified wood logs. We named this locality the Twin Butte Site because of two small, cone-shaped clay remnants in the midst of it. Probably occupied between A.D. 600 and 700, this site is similar in its architecture to that found widely in northern Arizona from that time period. It consisted of several small units; each had a deep pit house or kiva in front of five to ten surface rooms with walls of vertical sandstone slabs reinforcing a course of clay. The surface rooms formed an arc that was open toward the pit house. We dug only one of the units at this locality. The pit house/kiva was about 20 feet in diameter and 6 feet deep, with a surrounding bench raised about 3 feet off the floor, and a ventilator shaft on the east side. There were five rooms in the nearby surface component. In its architecture, the unit was typical Anasazi, the name given to the prehistoric puebloan groups who lived in the Four Corners Area of northern Arizona and New Mexico, and southern Colorado and Utah.

But the pottery was almost evenly divided between brown wares found in many sites in east-central Arizona and adjacent New Mexico, in a cultural complex Emil Haury named the "Mogollon," and the gray, black-on-white decorated pottery of the Anasazi, commonly found in northeastern Arizona and adjacent New Mexico. In my interpretation, an Anasazi group had occupied this site and had obtained the brown pottery by trading with their neighbors to the south and southeast, possibly exchanging pieces of the abundant and colorful petrified wood for pottery and other things from distant sources.

We also dug several burials, all of them accompanied by pottery vessels, both black-on-white and red or brown in color, and numerous shell beads and ornaments made of shells from the Pacific Ocean, including several pieces of abalone, *glycimeris* bracelets, and over 2,000 beads, including several hundred *olivella* beads. We theorized there had been an active trade network to explain how these Pacific shells and the Mogollon pottery reached the Petrified Forest area.

We had two visitors to our camp in the 1950 field season. One was Ned Colbert, the "dinosaur man," a famous paleontologist at the American Museum of Natural History in New York. He had discovered many dinosaurs in the area of the Petrified Forest. He used his few days with us to look for more, but he was unsuccessful. The other visitor was Kirk Bryan, my geology professor at Harvard. He came to walk some of the arroyos with me in the area east of our camp. It was a great opportunity for me because I thought he would teach me a few things about sedimentary stratigraphy, which he did and more.

As we walked along an arroyo a few days after he arrived, I expressed my concern that two of the students were challenging my instructions. Bryan stopped and said, "I had a similar experience on my first job as a geologist mapping a mountainous area in western Nevada. I had a crew of six of the meanest-looking laborers you ever saw and a tough old cook. I was afraid of all of them. Every morning the cook would get up first, make some strong coffee, and drink a cup. He'd pour a second cup, come over to me, kick my bedroll to wake me, and hand me the second cup of strong coffee. I was too afraid of him not to drink it. Then he'd go over to the kitchen, pour more water in the rest of the coffee, and set the pot out for the men to drink. After a week of this, I asked the cook, 'Why'd you give me the second cup of strong coffee and then add more water for the men's coffee?'

"The cook looked at me and laughed. 'I always thought anyone who bossed a bunch like this, or cooked for them, had to have a lot of backbone. Have you noticed when you drink that strong coffee how it pours down and solidifies around your backbone?' Maybe, Fred, all you need is stronger coffee." It was great advice.

Bryan left a few days later to join a geology group in Wyoming. There, a few days after he left us, he had a heart attack and died.

Salvage Archaeology and the Museum of New Mexico

(1950–1956)

CHAPTER 7

B efore I describe my efforts at pipeline and highway salvage archaeology, I need to go back a few years to discuss the origin of the preservation ethic in American archaeology, which started in 1944–1945 with two men: Fred Johnson, a Naval Intelligence officer temporarily stationed in Washington, D.C., a highly regarded archaeologist who in peacetime was at Phillips Andover Academy; and J. O. Brew, director of the Peabody Museum at Harvard. Some archaeologists refer to what they created as "salvage archaeology"; others call it "archaeological preservation," and more recently, "cultural resource management." Bureaucrats prefer the last term; they feel it allows them to "control" the cultural resources. "Salvage archaeology" is probably the most appropriate term for what was going on during those first years when Johnson and Brew were active and there was neither a legal requirement nor adequate funds to save our nation's threatened archaeological heritage.

In the 1930s and '40s (and before), there had been no real interest among professional archaeologists or the public in preserving the archaeological data construction or other economic development projects were destroying. Poorly supervised emergency make-work projects in the 1930s destroyed numerous large sites, and both the archaeologists and the public watched without raising a cry. A few of the WPA excavations did good archaeology and resulted in major expansions of archaeological knowledge, but they were rare.

In 1944–1945 (the date is not firm), Johnson learned that the Army Corps of Engineers and the Bureau of Land Management were planning to build hundreds of dams as soon as World War II was over. These dams were to be constructed on every major waterway in the United States. There were no plans to preserve the thousands of archaeological sites that the flooding of the reservoirs behind the dams would destroy. Johnson contacted Brew, and soon both of them were spreading the word about the dams and urging archaeologists everywhere and various government officials to take action.

By the fall of 1945, Johnson and Brew organized the Committee for the Recovery of Archaeological Remains (CRAR) to carry the message. It was an informal organization, sponsored by the Society for American Archaeology, the American Anthropological Association, and the American Council of Learned Societies. They set it up to be independent of any governmental organization or supervision. At first, there were only two other members, William S. Webb, a prominent amateur archaeologist in Kentucky, and A. V. Kidder, the most distinguished archaeologist in the country. The founders, Johnson and Brew, did most of the work. In 1954 a few more members were added, but Brew and Johnson still ran the organization.

During its existence, the CRAR profoundly changed American archaeology. Through newspaper and magazine articles, it was responsible for the expansion of interest in archaeology throughout the country; it stimulated the enactment of several federal laws and judicial opinions reaffirming that the preservation of our cultural heritage was in the public interest; it was responsible for the gradual, but ultimately massive, increase in public funding for archaeology; and it altered the way we do archaeology by insisting on the highest standards of archaeological research. Our country, indeed the world, owes an enormous debt to Johnson and Brew for their efforts on behalf of our heritage.

It was my good fortune to become a member of the CRAR in 1954. The group usually met in Washington, D.C., in a park service seminar room. I met many archaeologists who worked for the federal government, particularly those in the National Park Service, where most of the money to carry out the goals of the CRAR was administered. At first I was critical of the park service for not being more aggressive in seeking larger appropriations for archaeological recovery efforts from Congress. Soon it became clear to me, however, that the higher managers in the park service were opposed to larger appropriations for archaeology because everyone in the Department of the Interior worked under a ceiling for expenditures, and significantly larger appropriations for archaeology would threaten the funding for other, also important, projects. As I came to understand the rules of the game I developed a greater appreciation for these federal archaeologists and their achievements. Since J. O. Brew had been my advisor at Harvard, I developed a strong interest in preserving our archaeological heritage. It began very simply.

I had a job as a teaching assistant waiting for me at Harvard in the fall of 1950, but I was not able to claim it. Instead, on August 2, 1950, as the excavations at the Twin

Butte Site were drawing to a close, an airplane circled over our camp. An hour later a car drove up. A big man got out and asked, "Is this Wendorf's camp?"

"Yes, sir," I said. "I'm Wendorf." The big fellow came over, held out his hand, and said, "My name is Jess Nusbaum and I want to offer you a job. I want you to start immediately."

Nusbaum said he wanted me to be the field director of the first archaeological salvage project ever undertaken during the construction of a natural gas pipeline. This pipeline was to go from near Farmington in northwest New Mexico to southern California, a distance of around five hundred miles. (See Map 2 on p. 50.)

Jess Nusbaum was the senior archaeologist at the Department of the Interior. With the help of the chairman of the Navajo Tribal Council, Nusbaum had "persuaded" El Paso Natural Gas Company to salvage the archaeology their construction activities threatened. He said Colton and Stubbs had recommended me. I accepted the offer; I knew it would be a great opportunity, and a great challenge.

I closed my camp a few days later and returned the borrowed camping equipment and the pickup truck. The Museum of Northern Arizona offered us one of their better staff houses, and Nancy and I moved in. The house was comfortable, but it wouldn't do later in the fall, when the weather was cold, since the house had no heat. Nancy would have our car, and she'd look around for a place to stay when it got cold.

Later that day I reported to the superintendent of the pipeline project, Lazy (R. W.) Harris. Harris said, "The company doesn't really want to do this archaeology bit, but the Navajo held our feet to the fire, and since we have to do it, we want it done right. You can have any equipment you need, bulldozers, backhoes, and any number of men, but I have one request: Keep the hell out of my way! We're here to build a pipeline."

We kept out of their way. I realized that what we were doing was an experiment that could be of great significance to archaeology in the future. All of the archaeologists working on that pipeline project shared that view. We were convinced if we could prove to the pipeline industry that archaeological salvage was important, feasible, cost-effective, and achievable with a minimum of disturbance to established procedures, then further opportunities would be forthcoming. We believed, too, the opportunities would not be limited to pipelines, but would apply to all other large-scale earthmoving development projects.

The first phase of the construction of the pipeline was already underway when Nusbaum began recruiting archaeologists. He was frantic, yet he wanted to recruit good people. He even went out himself and surveyed two days at the starting ends of the rights-of-way to see if any sites had been destroyed. I closed my camp in the Petrified Forest on August 16th, but it was not until August 19th that I began working on the pipeline. Things were moving fast everywhere, and everyone had to scramble to catch up. Fortunately, all of the archaeologists Nusbaum hired had a lot of experience, so we lost no time in training.

There were two construction crews building the pipeline; one began at the San Juan River west of Farmington, New Mexico. The other began where the pipeline crossed the Little Colorado River thirty miles northwest of Winslow, Arizona. Before I reported to Harris, Nusbaum had hired four other archaeologists for the project. The first two were Francis Cassidy, a graduate student at the University of New Mexico, and Bill Bullard, a Harvard graduate student who had been with me in the Petrified Forest. Both were assigned to the east end of the pipeline near Farmington. Nusbaum secured a Jeep for them from the gas company office there and started them surveying just ahead of the already working bulldozers.

Nusbaum also hired Wesley Bliss and Paul Ezell, both graduate students at the University of Arizona. They met him at Flagstaff, where he got them a Jeep from the company office and took them to where the pipeline crossed the Little Colorado River. The bulldozers had already started working there, too. Nusbaum put them just ahead of the bulldozers. Both teams found and began excavating archaeological sites before I reported in.

The construction of a long "big inch" pipeline is a closely coordinated and highly complex activity involving hundreds of skilled workers and heavy earthmoving machinery of every description. Each phase of the project has to be carefully scheduled, and any disruption of this schedule has far-reaching and expensive effects on the total program of construction. Obviously, archaeologists on such a project must coordinate their efforts as closely as possible with the construction activities.

From the time the San Juan pipeline archaeology project was authorized it would be over twenty years before there would be a legal basis that would permit archaeologists to hold up construction of a pipeline to save an archaeological site. In 1950 there was no such legal basis. We might in particular instances ask that the bulldozers bypass a section for a few days while we finished an excavation, but in general we had to respect the needs of the construction schedule and delay nothing. This meant we had to evaluate our efforts carefully and stay constantly alert for means and techniques whereby the maximum information could be obtained in the time available. We had to learn to estimate the number of men we needed to excavate a site and how much time these excavations would require. We learned to employ heavy equipment, such as backhoes and road graders, when it was feasible and appropriate. Those of us who participated in these first few pipeline archaeology projects learned our lessons through our mistakes. There was no previous large-scale pipeline archaeology project to draw on for guidance.

About two months into the project, our employer, the El Paso Natural Gas Company, received some favorable publicity about the efforts to save the archaeology that was to be destroyed by the pipeline. Long articles with a lot of pictures appeared in both *Life* and *Time* magazines in the fall of 1950. As a consequence, El Paso became much more supportive of archaeology on all their construction projects. Because of this positive publicity, the pipeline project had a profound impact on both public and professional awareness of the need for salvage archaeology on other kinds of large-scale construction projects.

Pipeline archaeology is tough work. It requires long hours, walking the right-of-way at least twice, once after the surveyors plant their stakes and again after the pipe trench is dug but before the pipe is laid in the trench.

There were two archaeologists on each crew, and two crews. There was also a supervisor (me) who worked with the crew who got behind or was excavating a site in the right-of-way and needed help. In areas where there was no archaeology the two men in the crew took turns walking and driving. They would walk and survey twenty to thirty miles a day. They might sleep in their Jeep or spend the night in a motel, if the distance was not too far from where they ended the survey that day. For meals they heated a can of beans or chili over a fire or brought sandwiches when they could.

The first effort was to go behind the surveyors, but ahead of the construction crews, to seek out all of the archaeological sites within the sixty-foot-wide pipeline right-of-way. When the pipe trench had been dug, but before the pipes were welded together and placed in the trench, we'd go back and walk the trench again. That way we found several sites and pit houses that had been missed during the surface survey. Once they were discovered, we usually had about a week to excavate the structures before the pipe was placed and the trench back-filled.

Walking in the trench sometimes brought us into close contact with rattlesnakes, which enlivened the work considerably. Some of the snakes would fall into the trench and work their way into small pockets in the walls near the floor. Sometimes they would get in the shade of the pipe after it had been placed beside the trench. In both cases they were never in a good mood when we came walking by. Those snakes lying beside the pipe were the most dangerous because our heads were about even with theirs. We soon learned to make a lot of noise as we walked along, giving the snakes plenty of warning. No one was ever bitten, although there were a few close calls. Usually, the snakes rattled in time to alert us to their presence so we could avoid them or kill them with a shovel when we couldn't.

....

In the spring of 1951, when the fieldwork on the first pipeline project was near-ing completion, Stanley Stubbs offered me a job as his assistant at the Laboratory of Anthropology of the Museum of New Mexico in Santa Fe. The pay was low, two hundred dollars a month, but it was a job, and I could supplement it with my army officer's retirement pay.

When I told Lazy Harris about the job offer, he said, "I'm disappointed to hear it, Fred. El Paso is planning to offer you a permanent job. We're going to drill a lot of gas wells in the Farmington area, and each one will have a pipeline connection to the main collection system. If you want to continue doing salvage archaeology, there'll be years of work for you. If not, we could train you to do other things."

"Lazy," I said, "I really appreciate your efforts to find me a place with El Paso. I admire this company and the dedication I see in you and everyone who works for you. It means a great deal to me to have been associated with you and El Paso. But I want to be an academic archaeologist. I want to do what I spent so many years training to do. I hope in the future if you need me, you'll let me know. I'd like to continue working for the company on small projects."

By this time Nancy was six months pregnant. She had been having some difficul-ties, but her doctor said it was safe for her to travel from Flagstaff to our new home in Santa Fe. We arrived one late afternoon in early May 1951. Stubbs and his wife had offered to put us up for a day or two until we could move into our apartment in a small compound near downtown the museum owned. Nancy was tired and immedi-ately went to bed.

During the night Nancy woke me and said, "Fred, my water broke." I jumped up, threw on my clothes, and rushed her to the hospital emergency room. The baby was still alive, they said, and moved Nancy to the maternity ward. I stayed with her through the remainder of the night and the next day. Stubbs had arranged for a gynecologist they knew to look after Nancy, and late that evening the doctor told me they would have to take the baby. It was dead. This was a tragedy for both of us, but particularly for Nancy. We had already named our daughter. I couldn't help but think, "Was it my fault? Should we have stayed in Flagstaff until our child was born? What should I have done?" I had no answers, but it was a terrible way to start a new life.

Several months later, in late 1951, Nancy was again pregnant, and by the summer of the next year we had a fine, healthy boy. We named him Frederick Carl, but we always call him Carl.

My first assignment at the Laboratory of Anthropology was to study the materials recovered a year or two earlier from the excavation of Te'ewi, a thirteenth-century pueblo in the Chama Valley, about ten miles northwest of Espanola, New Mexico. It had been dug because it was in the area to be flooded by a new dam, but after Te'ewi was excavated the dam site was moved upstream and it was never flooded. After analyzing the artifacts, I wrote up the results for publication.

Stubbs was always helpful when I worked as his assistant. Two things stand out to me. First, and most important, he was generous with his knowledge of Rio Grande archaeology. He told me many facts about the prehistory of northern New Mexico and gave me his interpretation of their significance. He discussed with me the details of the archaeology at Te'ewi, and compared those with what had been found at nearby and distant sites. He showed me how to use a shadow box to photograph lithic artifacts so that details of the flaking could be seen without shadows. He also taught me how to develop and print photographs.

Te'ewi was particularly interesting to me because, as Stubbs told me, several of the designs on the pottery, as well as some of the vessel forms, resembled those found on pottery of the same age at sites in eastern Texas and Oklahoma, suggesting a strong possibility of contact between the two areas. Stubbs discussed the implications of these similarities with me at some length. His knowledge helped me greatly in writing the conclusions to the Te'ewi report.

In the evenings and on weekends I worked on my dissertation, but I was often tired and progress was slow. A few days after I finished the Te'ewi report, Stubbs came to my office. Standing in the doorway, leaning against the doorjamb, he asked, "How're you coming with that dissertation, Fred?"

"It's coming along, Stan, but at this rate it'll take me another year to finish. I find it hard to keep my mind focused on the dissertation when I'm at home in the evenings. When I'm with Nancy and I've not seen her all day, it's very difficult. We need some time together."

Stubbs smiled and said, "I understand. Why don't you bring your dissertation to your office tomorrow and finish writing it here?"

Working on it during office hours and in the evenings, I soon was able to finish the dissertation. I sent a copy to J. O. Brew to read. He liked it. All I had to do was go to Cambridge to defend it. In those days, Harvard required that the dissertation be defended in an open examination, not by mail, but in person and on campus.

A year later, in March of 1953, Boaz Long, director of the museum, came by my office and asked me if I had my PhD yet. I said, "I'm afraid not, Mr. Long. I've finished writing the dissertation and Brew has approved it, but I need to save enough money to go to Cambridge and defend it." Boaz Long didn't say a word. He looked at me, nodded his head as if to say he understood, and left my office. About an hour later I received a call from the local travel agent, who said, "Boaz Long just bought a round-trip plane ticket for you from Albuquerque to Boston. When do you want to go?"

I made a quick call to Brew, told him what Long had done, and he agreed to set up the exam for the next week. I called Long, thanked him, and told him what Brew and I had arranged. He was pleased and wished me a successful defense. I made the plane reservations, picked up my ticket, and was ready to go.

When I arrived in Boston I had a room at a hotel across the river from Harvard. As soon as I got in I called Brew. "The defense is scheduled for tomorrow afternoon at 2:00 P.M.," he said. "Unless some students decide to sit in, there will be only three of us: Donald Scott, the former director of the Peabody Museum, you, and me."

I thanked him and went to bed. I had a fever. It felt like the flu. The next afternoon I didn't feel much better; certainly I wasn't in top form. I took a couple of aspirin, rode the subway to Harvard Square, and walked to the Peabody Museum and into Brew's office. There were only the three of us. Both Brew and Scott were interested in my ideas about the indications of trade and what that implied about the relationship between the Anasazi and Mogollon. Brew had never accepted Haury's idea that they were separate cultural entities, but I thought my work in the Petrified Forest supported Haury's interpretation. I don't recall any of the questions on other topics they asked me. Although I didn't tell Brew I was ill, he could tell I was not myself and closed the exam after about an hour of questioning.

Brew then said he and Scott were going to have a party at his house that night to celebrate my successful defense. He said a lot of the students wanted to meet me, and he thought there would be a good crowd. I told him I felt terrible and I wouldn't be good company, but Brew brushed my comment aside. "Never mind, Fred, take a couple of aspirin and come on. Let's have a few beers and celebrate."

I reluctantly agreed and went to my hotel to rest.

It turned out to be a good party, and I'm glad I went. The students were interested in what I had been doing, particularly in pipeline archaeology, but also in my dissertation topic.

I received my PhD at the next Harvard commencement, in May 1953, but I couldn't afford to be present. Several weeks later Harvard sent me my sheepskin. As I looked at the diploma I felt a wave of warmth and happiness. I'd done it. That diploma was the culmination of many years of planning and working. I was, finally, an archaeologist. Nancy and I hired a babysitter, went to a restaurant for a special dinner, and while we were there I thanked Nancy for all she had done to make it possible.

In October 1952, Nusbaum asked me if I would do a short (two-hundred-mile) pipeline to carry petroleum by-products from near Farmington south across the Navajo Reservation to Highway 66, about twenty miles east of Gallup. I knew Don Lehmer was looking for a job, and I asked Nusbaum to hire him to help me on the project. Lehmer and I got a Jeep and a set of maps from El Paso headquarters in Farmington. We found the beginning of the pipeline and headed south. About five miles south of the Chaco Wash, we began finding and excavating sites ranging in age from about A.D. 900 to A.D. 1250. Most of the sites were in a thirty-mile stretch near the middle of the survey area. The ceramics we found were interesting because of the diversity of design styles represented. In one area the right-of-way just missed a mile-long line of pueblo sites.

By November of 1952 it was much colder than when we started, and we spent several nights in our Jeep with the motor running and the heater on. It was a relief to both Lehmer and me when we came into the Puerco Valley, where El Paso was building a petroleum products terminal.

In July of 1953, El Paso asked Nusbaum to assemble a team of archaeologists to work on a new pipeline stretching from east to west all across New Mexico. It began at Plains, Texas, and angled northwest to beyond Fort Wingate, where it joined with the pipeline right-of-way our group had cleared in 1950. From there it went on to California, staying in the 1950–1951 right-of-way.

Nusbaum asked me to supervise the project, but I turned him down. I was tired of the hard life of a pipeline archaeologist. At my recommendation, he hired Don Lehmer. Nusbaum also hired two other archaeologists, neither of whom I knew. One was Franklin Fenenga, about my age, who had a lot of experience in both California and the Plains area with the River Basin Survey. The other was Tom Cummings, a recent graduate of the University of New Mexico, considerably younger than both Fenenga and I. They began work near the end of July.

In early August Nusbaum called me to tell me Lehmer had resigned from the survey and asked me to take over the project. I really didn't want to take on such a big project, but I owed Nusbaum. After a long pause and a sigh, I told him I'd have to see if I could get a leave. Nusbaum said, "I've already called Stubbs and Boaz Long. I told them this was a real emergency and they said they'd give you a leave." Reluctantly, I took the job, and with Fenenga and Cummings, we found and excavated several interesting sites.

I always urged the archaeologists doing pipeline archaeology with me to complete their analyses and prepare a report on every site they excavated. By and large they had done so because Nusbaum suggested that the gas company keep them on the payroll while they were writing the reports. As a consequence, I had accumulated a sizable number of manuscripts and illustrations. After the 1953 pipeline project was completed, Nusbaum asked for and received a grant from El Paso Natural Gas to publish these reports.

It took me several months to edit everything, but late in 1956 the Laboratory of Anthropology and the Museum of Northern Arizona jointly published *Pipeline Archaeology*, which contained the results of all three of the completed pipeline archaeology projects. Jess Nusbaum wrote the Introduction, which told the history of pipeline archaeology. It is a "must read" for anyone interested in the history of rescue archaeology in America.

In the spring of 1953 I was invited to give a talk on pipeline archaeology to the Rotary Club in Santa Fe. In addition to showing slides of the excavations on the pipeline project, I showed several slides of archaeological sites that had been destroyed years ago during the construction of Highway 66 near Gallup, New Mexico. After I showed the slides I offhandedly commented, "I think it's too bad private industry is more responsive to our antiquities laws than our state and federal highway agencies are."

W. J. (Spike) Keller, head of the New Mexico District of the Federal Bureau of Public Roads, was in the audience. As the meeting broke up, Keller came up and introduced himself. At first I was embarrassed by my criticism of the state and federal agencies, but he soon put me at ease. "Wendorf, I'm interested in archaeology, and two months ago I saw a large prehistoric pueblo between Chama and Espanola destroyed by one of my highway construction crews. It almost made me sick that we'd destroy such an important part of our past without making an effort to save it."

Keller went on, "Pete (C. O.) Erwin, the chief highway engineer of New Mexico, also has strong interests in archaeology, and he was with me when that site was destroyed. We've discussed what we might do to change this situation. Could you meet with Pete and me to explore what we might do to protect the archaeology in New Mexico?" I told him I would, and he said he'd get back to me about a date and time for the meeting.

Things were going fast, but before we separated, I remembered Nusbaum, the person responsible for the salvage archaeology I'd done on the pipelines, and asked if I could invite Jess Nusbaum to join us at the meeting. Keller thought that was a good idea.

Being a junior curator at the museum gave me no authority to make agreements with state agencies. Yet I knew this was something we needed to do because it could be a major breakthrough for archaeological preservation. I needed Nusbaum to support me if Stubbs or Boaz Long were to object to something I might agree to do at this meeting. I knew I could count on Nusbaum.

When we assembled at the New Mexico Highway Department headquarters, Keller introduced Nusbaum and me to Erwin and two of his senior managers. Erwin's blue eyes seemed to look right through me when he shook my hand.

Erwin started the meeting by suggesting a way a highway salvage archaeology program might be organized. Obviously, he had given the problem a lot of thought.

"Let's begin our highway salvage archaeology program by agreeing that we'll have an informal, unwritten agreement between the two highway agencies and the Museum of New Mexico. Such an agreement will establish the first statewide archaeological salvage program on highways in the United States. I propose that both highway departments agree to ask their engineering survey teams to be on the alert for archaeological sites, and when sites are found, they're to mark their locations on their survey maps. I want the survey teams to be instructed to avoid any large sites, or where that is impossible, they should notify the head of engineering and me about the problem."

The rest of the meeting was devoted to the mechanics of how a systematic program would work. After considerable discussion we agreed on the following:

Each month, when the New Mexico Highway Department and the Federal Bureau of Public Roads sent out requests for bids from contractors for new highway construction projects, the museum would get copies. The New Mexico Highway Department usually had from eight to ten new projects each month. Of those, many were for improving/repairing already existing roads. There would be only two or three requests for bids from the Bureau of Public Roads.

The museum would survey the remaining projects, those in new rights-of-way, from three to five each month, for archaeological sites within the construction zone. For those projects involving new alignments, the museum would collect sets of plans from the engineering departments as soon as the projects were announced. The archaeologists would take these plans and begin their surveys.

Because it would sometimes be difficult to examine every project area, the museum might find it necessary to create an informal priority for the surveys. Those projects in areas where the museum knew archaeological sites were numerous would have the highest priority.

It was anticipated that on occasion the museum might find several sites on two or more different projects. In that event the museum would salvage as many as possible, but recognize that some would inevitably be lost.

When a site was found, the museum would estimate how many laborers would be needed and for how long, and file a request with the highway engineering office in Santa Fe, which would notify the nearest maintenance office to provide the labor.

Of course, when we spoke of the "museum" it meant me. Initially, I was the only one at the museum available to do surveys for sites on highways and supervise their excavation. At first, there was no money to cover my expenses (mostly fuel and an occasional motel room) except what was in our research budget at the lab.

After the meeting at the highway department, I went over the main points of the agreement with Stubbs and the director of the museum, Boaz Long. Both were pleased and told me to go ahead. To get things started, I spent the next several months traveling all over the state surveying the rights-of-way for new highway projects and excavating sites I found during my surveys.

Pete Erwin noticed that it was a frantic scramble for me. Without telling me, but at his urging, the next session of the legislature made a special appropriation of $10,000.00 to the museum and earmarked it for the highway archaeological salvage program. Long was surprised and irritated when he read about the appropriation in the legislative record. But he accepted in good humor my truthful explanation that it was also news to me. I told him the appropriation was intended to help the museum and that Erwin knew I didn't have any money to hire assistance and knew I was driving all over the state. He just wanted to help out. Long seemed pleased with my explanation, said that he understood, and that he just wanted to be kept informed about what was going on.

During the last part of 1953, while I was doing all these highway archaeology salvage projects, Nancy was again pregnant and often home alone. I went home weekends and tried to spend as much time with her and Carl as I could, but it was a lonely period for her. In the spring of 1954, she had our second son. We named him Michael Andrew, and called him Mike. He, like Carl, was a strong, healthy baby.

In June 1954 an important new development began when I excavated two small pueblos and several deep pit houses with numerous burials and a rich assortment of grave goods at the right-of-way for a new highway already under construction in the mountains near Reserve, New Mexico. Because the road was in a National Forest, it was a Bureau of Public Roads project.

There were fifteen deep depressions scattered over the site, one very large depression near its center, and five small pueblos. I first saw the site in June 1953, just after the survey crew staked the right-of-way. I knew that two of the pueblos and three of the deep depressions would be in the new highway construction zone. The big depression, which I identified as a "great kiva," was beyond the right-of-way. I asked Paul

Martin of the Chicago Museum of Natural History to excavate those parts of the site that would be destroyed by the new highway. He did the excavations later that summer and reported to me that the work was completed.

In May of 1955, Spike Keller asked me to come to Reserve and see if the excavations were indeed complete. He thought not, and his crews were to start work on that portion of the highway later in the summer. I went immediately, and when I arrived I was dismayed. The two small pueblos had been excavated, but I could see evidence of unexcavated burial pits in the room floors of both pueblos, and a kiva or pit house immediately in front of one pueblo. I had to do something and time was short. I should have called Martin and asked him to drop everything and come finish the job, but I didn't. I took him at his word that he was through at the site. Nevertheless, my conscience told me I should have called or written to Martin, but since the highway construction activities had already begun, it wasn't feasible to delay.

I asked Keller to find ten laborers and arrange for a backhoe for two or three days about a week later. I began the excavation of three of the small, deep depressions the next day. The excavations quickly disclosed that all three were deep, square pit houses with rock-lined walls, and ventilators on their east sides. Each house had several long, rectangular pits dug in the floors. These contained extended burials with numerous pots and other grave offerings. An unusual feature was the wooden "pillow" placed under the head of each body. I had never seen pillows like those before.

As we were finishing up the mapping of the pit houses and their burials, I moved most of the crew to the two pueblos to excavate the subfloor burials. Again, each burial had several pottery vessels as grave furniture. The pottery in both the pit houses and the pueblos were the same types, which told me that very little time separated the pit house and the pueblo occupations. It looked as if the pit house dwellers suddenly decided to build five pueblos and move into them. But why five?

Although the rich grave offerings were interesting and important, I was more impressed by what I thought I could see of the community's political/residential structure. It seemed likely that the five pueblos were evidence of an invisible residential structure within the slightly earlier pit house community. On the basis of the five pueblos, I believe the pit house community consisted of five separate residential subgroups. Thus, when the community decided to move into above ground pueblos, they built five similar, but separate, structures. I wrote a small paper on this topic published by Gordon Willey in his 1956 book, *Prehistoric Settlement Patterns in the New World*.

The pit houses and pueblos were spectacular, and the site drew a lot of local attention around Reserve. One of those who saw it was an engineer working in the area with the National Forest Service. He told Keller that he had seen a small ruin in the alignment of a timber access road not far from Reserve. Keller arranged for me to see the site and talk with the forest service engineer, who told me he could reimburse the labor cost of digging the small pueblo if I thought it should be excavated. We agreed on the sum of three hundred dollars.

I dug the site and submitted a bill. The engineer turned in the bill to his office, expecting it to be paid promptly. Evidently a clerk in the Albuquerque office was not as friendly as the engineer thought. Instead of sending it to forest service headquarters in Washington to be cleared for payment, he sent it directly to the comptroller general of the United States for his opinion.

I told Keller, and he immediately called his boss in Washington, the commissioner of public roads, C. D. Curtiss. He had been briefed on our highway archaeology program in New Mexico and had given it his unofficial approval since he, too, was interested in archaeology. Curtiss asked Keller to send me to Washington to meet the comptroller general and plead the case that the salvage of this site was in the national interest. I agreed to go. Curtiss then called Joseph Campbell, comptroller general of the United States, and set up an appointment for me. Our discussion was tense.

I started out by telling him that Congress on several occasions, beginning with the Federal Antiquities Act of 1906 and the Historic Sites Act of 1935, and several others more recently, had passed legislation confirming that it is a national policy to protect our historical and archaeological heritage. With every point I made he countered with an opposing position, commenting that the Federal Antiquities Act had never been enforced. He wondered after all these years why it should be enforced now.

I responded that the country needs the Antiquities Act and the other congressional actions taken to protect our heritage, and it needs them to be enforced now. I left certain he did not support my argument. However, several months later, on December 6, 1955, the comptroller general issued an opinion saying that my three-hundred-dollar bill should be paid. He went on to say that the legislative history clearly showed it had been the intent of Congress to protect ruins with historical value.

Later, when I saw Commissioner Curtiss, he told me that though it was an important victory, we needed to get it reaffirmed by Congress. He said, "Comptroller generals have been known to change their minds."

In the spring of 1956, I learned that national legislation was being drafted to build a vast new interstate highway system and that there would be an opportunity to insert language into it about archaeology. Senator Dennis Chavez of New Mexico was chair of the committee drafting the bill. I was told that Commissioner Curtiss, who had been so helpful with the comptroller general, had asked the senator to include something on archaeology in the bill. A few days later, Erwin, Keller, and I met to prepare a draft of the language we wanted to see in the bill. They told me Chavez's chief clerk would call me and ask for the text we had prepared. On a small sheet of paper I wrote down our prepared wording. I carried that sheet of paper in my shirt pocket for about three weeks before Senator Chavez's clerk called and asked me to read it to him. Our exact language was included in the bill when Congress passed it and President Eisenhower signed it. It was an important advance for archaeological conservation.

Although I now had higher expectations, the new highway legislation didn't have much impact on the arrangements we had in place in New Mexico, except to give legal cover to what Erwin, Keller, and I had been doing for two years. What it did do was make it possible for highway archaeological projects to be developed in a few states, and to be paid for with federal highway funds. Some programs were soon underway, as in Arizona, but because it was not compulsory, only a few states took advantage of the opportunity.

By late spring of 1954, almost four years after I reported to El Paso Gas Company to begin the first pipeline archaeological salvage project, and then the highway archaeological salvage program, I had excavated or supervised the excavation of well over a hundred archaeological sites, far more than most archaeologists experience in a lifetime. Either I, or one of the archaeologists I supervised, described these excavations in appropriate publications. I was generally pleased at what I'd accomplished, and I thought what I was doing was in the best interest of archaeology. I believed my colleagues approved of what I was doing, but I didn't think that this new archaeological data was filtering into the wider body of archaeological knowledge. I took comfort in the thought that the data were all there. The collections, maps, notes, pots, and other artifacts were in the museum storage areas ready for someone to use and integrate into the body of Southwestern archaeological knowledge. I was too busy excavating and describing more threatened sites to do any integrating myself.

One of my closest archaeological friends was Chuck DiPeso, director of the Amerind Foundation at Dragoon, in southeastern Arizona. At a meeting in 1953, Chuck and I were talking about archaeology when he turned to me and told me that he didn't like what I was doing excavating all those sites on pipelines and highways. He thought it would be better if the sites were destroyed, unstudied. He said my reports were too brief and didn't inform us about what was going on at the sites. He said I seemed to have no feeling for the people who lived there and that I made no attempts to recover the pattern of human behavior that must have been present.

I was shocked, but I knew his criticism was fair. If Chuck thought my work was inadequate, others must feel the same way. His words also touched my general unease about where I was going with my work in salvage archaeology. In my defense I said, "Chuck, if we don't do something to save the archaeology now, in a few years there'll be none. It'll all be under asphalt or concrete and we'll never know what happened." But DiPeso had made his point. Soon afterward, I turned the survey of the planned construction rights-of-way and the excavation of the threatened sites over to my assistant, Stewart Peckham, who kept things going.

After my discussion with DiPeso, I visited with Stubbs in his office. We were talking about archaeology in the Rio Grande and speculating on where the four major language families in the modern pueblos might have come from and when. I wanted to do a synthesis of Rio Grande archaeology, and I asked Stubbs if he would join me in writing it. He agreed, and I offered to write the first draft.

By June I had finished the draft and given a copy to Stubbs. I waited two weeks, then asked Stubbs if he had read the text. He had not. I waited two more weeks and asked Stubbs again if he'd read the paper on the Rio Grande and if he had any corrections or comments. When he said he still hadn't read it, I was unhappy. I had waited a month, and I thought it was an important paper that should be published before someone else did a synthesis.

I told Stubbs I was going to go ahead and publish this paper. I said I still had to do the maps, and said if he wanted to join me as coauthor, to let me know before I submitted it somewhere. He never responded. A few weeks later I submitted the paper to the *American Anthropologist,* a highly regarded national journal of anthropology. I had decided that if he wasn't willing to write even an introduction, he shouldn't appear as an author. I was wrong, however. Although Stubbs should have helped me, many of the ideas in the paper came from the discussions I had with him. I could've simply added his name to the paper before I sent it to the editor, but I didn't, and I was wrong.

When the paper came out I received several letters of congratulations and praise, including one I treasure from Albert Kroeber, the dean of American anthropology. I enjoyed the comments, but I knew I hadn't been fair to Stubbs.

Two months later I was out on a field trip with Erik Reed, Southwest regional archaeologist for the National Park Service, a distinguished archaeologist and a good friend of mine. Erik told me he admired my paper, but that he had a different idea on the languages, their sources, and how they relate to the archaeology. He explained his ideas to me, and for the rest of the afternoon we discussed them and the conclusions I had reached in my paper. At home that evening I continued to think about Erik's position on the languages, and before I went to sleep I had reached the conclusion that the evidence supported his interpretation. I decided to revise the paper and include Erik's hypotheses about the language groups. It took only three days, and when I finished it I added Reed's name after mine and took a copy to him.

He glanced at the title and told me I didn't need to add his name to the paper; he said it was almost all my work. I said I wanted people to know the changes were his ideas. We published version two in *El Palacio,* a local journal published by the Museum of New Mexico. This new paper was widely read and generally accepted as a good working model.

CHAPTER 8

One of the most intellectually challenging studies I did while I was at the Museum of New Mexico was the excavation of the so-called "Midland Man," a partial Final Pleistocene human burial and an associated camp in the sand hills near Midland, Texas. As it happened, the Midland remains were among the oldest, if not *the* oldest, human remains yet discovered in the New World (since then there have been a number of skeletons discovered that may be as old or older than the Midland skull). Our work on the Midland discovery was the subject of national news coverage, including articles in both *Time* and *Life* magazines.

Before my involvement, Keith Glasscock, an amateur archaeologist from Pampa, Texas, found the fossil human remains in June of 1953. Three weeks later he went to Santa Fe to see if he could find someone who could tell him how to locate an early Holocene bison kill site known as San Jon, in far eastern New Mexico. The Smithsonian Institution had excavated there several years before. He went to the downtown museum, the Palace of the Governors, and finally talked to Boaz Long, director of the museum.

Boaz called several senior curators, but all refused to see Glasscock because of other commitments. In desperation Boaz called me, telling Glasscock, "Fred'll help you. He's too junior to turn me down."

Glasscock was about my age (at the time I was twenty-nine), fit and sunburned. When he told me he was a pipeline welder I knew why he looked so good. Pipeline welders lead a tough life, crawling around under those big pipes and moving heavy equipment.

After we shook hands, Glasscock came right to the point: "My hobby is going to excavated Early Man sites to look for artifacts the archaeologists may have missed. I want to go to the San Jon site and see if I can find more artifacts."

It just so happened that on a road trip with Jimmy Griffin of the University of Michigan I had been to San Jon and several other Early Man sites in the area the previous June. I said, "A few miles east of Tucumcari is a gravel road going south from the village of San Jon. It goes up and over the scarp of the Llano Estacado. Once you're on top, there's a windmill on the left side of the road. Turn there. About three hundred yards east of the road you'll see one of those deflated basins that dot the top of the llano. The retreat of the escarpment has breached this one, and several large, deep arroyos cut across it. At the top of the southernmost arroyo you'll see the outline of the excavations and the back-dirt pile. I looked at those piles carefully when I was there and I didn't find a thing, so I don't think you'll find much."

Glasscock smiled, but didn't say anything. He stood, ready to go, and I asked him what other sites he'd visited. "There were two localities where I found Folsom Points," Glasscock said. Then he elaborated. "The best one has never been excavated. It's in a wind-deflated hollow on the Scharbauer ranch, about five miles south and west of Midland, Texas. I found a fossilized human skull there, badly broken, probably stepped on by a cow, and two points that look like Folsom Points, though they aren't fluted."

I asked if he'd found any other points. "No others," he said. Then he paused and added, "Except about a mile away where there's a lot of camp debris on the surface of a large dune, I found a variety of points, including several Folsom Points."

As he was about to leave, Glasscock asked if I'd like to see the skull he found. With a chuckle, I said, "Yes, indeed, that skull may be important."

About a week later the skull arrived, tightly packed into a box, about five inches long, three inches wide and two inches deep. The largest piece of bone was about the size of a half dollar. I had no idea if the skull could be restored. It was heavily mineralized and crusted with gray sand and calcium carbonate. It certainly looked old. I decided that if it could be put together there was only one person I would trust to do it: T. Dale Stewart, a renowned physical anthropologist at the Smithsonian Institution. I had met him once when I was in Washington, and I knew he was a highly skilled anatomist.

I picked up the phone and called Stewart, introduced myself, and asked if he would look at an old skull from West Texas. He told me to send it on. Then I called Alex Krieger, a distinguished archaeologist at the University of Texas whom I had known for several years, and explained the situation to him. I asked if he would join a small group at the site where it had been found. He agreed. I called Glasscock, told him what I was doing, and asked if he would mind taking a small group of archaeologists to the Midland site to show us where he found the skull. "When do we go?" he laughed. "I'm free anytime, but I'll need to get permission from Clarence Scharbauer for us to go onto the ranch."

I thanked him and told him I'd get back to him about a date when everyone could join us.

I went over to the park service building where Jess Nusbaum, my boss on the pipelines, and Charlie Steen, a senior National Park Service archaeologist stationed in Santa Fe, had their offices about three blocks from the Laboratory of Anthropology. I asked both of them to join my little group, along with Ed Jelks and Ed Moorman, archaeologists with the River Basin Surveys in Texas, and Jack T. Hughes at the Panhandle Plains Museum in Canyon, Texas. Hughes asked if he could bring his wife, Polly Hughes, and a photographer along. I acceded to his request, though I worried that the group might be getting too large.

We assembled in Midland late on the afternoon of October 28, 1953, and went to the site immediately after breakfast the next morning. As we walked into the blowout, we noted that the bottom was a dry streambed with a floor of firmly cemented white-colored sand. On the surface of the white sand and embedded in it were many mineralized vertebrate fossils, mostly horse, but also scraps of bison, turtle, and even a small antelope. We knew the fossils were old because horses became extinct in North America at the end of the Pleistocene. They were gone from the New World by about 11,000 years ago.

At the east end of the blowout we could see a unit of gray-colored sand that appeared to overlie the white sand. Slightly embedded in a shallow wind-scooped hollow in the gray sand was the place Glasscock had found the crushed skull. A thick bed of dark red sand rested on the gray sand around the margins of the basin. At the top of the red sand was a thick, dark gray soil.

Fossil bone occurred in each of the sand units. Jack Hughes and I both made rough sketch maps of the visible geological deposits in the blowout. We collected and numbered several of the bones on the surface and marked the location of each piece on both maps. We bagged and marked the fossils as to location and unit. Jelks found a fragment of another unfluted Folsom Point closely similar to the two points Glasscock had previously found there.

We cleared a pit 6 feet square around the spot where Glasscock had found the skull along with an almost complete unfluted Folsom Point (after which we soon named "Midland Points"). We excavated to a depth of 6 inches. We passed all of the sand through a 0.125-inch screen to be sure we got all of the bone scraps. The screen yielded several dozen tiny fragments of bone, possibly human, but too small to be identified, and three more human skull fragments, a piece of rib, and a metacarpal.

We could not rule out the possibility that the human remains had been in a pit excavated from a later surface into the gray sand, and as we walked around, several of my colleagues expressed concern that we wouldn't be able to learn much about the human remains at the site.

We visited four other blowouts in the general area, where only red and tan sands were visible. Considerable archaeology was visible on the surface of the red sand in two of these. Glasscock reported that he had collected several Midland Points, and several Folsom Points, as well as more recent points from the surface of the red sand.

By early afternoon we moved our discussion to a restaurant in Midland for lunch and beer. I went around the table asking, "Do you think we can do anything useful with the site and the human remains?" Each one said no. The last person at the table was Krieger. Before I asked him I said, "Well, I think I can do something. I'm not sure just what, but I'm going to try to get some funds and do a small excavation at the site. Is there anyone here who'd like to join me?"

Krieger spoke up. "I'd like to join you, Fred, because I, too, believe something can be done here." Krieger was a Viking Fund Medalist, one of America's most highly regarded archaeologists, and his support meant a great deal to me. Glasscock said nothing, but when I told them what I planned to do he smiled and gave me a "thumbs up" sign. I had more than enough work already, with pipeline and highway projects, but this was an opportunity to do something new and different.

In early November 1953 I wrote a one-page letter to Paul Fejos, director of the Wenner-Gren Foundation for Anthropological Research, and described in detail the geological setting at the Midland site and told him what I would like to do. I said I needed $2,500 for the project, and I closed by asking him to send me a grant application form.

Four days later I received a telegram that read, "The sum of $2,500 is hereby awarded to you for archaeological research near Midland, Texas. Congratulations. Paul C. Fejos, Director of Research."

When I called Alex Krieger to tell him the good news he suggested that I contact Claude C. Albritton, a geologist at Southern Methodist University who had worked in the sand hills near Monahans, Texas. I wrote Albritton and asked if he would be interested in doing the geology of the site. He said he would be delighted to work with Krieger and me. I asked him to join us at the site sometime in February 1954, at his convenience, preferably during the last two weeks when most of the trenches would be open.

By this time I had decided I would try to establish the stratigraphic position of the human remains found in the blowout by using microchemical analyses of samples of the faunal remains in each of the stratigraphic units and comparing the results with the results of the analyses on the human remains. Although the technique was not yet well known among archaeologists, it wouldn't be the first time that similar chemical analyses had been used to establish the age of human remains. The mountains of reading J. O. Brew assigned had told me that the first use of microchemical analysis in archaeology had been in the 1840s at Natchez, Mississippi, when fluorine analysis was used unsuccessfully in an effort to determine the age of a presumably old skeleton. More recently, in the 1940s and '50s, chemical analysis, including fluorine, had been successfully used to establish the association of human remains found in shell-mounds on the California coast, and in England, in the exposure of the Piltdown fraud.

Fluorine analysis is particularly useful where the true association of human remains is unknown because fluorine enters bone with the groundwater, and when fluorine ions come into contact with the crystalline mineral matter of bones and teeth, the fluorine is absorbed and locked in. Thus, fluorine increases in buried bone through time. The idea is that two bones in the same deposit for the same period of time should have closely similar chemical contents, and conversely, if one bone is buried in a deposit longer than another, then the chemical contents should be different.

The California studies also led me to think that several other analyses might be useful for comparative dating purposes, in particular, analyses for carbon, nitrogen, and water content. Whereas the fluorine intake in bone occurs through a process of absorption and fixation, the alterations in the carbon, nitrogen, and water are disintegrative processes, a decomposition of bone protein accompanied by a loss of water. I thought chemical analysis was worth trying.

Fortunately, I was acquainted with Norris Bradbury, the director of the nearby University of California Los Alamos Laboratory. I knew he was interested in archaeology, and I thought he might be willing to arrange for the microchemical analyses we needed. When I returned to Santa Fe, I called him and explained the problem and what I proposed to do, and asked if he could help. He said he thought he could and he would call me back in a few minutes. When he called he had four names of chemists in the laboratory who could do the analyses and who said they would be pleased to do the tests. He suggested that I call Frederick Worman, a chemist on his staff, to coordinate the tests. When I talked with Worman I told him I was returning to the Midland site in a few days and when I came back to Santa Fe I would bring more bone samples to him at Los Alamos.

It took a few days to contact Clarence Scharbauer in Midland and get his permission to excavate on his property, but once I reached him he quickly gave his approval. I had to borrow a car from the museum, as well as a plane table and telescopic alidade, shovels, picks, trowels, screens, and various other items for digging. I called Ed

Moorman and asked him to take a leave from the River Basin Survey to assist me for a month.

Finally, all was ready, and in late January, I drove to Midland, found an inexpensive place to stay, and went to meet Moorman. Then we went to the local labor office and hired two laborers. The next day, February 1, 1954, we began work.

The first thing Moorman and I did was to check the surface for any new fossils or points that might have been exposed after our earlier visit. Then we made a plane table map of the site and, using our earlier sketch maps, plotted on the new map all the fossils we'd collected on that October 1953 visit.

I laid out several trenches extending from the 6-foot-square area we had dug in 1953, and started the men digging with trowels and screening the sand as they went. Some of the trenches were over 40 feet long. All of them were laid out to facilitate determining the sequence of the units in the blowout. In each instance the base of the trenches was dug a few inches into the white sand.

The excavations confirmed our previous impressions of the stratigraphic sequence in the blowout: the red sand was laid over the gray and white sands. However, we found no additional fragments of human skeleton. The only new archaeological artifacts we recovered from the excavations were three small chert chips from the gray sand, as well as several teeth and bone fragments of fossil horse and bison, also from the gray sand. We found a horse lower leg-foot bone (?) bearing several cut marks. I thought this cut bone probably was from the top of the white sand, but the exact position was unknown. The fossil had been exposed while we were excavating the base of the gray sand at the contact with the white sand. One of the workers picked it up before I saw it, so it could have been in the bottom of the gray sand. The red sand also yielded several horse teeth articulated with fragments of the jaw.

Albritton arrived at the site in late February. He spent several days with us, examined each trench carefully, drew profiles, and sampled each unit of sand. He was a careful, methodical stratigrapher. On the afternoon before he left he described each of the stratigraphic units for me.

In early June of 1954 I received the exciting results of the microchemical analyses from Fred Worman at Los Alamos. They showed that the extinct fossil horse bones in the gray sand, and the human remains, were the same age. Thus, the Midland skull was at that time the oldest known fragment of human remains found in the New World. I sent a copy of the analyses to Krieger with a note suggesting that we meet soon and begin writing our report on the Midland site. Krieger called me a few days later and told me that he would like to come to Santa Fe around July 1st and stay over the July 4th weekend.

Alex and I began working as soon as he arrived. We spent an hour or two going over the data to be sure we were in agreement about the interpretation of the stratigraphic sequence. Krieger sat down at my typewriter to write the Introduction. I provided the names and other data he needed. He was a genius on that typewriter, faster than any secretary I have ever known. We worked together on the description of the stratigraphy, taking turns dictating, then writing. At the end of that first day I contacted all the people who had visited the site in October and told them the results of the chemical analyses and our interpretation. By the end of the second day we had made considerable progress with our report.

At this point Krieger suggested that I write a press release and call the local paper to see if they'd like to send out a reporter to interview us. I made the call. Then I wrote a press release, about a page long, and made a list of everyone connected to the project and their affiliations. I made several copies of both items in case other news outlets were interested. A reporter and photographer from the Santa Fe newspaper came out the next day, July 3, 1954.

Alex told them what we were doing, about Keith Glasscock, the pipeline welder from Pampa, Texas, who had found the site and why his discovery was important. "These are the oldest known human remains found in the New World," Krieger said. I told the reporter about the fluorine and other chemical analyses the Las Alamos Laboratory had done for us and how the results told us that the human remains were contemporary with the bones of the extinct animals we had found in the blowout. I said, "The Midland skull is at least 10,000 years old, probably several thousand years older." I gave her a copy of the press release.

When they left I called Polly Hughes in Canyon, Texas, a stringer for *Time* and *Life* magazines. I told her the results of the chemical analyses and that the story would probably be on the Associated Press wire that day and in the local Santa Fe and Albuquerque papers on July 4. I sent her my press release and the list of names.

"My editors would like me to write a major story," Polly said when she called me back. "If they accept my draft and like the pictures, the story will soon appear in both *Life* and *Time*." Krieger and I then wrote a letter to Paul Fejos at the Wenner-Gren Foundation to alert him to the story and thank him for his support.

I enjoyed working with Krieger. We'd sit for a few minutes discussing the pros and cons of some point, and when we reached agreement, he would turn to the typewriter and, at unbelievable speed, write a section on the data we had just discussed, sometimes giving both sides of the problem. We finished the text portion of our part of the report on July 5, 1954, his last afternoon in Santa Fe.

I spent the next several weeks getting the illustrations together, drafting the maps and profiles, and pressing Albritton, Worman, the paleontologists, and other contributors to send me their manuscripts.

After I closed my excavations at the end of February, a noted academic paleontologist decided, without telling Krieger or me, to do his own excavations at the Midland site. In late November he brought in a road grader and a trenching machine and began digging. The grader scraped off the upper two feet or so of the white sand in the bottom of the draw. With the trencher, he cut five long trenches across the gray and red sands at the east end of the blowout. The dirt from his excavations was piled on one side of the trenches to be screened later. He found two chips in the white sand and eighteen flaked stone artifacts and several burned caliche rocks in the gray sand, as well as several fossilized bones. He did not record the precise locations and depths of any of these finds.

When Krieger found out what this paleontologist had done he had a hostile confrontation with him, threatening him with various consequences. He explained that what he'd done was a breach of professional ethics. Krieger extracted a promise from him that neither he nor anyone else in his employ would ever again work at the site, and to punish him for what he had done at the Midland site, he got him to agree that I would be free to excavate where he was working at the Blackwater Draw Clovis site, near Portales in eastern New Mexico.

I was furious when Krieger told me what had happened. I calmed down when I realized there was nothing to be gained by a public confrontation with the offender. The damage was done. At Krieger's insistence, the paleontologist wrote a short report on his excavations and sent it to me. Resisting the temptation to write the full story about his destruction of the Midland site and attach it to his manuscript, I included his text—as written—as an appendix in our report.

At last, in February of 1955, I sent Krieger the completed manuscript, including seven appendices. He took it to the University of Texas Press for their review. In the fall of 1955 they published *The Midland Discovery: A Report on the Pleistocene Human Remains from Midland, Texas.*

Unfortunately, the saga of the Midland site was not yet over. Between October 24 and November 6, 1955, I returned to the site to salvage what I could after the destruction. With a crew of two men I dug eleven pits, each 8 feet square, adjacent and parallel to his Trench V. We dug each pit down to the top of the white sand layer. Most of the artifacts had been found in the gray sand clustered in an area about 25 feet north of where Glasscock had found the human remains. I placed my pits uphill from where the hapless paleontologist had found the cluster of flakes and chips. At a depth of an inch or so, possibly on the surface of the gray sand, I recovered a fragment of a maxilla, a human face bone, crusted with gray sand and carbonate, almost certainly from Glasscock's skull. In addition, I found several flakes, two sidescrapers, the base of a Midland point, two buried piles of burned caliche rocks, two horse teeth, a burned bone from an extinct small antelope, a mud turtle carapace, and several rodent bones. The thin cluster of stone artifacts and the piles of burned rocks and bones probably indicate a camp that was occupied while the gray sand accumulated.

By the end of my 1955 excavations I had a new interpretation of the stratigraphic sequence at Midland. I had concluded that the red sand was more complex than Krieger and I had previously thought. I had observed that the gray sand contained small pieces of red sand, indicating that the red sand had been present before the gray sand dune accumulated. I thought the red sand was a complex unit that probably formed the margins of the valley, and that part of the margin collapsed onto the gray sand after that unit was deposited.

This interpretation was a better fit with the archaeological evidence. Our previous interpretation was that the Midland Points in the gray sand were several thousand years older than the Folsom artifacts Glasscock found on the surface of the nearby red sand dune. To me this was highly improbable. Krieger, however, rejected my new interpretation of the stratigraphy.

Krieger and I never reconciled our differences over the age of the Midland skull and the Midland Points. It was partly my fault. I made several efforts to obtain radiocarbon dates from the burned limestone (caliche) rocks. I discovered that when these black hearthstones were dissolved in hydrochloric acid they left a thick oily scum on the top of the acid. In hopes of dating the scum I submitted several of the hearthstones for radiocarbon analysis. All of them yielded age measurements between 18,000 and 20,000 years old, which greatly pleased Krieger. I was still skeptical of these dates because they implied that Midland Points were present by 18,000 years ago and survived until Folsom, which was at the time dated around 10,000 years old. We remained good friends, but we never again worked together.

Today, I'm still convinced my interpretation of the stratigraphy is correct. I believe that the Midland skull is somewhere between 10,800 and 9,500 years old and contemporary with Folsom, perhaps a variety of Folsom. On the basis of the results of the microchemical analyses, I believe the skull is of the same age as the extinct fauna in the gray sand, the Midland Point found near it, and the fragments of other Midland Points I found in my excavations of the gray sand near the spot where Glasscock found the skull. The stratigraphic position of the Midland Points that Earl Green found at the Clovis site supports this conclusion. At the Clovis site, Midland Points occur in the same horizon as Folsom and are dated around 10,000–10,500 years old.

One of the most useful things I learned from the work at the Midland site was that the changes in the environment were far more complex on the Southern High Plains during the Late Pleistocene and early Holocene than was generally recognized in 1955. This knowledge prepared me to have an open mind when an opportunity came a few years later to conduct a large-scale research project on the past environments on the Llano Estacado.

Today an official Texas State Historical Marker is posted outside the Midland County courthouse, describing the Midland discovery and explaining its significance to residents and visitors to that West Texas town.

Teaching at Texas Technological University
(1956–1958)

CHAPTER 9

In February of 1956 I received an offer from Curry Holden, director of the museum at Texas Technological University in Lubbock, to become the associate director of the museum and associate professor of anthropology at the university. The position was to begin on September 1, 1956, with a salary considerably more than I was being paid at the Museum of New Mexico. Holden and his wife, Fran, were old friends, and I accepted the offer even though it meant that the highway archaeological program I had started in New Mexico might not continue.

At the end of August, Nancy and I sold our home in Santa Fe, packed our belongings, and called a mover to take our furniture to Lubbock. Although I was excited about my new job at Texas Tech, I was also sad. The house was only three years old, and it had been built to our specifications. I loved Santa Fe, then a small city of fewer than fifty thousand people. It had an artistic atmosphere, and the community included many people with interests in Southwestern archaeology. Nancy and I had made many friends there, and we would miss them. I would also miss the mountains that I enjoyed greeting every morning.

In early September of 1956, Nancy, our two children, Carl and Mike, and I arrived in Lubbock. We found an older adobe house north of the city limits that needed a lot of work, but was within our budget, and Curry Holden persuaded me to buy it. He saw an opportunity to introduce me to the advantages of adobe construction. We bought the house, and with Holden's guidance, I took on the major job of renovation, including the addition of a large living room and an adjoining dining area. We used adobe bricks, of course.

Adobe construction was not difficult, provided you dug a deep foundation trench and filled it with steel-reinforced concrete. I wired the new part of the house myself using a "How to Wire Your House" booklet from Sears. (If a house was outside the Lubbock city limits a homeowner was allowed to wire his own house. A licensed electrician was required to wire a house inside the city limits.) With Holden's help, I hired two local workmen. I worked with them on the new construction and together we built the foundation, placed the window frames, and put up the board and viga ceiling. The workers finished the floors and laid the adobe bricks. I hired a plumber to install the heating ducts, and a local contractor put on the tar and gravel roof. While this was going on I taught two courses at the university and worked with Holden at the museum.

One of my classes was Introductory Anthropology, a general ethnographic survey including political, kinship, and economic systems of hunter/gatherer groups and simple farmers throughout the world. There were about forty students in the class, many of them teacher trainees from the Department of Education, which required the course. My other class was Archaeology of the American Southwest, which dealt with the archaeological data from the earliest sites to the Spanish entrada. This class was smaller, with ten to fifteen students. The subject matter was very interesting to me, and my presentation was probably too detailed, but I felt these students had a special interest in the archaeology of their surroundings.

Although Holden had an interest in archaeology and had conducted several archaeology field schools, I was the first member of the Texas Tech faculty with a PhD in anthropology. At the end of the first week of classes two of my students told me there was an informant from a local church in my introductory anthropology course. I was not surprised. I had expected that religious fundamentalists in the community might want to monitor my classes, and I didn't feel threatened.

About three weeks into the semester, while walking to my class one morning, I saw a sign announcing Religious Emphasis Week. I decided to celebrate the event by giving three lectures titled "The Origins of Religion." The lectures seemed to be well received by the students, and the number of visitors increased from one lecture to the next. Some of them were faculty, and by the third lecture there was standing room only. At the end of the third lecture the informant raised his hand.

He said, "Tell us, professor, what is your religion?"

"I believe my religion is a private matter," I said. And then after a long pause, I continued, "But since this is Religious Emphasis Week, and we've been talking about the origins of religion, perhaps I should tell you about my religion."

Without giving my words adequate thought, I said, "I'm a Druid."

The informant didn't seem to know what a Druid was. When the snickers started in the back of the room, I said, "But I've become disenchanted with my religion because I've been a Druid for many years and so far no Druid priestess has ever called on me." The class broke up with laughter, the bell rang, and I went off to my office.

Two hours later the phone rang. The secretary to the president of the university told me that President Jones would like to see me. I walked over to his office, and his secretary told me to go right in. President Jones sat behind a big desk across the room from the door. He looked up and said, "It's SOBs like you that make my life difficult. Please don't make jokes about religion again." There was a slight twitch of his mouth. I thought I saw the start of a grin.

Over the next few days I received invitations to join several faculty clubs. I was no longer an unknown entity on the Texas Tech faculty: I was the campus Druid.

Beside Curry and Fran Holden, my closest friends in Lubbock came to be members of the history faculty, particularly Bill Pearce, chairman of the department, Ike Connor, and Sylvan Dunn. In the fall Bill Pearce and I took up duck hunting at some of the small ponds around Lubbock. We'd get up at 5:00 A.M. and go in Bill's car because he knew where all the ponds were. We'd arrive when it was still dark and find a place to hide in the brush near the water. There we would wait until dawn when it was legal to hunt ducks. I had only a double barrel twenty-gauge shotgun I had bought when I was fourteen to hunt doves and quail. My gun was a little light for killing ducks flying overhead. Bill had a twelve-gauge automatic shotgun; he got a lot more ducks than I. It was so much fun it never mattered to me who killed the ducks. We'd have about an hour to hunt, and then we had to hurry back for our classes, muddy shoes and all.

One of the best aspects about being an archaeologist in West Texas was that everyone seemed to be interested in archaeology and wanted to talk about it. One of my new amateur archaeologist friends was a state game warden whose name I do not remember. From time to time, he would come by my office to talk about archaeology, particularly about where the best sites were. One day in November of 1957 he noticed the mud on my shoes, and I explained that Pearce and I had been duck hunting.

He asked if I'd like to kill a goose, and I said that would be great. "Well," he said, "the Muleshoe Game Refuge has thousands of geese." I stopped him. "Hold on there, Mr. Warden. I'll be arrested if I kill anything on the game refuge." He laughed and said, "That's true if you hunt on the game refuge, but every morning at dawn the geese fly out of the refuge in big swarms over to the sorghum fields beyond the game refuge boundary. You're permitted to hunt them if they land in the sorghum fields."

It was getting close to Thanksgiving, and a goose feast sounded great. Two days before the holiday, Ike Connor, Sylvan Dunn, and I went out to an area adjacent to the game refuge to check it out. As reported, the sorghum fields were alive with gray geese. When we returned I told Pearce what we had seen, and I asked if he wanted to join us in this great goose hunt. "Hell, yes," he said, thinking of a goose for his Thanksgiving table. "What time do you want to leave?"

The day before Thanksgiving, about an hour before dawn, the four of us arrived at the place where Connor, Dunn, and I had seen lots of geese. We walked in about a quarter of a mile from the road, spread out along the edge of the sorghum field, squatted down, and waited. Just after dawn here they came. One swarm looked as if it was about to land on top of me, honking like mad. I almost shot a protected snow goose, but recognized my mistake in time. I swung my gun around and with two quick shots killed two geese while they were still over my head. I gathered up my kill and started walking back. I called out to the others, "I have my two geese. I'll see you at the car."

A few minutes after I got to the car a farmer walked up and asked, "What are you guys hunting?" And I said excitedly, "Geese. That field is full of them." He looked at my two geese and said, "They look to me kinda gray to be geese." And he walked away. "Dumb farmer," I thought. My fellow hunters came back to the car. I counted the number of geese in the trunk and said, "The four of us have killed seven geese. This was great shooting. There are so damn many geese I thought they were going to land on top of me!"

Connor's wife, Ann, had agreed to clean our birds. Later that afternoon, Nancy and I planned to join the Connors and cook them together. About mid-morning the phone rang. It was Ann Connor. She had cleaned one of the birds and was starting on the second when she decided to call me. "Fred, these are the strangest geese I've ever seen."

I said, "They honk like geese, they're the same color as geese, and they fly in lines just like geese. What's wrong?" Ann got out her bird book and read to me, "Geese have webbed feet. These birds don't." She turned the page and saw a bird that looked and sounded like a goose, but didn't have webbed feet. The title at the top of that page read, SANDHILL CRANE. Oh hell! We had killed seven protected birds. Killing even one could result in a seven-hundred-dollar fine.

Nancy and I and our two children, Carl and Mike, sped to the Connors' house, and the four adults began scrubbing the counters and tables and vacuuming up all the feathers and other traces of the birds. We called Pearce and Dunn. Pearce was at the dinner table eating his "goose." I could hear Bill take another bite and smack his lips. He said, "Tastes pretty good to me." None of the rest of us had the courage to eat them. We took the large bags containing all traces of the birds to the city dump and buried them as deep as we could. All four of us took an oath never to mention this episode to another living person.

About two weeks later we four "goose" hunters were having lunch in a restaurant across from the campus that was popular with the faculty. In walked my game warden friend who came right to our table and greeted us warmly. "I haven't seen you for a couple of weeks. What've you been doing?" I asked, trying to sound casual. He laughed and said, "I've been out at the Muleshoe Game Refuge shooting sandhill cranes. See you later, Fred."

The four of us were speechless. Lunch was finished as far as we were concerned; none of us could eat a bite. It was clear my friend knew what we'd done. How could four reasonably intelligent professors have made such a mistake? Bill Pearce had been born in West Texas and had seen many sandhill cranes, yet he'd been completely fooled. Dunn, who is a sociologist and a specialist in such things, says it was mass hysteria: an authority figure had said there were geese, and thus they became geese to us. That may be as good an explanation as any.

About four years later the sandhill crane was removed from the protected list, and a hunting season was established. A few days later I received in the mail a clipping about the new hunting season. The envelope was postmarked Lubbock, but there was no sender's name or address. Each fall I continued to receive a clipping about the sandhill crane hunting season from this anonymous source until about ten years ago when they stopped. I never found out who sent them, although I suspected my former game warden friend.

Despite the notoriety of being the campus Druid, I settled into my new life in West Texas. Our third child, Gail Susan, was born in Lubbock in 1957. She was a beautiful baby girl who stole her father's heart. The renovation of our home continued, with occasional breaks since it was a pay-as-you-go project. By this time the walls were up, and we would soon put on the ceiling deck and the roof.

Cantonment Burgwin |
(1957–1958)

CHAPTER 10

I n Lubbock two new, unanticipated, and important research opportunities arose even before I arrived at Texas Tech. Both continued for many years after I'd left Lubbock. To avoid confusion I'll first discuss my role in the initial two years of the Fort Burgwin Research Center, an institution created to enrich the intellectual and cultural life in northern New Mexico. Then, in the next chapter, I'll tell the story of how I became involved in an exciting, long-term research project to study the Late Pleistocene environments on the Southern High Plains of eastern New Mexico and western Texas.

When I was still in Santa Fe, in April 1956, I had been invited to give a paper on highway salvage archaeology at a regional meeting of highway construction people in Phoenix, Arizona. The evening of my presentation the Concrete Products Association hosted a party for the New Mexico delegation. I was seated next to the chairman of the New Mexico State Highway Commission, George Lavender.

Late in the evening, after several rounds of drinks, he said, "Fred, I hear you're leaving us and moving to Lubbock to teach at Texas Tech University." I said that was true. He asked if I'd like to have a place in New Mexico where I could bring my students to teach them how to do archaeology. "That would be great," I said. "But where?"

"Well, when we sober up, come and see me and we'll see what we can work out."

I waited a week and then called Lavender at his lumber mill office in Santa Fe. The party had been so raucous I feared he might not remember our conversation, but he did. As soon as I introduced myself he invited me to come out to his office. When I arrived fifteen minutes later, he asked, "Do you know about the big pueblo ruin on Pot Creek, about ten miles south of Taos?" I said I did and that we had a collection of pot sherds from there in the Laboratory of Anthropology. Lavender went on, "The ruin is about two hundred yards north of our sawmill office at Pot Creek. Why don't you bring your field school to the Pot Creek Pueblo? If you do, I'll assist you financially."

I said that would be a great help, and I told him that to attract the best students I needed to offer scholarships to cover their expenses. Lavender nodded to let me know he understood, and said, "My business partner, Ralph Rounds, owns the land where the site is located, and he has a lot more money than I do. He's also interested in archaeology. Rounds keeps an apartment above the sawmill office at Pot Creek, where he spends several weeks each summer. I think he's likely to help you with your plans to excavate the pueblo. He is, however, primarily interested in an old presidio he thinks was once on his property. Before you talk with Rounds I think you should see if you can find any information about an old fort somewhere in the Taos area."

Rounds owned about 91,000 acres southeast of Taos. Much of it was high mountain country, timbered, rough, and difficult to cross. The thought of spending several months searching for an old army post in such mountainous terrain was not attractive to me. Nevertheless, I decided to see what I could find in the library. I spent the next few weeks researching old forts in New Mexico, reading, among other works, *Forts and Forays,* a much-edited diary by James A. Bennett, who had been a supply sergeant in the First Dragoons. In 1852 he had helped build a post near Taos known as Cantonment Burgwin. The army used the term "cantonment" to designate a temporary post. I read Lydia Spencer Lane's *I Married a Soldier; or, Old Days in the Old Army* (1893). She'd married First Lieutenant William B. Lane of the U.S. Mounted Rifles on May 18, 1854, and they were sent to New Mexico, where they spent October and November of 1854 at Cantonment Burgwin. In her diary Lydia Lane described the cantonment as a "very small post, most beautifully situated, being surrounded by high mountains. It was nine miles from Taos, New Mexico" (Lane 1893, 50).

This research was helpful, but the most important information I found came from an unpublished document, a copy of which happened to be in the Laboratory of Anthropology library. Kenneth Chapman, a famous artist and the senior curator at the laboratory, brought the document to my attention. The manuscript carried the lengthy title of "Report of Jos. K. F. Mansfield, Colonel and Inspector General, United States Army, Regarding His Inspection of the Department of New Mexico During the Summer and Fall of the year 1853." This report gave a brief description and included a simple sketch map of each of the army posts in New Mexico at that time, including Cantonment Burgwin. Mansfield's map showed that Cantonment Burgwin was at the confluence of the Little Rio Grande and an unnamed eastern tributary. The Mansfield map identified and marked the location of every building at Cantonment Burgwin, as it had existed in 1853.

A quick study of the United States Geological Survey (USGS) topographic sheet for the Taos area indicated there were two significant streams entering the Little Rio Grande from the east, only one of which matched Lydia Lane's description as "beautifully situated, being surrounded by high mountains." The matching stream was Pot Creek, where the Rounds and Lavender sawmill was located. During the course of my reading I learned that Cantonment Burgwin was named after Captain John Henry K. Burgwin, who had been killed in 1848 leading the assault on the church at Taos Pueblo. This assault ended the Taos Rebellion, an uprising of local Spanish and Taos Indians unhappy over the American army presence. I also found out that the cantonment had been established on August 14, 1852, and abandoned on May 18, 1860.

In June of 1956, shortly after reviewing the Mansfield report, I received word that Ralph Rounds was in Taos and wanted to meet with me. I took the Mansfield manuscript and the USGS sheet and drove up to Taos and out to the sawmill. The office building was on the south side of Pot Creek, about a hundred yards east of the highway to Las Vegas, New Mexico. To the south of the office was a huge sawmill, covering about twenty-five acres, with a millpond, vast piles of logs, and stacks of sawed lumber. The area was bustling with people, loaders, and logging trucks. When I got out of the car I saw Rounds standing on his porch above the sawmill office. "Come on up," he called.

At the time, Ralph Rounds was sixty-seven, of middle height, and solid. He was almost bald except for arcs of sandy-gray hair above his ears, with a few tufts on top. He stood erect, his shoulders back, and he looked directly at you, right in the eyes. He had a round, friendly face.

"Please sit down here, at the table," he said. He seated himself in the other chair and immediately put me at ease, saying, "I know you want to bring a group of students from Texas Tech to excavate the old pueblo across the creek. It's only about two hundred yards north of here." He gestured vaguely in the right direction. "I like the idea and I'll help financially."

"That's great, Mr. Rounds," I said. "With your help we could have one of the best archaeological field schools in the country. This beautiful setting will be attractive, but even here, to attract the best students I'll need to offer scholarships."

Rounds nodded. "I like your plan to study the old pueblo," he said. "But what really interests me is finding and possibly restoring the old fort I'm sure is somewhere on this property. The presence of a 'presidio' is recorded in the abstract to this property." He waved his arms to show he meant the vast area of hills and mountains around us.

"I'm also interested in the old presidio," I said, "and I've found a map that might help us find it." We looked first at the Mansfield map showing Cantonment Burgwin at the junction of the Little Rio Grande and an unnamed creek coming in from the east side. We checked the USGS sheet, and we saw that there were only two creeks entering the Little Rio Grande from the east. One of them was the Rio Chiquita at the mouth of the Little Rio Grande Valley, an open area with many houses and few trees. I told him about Lydia Lane's book and her description of the cantonment as "a small post surrounded by beautiful, timbered mountains." That description didn't match the area around Rio Chiquita. It left only Pot Creek.

Rounds agreed. "The cantonment seems to have been located where Pot Creek joins the Little Rio Grande, about a mile northwest of where we are now. Let's get into my car and find out," he said. He drove across the highway and down a small dirt track that bordered Pot Creek on its south and west banks. A hundred yards after crossing the highway I noticed a group of low mounds in the sagebrush flat just off the track. "Those look like the ruins of small pueblos," I said.

We followed Pot Creek to its confluence with the Little Rio Grande and got out of the car. It was a marshy area, not at all a suitable setting for a military post. We searched for about an hour but found no trace of anything that might have been a fort. Disappointed, we returned to the car. On the way back to his office I asked him to stop at the Indian ruins we had seen on the way down. Once we got there we walked about fifty feet when I reached down and picked up a uniform button from the First Dragoons.

"Look at this," I said. We began looking carefully and found several horseshoes, a few fifty-caliber bullets, handmade nails, and a lot of broken glass and china. There was no Indian pottery. "I think we've found Cantonment Burgwin, or at least some part of it," I said. "The numerous small mounds we can see in the sagebrush are probably collapsed chimneys, indicating the presence of buildings."

We returned to Rounds's apartment in high spirits. He was so happy he hugged me. He recounted all his previous unsuccessful efforts to find the presidio. He said one historian had told him the post was under his sawmill. I cautioned Rounds that the sawmill might have destroyed a major part of the cantonment, and that only a careful archaeological study could resolve the question. I suggested that one of my first steps should be a search of the military records relating to Cantonment Burgwin in the National Archives to find out as much as I could about the post and its history. He asked me to prepare a plan and a budget for the work as soon as I could after establishing myself in Lubbock.

Before I left, Rounds explained why the old fort was so important to him. "I'm fond of the people of northern New Mexico, and I want to do something to help them. I've made a lot of money from this sawmill here at Pot Creek, and I want to return some of it to the area, but do it in a way that will help the people. I have dreamed that I might develop the old fort to attract scholars and scientists to the Pot Creek area."

I thought it was a bold and attractive concept. Rounds asked, "Will you be willing to excavate the cantonment next summer, in addition to excavating a part of the old pueblo?" I told him it would be a pleasure.

I wrote to the National Archives, outlined our project, and asked for assistance. Back came a form letter indicating that I was welcome to use the archives, but that the search was up to me. I could not expect any help from the staff. As an archaeologist with no experience with either old military documents or the National Archives, I knew that if I undertook the job alone it would be time-consuming and probably not productive.

Near the end of September 1956, three weeks after I arrived in Lubbock, I was recounting my unsuccessful efforts to recruit help from the National Archives to Seymour (Ike) Connor, a professor in the history department at Texas Tech. Connor said, "Why don't you ask Senator Johnson to help you? I'll introduce you to a friend of mine who's a senior clerk on Senator Lyndon Johnson's staff."

Connor thought the senator might be willing to help, and in any case, it wouldn't hurt to try, he said. We placed a call to Johnson's office, and soon we were speaking with Connor's friend. Connor briefly described my project and then handed me the phone. I gave him a few more details and asked if he thought Johnson might be willing to help me with the National Archives. He promised to talk with the senator and get back to me the next day.

Johnson was then Senate majority leader and one of the most influential men in Washington. The next day I learned that Johnson had agreed to help, but in exchange, he wanted me to pose for a photograph with him and help prepare a press release about his assistance with our project. I agreed and scheduled a trip to Washington for two weeks later. When I arrived at Johnson's office, the director of the National Archives was also waiting. A few minutes later a photographer appeared.

Senator Johnson emerged, said "Hello," and the photographer took a photo of Senator Johnson, the director of the National Archives, and me. Then, with only a nod to the others, Senator Johnson said, "I believe everything is taken care of," and left, his objective met.

The director invited me to go with him to the National Archives. We got into his limousine, and as we sat down I said, "I am acutely embarrassed over the trouble I have caused you." He replied, "Think nothing of it. When the Senate majority leader asks me to do something, I do it." At the National Archives the staff had laid out everything they could find about Cantonment Burgwin on several long tables. After a brief inspection I arranged for all the material to be copied on microfilm for later study. I paid the standard fee and arranged to come back the next day for the microfilm.

There was an unexpected benefit from the assistance I received from Senator Johnson. The senator's news release about our plans to restore Cantonment Burgwin went out nationwide, which led to a letter I received from Mrs. Virginia S. White of Sumter, South Carolina, the daughter of W. W. Anderson, who had been stationed at Cantonment Burgwin as post surgeon between 1855 and 1857. Mrs. White told me that during the Civil War Anderson became the assistant surgeon general of the Confederate Army. Mrs. White said she had two sketches her father had made of the cantonment, copies of which she was sending to me in Lubbock.

W. W. Anderson had been a well-educated, curious, and talented man. He assembled collections of birds and old Indian pottery that he sent to the Smithsonian Institution. He discovered an entirely new species of songbird in the environs around the cantonment. He made a drawing of it and named it Virginia's warbler *(Vermivora virginiae),* in honor of his wife, a cultured woman who had brought her piano from St. Louis to Cantonment Burgwin and played it regularly.

Anderson was an excellent artist and a careful draftsman. His drawings proved to be extremely useful. One sketch was of the parade ground looking toward two small buildings. It showed that the walls were constructed of upright logs, and that the buildings had rectangular four-paned windows and flat roofs.

Another drawing was a scene from a hill south of the cantonment, with the buildings of the post in the middle ground and the lower valley and the Taos Mountains in the distance. Because of Anderson's precise draftsmanship I realized I might be able to find the actual place he had been standing when he drew the picture, and I knew that with his drawing I would be able to locate the exact position of the cantonment and many of its buildings.

A few days after receiving the Anderson drawings I drove out to Taos and climbed the hill where I thought Anderson had probably stood when he made the sketch. It was about a half-mile south of where Rounds and I had found what we thought were traces of the cantonment. Anderson's drawing was a northward view down the Little Rio Grande Valley, showing two easily identified ranges of hills and mountains in the distance. By moving up or down the hill, and then from side to side until I could see the hills in the exact same spatial relationship to each other as shown on the drawing, I was able to find where Anderson had stood to make the sketch. By holding the drawing up to match the scene below, I noted the sagebrush flat where Rounds and I had found traces of old structures, and there on the Anderson drawing were the main buildings of Cantonment Burgwin in the exact same place. It was a relief to me to learn that the post was not under the sawmill after all. I immediately contacted Rounds with the good news.

A few days later I submitted a proposal to Rounds outlining all I had learned from my research, particularly the conflicting information from Bennett in *Forts and Forays* indicating that Burgwin had been built of adobe, and the Anderson drawings that showed walls made of upright logs. I was skeptical of Bennett's description, despite his participation in the construction, because his editors noted that Bennett wrote the diary late in his life from notes and that they had found several errors. In their Foreword, the editors confessed that they had done "some rearranging" of the text. I concluded that the description of the construction of Cantonment Burgwin must be one of those editorial changes. Excavation alone would resolve these discrepancies and would provide the accurate information we would need to reconstruct the buildings.

My plans were first to excavate and then restore the rectangular compound, which according to the Mansfield map, had been used for the enlisted men's quarters and the stables. At first I thought this large structure might be used as a museum, but a museum would require bringing in artists and exhibit designers and a staff to manage the collections. When Rounds heard this, he told me to set aside the museum idea for now, because his first priority was to develop housing and laboratory facilities for the scholars and scientists he hoped to attract to the area.

I thought we would hire a local building contractor in Taos to construct the first building. But Curry Holden, who had extensive experience in constructing adobe buildings, told me, "From the indicated size of the building, no contractor will agree to do the job for the money in your budget." Rounds had been talking about providing ten thousand dollars, of which two thousand was earmarked for the field school. Neither figure would be enough. Holden said, "You'll have to hire a crew and build it yourself, Fred. We know that the original walls were almost certainly made of upright logs and wouldn't be suitable for a permanent structure. Why not build it of adobe? When you put up the walls you could lay three horizontal courses of two-inch-by-twelve-inch planks in the adobe walls, one at the bottom, another in the center, and a third just below the concrete bond beam at the top. These three plank courses would provide a way to attach split logs to the exteriors so you could simulate the appearance of the original vertical log walls."

Curry and I made up several cost estimates for the building, assuming a one-hundred-by-one-hundred-foot building with a courtyard at its center. Each time we varied the cost of items to be purchased, the roofing, heating, plumbing, and electrical subcontractor fees, the length of time needed to build the structure and thus the labor costs, and the result always was that we would be short several thousand dollars.

A few days later, during a visit to Lubbock, Rounds asked, "How much reconstruction do you think you could do for the eight thousand dollars I plan to give you?" I told him I didn't know yet because there was still some doubt about the size of the structure, but I intended to build until I ran out of money. I went on, "Unless you're willing to put considerably more money in the project, it can't be done using a general contractor. So, unless there's more money, I intend to supervise personally the construction of the first building."

He liked the plans, but I could tell he was worried about my lack of building experience. So was I. I had never built anything, except the addition to my house in Lubbock. Despite his concerns, Rounds said, "Okay, then. I'll raise the total amount of my gift to twenty thousand dollars. You should at least try to get the walls up and the roof on the building by the end of next summer."

I agreed, and said, "To get this done within the budget I need some more help from you, Mr. Rounds. Can you arrange for the windows to be built to my specifications at your factory in Wichita, Kansas? I'll have the details of the window sizes early in our excavations. The windows should match those in the original building, and with luck in the excavations, I'll find broken glass that will even tell us the dimensions of the glass in the windows. We already know from Anderson's drawings each window had four panes.

"Can the Pot Creek Lumber Company loggers cut the vigas for the building? They need to be almost straight logs with the bark removed, and from ten to fourteen inches in diameter. They can be peeled and dried down at the construction site. I'll get you the length and number of vigas we need as soon as I have the dimensions of the building."

And finally I asked if he would arrange for the sawmill to supply whatever lumber we needed at a wholesale price. He agreed to all of these requests, and a few days later the West Texas Museum Association received a check for twenty thousand dollars from the Wichita Foundation.

Later that spring, I learned that I had overlooked several things I needed from the sawmill if I intended to build the enlisted men's quarters. I received a call from Mrs. Lorraine Lavender, George Lavender's wife, a good friend and the business manager for the Pot Creek Lumber Company. She said, "We'll give you the help you asked for from the sawmill. We also think you'll need water, so Winton Bernardin, the manager of the Pot Creek sawmill, and I have arranged for a shallow well to be drilled next to where you're going to work. It will provide water at the site for drinking and construction purposes. I've also made arrangements for you to use the abandoned Pot Creek School. It has a kitchen and room to house and feed the students in your field school."

I realized we'd need bathing facilities, too, so I borrowed a tent from the museum at Texas Tech, and when I returned to Pot Creek I put it up near our new well. We ran a hose from the tent to the faucet that had been set up at the well, put down a few boards to stand on, and all was ready for our very cold showers. With this, the excavations could begin at Cantonment Burgwin.

On June 1, 1957, I went to Taos to make final arrangements for work to begin on the Texas Tech Archaeology Field School at Cantonment Burgwin and Pot Creek Pueblo. I planned to reconstruct the largest building in the cantonment. Eleven students were enrolled in the field school from six different universities around Texas. Our first project would be to excavate the enlisted men's quarters.

Work began by clearing the brush with heavy mattocks. With the help of the Mansfield map and the Anderson drawings, we identified all of the major structures of the old post. Then we began the excavation of the building we identified as the enlisted men's quarters with its adjoining stables. Almost immediately we were able to confirm that the walls had been of vertical pine logs, from 12 to 16 inches in diameter, with bark intact. The logs were set into trenches 4 feet deep, and chinked with mud. In most cases the walls were identified by the presence of a ghost of the bark; the core of the logs had long since decayed and disappeared completely. Finding and following those walls proved to be a challenge.

The floors had been made of leveled, packed earth. The interiors of the walls had been plastered with micaceous clay, available locally and known as "*tierra blanca* (white earth)," traces of which occurred as a minute lip on the floor along the walls in almost every room. From the areas of broken window glass we found in the excavations I was able to determine the size, number, and locations of the windows. We ordered specially made windows and frames of those sizes.

Now that I knew the dimensions of the building, I could ask Winton Bernardin to arrange for vigas of the proper length and size to be cut and brought to the building site, where they would be peeled, cleaned, and set up to dry.

After the walls had been located and the building outlined, and with the guidance of state representative Bish Trujillo, who was yard superintendent at the sawmill,

I employed six local laborers to assist with the work. Since they were young men in their twenties, and hard workers, it took them and the students only four weeks to clear the walls, fireplaces, and floors of the entire 80-by-100-foot building and a 40-by-60-foot interior open courtyard of the enlisted men's quarters.

Work shifted to Pot Creek Pueblo, where several test pits were dug and two rooms excavated. The test pits showed there had been at least two occupations and that there were pit houses below the pueblo.

The field school, however, was not all excavation, mapping, and recording. We were privileged to hear four distinguished archaeologists lecture on their special areas: Alex Krieger from the University of Texas, Luther Cressman from the University of Oregon, and E. N. Ferdon and Stewart Peckham from the Museum of New Mexico. My friend Norris E. Bradbury, a physicist and longtime director of the Los Alamos Scientific Laboratory, also came. Bradbury discussed the application of physics to archaeology, particularly the recently developed technique of carbon 14 dating.

As soon as the stable area was cleared, about three weeks into the field school, I calculated that we would need 36,000 adobe bricks to rebuild the quadrangle of the enlisted men's quarters. So, again with the assistance of Bish Trujillo, I hired a local Taos family to make the bricks, using dirt removed during the excavation of the stable. Our plan was to erect a permanent structure that on the outside would have an appearance close to the original, while on the inside it would be modern, with plumbing, heating, electricity, and permanent floors.

By this time we were referring to the new building as "Fort Burgwin" to signify its change of status from a temporary to a permanent facility. While the excavations of the enlisted men's quarters were still underway, I found a heating and plumbing contractor, a roofing contractor, and a local builder who would pour the concrete foundations and floors. My efforts to find an electrical contractor at a reasonable price were unsuccessful, but I wasn't concerned because I had learned how to do simple wiring when I'd worked on my house outside Lubbock. If I had to, I thought I could wire the building myself.

As soon as the field school was over, we began the reconstruction of the main quadrangle, using our six laborers and two students who elected to stay and help with the work. Including myself, nine of us were working. We dug 4-foot-deep footings following the original alignment of the walls. The plumbing contractor installed heating ducts and plumbing pipes, and the concrete contractor poured 5,600 square feet of steel-reinforced concrete foundations and floors. We had agreed to install the reinforcing steel ourselves if he would pour the concrete foundations and floors. Then we planned to finish the concrete.

Unfortunately, not one of us knew anything about finishing concrete. The floors were poured every day for ten days (during an unusually wet summer) in sections ranging in size from 600 to 800 square feet. No sooner would we finish the floor for that day than a rainstorm would come up and ruin the smooth surface. We would have to refinish that section, sometimes two or three times as new storms appeared, one after another. We learned a lot about finishing concrete floors, and someday I hope to forget it all.

We finally finished the floors and then began laying adobe bricks to form the walls, leaving spaces for the door and window frames. When the walls were the correct height, we capped them with a steel-reinforced concrete bond beam that tied everything together.

I had some important help during this period from Ben Gonzales, who operated La Lomita, a small bar and café in Taos. Mrs. Isabel Gonzales was the cook there, and she made delicious enchiladas, which my two students and I ate almost every night. One night Ben could no longer contain his curiosity. He asked me what we were doing in Taos. I told him we were constructing a building near the sawmill at Pot Creek. "What kind of building?" Ben asked.

"Adobe. We are rebuilding part of an old U.S. Army post," I replied. Then I told him about our trouble finishing the concrete floors. "We're about to start laying the adobe bricks for the walls," I said, "and I'm not familiar with adobe buildings. I'm learning as I go."

Ben told me he'd once been a building contractor and said he might be able to help if I had any questions. After that, each evening over a beer, I told him what we'd accomplished during the day. Then I'd ask, "What do I do tomorrow?" Ben was always able to come up with a good working plan for each stage of the project.

Rounds and his wife came out the second week in August to see how the construction was going. He was delighted when he saw how far along we were. We had almost completed placing the vigas to hold up the roof, and he could see we would probably finish on schedule. I had to, because in three weeks, classes in Lubbock began.

Rounds asked me how things were going with expenses. "We are going to be close, but I think we will be within budget," I said. He said, "Don't hesitate. Let me know if you need any more money."

The only crisis occurred a few days after Rounds had returned to Wichita. We started to lay the ceiling deck above the vigas when I realized that the electrical wiring had to be placed before we could install the insulation or put on the roof deck. A quick recheck of the local electrical contractors failed to find anyone who would do the job at a decent price, so I decided to do it myself.

I still had my "How to Wire a House" booklet from Sears, and I reread it carefully. On a map of the building I laid out the twenty-six electrical circuits I thought would be needed for the building, being careful to keep the number of outlets on each circuit well below the limit mandated by the national electrical code. I went to Santa Fe and purchased the necessary supplies and installed the complete system. We proceeded with the insulation and the framing for the roof. Then I called the Kit Carson Electric Cooperative to hook us up and turn on the electricity.

The first thing the Kit Carson crew asked when they got there was "Where's your tag?"

"What tag?" I asked. They explained that in New Mexico, unlike Texas, only licensed electricians can install wiring, even in rural areas, and that the electrician must attach an official tag confirming that the work has been done properly. One of the men said, "If I were you, I'd check with the state electrical board in Albuquerque to see what might be done."

I went to Albuquerque that day and met with the supervisor of the electrical board. I did the only thing I could: I told him the truth, the whole story, including my experience in Texas, and described what I had done. After a few questions he handed me a thick book, told me to read it, and come back the following week to take an electrician's licensing examination.

When I showed up the following week, I put the book on his desk, and he asked if I'd read the book. I said I had. He handed me a tag, saying, "Listen here, young man; don't ever do your own wiring again, because this is the last tag you'll ever get from me."

Much relieved, I returned to Fort Burgwin, hung my tag, and again called Kit Carson Electric. The same men came out, and with broad smiles, turned on the electricity. Miracle of miracles, there were no sparks, flashes of lightning, or dead wires.

A local contractor installed a twenty-year specification asphalt and gravel roof. Finally, we hung the windows and doors and installed the locks. I had two days before I had to be back in Lubbock, and I had $234.00 left in my account. It was a wonderful feeling; we'd done it!

Although the building was now protected from the elements for the winter, much remained to be done before it could be used. The exterior walls needed to be covered with cement stucco, and the vertical log slabs had to be nailed to the horizontal boards we had set in the adobe walls for that purpose. The interior also had to be plastered and painted to match the *tierra blanca* of the original walls. Lighting and plumbing fixtures would have to be installed, water and sewer lines laid, septic tanks constructed, and partitions erected. As soon as those things were done, Fort Burgwin would be ready for use as the 1958 Texas Tech Archaeology Field School.

Pollen Studies on the Llano Estacado |
(1956–1962)

CHAPTER 11

A second new research opportunity unfolded only a few weeks after Rounds and I had found Cantonment Burgwin, in late June of 1956. It began when I attended a large conference on the past and modern environments of the Southwestern desert, held at the University of New Mexico in Albuquerque. During a break in the proceedings, I introduced myself to one of the participants, Mrs. Kathryn Clisby of Oberlin College. She and Paul Sears of Yale University had given a paper on the results of the pollen analyses they had done on sediments from the San Augustine Basin of south-central New Mexico. These pollen studies yielded interesting new data on the changes in the vegetation in that area. I congratulated her on her research.

Clisby was in her early fifties, full of energy, and intense. I told her about my work at the Midland site. She knew that our book on the Midland site had been published the year before, but she had not read it. I mentioned that we had failed to recover pollen from the sediments there. Clisby was abrupt and direct. "You need a new pollen analyst."

There was an awkward pause. I mentioned the numerous large playa lake basins on the Llano Estacado (Staked Plains) of eastern New Mexico and western Texas, and she became visibly more interested. I offered to take her to see the basins sometime. To my surprise, she said, "No, let's go now. Tomorrow, if you can."

I checked with Stubbs and the business office at the Museum of New Mexico, and got their approval, and Clisby and I headed out the next day to Clovis, Portales, and Blackwater Draw. She looked at Blackwater Draw where it crossed the Clovis-Portales Highway and examined the exposures of sediments in the Arch Lake Basin southeast of Portales, near the New Mexico–Texas border.

When we had finished looking around at Arch Lake, Clisby said, "Take me back to Portales and let's find the Department of Agriculture Soil Survey office."

She walked into the office and asked, "Who's in charge here? I'm Kathryn Clisby and this is Fred Wendorf." When the man in charge came out she repeated herself: "I am Kathryn Clisby, a fossil pollen specialist from Oberlin College in Ohio, and I've just seen some interesting sediments in two basins near here. Do you have a punch-coring device?" He answered that he did have such a device on the back of one of the agency's Jeeps. Clisby asked if he would loan it and its operator to us for about an hour that afternoon. She told him we needed it to collect samples from these fossil lake beds for pollen analysis and that if they contained pollen it would be a major discovery of considerable importance to his work.

After a brief pause, he agreed and offered to come with us in his Jeep with the punch-coring device attached to the back. We collected a series of samples from four localities: the Blackwater Draw site, the Blackwater Draw channel near the highway, and two localities at Arch Lake.

The core samples were about 1.5 inches in diameter, and from 3 to 4 feet long. Clisby cut them into 6-inch lengths that she identified with a number on a diagram in her notes, and wrapped each one in tinfoil with its identification number on a slip of paper placed inside the wrapping. She packed them in small mailing tubes the soil survey staff provided and put them in our car. Clisby then thanked everyone, announcing she'd seen enough and would return to Oberlin to analyze her samples.

On the way back to Albuquerque she told me that if the samples were rich in pollen, as she strongly suspected they were, I must apply for a large grant from the Environmental Biology Section of the National Science Foundation (NSF). When we returned to Albuquerque, Clisby took me to meet Paul Sears, her colleague and one of the important participants in the symposium. Sears was past-president of the Ecological Society of America, and in 1956 he was president of the American Association for the Advancement of Science. He was also a member of the National Science Foundation board of directors. Sears, a tall, lanky, sixty-five-year-old, was a professor at Yale.

A few days later Clisby returned to her lab at Oberlin and began processing our samples. She discovered that all of the samples, except those from the Blackwater Draw site, were rich in fossil pollen. She wrote to me in Lubbock, urging me to begin a study of the Late Pleistocene sediments on the Llano Estacado, with an emphasis on pollen analysis. She was sure the National Science Foundation would support such a project, including the hiring of an experienced European specialist to do the pollen work. Clisby was insistent, calling me several times from Oberlin to ask if I had written a proposal yet. Between her letters and phone calls, I finally sat down and wrote the proposal and submitted it to the NSF through the Texas Tech grants office, as required. (Almost all universities insist that the university administer all grants to their faculty. This provides them some financial control, and assures the school it will receive the overhead money that most federal granting agencies provide as a way of supporting higher education.)

The proposal emphasized the importance of the discovery of well-preserved fossil pollen in the Late Pleistocene to early Holocene lake sediments on the Llano Estacado and described how this would provide strong evidence enabling us to reconstruct the vegetation sequence on the Llano during this period. I noted that this knowledge would help us understand the food economy of the Paleoindians who lived there. I also described the results of my work at the Midland site and, in particular, the evidence there of a more complex climatic sequence than that of the generally accepted Bryan/Antevs model. I also emphasized the fact that it would be a multidisciplinary project involving several kinds of earth-science specialists. I submitted the proposal to the Environmental Biology Section of the NSF, not the anthropology section.

Writing the proposal took longer than it should have because I was learning my new jobs as an associate professor at Texas Tech and associate director of the museum there. Despite the pressure, I appreciated the encouragement I received from Clisby, because I was interested in studying the Late Pleistocene and early Holocene environments on the Llano Estacado. I had learned enough to know that the reconstruction of the vegetation history of an area through the recovery of fossil pollen was a new, highly promising, and relatively inexpensive technique for paleoenvironmental studies.

The research area was within easy driving distance of Lubbock, and there were numerous places where promising samples could be collected. The proposed study area, the Llano Estacado, is topographically a large plateau isolated from the surrounding highlands on the west and south by the Pecos River, on the north by the Canadian River, and on the east by the erosion of several Texas rivers, including the Brazos and Colorado. The only water available on the Llano today and in the Late Pleistocene is what falls as rain or snow. Today's modern economy depends on an extensive and thick underground aquifer that has been tapped by numerous deep wells. The water from these wells is used to irrigate large farms, most of which grow sorghum and cotton.

This enormous plateau includes much of what is now east-central New Mexico and west-central Texas, one of the flattest areas on earth, with only a slight tilt to the south and east. The surface of the Llano is dotted with several thousand dry-lake basins, many of them filled with extensive remnants of fossil lake deposits. The sediments in these basins, the major focus of our proposed research, are known to range in age from Late Pleistocene to early Recent, and were formed by deflation during dry years and in the larger ones by both deflation and dissolution of the subsurface limestone bedrock. I was sure these basins would yield important new data on the past climate of this region.

The NSF grant was awarded in early May of 1957; it was my first grant from the NSF. On Curry Holden's recommendation, I asked Earl Green, a recent PhD in geology from Texas Tech, to be my field foreman, geologist, and stratigrapher, starting June 1st. To help our budget, Curry also appointed him as part-time curator of the museum. My second hire was Ulf Hafsten, a highly trained fossil pollen specialist from Bergen, Norway, whom Clisby sent to me.

Hafsten and his wife came for a six-month period beginning in July 1958. After stopping at Clisby's lab at Oberlin, where he processed the initial samples, they came to Taos in August and set up a pollen laboratory in the northeast wing of the enlisted men's quarters of Cantonment Burgwin. The timing was close because a few days earlier my family and the students in my archaeological field school from Texas Tech were living in those same rooms.

I had selected the Odessa Meteor Crater as the first place to be sampled for fossil pollen, because a mine shaft the Texas Memorial Museum had dug in the center of the crater in the 1930s had exposed 65 feet of interbedded aeolian and pond deposits. The crater was surrounded by an upthrusted rim, and I thought it would be an ideal collecting basin for pollen. I planned to ride a specially made cage down one wall of the shaft and collect samples as I went, but when I saw the huge blocks of loose dirt around the top of the shaft I changed my mind. I decided the shaft was unsafe, and that the best option was to drill for the samples. Hafsten processed these samples first and learned there was almost no pollen in the sediments.

Hafsten and Green turned their attention to the saline lakes, sixteen of which they sampled. Of these only thirteen yielded well-preserved pollen grains. The best results came from four of these saline lakes, ranging from Crane Lake in the south to Arch Lake, Tahoka Lake, and Rich Lake in the north, the last three located south and southwest of Lubbock.

This time Hafsten's analyses produced spectacular results. High frequencies of pine and spruce pollen were recovered from several pollen horizons we believed to be of Late Pleistocene age. From this evidence Hafsten inferred that pine-spruce parklands or woodlands existed on the Llano Estacado during the Last Glacial Maximum, about 20,000 years ago. The spruce was particularly important because several earlier studies had indicated that spruce pollen wind carries less than 20 miles from growing spruce trees. Pine pollen, on the other hand, can carry enormous distances, even out to the middle of the ocean.

Hafsten gave me his detailed report on the pollen data just before the end of December 1957. The other manuscripts on the results of the remaining studies, including the stratigraphy, vertebrate, invertebrate, and diatom analyses, came to me in late May 1958.

The results of the pollen studies were spectacular, but they were also highly controversial. Some scholars, not fossil pollen specialists, suggested that the high pine-spruce pollen zones in the pollen diagrams were the result of differential destruction of other kinds of pollen, such as those of sage and grasses. I didn't know how to evaluate these criticisms. Hafsten insisted that in Europe such zones would be interpreted as evidence of at least pine-spruce woodlands in the vicinity of the sampled lakes. I believed he was right, and the study of the paleoenvironments on the Llano Estacado continued to be one of my major research commitments for several more years.

Convinced of the usefulness of pollen analysis in paleoenvironmental studies, I applied for a second grant from the NSF to continue the Llano Estacado research. The requested funds were awarded in January 1961. The grant was more than twice as large as the first grant.

Earl Green, the field director on the first phase, was no longer available for the new project because by then he was a full-time curator at the Texas Tech Museum. I turned to Jim Hester, an archaeologist on the staff of the Museum of New Mexico. I knew Jim was interested in the study of past environments, and he was a natural choice for the field director of the Llano project.

Hester and I recruited a larger and more diverse group of specialists to work with us this time. They were Jerry Harbour (geology), Vance Haynes (geology), Loren Potter (botany), James Schoenwetter and Frank Oldfield (both pollen analysts), Bob Slaughter (paleontology), M. H. Holn (diatoms), and Robert Drake (invertebrates). We hired two pollen analysts because Oldfield was available only for the first year and I wanted the pollen analyses to continue through the second year. The results of the pollen studies by Schoenwetter and Oldfield were not much different from those of Hafsten. The major difference was that they collected their samples at closer intervals, resulting in greater precision and complexity. Their pollen diagrams indicated there were several abrupt climatic changes during the period represented in the samples. Both Oldfield and Schoenwetter found that the high pine/spruce zones overlay still earlier horizons dominated by sage.

We completed the field and laboratory work on the second phase of the High Plains project in the fall of 1962. The reports were written and submitted before the end of that year. As might be expected, such a large group of participants had a variety of conclusions about the interpretations of their data. Hester and I were reluctant to proceed immediately with publication. We needed time to sort the material out, and neither of us wanted to begin editing the reports until either some of these conflicts were resolved or we had decided how to deal with them.

I should have continued the paleoenvironmental research on the Llano Estacado, but I did not. I became involved in another challenging project. I also realized that although the information on the pine-spruce horizons was interesting, the pine-spruce preceded by several thousand years the earliest evidence for humans in North America. I told myself I am an archaeologist, and archaeologists deal with people.

Return to Santa Fe and the |
Museum of New Mexico

(1958–1961)

CHAPTER 12

At the end of my second year of teaching at Texas Tech, in May of 1958, the board of regents of the Museum of New Mexico offered me the position of director of research and associate director of the museum, to start on September 1, 1958. The offer was completely unexpected; there had been no negotiations or preliminary discussions. The board knew me and felt sure that I would want to return to Santa Fe. It was indeed an attractive offer. Archaeological research at the museum had declined after I left, and I felt that as director of research I could rebuild a strong program. Although I didn't want to leave Curry and Fran Holden and our other friends at Texas Tech, I accepted the offer and returned to Santa Fe.

In my new position I was responsible for two of the main units of the museum: the Palace of the Governors and the Laboratory of Anthropology. In addition, I was responsible for the state archaeological monuments and all anthropological research at the museum. I was to supervise a sizable staff, most of which (except for the janitors) had been senior to me when I'd left the museum two years before. I was aware that most of the senior staff at the Laboratory of Anthropology and the Palace of the Governors were probably not pleased that their former junior curator had been installed over them, but to their credit I never detected any hostility that affected our working relationships. On the surface, at least, everything was cordial. I think they were willing to wait and see what I would do. I knew the problem was not the staff; the potential problem was how I was going to juggle everything I had to do at the museum, keep my research going on the Llano Estacado, and still find time to keep excavating and rebuilding Cantonment Burgwin.

Nancy and I were delighted to make the move back to Santa Fe in early September of 1958, and our pleasure was increased when almost immediately we found and bought a beautiful old adobe house on the Camino del Monte Sol, the best address in town. Our family was growing, too, with the birth of our daughter Cindy in 1959. Like Gail, she was a beautiful baby girl who stole my heart. Without the pipeline work, I expected to be able to spend more time with my family.

There were many archaeologists in Santa Fe, including six who worked for the Museum of New Mexico, four with the National Park Service and Department of the Interior, and one who had retired to Santa Fe. Soon, with these and our other friends in the community, Nancy and I had an active social life.

A few weeks after we moved to Santa Fe, Jess Nusbaum gave me a puppy, a Dalmatian–German pointer mix. A delightful and gentle dog, he was covered with small brown spots. His name, naturally, became "Spec." He soon grew into a big, even-tempered dog. He was given free rein in the house, but he spent most of his days outside, coming into the house before dark. He had many good qualities and soon appointed himself guardian of the children. When he found the children playing in the street in front of the house, against all orders, he would go out and get between the children and any traffic on the road, forcing it to slow down. When the children were at school, he ranged over a large area, but he always came home when school let out.

Spec was also useful to me on several occasions. We would frequently have small groups in for dinner, and sometimes the company wouldn't realize that I needed my "beauty sleep" and would continue talking beyond my usual bedtime. Spec would get sleepy, too, but he wouldn't go to his bed until everyone left. On several occasions when the hour grew late Spec would sit in front of the guests, look directly at them with his sleepy, baggy eyes, open his huge mouth as wide as he could, and give a loud yawn, followed by a snap of his teeth. If they didn't get the hint with that yawn, a few minutes later he would repeat it. No one ever stayed for his third yawn.

My first professional effort in Santa Fe was to try to revive the relatively small salvage archaeology program at the museum. The most critical of the salvage archaeology activities was the Navajo Project, because it was grossly underfunded. It focused on a huge reservoir basin on the San Juan River in northwestern New Mexico and extended northward into southern Colorado. A preliminary survey showed that the basin contained hundreds of archaeological sites, but unfortunately, by the time I arrived at the museum, the Navajo Dam was already under construction. In a few years it would be too late. I had to find funding quickly or there would be an enormous archaeological disaster.

Despite knowing that the Navajo Basin was full of archaeology, the National Park Service had for two years allocated only $10,000 a year to the Museum of New Mexico to salvage that archaeology. This was the approximate amount needed to dig and analyze the materials and other data from one pit house, and there were dozens of pit house villages and hundreds of pit houses in the area about to be inundated.

Shortly after I returned to Santa Fe, I told Ed Dittert, our senior archaeologist in charge of the Navajo Project, that I wanted him to prepare a budget for $100,000 for the project for the coming year, and to have it on my desk by the beginning of next week. Ed protested, "I could never spend that much money, Fred."

"Then I'll find someone who can," I said. He became quiet, but a good and thoughtful $100,000 budget for the Navajo Project was on my desk when I came in on Monday morning.

I didn't know where I was going to get $100,000, but I was determined to try. The first person I went to was Spike Keller, head of the Federal Bureau of Public Roads, New Mexico office. He and Pete Erwin had helped me establish the highway archaeological salvage program in New Mexico. I explained my problem, and we had a short discussion about how the money would be spent. I told Keller that not only did I need $100,000 for the coming budget year, I was also going to need $200,000 a year until the reservoir was completed. Spike said, "Let's go see U.S. Senator Clinton Anderson. He'll be in his Albuquerque office for the next week or so." He picked up the phone and made an appointment for us later that week.

When we went in to see Senator Anderson, Keller asked me to explain the problem. I told him about the numerous sites known to be present in the Navajo Reservoir, and the woefully inadequate amount of money the park service had allotted to save our important heritage. He looked at me for a few moments, and then asked, "How much do you need and when?"

"One hundred thousand dollars at the beginning of the next fiscal year, and $200,000 a year each year after that until the reservoir is completed," I said. Anderson said, "Okay." And then told me to go to the outer office, and wait a few minutes. He added that he had some other business to discuss with Spike.

My interview with Anderson had taken about ten minutes. When he came out, I asked Spike how much that conversation had cost him. He laughed and said, "A hell of a lot more than you got for the Navajo Reservoir."

The laboratory staff was elated when I returned with the news that afternoon. I enjoyed seeing the look on Dittert's face when I told him we had the $100,000. Later that week I asked him to prepare a $200,000 budget for the Navajo Project for the following year.

As it turned out, we did not receive the full $100,000 or $200,000 I had requested from Senator Anderson. The park service took a substantial amount for "administrative expenses" each year. Yet what remained was sufficient for Dittert to have a major project. Given the necessary resources, Ed Dittert was a superb manager. He recruited a large, competent staff of archaeologists and support personnel, and soon a massive salvage program was underway in the Navajo Basin.

Soon after the funding of the Navajo Project I began looking for other salvage archaeology projects. The first was a coal strip mine and power station near Farmington, New Mexico. It was a small project that would require a small team of archaeologists for three or four weeks.

I also negotiated with the highway department to fund a long-term archaeological survey of a wide strip of land on both sides of existing highway rights-of-way throughout the state. Since most new highways were likely to be built within these existing rights-of-way, and adjacent to them, I reasoned that knowing the presence of archaeological sites in and adjacent to these highways would facilitate avoiding the sites, or allow adequate time to do an appropriate excavation before they were destroyed.

The most important project, however, was the archaeological project about to begin on the new Interstate Highway 40 that would go from Albuquerque to the Arizona state line. Numerous small-to-medium-sized pueblo sites were known to be present in the area, and I knew that a large staff would be needed to complete the archaeological study and not delay highway construction. I hired Joel Shiner, a senior archaeologist with long experience in the Southwest, to oversee the excavations and to recruit the staff he would need to supervise the excavations.

After consulting with Shiner, I employed Lyn Hargrave to manage the laboratory analyses. Hargrave was an old-timer who had been a junior author with Harold Colton in their classic *Handbook of Northern Arizona Pottery Wares*. He had dropped out of archaeology in 1939 to become the owner/operator of a motel in Benson, Arizona. He had made a lot of money as a motel owner during World War II, and he was eager to get back into archaeology.

By the summer of 1961 Shiner had recruited most of his staff and the fieldwork was underway. After it got started I had almost no personal participation beyond an occasional brief visit to meet the people and see what they were finding. There were so many people now working at the laboratory that parking became a problem; the staff began to joke that it looked like a used car lot.

During this period the museum received an additional appropriation from the state legislature to renovate the exhibits in the Palace of Governors and the adjoining Hall of Ethnology. Marge Lambert was the curator in charge of the archaeology exhibits in the palace, and Bertha Dutton was curator of the Hall of Ethnology. Both curators prepared detailed plans of the new exhibits. It took over a year to design and install both halls. The exhibits were exceptionally well done and received a lot of favorable public response. In this instance, as in the research projects mentioned above, because I had confidence in those doing the work, my management technique was to provide support and encouragement and avoid direct intervention.

At about this same time, I decided to survey an electrical transmission right-of-way from near Farmington, New Mexico, to the Arizona boundary. I wanted to do this myself because the construction company offered to provide a helicopter for the survey. I am not sure if it was the first time a helicopter was used for an archaeological survey, but it was new to me and I wanted to see if it could be an effective tool. It was.

Instead of the week or more I had scheduled for the survey, it took only a day to complete the project. We flew at slow speed into the wind and twenty-five to fifty feet above the ground, easily following the stakes that had been placed by the survey crew. The archaeology was clearly visible as well. When we found a site in or near the right-of-way, we'd land, I'd hop out, identify a sample of the sherds on the surface, make my notes, record the count of each ceramic type, locate and number the site on my map, and get back in the 'copter.

I thought about situations where a helicopter rental might be cost-effective, but I put those ideas out of my mind when my helicopter pilot was killed ten days later while he was working on San Francisco Mountain near Flagstaff, Arizona.

Another world of research opened up for me while the Llano Estacado project was still underway. In the summer of 1960, while I was in Washington on other business, I called on Luna Leopold, who was then head of the Water Supply Division of the U.S. Geological Survey and a casual friend from my Harvard days. He invited me to have dinner with him and his family and mentioned that there would be another guest, Brigadier General Ralph Bagnold, famed explorer of the Egyptian Sahara and author of several superb books, including *The Physics of Wind Blown Sand*. He had been commander of the Long Range Desert Group, which had given the Germans and Italians a lot of trouble in the desert during World War II.

During dinner Bagnold recounted his early explorations in the Western Desert of Egypt and Sudan. He and his crew had gone everywhere, even into the Great Sand Sea, carrying fuel and water to depots they placed at several locations around the desert and stockpiling them there. They employed two-wheel-drive Ford pickups, using sand tracks and a lot of pushing to get them over places of soft sand. They used sun compasses to navigate. It was a fascinating evening, a harbinger of my future work in Egypt, though I didn't know it at the time.

A few weeks later Leopold contacted me and asked if I would like to join a project with him and his sister, Estella Leopold, a pollen analyst working in Denver with the U.S. Geological Survey. They wanted to do a study in the Tesuque Valley, north of Santa Fe, and they wanted me to dig a trench in a kiva so they could take a series of pollen samples from the fill. They wanted a kiva that had been occupied around A.D. 1225 and abandoned shortly after A.D. 1300. Their goal was to look for pollen evidence in the northern Rio Grande area for the Great Puebloan Drought of A.D. 1275–1300 that might have caused the abandonment of many of the pueblo villages in northwestern New Mexico, northeastern Arizona, southern Colorado, and adjacent Utah. I agreed to help.

I checked the survey records in the Laboratory of Anthropology, and on the basis of the ceramic typology, identified a site that fit what they wanted. I told Luna I'd get a permit from the Department of the Interior and dig a trench when they were ready. When Luna called and told me they were coming, I got a permit and hired a couple of workers for a day to dig the trench. A few days later I took Luna and Estella to the site and stayed with them while they collected the samples.

I didn't hear anything more until late in the spring when Luna called and asked me if I'd like to join him and Estella at a meeting in Rome next June. He said his office would cover the cost of the tickets and other travel expenses. I said I'd love to go, and added that the last time I was in Italy was in April of 1945, when I was an army second lieutenant.

But my dreams of returning to Europe would have to wait. I had a lot to do at the museum. In addition to the large highway salvage program on Interstate 40, and a new project surveying areas adjacent to existing highway rights-of-way, I was coordinating an important new exhibit program at the Palace of the Governors, and I was involved with Fort Burgwin, where I was still director.

Fort Burgwin Field School | and Research Center
(1958–1963)

CHAPTER 13

W hen I had told Ralph Rounds I was leaving Texas Tech for a new job at the Museum of New Mexico in Santa Fe, I had offered to resign as director of Fort Burgwin. He rejected my offer and insisted that we proceed as planned. Even though I would not be spending as much time at Fort Burgwin as I had in the past, he wanted me to remain as director.

At Rounds's request, at the beginning of the 1958 season we had shifted our emphasis toward research. The new long-range plan called for a half dozen of the smaller buildings of the cantonment to be excavated and restored as quickly as possible to serve as summer homes for a research staff. We decided initially to support those scientific disciplines that had a field emphasis: geology, botany, zoology, and ethnology, in addition to archaeology.

To provide the necessary work areas, partitions for laboratories and offices were set up in what had been the southern and eastern sections of the enlisted men's quarters and the small projection in the northwest corner of the stable area. Rounds thought these facilities, in addition to small stipends for the scholars, and the natural beauty of the Rancho Rio Grande Grant, would be enough to bring outstanding scholars to Fort Burgwin in the summer months to work on problems related to the Taos area.

We would use the shell of the enlisted men's quarters erected the previous summer to house my family and the students of the Texas Tech Archaeology Field School during June and July of 1958. The first thing I had to do was get the kitchen and toilets set up. The kitchen needed a sink, stove, and refrigerator. Work began on these facilities on June 1, 1958.

I hired a Taos carpenter to build partitions, countertops, and cabinets, and I arranged for a plumber to put in a septic tank and distribution field and run a water line from the pump house to the main building. He also installed the sinks and toilet fixtures. All of this was still underway when Nancy, our three children, and the students arrived on June 7th.

A few days later, as soon as the kitchen was operational, I hired Florida Archuleta to be our cook. The dining area was in the northeast corner of the enlisted men's building, next to the kitchen. We sat on benches and ate at a big table the carpenter made using lumber from the sawmill.

During the summer of 1958, in addition to extensive excavations at Pot Creek Pueblo, the field school excavated the "Commanding Officer's House," a small, square vertical log building just beyond the northwest corner of the enlisted men's quarters. This was to be my future summer home at Fort Burgwin. In August of 1958 I hired a local Taos architect to draw up construction plans for the house, using the same adobe-plus-board technique we employed on the enlisted men's quarters. By the end of September in 1958 Rounds and I had approved his plans and selected a local Taos contractor. The house was rebuilt over the fall and winter and was ready to be occupied in May of 1959.

In the summer of 1959 Rounds had formally designated Fort Burgwin as a division of the Wichita Foundation. A nine-member board of trustees was appointed to establish policy and oversee operations. I had urged Rounds to appoint such a board, and he asked me to help select the initial slate of trustees. The board included representation from the Rounds family, as well as some of the most influential citizens of the Taos and Santa Fe areas. It was a strong and diverse board. I had worked with most of the local members in the past and felt that they would be a powerful force for the future development of the center. None, however, were people of great wealth who might become major benefactors.

The first meeting of the board was held in Taos on August 25, 1959, where it was announced that Ralph Rounds had made a gift of one thousand shares of Santa Fe Railroad stock to establish an endowment for Fort Burgwin. This was a good start, but we knew that a much larger endowment was needed to ensure the survival of Fort Burgwin.

The report I prepared for 1960, the third fiscal year for Fort Burgwin, refers for the first time to "The Fort Burgwin Research Center," reflecting our decision to emphasize scientific research at the new facility. Later, Rounds told me he was pleased with the work that summer; he thought it was the most productive yet. Rounds continued to be generous with Fort Burgwin and sent us a check for twenty-five thousand dollars in June of 1960, at the beginning of our fiscal year.

In 1958 and for several summers thereafter, the excavations at Pot Creek Pueblo were extensive. We soon discovered that the pueblo consisted of several separate room blocks, each with one or more small kivas, or subsurface ceremonial rooms. There was also at least one very large depression I thought might be a great kiva for community ceremonies. All of the rooms were built with "coursed adobe," a technique in which the walls are formed one thick layer at a time. The courses often joined several rooms together, indicating that most of the units of the pueblo had been built at the same time. We noted that all of the rooms in the southeast section of the pueblo had been burned. Many of the rooms contained quantities of burned corn.

Other interesting features were the clay-lined basins in the center of most rooms, and the upright posts in the centers of the basins. The posts undoubtedly functioned as reinforcement for the roof supports, indicating at least two, sometimes more, floors. On a visit in 1957 to Picuris Pueblo, about twenty-five miles from Pot Creek Pueblo, on the south side of Picuris Mountain, I saw several similar "basins with posts" in the abandoned section of the pueblo. This was my first clue that the inhabitants of Pot Creek Pueblo may have moved to Picuris when they left Pot Creek.

Since I no longer worked for a university, there was no formal field school during the summers of 1959 and 1960. Archaeological research continued, and I hired local laborers to do the excavations and graduate students with previous field experience supervised the work. This was an advantageous arrangement. In most cases the students had enough experience that they could supervise a field crew with minimum oversight from me, thus greatly expanding the research that could be done. I strongly urged the students to write reports on their excavations for publication by Fort Burgwin, and several did.

Five graduate students from four universities participated in the first "non-field-school" summer of archaeological excavations. One of them was Ron Wetherington, who recently had been accepted as a graduate student in anthropology at the University of Michigan. I asked him to do more excavations at Pot Creek Pueblo and he agreed. Later, when he completed his classwork at Michigan, he used the results of his excavations at Pot Creek for his PhD dissertation. Another was Natalie Veitlacel, an anthropology graduate student at the University of New Mexico. She excavated a pit house on a bench a few hundred yards north of the fort.

One of the larger excavations during the summer of 1959 was the complex of officers' apartments at the west end of the parade ground. The excavations were completed by the end of July. I contracted with a Santa Fe architectural firm to prepare the reconstruction plans for the apartment complex. The architects told me that cement blocks filled with pumice would be better insulation than adobe for the walls. I decided to use cement blocks and pumice for the officers' apartments. I specified that two-by-twelve boards were to be attached horizontally to the cement block walls with long bolts. These made it possible to attach split logs to the exterior as in the other buildings.

The plans were ready by September, but my job at the museum required that I return to Santa Fe. Rather than getting bids from several contractors, I hired a carpenter who had worked for me in Santa Fe to come to Taos and supervise a local crew that would construct the building. When the walls and roof were on, I asked the carpenter to stay as late as possible into the fall and put in as many of the partitions and as much of the cabinetwork as possible. I also arranged for other subcontractors to put in the plumbing, heating, electrical service, and roofing.

I came up from Santa Fe a few times to see my carpenter-supervisor, and I realized that the finish work was taking longer than I had planned. By early December cold weather forced the carpenter to close down operations until the beginning of April. The building was finally finished at the end of May in 1960. It had five apartments, three of which were single bedrooms; the fourth had two bedrooms, and the fifth had three. Five researchers and their families occupied those quarters that summer.

At the end of August in 1959 the research center sponsored the Pecos Conference, an annual gathering of most of the archaeologists working in the American Southwest. Because of widespread interest among Southwestern archaeologists in what was happening at Fort Burgwin, the attendance at the conference was unusually large and included several archaeologists who worked in areas beyond the Southwest.

On the last evening of the conference Ralph Rounds hosted a Hispanic dinner, with entertainment that included dancers from Taos Pueblo and local Hispanic singers, guitar players, and flamenco dancers. With a big keg of beer, the party was a great success, maybe too much of a success. A delegation of Taos ladies called on me the next day to complain about the unrestrained gaiety that followed the party as it moved from the fort into downtown Taos. As they left, the ladies suggested that the Pecos Conference not be invited back.

Ralph Rounds joined my family and me for breakfast at the fort on July 23rd, 1960. After breakfast he walked back to his apartment over the sawmill office. A few minutes later the office staff heard him fall to the floor. Two of them ran upstairs to investigate and called an ambulance; then one of them came to get me. I was with him when he had a second heart attack and died, only a half hour after we got him to the hospital in Taos. He was sixty-nine years old.

It was a profound loss to me personally, to Fort Burgwin, and to the goals Rounds had set for the research center. Although the financial situation was tight, Fort Burgwin survived primarily because I received a large NSF grant to continue my study of the Late Pleistocene paleoenvironments on the Llano Estacado. Because the grant was administered by Fort Burgwin, the research center received the overhead funds from the NSF.

In late April of 1961, nine months after Rounds's death, I received a call from his sons, Bill and Dwight, in Wichita, Kansas. They wanted to talk about Marian Meyers, who had been Rounds's personal secretary. They wanted to find a place for her away from the Wichita office. I had known and liked her from the time she was the recording secretary for the meetings of the Fort Burgwin board. In her youth she had been a court reporter, and she still had excellent skills on the stenotype machine. She told me that she had placed first in a national transcription contest, and I believed her.

The Rounds brothers asked if I'd like to have her as my secretary. They'd pay her salary and Social Security contributions for three years until she reached sixty-five and could retire with full benefits. Two or three times they told me they weren't trying to force me to take her, but they thought she might be of help to me. I said I'd like to have her help here, and I told them I'd find a place for her at the fort.

She moved to Taos a few weeks later, and I put her in the Commanding Officer's House, where my family had been living for less than a year. With four children, I needed more space, and I moved my family into the three-bedroom apartment in the officers' quarters at the west end of the parade ground.

Meyers became my secretary and helped me with my correspondence regarding Fort Burgwin, as well as my research. She also took the minutes at board meetings. There was not much to do, but she looked after the place during the winter when no one else was there.

In June of 1961, Paul B. Sears, who had been a strong supporter of the Llano Estacado project, was elected to the Fort Burgwin board, replacing a member from Wichita who resigned shortly after Ralph Rounds's death. Sears had recently moved to Taos. Since he was a highly regarded botanist and fossil pollen specialist, a former member of the National Science Foundation board, and past president of the American Association for the Advancement of Science, he brought much-needed scholarly strength to the board.

In July of 1961 Bill Rounds sent the fort a check for twenty-five thousand dollars from the Rounds Foundation to continue the annual support that his father had started just before he died. When Bill and I were together a few weeks later, however, he warned me that he did not know if he could continue making annual gifts.

Fort Burgwin was a wonderful place for my children. By the time Carl was six he was spending most of his summer days fishing in the Little Rio Grande or Pot Creek. From the beginning, he was a good fisherman; he always caught more and larger fish than I did. Like his grandfather, he had the knack and patience to be a good fisherman. I'd sometimes take him and Mike, if he wanted to go, in my old Ford pickup far up Pot Creek where there was a big meadow and several beaver ponds. Carl would lie on the bank a few inches back from the edge of the pond, drop the fly into the pond, and suddenly a cutthroat trout would take his bait.

Mike's hobby was archaeology. When he was four or five he liked to watch the students while they were digging, and sometimes one of the students would invite him to help move the back-dirt. By the time he was seven or eight he began looking for sites in the hills surrounding the valley. He found many. At first Nancy and I tried to restrict his trips to the area near the fort, but that was impossible, so we settled for his telling one of us where he was going and when he would return, much like my mother did when I was eight and started collecting artifacts.

Gail, and later Cindy, stayed closer to the fort, except on those occasions when they would ask to go and watch the students dig. Like Mike, they would sit on the back-dirt or sit with the students while they cleared a floor. I had one firm rule: they must never go near the creeks. The only time I ever spanked either girl was when I found Gail standing by the bank of Pot Creek. She was three; I took her away from the creek and fussed at her. I lightly struck the back of her legs with a switch, and she went home crying. A few years ago she told me she still remembers that day. From that day on, she stayed away from the creek unless her mother or I was with her.

We had little jobs for all of the kids around the house. Marian Meyers employed both girls to look after her flower garden. I think she paid them ten cents an hour. Gail greatly improved Mrs. Meyers's garden, as well as the big garden in front of the main entrance to the fort. When she was about eight Cindy had an old wheelbarrow she'd push all around the fort at full speed. A few years later, both girls took turns staffing the sales desk inside the front doors of the main building. They made "god's eyes" using a couple of sticks and colored yarn, and sold them to the visitors. That became a major source of spending money for both girls. Everyone enjoyed the summers at Fort Burgwin. My four older children still tell me it was their favorite home.

Although no new buildings were constructed during the period of turmoil that followed the death of Ralph Rounds, I was determined that research activities at Fort Burgwin would continue. In May of 1961, we issued our first scientific publication: *The Paleoecology of the Llano Estacado.* I assembled and edited the work, which was jointly published by Fort Burgwin Research Center and the Museum of New Mexico, Santa Fe. It contained several major papers, including the report on the pollen study by Ulf Hafsten.

In several significant aspects, the Llano Estacado research was a pioneering interdisciplinary project. Paul S. Martin, in his review of the book in *Ecology* 1962, described it as "the new Paleoecology . . . a bold, pioneering, interdisciplinary study."

Other research activities at the fort began to accelerate. There was more money available, which allowed me to seek more diversity in the fields we studied. The overhead from the NSF grant not only provided support for the maintenance of the fort, but made it possible to offer several small grants to support other projects in the Taos area. Faculty from several different universities conducted the research and submitted their reports to Fort Burgwin for publication. This was a difficult period financially, but we made it because we had no big salaries to cover. The only salary, other than the laborers', was that of the custodian, Toribio Mondragon.

Herb Dick, an archaeologist I had known while we were students at Harvard, came to see me in June 1961. When I'd met him at Harvard he had just finished his excavations at Bat Cave in west-central New Mexico and was completing his analyses and writing his dissertation. Bat Cave was a spectacular site. It yielded what was then the earliest known corn in the American Southwest. When Dick left Harvard he took a job at Trinidad College in southeast Colorado, about a hundred miles from Taos. He asked me if Fort Burgwin would sponsor his excavation of an eighteenth-century Spanish farmhouse near the village of Talpa, about five miles north of the fort. It sounded like a good project, and I not only agreed to sponsor his excavations, but I gave him a small grant to hire extra labor.

In the fall of 1961 I offered Dick a place to analyze his excavated collection. One afternoon as he was showing me some of his material, he told me that for several years he had been planning to excavate at Picuris Pueblo, a small Tiwa village about twenty miles south of Fort Burgwin, on the other side of Picuris Mountain. He felt sure he could get permission for the excavations from the Picuris Tribal Council. I was interested in his proposed project because on several visits to Picuris I had seen a number of architectural features in the old part of the pueblo similar to those we had found at Pot Creek Pueblo. I urged Dick to apply for an NSF grant to excavate at Picuris. I invited him to join me as an associate director of Fort Burgwin without salary, but with a place to work. If he wished, I said, Fort Burgwin would sponsor his proposal to the NSF. He readily agreed.

That winter Dick wrote a proposal to the NSF for a two-year project at Picuris. It was approved, and the overhead from that grant came to Fort Burgwin just in time to help us through a difficult financial situation. Bill Rounds had just stopped making the $25,000 annual contribution begun by his father.

Dick's excavations at Picuris were very successful. At the end of the second field season he moved his archaeological staff and his collections to Fort Burgwin. He had budgeted for one year to complete his report. The staff began sorting their collections and writing their reports, but they weren't finished when the funds for writing the reports were exhausted. Dick asked me for money to finish the report, but I didn't have it to give. A few weeks later he resigned as associate director and told me he would finish the reports at home. It was not a happy ending for what I had hoped would be a major new activity at Fort Burgwin.

In 1963, with the encouragement of Bill Rounds, the Fort Burgwin Research Center was incorporated in the State of New Mexico. The fort was no longer a part of the Wichita Foundation, although the foundation retained custody of the Fort Burgwin endowment until 1979.

When Ralph Rounds's estate was probated, Fort Burgwin received the sawmill site and the area around the old schoolhouse, which, with the 25 acres previously given to Fort Burgwin, resulted in a total campus area of 75 acres. He also left $225,000 for the Fort Burgwin endowment.

During the period when the Rounds estate was in probate, the Rounds family decided to sell the Rancho Rio Grande Grant to the National Forest Service, but before that sale was completed, the family offered to sell Fort Burgwin whatever land it wanted in the valley at the value the Forest Service placed on it. This was a great opportunity, and the Fort Burgwin Advisory Board decided to use half of the new endowment money to purchase 225 acres around Fort Burgwin for future development. With the new additions, the fort then owned 300 acres.

When Ralph Rounds was alive, our goal had been to develop a research center to attract productive scholars with interests in New Mexico and its history. For several years after his death I tried to implement his vision by encouraging scholars to bring projects to Fort Burgwin, with the possibility of later publication of their findings. We offered small grants to supplement their resources. This plan was developing even after Rounds's death, as long as funds came in from the Wichita Foundation and we received grants with overhead funds from the NSF.

In my view there was now one major problem for Fort Burgwin. The Pot Creek sawmill partnership had been automatically terminated upon Ralph Rounds's death. Buddy Bostain owned a small sawmill operation affiliated with the Pot Creek sawmill, and it, too, was shut down with the death of Ralph Rounds.

Through George Lavender, Bostain went to Bill Rounds and obtained a one-year lease to operate a sawmill on the old site. Bostain brought in about twenty men and began producing lumber. At the end of the contract year I asked Bill Rounds to arrange for Bostain to move his sawmill elsewhere. Nothing happened. I went to Bostain and asked him to move, and he said he had gotten a one-year extension. By the time that second year was over, Ralph Rounds's will had been probated, and Fort Burgwin became the owner of the sawmill site. Again I went to Bostain, told him we needed to develop the sawmill site, and asked him to move. He declined. I went to our lawyer, the son of Steve Mitchell (who was president of the Fort Burgwin board), and asked him to have the courts remove Bostain from our land. Although the court action was successful, Bostain did not have to pay the two years' rent he owed the fort for the use of our land. He only had to pay court costs. Not only that, we had to clean up after him. He left a mess—old car bodies, washing machines, refrigerators, anything big, heavy, and useless.

Nubia Catches My Eye
(1961–1964)

CHAPTER 14

I n the fall of 1961, while I was working at the Museum of New Mexico, a newspaper story about a UNESCO program in Nubia caught my eye. Plans were being developed to record and excavate the archaeological remains threatened by the new dam under construction at Aswan and the three-hundred-mile-long reservoir behind the dam. The U.S. Congress had appropriated the funds needed for American participation in the project. Jim Hester, the field director of the second phase of the study of the paleoenvironments on the Llano Estacado, had seen the story, too. A few days after the piece appeared the two of us were on a short trip to look at a basin in eastern New Mexico we were considering sampling for fossil pollen.

He brought up the topic, saying he thought we should look into the possibility of participating in the new project in the Aswan Reservoir in Egypt and Sudan. He believed we had the skills to manage large-scale archaeological salvage projects. And he said if I made an effort to be involved, he wanted to be included. He said the work would be useful, not only to the museum, but to several of us who, as archaeologists, might gain this kind of international exposure and experience.

I objected that neither of us knew anything about Egyptology. He said he wasn't thinking about Pharaonic remains, but the earlier prehistoric materials. He added that almost nothing was known about the Paleolithic period of the Nile Valley. After further discussion, I decided to look into what might be possible.

In November of 1961 I called J. O. Brew, my old professor at Harvard, who was the cochair of the UNESCO commission organizing the Nubian salvage campaign. I told him I was interested in organizing a project to work on prehistoric sites in the Aswan Reservoir, with projects in both Egypt and Sudan. Brew responded positively. But he warned me that he'd tried to get several senior archaeologists with experience in the Old World to lead a project to salvage the Paleolithic sites in the reservoir area. No one was interested because there were at the time almost no known Paleolithic habitation sites. He said the senior archaeologists were convinced there would be few sites found in the Nile Valley, since they thought the sites had been destroyed by erosion during the Nile floods or were buried below the modern floodplain.

Furthermore, Brew said that the few known sites indicated that Levallois technology, a characteristic feature of many Middle Paleolithic assemblages, had persisted into the Final Paleolithic, suggesting that the prehistoric societies of the lower Nile Valley were somehow culturally stagnant. These archaeologists assumed if prehistoric sites could be found, the associated stone artifacts would be so primitive as to have no bearing on either the origin of the Upper Paleolithic or the beginning of food production. I knew both were hot issues among many Old World prehistorians.

He outlined all possible negative aspects of working in Nubia. He paused, and then asked if I was still interested. I said I wanted to accept the challenge, and that I was making this decision because I thought those other archaeologists were wrong. One of the world's great waterways had to have a lot of associated archaeology. He told me to write two proposals, one for Egypt and the other for Sudan, and to submit the Sudanese one to the National Science Foundation for U.S. dollars, and the one for Egypt to the State Department for Public Law 480 money (Egyptian pounds, held by the United States as payment for wheat and other food supplies given to Egypt, and spendable only in Egypt). He said he'd send me the address for where I should send the Egyptian proposal.

As he was about to hang up, he added, "Oh, one other thing, Fred. See if you can raise some private money. Things may come along that cannot be covered by NSF and State Department grants."

I went to work drafting the proposals, drawing on what I could remember from the dinner at Luna Leopold's home with Brigadier Bagnold and what he'd told us about living and working in the desert. In both proposals I budgeted for three new four-wheel-drive Land Rover pickups to survey in the desert. I requested funding for three field seasons, each of six months' duration. With salaries, international transportation, vehicles, excavation equipment, camp gear, fuel, food, and publication costs, each proposal totaled several hundred thousand dollars. I submitted both proposals in the name of the Museum of New Mexico.

The texts in both proposals were essentially the same except for the budgets. Both emphasized my belief that the Nile Valley, fed by one of the great rivers of the world, must contain a lot of archaeology. I noted that with deserts on both sides of the river, the archaeology would be restricted to the edges of where the floodplain was at the time of settlement, and that geological studies indicated that at several times in the past the floodplain was often much higher than today. I emphasized the fact that the Nile Valley was the most likely route people would follow in moving from Africa to the Near East and beyond, or in moving south into Africa. I attributed the lack of knowledge about the archaeology in the Nile Valley to the limited research in the reservoir area. In both proposals I discussed the studies of the amateur archaeologist E. Vignard, who, in a book-length work, reported the presence of many Late Paleolithic sites at Kom Ombo, a Nile embayment fifty miles north of Aswan. I also summarized S. A. Huzayyin's useful *The Place of Egypt in Prehistory* (1941). His discussion of the Paleolithic was based, in large part, on Gertrude Caton-Thompson's work. In the 1930s and '40s, she had published several short papers on several localities in the Nile Valley. Some yielded Acheulean hand axes; others had scattered Middle Paleolithic tools. I noted that all of these materials were found in Nile silts or gravels and none were in primary position. I summarized the multiyear work by K. S. Sandford and W. J. Arkell. They found many scattered Paleolithic stone artifacts during their study of the Quaternary Nile sediments between Nubia and the Mediterranean.

Despite the limitations of these earlier studies of the Paleolithic in Egypt and northern Sudan, in my proposals I emphasized my belief that much of the archaeology along the Nile would be found high up on the margins of the valley, where settlements would either be buried in the remnants of Pleistocene-age Nile deposits, or just beyond, on the edge of the then floodplain. Some of my discussion concerned how I proposed to search the vast area to be inundated, and how I planned to recruit the necessary staff. I said we would use four-wheel-drive pickup trucks and utilize sand tracks where needed, ideas I acknowledged I'd borrowed from Brigadier Bagnold. For Sudan I thought it would be possible to live in houses in Wadi Halfa, but if not, I budgeted for tents and other camp gear. In Egypt, I knew a tent camp would be necessary. There were no suitable villages nearby.

After I submitted the two proposals I called Bill Rounds and told him about the project. I asked him to pledge ten thousand dollars toward it. If he made that pledge and my proposals were funded, I promised that the results would be jointly published by Fort Burgwin Research Center and the Museum of New Mexico. He agreed to give me the money, and I passed the good news on to Brew.

Going to Nubia was perhaps the riskiest decision I had made since I'd volunteered for combat with the 10th Mountain Division. If I got a big grant and we found no sites, my reputation would be ruined.

Brew failed to tell me that he and UNESCO had sent two other archaeologists, Charles Reed, director of the Peabody Museum at Yale, and Phillip Smith of the

University of Ontario (and a Harvard graduate), to the Aswan Reservoir to look for prehistoric sites south of Aswan. They had just completed their survey, using a houseboat between Aswan and Wadi Halfa, and submitted a report to UNESCO saying that they had not found a single site. They recommended that no funds be allocated to survey or excavate prehistoric sites in the reservoir area.

When Reed and Smith learned of my proposals, they were incensed that I had the effrontery to submit not one, but two, proposals to study the prehistory in the Aswan Reservoir. They wrote several critical letters about me and sent copies to everyone in North America and Europe who might review my proposals. Some of what they said bordered on slander.

A short but harsh controversy immediately developed over whether or not I was qualified to study the prehistoric archaeology in the Aswan Reservoir. The flurry of letters by the two "houseboat archaeologists" opposing my participation in the Aswan project led me to consider withdrawing my proposals, but on reflection I decided to let them stand. I knew that a riverboat was not the best means of doing an archaeological survey of a large reservoir basin.

A few weeks later I learned of yet another complication. In the fall of 1961, at the request of the UNESCO commission, Ralph Solecki had conducted a small survey of the area around Wadi Halfa, in the Sudanese portion of the reservoir. His team had found several interesting sites, but nothing Solecki considered significant. At his request, I met with him in New York in late March of 1962. At that time he told me he wanted to avoid the brewing conflict. He did not wish to continue with the project in Sudan. He had done the initial survey as a favor to J. O. Brew, and now he wanted to return to his main research area in Iraq. He suggested that I take over responsibility for the prehistory in the Sudanese area.

I accepted Solecki's generous offer and asked him to contact the staff he had assembled for his project to urge them to stay with me. As a result, Jean de Heinzelin, a geologist with extensive experience in Africa; Anthony Marks, a graduate student at Columbia University who was studying for a PhD with Solecki; Roland Paepe, a geology graduate student working with de Heinzelin; Dexter Perkins, a paleontologist who had worked several years with Solecki in Iraq; and John Waechter, a senior prehistorian with the University of London, all agreed to work with the Sudanese section if I received funding from the NSF. The most senior archaeologist in the group was John Waechter; I asked him to be the field director in Sudan.

The Aswan project was developing rapidly, and it raised a difficult problem. If my proposal was funded, should my family go with me, or stay in Santa Fe? I thought I would be away for only brief intervals. We knew almost nothing about conditions in Wadi Halfa, where Nancy and the children would probably have to stay while I was in

Sudan, or what camp life might be like in Egypt. As parents we were concerned that the children might contract some strange African disease. There was also the problem of school. Carl, Mike, and Gail were in school, and Cindy was still little and would have to be watched all the time. Nancy and I discussed our options at some length, and we decided that because of the children she would not try to go with me.

In hindsight, it was the wrong decision. I had to stay in the field longer than I had planned. Many of the staff in the other expeditions based in Wadi Halfa had brought their wives and children. It was a remarkably clean town, and none of these children became ill. Our camp in Egypt would have been more difficult. There would have been nothing for the children to do in camp all day; the tents would be hot during the day and cold at night. If Nancy came, she and the children would have had to stay in Cairo, far away from where I would be working.

Looking back, I don't know how I thought I could manage to do my job at the museum, take care of Fort Burgwin, and run two large and complicated research projects in North Africa, but with the optimism and drive of youth I was sure I could do it all.

I later learned that when the special UNESCO panel assembled for the Nubian project met in May of 1962 to decide whose projects would receive money, there was considerable discussion as to whether mine should be funded at all. For some time Brew and Walter Emory, a distinguished British Egyptologist, were the only two supporting me. Reed and Smith had been persuasive against me, and most of those present were convinced no Paleolithic sites would be found. In desperation, Brew said, "Why don't we let Fred find out?" Emory joined Brew in this appeal and that carried the day.

There was only one other proposal to study the Paleolithic sites in the project area, and Reed and Smith submitted it. They requested funds to survey in the reservoir and to excavate at Kom Ombo, where Vignard, the French amateur, had found numerous Paleolithic sites in the 1920s.

In June of 1962 the UNESCO panel awarded me two large grants, not quite as much as I had asked for, but enough for two expeditions for two years, one project in Egypt, the other in Sudan. A month later, Nancy and I left the four children in the care of Nancy's mother, and the two of us went to Europe to participate in a small conference on salvage archaeology at Berg Wartenstein in Austria and to meet with François Bordes, a distinguished French archaeologist who had agreed to help me find two archaeologists to join me on the Sudanese project. By the time we arrived in France, he'd arranged for Jean and Genevieve Guichard, two of his most advanced graduate students, to work with me. While we were in the Dordogne we also visited with Jean de Heinzelin, the Belgian Pleistocene geologist who had been with Solecki on the 1961 survey. We met his wife, Francine Martin, a beautiful young woman who was about to complete her PhD in invertebrate paleontology. De Heinzelin suggested that she join our group, and I agreed.

In late July, Nancy and I went to Austria for the meeting that J. O. Brew and I had organized, which was hosted by the Wenner-Gren Foundation. Nancy was to be the recording secretary for the conference. While I was at the conference I met Waldemar Chmielewski, a Polish prehistorian, who impressed me as being exceptionally competent. I invited him to join our group, and he accepted. I asked him what I needed to do to help him join us in Sudan, and he told me I needed to write him a letter. We drafted the letter together, and he took it with him to Warsaw. It took about two months for him to get the necessary permissions, but he was in Wadi Halfa by early October.

I had no experience in Paleolithic archaeology, but I recruited a staff of experts in Pleistocene geology and European Paleolithic typology. I needed them, and I expected I would be able to learn much of what I needed to know from them.

After the Austrian conference, in August, Nancy went home, and I went on to Cairo and Khartoum to meet officials in the antiquities organizations of both countries and to apply for the appropriate permits. Two old friends, Kathryn Clisby, the pollen specialist who helped me begin what turned into the Llano Estacado Project, and Dick Daugherty, a highly regarded American archaeologist, accompanied me. I hoped both of them would participate in the Nubian project at a later date.

The trip to Egypt did not start off well. In Cairo I had a hostile meeting with Anwar Shukry, head of the Egyptian Antiquities Organization, who bluntly told me he was disappointed I received funds to work in Egypt on prehistoric sites. He'd wanted to spend that money on the salvage of Pharaonic materials. To which I didn't respond. Then he said if he gave me a permit he wouldn't allow me to use trucks for my surveys, or to live in tents. I'd have to use camels and live on a houseboat. I was determined, however, to use vehicles and have a field camp if we were going to work in the Aswan Reservoir. Using camels and living on a houseboat would tie us to the shore of the river and be inefficient.

Discouraged, Clisby, Daugherty, and I left the antiquities office and called on Vivi Tackholm, a renowned Swedish botanist at the University of Cairo. Clisby wanted to obtain pollen samples from Tackholm's herbarium so she could identify the local pollen. Tackholm was interested in Clisby's project and agreed to help her assemble a pollen library.

While I was visiting Tackholm, I ran into an old friend, Rushdi Said, who happened to be visiting with her when we arrived. Said and I had sat next to each other in Kirk Bryan's Pleistocene geology classes at Harvard. We greeted each other warmly. It didn't take long for me to learn that Said was a frustrated assistant professor of geology at Cairo University. It was clear to me, also, that Said had a quick mind and would be a great asset to our project. I asked him if he'd join us as the geologist for our Egyptian team on this new project. Without hesitation, he said yes.

Said was amused when I told him what Anwar Shukry had said. He suggested that I accompany him and a student of his, Bahay Issawi, on a weeklong trip into the reservoir area to see if we could find any prehistoric sites. He said we'd join Issawi's Egyptian Geological Survey field party in the reservoir area, and I'd be able to see for myself if we'd be able to survey from trucks and live in tents, if Shukry gave us the permit.

I told him that was a great idea, but I was on my way to Khartoum and I expected to be back in Egypt in early January. I asked if we could do the survey then, and if he would make the arrangements. He said we should go meet Issawi to see if he could help us. Issawi was in Rushdi's lab down the hall. After a brief discussion, Issawi agreed to take us on a weeklong preliminary survey of the reservoir area. We'd go in early January. He also offered to include some of the adjacent oases in the trip. Issawi suggested that I meet him and his group at the Aswan airport at a time and date he'd work out with Said. They'd let me know by letter or telegram confirming the details in time for me to make my plane reservations.

The next day Clisby, Daugherty, and I went to Khartoum. There, in contrast to the meeting we'd had with Shukry in Cairo, Thabit Hassan Thabit, the head of the Sudanese Antiquities Service, greeted me warmly. He offered me full access to all of their facilities. No doubt he extended this warm reception because an old friend of mine from the Navajo country, William Y. Adams, was in Khartoum as a UNESCO representative and advisor to the Sudanese Antiquities Service.

Khartoum in 1962 was an open market. You could buy anything there. Among the items I purchased were three new Land Rover pickups. I arranged with the dealer to have them delivered by train to Wadi Halfa a month later.

When all the arrangements had been completed, we took the train to Wadi Halfa, where, again with the assistance of Bill Adams, I rented a house with eight rooms that opened onto a large interior courtyard. It would serve as the expedition headquarters, dormitory, and field laboratory. With Adams's help, I hired a cook named Biseri Ali, and a servant named Mohamed (what else?). Biseri spoke excellent English, was a hard worker, and an excellent cook. He was a real find.

When everything was ready to go, Adams loaned us his truck to look for sites. After a few unsuccessful trips in the desert north of Wadi Halfa, we gave up. In August, by 10:00 A.M., the rocks were too hot to pick up with our bare hands, and the sand burned our feet through our shoes. We'd learned a valuable lesson about the heat in Wadi Halfa: we should stay away from there in August. The next day we took the tourist boat to Aswan and from there we proceeded to Cairo and back to the States.

In late September John Waechter arrived in Sudan, collected additional maps and other supplies in Khartoum, and went to Wadi Halfa, where he set up our field headquarters. John looked exactly like an English fighter pilot, which is what he had been in the Near East during World War II. In 1962 he was a professor at the Institute of Archaeology at the University of London. His major task on the Sudanese project was to survey the reservoir area between the Egyptian-Sudanese border and the Second Cataract of the Nile. Every week Waechter sent me a report; none of them was encouraging. By the end of November, he had not found a single site. I was concerned and made plans to return to Sudan in January.

The two Guichards and Chmielewski had arrived in Sudan in late September and had begun to look for sites. The Guichards concentrated their efforts on the east bank north of Wadi Halfa. There they discovered several rich, still embedded, Lower and Middle Paleolithic workshops.

Chmielewski went to the west bank near Arkin, where Peter Shinnie, the director of the University of Ghana's archaeological expedition, offered him a place to live at his group's headquarters. From there, he surveyed entirely on foot. Chmielewski found an important sequence of Terminal Paleolithic sites at Arkin and a group of early Middle Paleolithic workshops farther out in the desert. Neither Chmielewski nor the Guichards informed Waechter of their discoveries.

About this time Jean de Heinzelin, Francine Martin, and Roland Paepe arrived in Wadi Halfa to begin a study of the sequence of Nilotic sediments in the area north of the Second Cataract. Except for me, the team was in place and working in the desert.

In early January 1963, I returned to Egypt, proceeding directly to Aswan, where Rushdi Said and Bahay Issawi and the men of Issawi's Egyptian Geological Survey field team met me at the airport. Issawi and Said had decided that they would go into the reservoir area ahead of me to see if they could find any archaeological sites. Unfortunately, neither Said nor Issawi knew anything about Paleolithic artifacts. They collected a boxful of wind- and water-shaped rocks, one of which had the general outline of a pistol. They thought the rocks were Paleolithic tools. During the week they were out collecting rocks by themselves, they hadn't bathed or shaved. My welcoming party consisted of as rough a group of dirty, bearded men as I had ever seen, and I wondered what I had gotten myself into. I had made a commitment, and although I was dismayed, there was no way out of it.

We left the airport and went directly into the desert. Before we left Aswan, however, I took a moment to throw away the box of useless rocks they had collected. Said and Issawi looked on sheepishly as I cast out the rocks. We traveled in two old beat-up two-wheel-drive Ford pickups. There were three men in the cab of each truck and two more in the back, with a drum of petrol, a can of water, a canvas tent, and miscellaneous camp gear.

We drove southwest from Aswan across a trackless waste, using a compass and the sun for direction. We got stuck from time to time, but with sand-tracks and strong pushers we were soon moving again. That day I received a superb education in how to drive across the Egyptian desert. It was nothing like our American deserts; this was a desert seemingly devoid of all life. Our first planned stop was ninety miles from Aswan, at Dungul Well, where we found a few palm trees and a small pool of water on the edge of the Eocene scarp. Flint workshop debris was scattered over much of the area. We collected a few pieces, and later that day we drove back toward the Nile. We set up camp in the desert west of Ineiba, halfway between Aswan and the Sudanese border.

I was entranced, not that the desert gave us an easy time, far from it. For six days we rose at first light, had a brief breakfast of bread, beans, and tea, and then surveyed for sites, alternately driving along the Nile, then out in the desert. We returned to camp long after dark each day. We found our way by following the navigation instructions of our Bedouin guide, Eide Mariff, who used the stars to take us back to our camp at night. Once we sat there, we immediately fell into bed. Issawi, Said, and I shared the tent. The others slept outside in their bedrolls. It was cold at night, but I was warm on the cotton mattress under the three blankets Issawi thoughtfully provided for me.

One of our more memorable side trips was to Abu Simbel, an enormous and beautiful Pharaonic temple that was to be moved to the top of a cliff before it could be inundated by the rising water of the Aswan Reservoir. The antiquities crews were beginning to record the temples in preparation for moving them when we approached the monument by driving to the cliffs above the temple. Issawi asked me if I wanted to go down and see the Temple of Abu Simbel. And I said yes, if it wasn't too difficult, thinking he'd park and we'd work our way down the cliff on foot.

Instead, Issawi turned abruptly into the steep, sand-filled gully that ran from the top of the cliff to the edge of the river in front of the temple, and headed down. There were some startled Egyptologists present when our two pickups drove up to the front of the temple where they were working. Ours were probably the first vehicles ever to come right up to Abu Simbel, and perhaps the last.

The temple consists of two parts, one for Rameses II, the other for his favorite wife, Nefetari. The front of the Rameses temple has four enormous statues of Rameses, seated in a row, all carved in the round in the face of the cliff. A long tunnel, about two hundred feet deep, had been carved out at the base of the cliff between the two center statues. At the back of the tunnel was a stone altar and on top of this was another statue of Rameses. Each year, at sunrise, varying between the 21st and 23rd of February, the rays of the sun enter the tunnel and shine on the face of Rameses's statue.

Nefetari's temple is much smaller than that of Rameses. It has four statues of Nefetari carved into the face of the cliff at its base. She stands upright in a graceful pose, looking at Rameses. There is no tunnel for the sun's rays to reach her like that at the Rameses temple.

By now, I was sure Issawi was crazy and we would have to leave the trucks and take a boat back to Aswan. Instead, we examined the temples, got back into the trucks, the drivers gunned their motors and drove back up the dune to the top of the scarp. I knew then a modern truck and a good driver could go anywhere in the desert.

On the way back to Aswan, the driver of the pickup behind Issawi's hit a rock and broke a front axle. We were fifty miles from Aswan and the nearest place the vehicle could be repaired. We had water, but I doubted if we could walk that distance. Before I really got worried, however, the driver got out a jack and a piece of rope about seven feet long, lay down beside the broken axle, placed the jack, and told one of the workers to work the jack handle until he said to stop. When the two pieces of axle were lined up and slightly overlapping, he told his helper to stop. He took the rope, wrapped it around the two pieces of axle, and tied the two ends together into a firm knot. The whole operation took about thirty minutes. I thought it might hold for a mile or two, but the repair took us all the way to Aswan.

These were exciting days because it seemed Paleolithic sites occurred in almost every wadi mouth, some close to the Nile, others embedded in silts several miles from the river. I collected a dozen bags of lithic artifacts, enough to demonstrate that Paleolithic sites were present in the reservoir area. When I returned to Cairo I took the sacks of artifacts to Anwar Shukry.

His reaction was to ask me what value the rocks had and how I managed to get into the reservoir area. I told him that I'd gone as a guest of the Egyptian Geological Survey in two pickup trucks. At first he looked surprised, then skeptical, and finally, he dismissed me.

After my meeting with Shukry, Pete Erwin joined me in Cairo. He had recently retired as head of the New Mexico Highway Department and wanted to see some of the archaeology we hoped to find in the reservoir. Erwin had played a key role in developing the New Mexico highway archaeological salvage program. He had traveled by freighter to Egypt. But it had been a rough crossing, and he had fallen and hurt his back. We stayed in Cairo for several days while he recovered. When he was able to travel we took a train to Aswan and a riverboat from there to Wadi Halfa, with a brief stop for him to see Abu Simbel.

When we arrived in Wadi Halfa I discovered that Waechter had gone to Khartoum to rest and buy supplies. With nothing else to do, I took one of the new Land Rovers, and Erwin and I drove south from Wadi Halfa to the mouth of the Khor Musa, near the Wadi Halfa airport. There, and almost in the road a few miles south of Wadi Halfa, we found several Late Paleolithic sites embedded in sandy sediments covered by Nile silts. I also found a Middle Paleolithic site buried in dunes under a very thick unit of silts. Farther up the wadi these silts were over ninety feet thick. Waechter hadn't seen these discoveries, and this fact, together with the reports by the Guichards and Chmielewski, led me to decide the arrangements with Waechter were not working. I took the opportunity to question Biseri about Waechter. I asked him how often Waechter went surveying along the river. Biseri told me only once or twice; mostly he stayed in the house.

I returned to Khartoum to search for Waechter. I found him on the roof of an inexpensive hotel wearing shorts, reading a newspaper, and taking a sunbath. After a none-too-friendly discussion, Waechter asked to be relieved as field director. I agreed. Since he was on leave without pay from the university until the end of April, he asked to stay on as an archaeologist until the end of the field season. I didn't know if he would be useful, but I agreed to let him stay as a senior archaeologist until the end of the season.

At the Nile Hotel in Khartoum I found an international telephone and called Dick Daugherty at his home in Pullman, Washington. I asked him if he'd come to be the field director until April, when the project would close down for the season. He agreed to come as soon as he could.

After we returned to Wadi Halfa, I was upset about the business with Waechter. I told Erwin what I had done and asked his advice. Erwin told me the hardest part of his job as head of the New Mexico Highway Department was when he had to demote or terminate someone. His commiseration helped, but I was still worried.

Erwin and I stayed on for a couple weeks in Wadi Halfa to help Daugherty get organized. In late February we left on the tourist boat for Aswan. From there we took a plane to Cairo, then another to Brussels for a night, and another to London for two nights. From there we went to Santa Fe and home.

After I left, the Guichards, Chmielewski, and Waechter excavated several sites. Almost all of their work was in Lower and Middle Paleolithic localities. Ironically, the most interesting to me was the late Middle Paleolithic site Waechter excavated. It was embedded in Nile sediments and had a rich associated fauna and a lithic assemblage consisting of numerous retouched tools made on Levallois flakes, as well as many end-scrapers and gougelike tools, or burins. Waechter's site appeared to combine several Middle and Upper Paleolithic traits.

I realized Waechter's data could be very important. The timing and place where modern humans and modern human behavior first emerged was highly controversial. At that time, most European and North American specialists assumed, of course, that the transition occurred either in Europe or in Southwest Asia. They were wrong, but I'll discuss this topic in a later section.

After I began studying the archaeology in the Aswan Reservoir I realized the potential our data had for significant new additions to our knowledge of African and Nilotic prehistory. At the same time I began to lose interest in the archaeology in the American Southwest, even the so-called Early Man studies. I had dug two Early Man sites in New Mexico and Texas, and surveyed several large areas in hopes of finding more sites of that age, but as most archaeologists with interest in Early Man in the New World will agree, good sites of that period are rare. In contrast, in the Nubian Nile Valley the sites dating between 20,000 and 12,000 years old are numerous, and the associated artifacts abundant and diverse. As an anthropological archaeologist I was intrigued by the opportunity to study how Late Paleolithic and Final Paleolithic societies functioned and to learn about the relationships among the various Paleolithic societies present in the Nubian Nile Valley.

While I was in Wadi Halfa, Rushdi Said called on Anwar Shukry to see if he could persuade Shukry to be less hostile to our project. Rushdi told him that he was a participant in one of the Aswan Reservoir salvage projects and wanted his help. Shukry asked him which one, and Said told him he was the geologist on the Wendorf expedition.

After Shukry recovered from the shock of learning Said was part of my expedition, he finally agreed to give us a permit for Dungul and Kurkur Oases, and a "small window" along the west bank of the Nile, from Ineiba to the Sudan border, the area our survey had shown to have the greatest concentration of Late Paleolithic sites. Said told me Shukry changed his mind because of the opportunity we offered for collaboration with the geological survey. I think his decision to be cooperative may have been influenced also by President Nasser's appointment of Said to

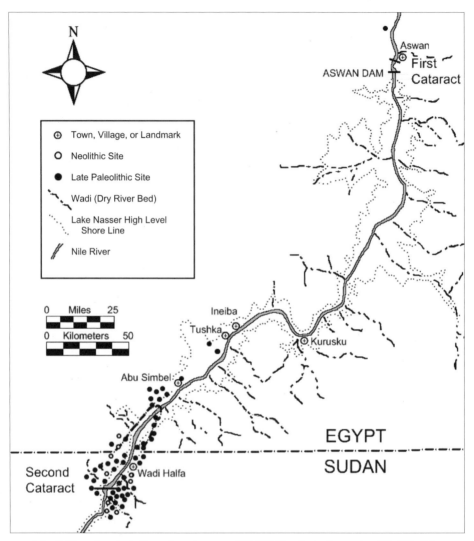

Map 3. Map of southern Egypt from Aswan and Wadi Kubbaniya in the north to Wadi Halfa in
northern Sudan. Sites excavated by the Combined Prehistoric Expedition from 1962 to 1975
are indicated by solid and open circles. Drafted by Chris and Cheryl Hill.

the Egyptian Parliament, and Said's new position there as chairman of the Finance
Committee.

Whatever the reason, from that point on, the problems I'd had on my first trip to
the antiquities office disappeared, and we got the complete, often enthusiastic, cooperation of all antiquities personnel. The demand that we use a houseboat instead of
tents and camels rather than trucks never came up again.

There was nothing esoteric about the way we located sites: we simply looked in areas where older Nilotic sediments were preserved, or where our reconstruction of the paleoenvironments suggested there might have been suitable habitation spots. I soon learned that areas of contact between older dunes and overlying Nile silts were good places to look. I called that my "tender tootsie" hypothesis. We had much more success on the sandy outer margins of the silts or around outcrops in the valleys. I find it difficult to understand why numerous Paleolithic sites had not been found previously in the Nile Valley. Part of the problem may have been the riverboat approach, coupled with a lack of vehicles and a reluctance to move away from the modern floodplain into the stark desert beyond.

Professionally, everything seemed to be going exceptionally well for me, but not so in my personal life. In my hospital days, and later in Tucson and at Harvard, Nancy was always there with me, even cooking for our group in the Petrified Forest. The work on the pipelines had been the first to break this pattern. She did not go with me on the pipeline projects because she was pregnant and we were both worried about a miscarriage. Even so, the times we were apart were short, a week or two, and then I would return home for two or three days. Later, after Carl was born, I knew we were not as close as we had been, but I didn't think we had a serious problem.

Nubia was different. The separations lasted two months or more, and the long absences made it difficult for Nancy and me to stay close. By then we had four children, and they were a full-time job for Nancy, who was excluded from the exciting new life I was leading in Africa. She was almost a stranger to me when I did get back home, as I was to her. With all the traveling back and forth to Africa, I felt us slipping apart, yet I did nothing to stop it. Each of us had begun to drift toward separate lives. I was very unhappy.

While I was feeling most estranged from Nancy, in late February of 1963, I met a woman whom I found attractive, and we had an affair. Peta was a young, charming, pretty English girl living in San Francisco. We met flying across the Atlantic. She was a kind and gentle person who made friends everywhere. I made several trips to San Francisco to see her. I was soon hopelessly in love with her.

I couldn't believe what had happened to me. I had sworn I would never divorce my wife or subject my children to the tragedy of being part of a split family. I knew what that was like, since I'd experienced a divorce in my childhood. For months my emotions were in turmoil. I began to leave the office and go for two-hour walks in the wooded area behind the Laboratory of Anthropology, weeping and cursing my weakness. How could I leave my children, whom I loved so dearly? For the first time I quarreled with my boss and several of those who worked for me. Nancy must have noticed how disturbed I was, but she never guessed why. I thought I might take a leave and go somewhere alone with her and we would try to find our love again. I even confessed my problem to a good friend of mine, but he was no help. He was in the midst of an affair himself. I concluded that I had to make a life with Peta.

I asked her if she would marry me, and she said yes. A few days later I told Nancy I wanted a divorce, and she agreed without any discussion, except to say that if I had to go, I should just go and take whatever I wanted. I didn't want much, just my clothes. I told her I would leave her the house, our car, and whatever the court decided for child support.

And so it happened, my marriage of eighteen years was over, and Nancy and I were divorced in the summer of 1963. That was the beginning of many years of pain and guilt that I carry to this day. Most of this guilt was from knowing that my children would have a difficult adjustment. And they did. I don't know who had the hardest time—maybe Cindy. Only four years old when I left her, Cindy told me years later she felt I had abandoned her. Fortunately, Nancy did all she could to be sure that our children didn't lose their father's influence. The most important of those efforts was the encouragement she gave them to spend every summer with me at Fort Burgwin.

In September 1963, Peta and I had a simple marriage ceremony at the home of one of my friends in Santa Fe. My staff met my new wife when she came with me to the Pecos-Plains Conference at Fort Burgwin a few days later. I was standing behind one of my staff when she got her first glimpse of Peta. Not knowing I was there, she gasped, "Oh, she's so pretty, but so young." Despite the obvious curiosity about her, Peta soon won over all those she met with her charm and poise. A few weeks later Peta and I left for a long field season in Egypt and Sudan.

When we returned to Santa Fe I asked Joel Shiner, a senior archaeologist at the museum, to be the new field director in Sudan. He accepted, and he and his wife, Maxine, and their young son left for Wadi Halfa in mid-September 1963. I recruited four graduate students in archaeology from three different universities, Philip Evans, Bill McHugh, Harvey Rice, and Jay Ruby, and four laboratory technicians, Jane Nettle, Catherine Newman, Bill Merrill, and Mary Beth Stokes, three of whom came from the museum, to work at Wadi Halfa. This group arrived in Wadi Halfa in late September, joining the Guichards and Chmielewski, who had returned with his wife, Maria Chmielewska, a distinguished prehistorian in her own right, as well as a young associate at the Polish Academy of Sciences, Romuald Schild. Nadia Mustapha, an Egyptian archaeology graduate student at Columbia University, also joined the Polish group.

Dexter Perkins, a paleontologist who had been with Solecki's project during the 1961 survey, also returned, and de Heinzelin came with his wife, Francine Martin. Maxine Shiner immediately took over as "house mother," quickly making a name for herself among the merchants of Wadi Halfa. The full staff for the Sudan project was now assembled.

In early October of 1963, Peta and I arrived in Wadi Halfa a few days after the Shiners and Tony Marks and his wife. Maxine Shiner greeted Peta warmly. Soon they became close friends. Most days I stayed at our headquarters, and Peta would help in the lab. But on those days when I had to make a long trip to see sites, she would sometimes stay behind, and Maxine would take her shopping, where she would meet the merchants with whom Maxine traded.

I was eager to show Joel Shiner and Tony Marks the sites I'd found in the Khor Musa the previous year, so shortly after I arrived, the three of us drove out in the desert. We had no trouble finding the sites and several others in the same area. When we got out and started searching for sites we crossed a large, rocky, flat bed of quartzitic sandstone. We heard a low growling and hissing about seventy feet ahead of us. An aroused cobra with its hood up stood about two feet tall. Shiner and I had spent years around rattlesnakes and knew that if you were reasonably careful they were no great danger and were easily dispatched with a long stick or a rock.

But you should never threaten a cobra, which is dangerous when antagonized. We discussed leaving the snake alone, but we thought someone might come by and be bitten. There was a well-traveled track fifty yards away. We decided to try to kill the cobra with rocks. No sooner had the rocks landed than the snake was coming with the speed of a racehorse straight toward us, hissing and growling. Shiner, Marks, and I, in a panic, scattered in three different directions. The snake reached where we had been standing and stopped, hood up, growling and hissing, looking at each of us in turn.

My first reaction was to leave the cussed thing alone, but after my heart slowed down, I said, "Let's quit fooling around and kill that snake!" Marks agreed, and Shiner was the first to come up with a plan. "Let's each gather some big rocks and take turns throwing them at the snake."

But this was complicated, because as soon as a rock landed near the snake, it would start toward the thrower, so it was necessary as quickly as possible to throw another rock at the snake from another direction. This confused the snake, and it stopped chasing the assailant who threw the last rock. After several rounds Shiner hit and killed the snake. None of us dared go near enough to be sure. The next day Marks passed the spot where we encountered the cobra, and he roused another one, or was it the same snake?

The day after our experience with the cobra, Shiner, Marks, and I went out to survey systematically those Sudanese portions of the reservoir we'd not previously examined. Excavations would begin six weeks later. At this point I realized, even more than before, how little I knew about Paleolithic flaked stone typology. I needed to become proficient in the classification of lithic artifacts if I were ever to make a contribution to our knowledge of the Paleolithic in Northeast Africa. I made every effort to participate in the surveys and excavations conducted by those who had strong backgrounds in Paleolithic stone typology. Four people were particularly helpful in teaching me the basics of Paleolithic typology: Jean and Genevieve Guichard were patient teachers of Lower and Middle Paleolithic typologies; Tony Marks was a great help with Middle and Late Paleolithic typology; and later Joel Shiner quickly taught me the basics of Late Paleolithic typology. With their help I gradually began to understand some of the interesting problems the Paleolithic archaeology in the Nile Valley presented. Chmielewski and Schild would've been equally helpful; however, they were living and excavating on the west bank, while I spent most of my time on the east bank. Much of the tutoring I received on Paleolithic typology occurred in the laboratory during the evenings.

When he returned in the fall of 1963, Chmielewski excavated several early Middle Paleolithic workshops in the desert west of Arkin, an area where he'd started working the previous fall and spring. Schild, Chmielewska (Chmielewski's wife), and Mustapha excavated a series of stratified Final Pleistocene sites embedded in fossil Nile beach sediments at Arkin. The earliest of these Arkin sites dated around 10,500 radiocarbon years ago. Among the other sites the Polish group excavated were several early Holocene localities they identified as Epipaleolithic. The charcoal recovered from these early Holocene sites dated between 8,500 and 5,000 years ago. Some of the late sites in this group yielded a few sherds of pottery, and we identified these sites as Neolithic. On the east bank, the Guichards continued excavations at several Lower and Middle Paleolithic workshops. Shiner and Marks concentrated their efforts in the Khor Musa. I asked Shiner to work with Marks because Marks had a lot of experience in Paleolithic archaeology with Solecki.

With large numbers of Paleolithic sites in the Sudanese section of the reservoir, and the excavation of many of these sites underway, our next problem was how to deal with the typological complexity represented in the collections, particularly in the material we regarded as Late Paleolithic. We solved this problem using classic archaeological methodology: we laid out the tools and cores from every site on large tables, then looked for similarities among them, and grouped similar assemblages. Although the assemblages in each of our groups were similar, there were always small differences between them. Our working hypothesis was that each group of similar assemblages represented the product of a group of closely related social units that shared a common way of life. The minor differences were regarded as reflections of either seasonal variations in economy or subgroup diversity. We called these clusters of assemblages "industries," naming them after prominent local geographic features, such as Khormusan, Halfan, and Qadan. These new ideas were first discussed in the two-volume study *The Prehistory of Nubia,* which I assembled and edited.

I regard the definition and naming of these various lithic complexes to be among the most important contributions our group made during the work in the reservoir. I consider recording the almost-lost Pleistocene past of the Nubian Nile as one of the highlights of my career.

We were dealing with hundreds of sites. The sites represented a wide variety of different lithic technologies and typologies. Classifying "industries" was our attempt to bring order out of the chaos, to group those localities similar in both typology and technology, and then to determine if the groupings were of a similar age. Initially, we were not prepared to say what these industries represented; we didn't think they reflected seasonal differences in activities, because the associated fauna in the various industries was closely similar. Eventually, we began to think the industries were reflections of different social entities. It was an idea radically new in Paleolithic studies, because the Late Paleolithic in Europe, the Maghreb, and Southwestern Asia were regarded as characterized by relative stability and continuity, with only minor changes through time. This was not so in the Nile Valley, at least northward from the Second Cataract. Why? we asked.

We had a major problem in trying to determine the chronological and stratigraphic positions of the industries. The radiocarbon dates were essentially useless. All of our dates were based on wood charcoal, but because the samples did not receive adequate pretreatment by our radiocarbon laboratory (at Washington State), sites of the same industry often had widely different radiocarbon dates. Without reliable dates, the correlation of one isolated body of silt with another that looked the same, but with different lithic industries, was insecure. Jean de Heinzelin, our geologist, could not determine whether during the Late Pleistocene there was a single episode of silt aggradation, or several, separated by intervals of downcutting. This was not resolved until we completed the stratigraphic work at Wadi Kubbaniya in the early 1980s.

In the fall of 1963, upstream along the Nile, near the Second Cataract, Shiner found and excavated two sites he named "Gemaian." He collected artifacts from the surface of six more deflated early Late Paleolithic living sites with the same distinctive Gemaian lithic industry. This entity used Nile chert pebbles and Levallois technology to make tools, many of which were retouched microlithic blades. The Gemaian emphasized points removed from small Levallois cores. Although there were resemblances to the Levallois cores in some Middle Paleolithic sites, the Gemaian microlithic tools were clearly not Middle Paleolithic, but very early Late Paleolithic.

While the Gemaian sites were being excavated, Marks dug three stratigraphically later Late Paleolithic sites in the same area that had another, different stone industry he named "Halfan." Stratigraphically, the Halfan sites were from 24 to 30 feet above the level of the Gemaian sites. They contained a lithic assemblage that included many "Halfa Flakes." These distinctive pieces were short, with a wide, sharp distal end. Many were smoothed on both lateral edges near the base, presumably for hafting. The Halfa Flakes had been removed from Levallois cores made on small chert pebbles. There were several radiocarbon measurements on charcoal from the Halfa sites that dated between 19,500 and 17,500 years ago. We found no charcoal in the Gemaian sites, so we have no dates, but obviously they were stratigraphically much earlier than the Halfan. We regarded the Gemaian as the oldest of the Late Paleolithic complexes we found in the Nile Valley, probably dating between 20,000 and 22,000 years old.

In 1963–1964 Marks also excavated five late Middle Paleolithic sites that contained an industry he named "Khormusan." One of them was the locality tested by Waechter in the spring of 1964. Now we had a name for Waechter's material. All of the Khormusan sites were embedded in stream channels in the upper part of a thick deposit of Nile silts. They contained tools made on large, typical Middle Paleolithic Levallois flakes, together with well-made burins and endscrapers, both tool classes more characteristic of the Upper Paleolithic. The abundant fauna associated with these Khormusan sites included wild cattle, the most common, followed by hartebeest, gazelle, ass, and hippo. Three of the Khormusan sites also contained numerous fish bones, including several from large, deepwater species.

In the spring of 1964, Shiner excavated the nearby and much older Middle Paleolithic locality (Site 440) with two cultural horizons embedded in a fossil dune, covered by 90-plus feet of Nile silts. This was one of the sites I'd found near the mouth of the Khor Musa the year before. The stratigraphy suggests that both cultural horizons are much older than the Khormusan sites Marks excavated near the top of the same body of silts.

The lower occupation at Site 440 yielded an associated fauna dominated by wild cattle. The upper horizon, 2 feet higher in the same dune bed, contained a fauna that was mostly fish, including several bones from large, deepwater species. The fish from Site 440 and from the much later Khormusan sites suggest the presence of a well-developed fishing technology in the Nile Valley during the Middle Paleolithic. I've often wondered if the large, deepwater fish in these sites were scavenged, or if their presence indicated the use of boats or rafts.

One of the most interesting and perhaps the most recent of the Late Paleolithic industries Shiner studied in the Wadi Halfa area is the Qadan, represented at numerous localities. It has a microlithic toolkit; that is, most of the retouched tools are less than three centimeters long. The Levallois technique also was used, mostly for the production of points. Grinding stones occur in many Qadan sites, and in some sites they are numerous and well made.

Many of the Qadan localities yielded large faunal collections in which fish, mostly catfish, were abundant. The few radiocarbon dates available for the Qadan indicate an age between 12,000 and 14,500 years ago. It may have been the most recent Late Paleolithic entity in the Nubian Nile Valley.

Marks dug two other Late Paleolithic localities that had a very different lithic assemblage. He called these sites "Sebilian." The artifacts closely resembled those found at Kom Ombo, between Aswan and Luxor, that Vignard (the French amateur archaeologist) had given the name of Sebilian I in the 1920s. The Sebilian is interesting because it has a high frequency of Levallois technology and a toolkit based on large, flat flakes removed from large Levallois cores. It is also distinguished by the almost exclusive use of hard basement rocks, such as basalt, diorite, and quartzitic sandstone as the preferred raw materials.

It was Vignard's Sebilian that caused those "experienced Old World archaeologists" Brew contacted to assume that the Late and Final Paleolithic along the Nile was backward, and thus of little interest. As it turned out, the Sebilian was a minor and late player in the Late Paleolithic of the Nile Valley. The Sebilian sites were still interesting, however, because the people who made and used the Sebilian technology were probably recent migrants into the lower Nile Valley. It is likely they came from farther south. Their technology, raw material preference, and toolkit are closely similar to those found in contemporary sites in several areas in central Africa. Despite the abundance of Sebilian sites, they are not well dated, because many of them had been deflated by wind erosion. The available evidence suggests they may have been contemporary with the latest Qadan, and probably date between 13,000 and 12,000 years ago.

The gamble I made that there would be numerous, diverse, and interesting prehistoric sites in the Aswan Reservoir paid off. What a terrible loss it would have been to our cultural patrimony had there been no study of the prehistoric sites in the Aswan Reservoir. This superb record of the Pleistocene past in the Nile Valley would have been lost forever. I consider the work in Nubia to be among the most significant contributions I made during my entire career.

Excavating Aswan Reservoir Sites |
(1963–1964)

CHAPTER 15

Thanks to Rushdi Said, by the summer of 1963 we had a license to work in a large, extremely promising area along the west bank of the Nile, Said's "little window," and the two desert oases closest to the river, Dungul and Kurkur. We'd always planned that Jim Hester, Frank Eddy, and Philip Hoebler, all archaeologists on the staff of the Museum of New Mexico, would do the Egyptian part of the project. Said, with the assistance of Issawi, arranged with G. H. Awad, the undersecretary of state in charge of the Egyptian Geological Survey, for the survey to cosponsor our work and manage our field camps.

Hester, Hoebler, and Eddy, with their wives and Hester's two children, arrived in Cairo in early October. They cleared two new Ford pickups and other equipment through customs. (I bought Ford pickups with two-wheel drive, rather than Land Rovers I initially planned to buy, because Bahay Issawi told me his men were accustomed to working with Fords, and spare parts would be easier to obtain in Egypt.) By November everyone, except Hester's wife and children, who had decided to stay in Cairo, joined Issawi and his crew in the geological survey camp, initially sited in the desert at Dungul Oasis.

We had an antiquities inspector with the group, Ahmed Said Hindi. Ahmed was usually easygoing, but he had a run-in with Issawi during his first week over who was running the camp, and threatened to leave. The conflict lasted only a few hours, and soon they were friends again. Bahay was in charge of the camp. Ahmed Hindi and Hester were in charge of the archaeology.

Said, Issawi, Hindi, and the other members of the Egyptian crew, plus Hester, Eddy, and Hoebler (and Eddy's and Hoebler's wives), spent the last two months of 1963 working at Dungul and Kurkur. Peta and I visited them near the end of their work at Dungul, but we only stayed a few days and moved on to Aswan and from there to Cairo.

Hester's group found numerous Early and Middle Paleolithic and Neolithic sites, mostly badly eroded by wind. Significantly, there were none of the Khormusan, or Upper, Late, or Final Paleolithic sites so common at Wadi Halfa. We now know that the absence of these later Paleolithic entities was almost certainly attributable to the hyperaridity of the Sahara between ca. 65,000 and 13,000 years ago. There was no one in the Western Desert during this interval. The desert was lifeless, with deflation and dune deposition. For the northern latitudes, this was a period of cold temperatures and glacial advance. We did not understand this relationship until after we had spent several seasons in the desert.

In 1963, on one of their surveys of the desert south and west of Dungul Oasis, Issawi and Hester took a little diversion from archaeology. They found and followed the tracks Prince Kamal El Din, a member of the Egyptian royal family, had left on his trip to the desert in 1933–1934. Soon they came upon a 1933 Fiat touring car the prince had abandoned when the transmission failed. Blowing sand had scoured off all the exterior paint. The windows were frosted over by the sand. The tires were in shreds, but inside the car everything, including the beautiful walnut interior trim, was intact and in good condition.

Issawi took one look and told his driver to get the lorry, load the Fiat onto it, and take it back to camp. Once in camp, Issawi had the driver/mechanic completely strip the car, taking every bolt and nut apart. He cleaned everything. Then he reassembled it, fixed the transmission, loaded it back on a lorry, and took it to Cairo, where the restoration was completed. By some magic, Issawi got it licensed and then he sold it. For several years that Fiat ran as a taxi on the streets of Cairo. Hester and I always regretted that we didn't make a deal with Issawi to take the car to the United States, where we could've sold it and all three of us could have made a little money.

Issawi and Hester also found a partially buried Canadian two-engine bomber that had crashed in 1943. Everything was still intact, including the water bottles. Footprints exiting the plane indicated that the crew had survived and walked to a nearby hill where a vehicle picked them up. How had those tracks survived for twenty years? Except for the sand dune that partially covered the plane, the surrounding landscape consisted of hard-packed sand and small gravel. Footprints or any other disturbances are visible for many years on such a surface, much longer than the twenty years between the crash and Issawi and Hester's discovery of the plane.

The Bedouin workers removed what aluminum they could from the plane and sold it in Cairo. They took out the fifty-caliber machine guns and sold them in Chad. The group intended to return to the plane the following year for more aluminum, but in the meantime the dunes that partially covered the plane had moved and buried it again. Even Eide Mariff could not find it.

After the brief Christmas break when everyone went to Luxor or Cairo, Said, Issawi, Hester, and the rest of the group moved their camp closer to the Nile to survey the area between Ineiba and the Sudanese border. They found two major clusters of Late Paleolithic sites, one at Ballana, just north of the Sudan border in a narrow canyon with high sandstone escarpments on both sides, and another at Tushka, a wide embayment where a major wadi entered the Nile from the west. These localities were much more promising than the sites I had found on my preliminary survey, and Hester decided to concentrate most of their efforts in those two areas.

Hester and his group initially excavated at Tushka in January of 1964, where they cleared an interesting graveyard and trenched several carbonate-cemented mounds. The graveyard contained twenty-nine human burials. All of the bones were encrusted with carbonates deposited when Late Paleolithic silts covered this area. The burials were *Homo sapiens*, equivalent to the Cro-Magnon skeletons of Late Pleistocene age in Europe. There are several radiocarbon dates from this locality, ranging from 14,500 to 2,000 years ago, but all of the dates are suspect because the dating laboratory inadequately processed the charcoal samples. The lithic industry, which Shiner identified as Qadan, is similar to the Qadan he found in many sites near Wadi Halfa in Sudan.

The Tushka graveyard was unusual, first, in the number of people buried there, and, second, in the presence of skulls of wild cattle placed at the heads of several of the human burials. What the placement of the cattle skulls means is not clear, but there may have been a close, perhaps religion-based, relationship between the Qadan people at Tushka and their cattle. It is tempting to suggest that this may indicate an early phase of cattle taming and association preceding domestication, but I doubt it. The earliest evidence for cattle domestication appears in the nearby Western Desert around 3,000 years later, about 9,500 years ago.

Hester and his group decided they should move on to Ballana, with its complex stratigraphy and archaeology. It was a good move, but I was concerned that they had left a great deal of unstudied archaeology behind at Tushka.

Hester was right, however, because they found a more diverse group of lithic industries at the new area. Most of the sites at Ballana were buried in an enormous aggrading dune with interbedded layers and lenses of silts. The earliest industry in this aggrading dune was Halfan. It had the same stone tools, mostly backed microblades and Halfa Flakes and cores, that Marks had found in the Halfan sites near

Wadi Halfa. Charcoal from this site dated 18,600 years ago, about the same age as the Halfan sites near Wadi Halfa.

Three other localities at Ballana, found in February and early March of 1964, slightly higher up in the aggrading dune, yielded a lithic industry unlike any of those found to the south in Sudan. We named this lithic complex Ballanan. We excavated two of these sites. The Ballanan stone technology was unusual: Most of the tools were made on thick blanks. Some had abrupt, vertical retouch along one lateral edge, while others had abrupt retouch at an angle across the distal end of the bladelet. Gougelike tools, or burins, were also common.

Charcoal from one of the Ballanan sites gave a date of 14,000 years ago, but the measurement was from the same lab that had not properly pretreated our samples. The date is too young for the stratigraphic position of the site and for the associated lithic assemblage. The true age is probably 2,000 to 1,500 years older, around 15,500 to 16,000 years ago.

Moving to Southern Methodist University and Creating a New Anthropology Department
(1963–1964, 1966)

CHAPTER 16

I n the fall of 1963, after my marriage to Peta and before we left Santa Fe for Egypt, I'd had a major dispute with the director of the Museum of New Mexico over his policies with regard to the anthropology program. I confess that it occurred largely because I was so upset over my divorce that I was irrational. The argument was totally unnecessary, but it angered the director more than I thought. Had I realized how disturbed he was I would have apologized. After I left for Egypt, he went to the museum's board of regents and demanded that I be fired or he would resign. This gave the board no choice, and while I was in Egypt the board fired me. Someone sent an official letter to Egypt, but I received it only after I had returned to Santa Fe, where my secretary called me with the news.

It was a shock to hear that I had no job. Shortly after I walked into my office, Ed Dittert, who was given my job, asked me to clean out my desk, turn in my keys, and leave the office. I felt as if he had hit me in the chest. I could not believe that I was fired—without a hearing, and without a chance to tell my side of the story. I thought I had failed everyone, my children, Peta, Nancy, my staff, and my friends. I was sure everyone regarded me as a total failure.

The first thing I did was to tell Peta. Then I went to Nancy to tell her what had happened. I promised I would continue paying her child support every month as long as I had any money. She was sympathetic and told me not to worry. Before we'd gone to Egypt, Peta had found a nice apartment within our means two blocks down the street from my house on the Camino del Monte Sol. The location made it convenient for me to see my children and for them to come to see me. They came with Spec to visit almost every afternoon after school. On Saturdays, with Nancy's approval, Peta would prepare a lunch and the kids would spend most of the day with us. It must have been difficult for them, but they soon were friends with Peta. As I look back at this time, I realize how fortunate I was that Nancy and Peta forged a bond over their mutual concern for the well-being of my children. There was never any squabbling over their visits. Later, when Peta and I had our children Kelly and Scott, Nancy would send the older children by bus from Bisbee to Dallas to spend Christmas with us. It was a long bus ride, but they enjoyed being with us. I knew they missed me, and I missed them terribly, too. At Fort Burgwin and in Dallas, all six of my children would play together and seemed to like each other. I credit both Nancy and Peta for the harmony we enjoyed. So far as I know, neither Nancy nor Peta ever said a bad word to them about me, and Peta was careful to treat my older children the same as the younger two. (Later, in May of 1970, Carl, my oldest child, graduated as covaledictorian of his high school class. I wasn't there for the ceremony, but Carl sent me the big story in the local Bisbee newspaper with pictures of the two scholars. It was one of the proudest moments of my life. I knew then that Carl was going to be fine, despite not having had me around as a full-time father. He won a full four-year scholarship to the University of Arizona.)

Now, though, at this critical juncture when I found myself without a job, it was fortunate that I had saved enough money to last for several months while I looked for a job. I didn't know where to turn. After several days of near panic, I called Claude Albritton, my old geology friend and colleague from the Midland project. Albritton was dean of the faculty at Southern Methodist University in Dallas. I told him exactly what had happened and asked him if there might be a place for me at SMU. Claude told me there might be, and that the university had already been talking about hiring an anthropologist. He said he'd call me back in a day or two.

Two tense days later Claude called me. He said, "I'm authorized to offer you a full professorship, with tenure, beginning September 1, 1964. I hope you'll accept our offer. I want to assure you we'll do our best to make it possible for you to continue your research in Egypt and Sudan and the directorship of Fort Burgwin. If you do come to SMU, I'll arrange for you to be paid ten months a year. You'll teach three classes one semester a year. You'll be free during the other semester to do your field work and research. Whenever possible, however, I'll expect you to cover your salary from grants when you are in the field."

The salary was two thousand dollars a year more than I was making at the Museum of New Mexico. I accepted the offer, with pleasure and profuse thanks. As we talked, I told Claude more about my research in Sudan and Egypt, and how well it was going. I asked if I could bring several of my staff with me. I explained that I had two large grants, one from the NSF, the other from the State Department, and I told him I could cover their salaries until he could find places for them.

Claude asked how many I thought would come. I told him between four and six, and that two of them would have PhDs, and a third would have his the next year. A few days later he called and said, "Fred, I've found a place for you and your staff on the third floor of Smith Hall, a nearly empty dormitory of the Perkins School of Theology. There are rooms you can use as labs where you can study your collections; others can be offices."

Four weeks later, in late May of 1964, the ten members of the American staff I had left in Sudan and Egypt returned to Santa Fe. I contacted each one to tell him or her that I had been fired, and that I had a new job at SMU. I told them that I had arranged for all of them to join me at SMU if they wished. After some discussion about salaries, where we would work, and job security, the two senior people, Jim Hester and Joel Shiner, and three others, Phil Hoebler, Tony Marks, and Mary Beth Stokes, decided to come with me to Dallas. I moved them all, with all of our archaeological collections, to Fort Burgwin, where we could begin the analyses and report writing. Five others, Frank Eddy and four lab technicians, decided to stay in Santa Fe.

Having a good job once again brought me out of my depression; I had been knocked down, but now I was determined to succeed and to fight if necessary. I didn't realize it at the time, but the museum board did me a great favor when they fired me. They forced me to leave Santa Fe and go to SMU, where the opportunities and resources were much greater.

My departure from the Museum of New Mexico and the move to SMU took place with few problems. At first the staff at the museum thought they might like to keep the Nubian project there along with its overhead funds. They made a tentative overture to Jim Hester to take over as principal investigator, but Jim rejected their offer. The museum released the project to SMU without further discussion.

After we were settled in for the summer at Taos, I began assembling and editing the manuscripts I had asked each archaeologist to prepare at the close of the spring 1963 field season. They were all major reports. Two of them, both with many illustrations, were on the Acheulean and Middle Stone Age sites the Guichards excavated. Chmielewski wrote a similar report on another group of Middle Stone Age quarries on the west bank, also well illustrated; John Waechter wrote a fine description of the late Middle Paleolithic site he excavated on the west side of the Nile; and I wrote an introduction and conclusions. I wanted to get these reports published as soon as possible. I thought it was important that the archaeological community, as well as the staff at the NSF and the Foreign Currency Program at the State Department, know there was a lot of archaeology threatened by the Aswan Reservoir.

Mrs. Kirk Bryan, the widow of Kirk Bryan, my geology professor at Harvard, was living in Santa Fe when I began assembling the reports. I went to see her and asked if she would be my editorial assistant. She agreed and refused to take any money for her services. With her help we quickly prepared the volume for publication. It was the first significant report on the prehistory of Nubia, the first strike in my struggle to convince the archaeological world that there were many interesting Paleolithic sites in the Aswan Reservoir.

Our group stayed at the fort until the end of August 1964, when we gathered the collections and moved everything and everyone, including Peta and our beautiful baby daughter, Kelly (who had been born that year), to Dallas. The move to Dallas occurred without a break in the research because Albritton had allowed me to bring the key members of the Nubian project staff to SMU.

At the same time we came to Dallas, SMU hired Ronald Wetherington as an assistant professor of anthropology. Ron had been my assistant in some of the excavations at Fort Burgwin and had just received his PhD from the University of Michigan with a dissertation based on Pot Creek Pueblo.

SMU's interest in anthropology can best be understood in the context of other events at that time. President Kennedy had been assassinated in Dallas the previous November. The city was still in shock, and city leaders were trying to rediscover the soul of the community. They wanted to divert attention from the assassination and find a way to make the community more aware of the rest of the world. As Albritton had mentioned when I asked him about a position, SMU had decided to develop an active anthropology program. When our group became available, the university administration responded positively.

In early October 1964, a month after we arrived in Dallas, the *Dallas Morning News*, the most important (and conservative) local paper, ran an editorial warmly welcoming our group to SMU and Dallas. Until then I had been apprehensive as to how the people of Dallas would receive us. I knew the community was politically conservative and might not appreciate my teaching evolution, race, and the great antiquity of man to their children. After the editorial, however, I had no doubt that the local community welcomed us.

We were brought in to SMU as part of the Department of Sociology, but we were housed separately in Smith Hall. Soon the sociologists added anthropology to the name of the department. From the beginning it was a good relationship.

That first semester I taught three classes. One was "The Nature of Man," a required course for all freshmen. It was team taught, and Shiner and I jointly gave one general lecture each week. In addition, each week I taught two discussion sections of the Nature of Man with forty students. The first part of the course was devoted to philosophy, and I found the text obtuse and difficult. My second course was an ethnographic survey of simple societies throughout the world, not very different from the introductory course I taught at Texas Tech. The third course was a survey, "The Archaeology of America North of Mexico." Both of these survey courses were very popular: the first had more than thirty students; the other, forty, including two registrants who were members of the Dallas Archaeological Society, an amateur group. I taught one or more of these courses every year for nearly forty years.

With the move to SMU I was back in Texas, not far from my childhood home in Terrell. My mother had moved from Terrell to Fort Worth while I was in the army, but she was not there long. Her older sister, Tot Hall, owned a nursing home on the outskirts of Washington, D.C. She wanted my mother to help her run the nursing home. Mother made the move in 1947, about the time I was discharged from the army hospital. While I was in graduate school at Harvard I was able to visit her in Washington when I was traveling to and from Cambridge. The visits became rare, however, after I went to Santa Fe. At most, I was able to see her only once a year, usually when I was in Washington on archaeological matters. About 1970 Tot sold the nursing home for a large sum, and she and my mother moved to Tyler. My mother was not very happy living with Tot, who soon went to stay with a daughter in Mississippi, leaving my mother alone in Tyler. My visits with her became more frequent, about once a month. I tried to persuade her to return to Terrell, but she refused. My mother died on February 18, 1977, while I was in our field camp far out in the Egyptian Sahara. She was seventy-five years old. By the time the news of her death reached me, she was already buried. She was alone when she died, but my sister Millie gathered up her belongings, put the things she knew I would want in a box for me when I returned from Egypt, and sent the rest to the Salvation Army.

In the fall of 1965 I received a call from George Trager, a professor at the State University of New York at Buffalo and an internationally recognized linguist. He and his wife, Felicia, did linguistic research at Taos Pueblo and often visited me at Fort Burgwin. It was Trager who told me that the dean of arts and sciences at his university would like to meet with me. He was looking for a new chair for the Department of Anthropology, and Trager had recommended me.

I had gone to SMU telling myself I'd stay for two or three years, no more. The university had a reputation of being strong on athletics and a good party school, neither of which was important to me. By the end of my second year, however, I knew I liked Dallas, SMU, its students and faculty. Even so, I went to the meeting with the dean in New York with an open mind. We had a good meeting, and he made me an offer that included considerably more money than I made at SMU. He also agreed to find places for those who might come with me from SMU.

When I returned to Dallas I called a meeting of our group and explained the offer. I wasn't surprised when everyone said they didn't want to leave SMU. It was a great place to work, and they liked Dallas. I felt that way myself, and I knew that I would never find a better boss than Claude Albritton.

There was, however, one thing we wanted: we were all dedicated research scholars, and we wanted to teach in a PhD program where we would have good graduate students and the financial resources needed to make such a program successful. I decided to discuss the offer with Neil McFarland, SMU's provost. I told him we wanted to stay at SMU—if we could have a PhD program. He seemed supportive and asked if I could give him two weeks to discuss the matter with the board of governors. I agreed.

A week later McFarland called and told me the board had approved the PhD program in anthropology and had authorized the creation of a Department of Anthropology with me as its chair. I thanked him profusely and assured him we would stay. I called the dean at the New York university and declined his offer.

I had not asked for a separate department. We liked our colleagues in sociology and had no particular reason to want a separate department. I went to Morton King, the chair of the Department of Sociology and Anthropology, told him what had happened, and offered to include sociology in the PhD program. Morton told me he would have to check with the other sociologists and would get back with me the next day. When Morton came to see me he said the sociologists didn't want to join us in a PhD program. They knew that the standards for research and teaching would be higher than they had been, and the faculty preferred to keep the program as it was. I understood the sociologists' position, but I urged him to reconsider, because together we would be a strong department.

He said that their decision was final. I was sure they were making a mistake, and time proved me right. Separately their department remained weak, and once the administration almost terminated the department.

The initial anthropology faculty consisted of Jim Hester, Tony Marks (who'd just received his PhD from Columbia), Joel Shiner, Ron Wetherington, and me. In the fall of 1966 we were authorized to bring one more person on board, and we selected Ed Fry, who had received his PhD from Harvard three years before. He had been teaching at the University of Nebraska.

Ed was a physical anthropologist with an interest in social anthropology. He had started his PhD research doing social anthropology in Polynesia, but he changed his plans and did a study of growth patterns among preadolescent youth in Polynesia. A dynamic teacher and a great favorite of our students, Ed was an asset to the department.

The semester after it was announced that SMU would have a PhD program in anthropology we received the first applications from potential graduate students. Most of them came from Texas and adjacent states, but one was from Illinois. All were good students.

Jim Phillips was my first PhD, and he came to SMU from the University of Chicago. He worked with me in Egypt for three long field seasons (1967, 1968, and 1969). Rushdi Said arranged for the Egyptian Geological Survey to publish his dissertation. He has remained a close friend.

Another early student was Jon Gibson, from Louisiana. His PhD dissertation was based on the late Archaic Poverty Point Complex in Louisiana and adjoining states. He was the first to document that the large mound group at the Poverty Point site was a religious center supported by a widespread trade network that specialized in small stone carvings of insects and animals. Trade in the carvings and other crafts extended from east Texas to Mississippi, and from Arkansas to southern Louisiana. Like all radical new ideas, Gibson's theories had many doubters.

When my old friend Jimmy Griffin, the "dean of archaeology in eastern North America," saw Gibson's dissertation, he called me. His opening words were "You're not going to accept Gibson's dissertation are you?" I said I was, that it had already been accepted. I told him I thought it was a great thesis. "But the idea of a widespread trade network is crazy, and wrong," Griffin said. "Let's wait and see, Jimmy," I answered. It took time, but the Poverty Point Complex today is a widely recognized feature in Southeastern archaeology.

In 1965, a few weeks after I had my discussions with Provost McFarland, Claude Albritton met with William P. (Bill) Heroy, president of a geophysics firm in Dallas, to discuss a new building to house the Departments of Anthropology and Geology. Heroy had acquired significant wealth when Teledyne, a large conglomerate of several diverse companies that was growing rapidly, bought his firm. Albritton knew that Heroy was not only a geologist, but he also had a strong interest in archaeology. After several discussions with Albritton, Heroy agreed to pay over half of the money needed for a new building to house the geology and anthropology departments (later the Department of Statistics was included as well). The remainder of the money needed to come from grants from two sources: the Department of Health, Education, and

Welfare (HEW), and the National Science Foundation. That fall, Albritton decided it was time for Frank Seay, assistant to President Willis Tate; Bill Heroy; Jim Brooks, then chairman of the Department of Geology; and me, as chairman of the Department of Anthropology, to meet to discuss this opportunity for a new building to house our departments and how we would obtain the two grants. We agreed that there needed to be an institute to coordinate and support the research activities in the new building. Heroy later went to President Tate to insist that the institute would be separately incorporated from SMU. We agreed to call it "The Institute for the Study of Earth and Man (ISEM)."

Heroy and Albritton were well connected to HEW in Washington, and they wrote two grant proposals, one to HEW, the other to the NSF. The NSF scheduled a site visit in late July 1966.

That May I had gone to Fort Burgwin to write my section of a new book, *The Prehistory of Nubia*. A few days before the SMU site visit, I spent the day writing, as was my habit. By mid-afternoon I was tired and decided to take a break for an hour. I found my fly rod and went trout fishing. I must've brushed against a juniper tree in full flower. I returned to my office and continued to write for another hour. I had never before had an allergic reaction to juniper pollen, but when I tried to stand up I lost my balance and fell against my desk. By holding onto the wall I managed to make it to my home and into bed. The next morning I couldn't hear and could barely see. Peta thought I'd had a stroke and called a local physician. After he heard a description of my symptoms, he suggested she take me to an allergist he knew in Albuquerque.

When we got to the allergist's office, and he had identified the source of my allergic reaction, I told him I had an important meeting the next day involving a half-million dollars and a new building for my university. The allergist explained that I'd damage my hearing if I didn't go to bed and stay there for several weeks. But I insisted that as chair of the new anthropology department, I had to get to the meeting. I asked him to give me something to relieve my congestion. He gave me a shot and a prescription, and late that afternoon I got on a plane to Dallas. Peta called John Chapman, a physician who taught at Southwestern University Medical School and a close friend of ours. He met my plane and took me home and put me to bed. Chapman arranged an appointment early the following morning with an ear specialist at the medical school. The specialist gave me more medicine, and by late morning my eyesight was normal and I could hear. My new ear specialist, as had the one in Albuquerque, urged me to get back in bed and stay there for a month, as soon as the site visit was over.

Two members of the NSF site visit team were old acquaintances of mine: Al Spaulding, the program director for anthropology, and Ray Thompson, who, with his wife, had shared an apartment with Nancy and me for a semester while we were at Harvard. The team also included a geologist I knew casually, Bill Benson, then head of the Earth Sciences Division of the NSF.

Although I was not at my best during the site visit, we got the money for the new building: $600,000 from the Department of Health, Education, and Welfare; $500,000 from the NSF; and $1,500,000 as a gift from Bill Heroy. The Heroy Building was constructed, furnished and equipped, and ready to move into in September of 1968. We moved from our quarters in Smith Hall into a great new building with faculty and student offices, labs, all the equipment we thought we might need, and conference rooms for all.

Peta and Kelly returned to Dallas about the same time the visitors left. With Peta's help I was able to stay flat on my back for over a month. My ear doctor did the best he could, but tests showed I had lost between 10 and 15 percent of my hearing.

My professional life was taking on a regular pattern. Starting in early January of each winter I was in Egypt for three months, where I directed the excavations of the Combined Prehistoric Expedition. (Winter is the only practical time to work in the Egyptian Sahara. From around the middle of March to the end of September it is too hot to work, with daytime temperatures over 130 to 150°F.) Back in Dallas in the evenings between classes during the fall, with the assistance of graduate students such as Jim Phillips, I analyzed the collections from my personal excavations the previous winter, wrote the description of the artifacts, and prepared a site report for each locality I excavated. Some of the writing spilled over into the summer, when I was in residence as director of the Fort Burgwin Research Center. In addition to writing, in the summers I supervised three or four archaeology graduate students and hosted from seventy-five to a hundred students in field schools from several universities. It was a full life.

Whenever we completed a project, usually after three or four field seasons of excavation, analysis, and writing, we began the preparation of a major book. We included site reports on excavations by every member of our group, as well as reports by specialists on such topics as fauna and dating. Mary Beth Stokes did many of the maps and profiles for our books and articles while she was with us at Smith Hall. I'd recruited her to join Shiner on the Sudanese project, and she was one of those who had come to Dallas with me. She left after three years and joined the Museum of the American Indian in New York. After she left, someone I never met did most of the maps and profiles in Poland. Later, another gifted Polish draftsman and artist, Marek Puszkarski, did the illustrations.

While the writing was underway, we had to select some artifacts for illustration.

For many years, beginning in 1964, and continuing until 1990, Lucy Addington, a gifted Dallas artist, illustrated most of the artifacts in our articles and books. She came to us initially as a volunteer. One day, not long after we set up shop in Dallas Hall at SMU, she walked in the door and offered her services as an artist. She quickly mastered the skills needed to illustrate a flaked stone artifact. After only a month working as a volunteer, she made such fine drawings that I put her on the payroll. Her work soon was widely recognized as the best anywhere. In 1986 she did a book called *Lithic Illustration,* in which she defined the rules she'd developed for drawing stone artifacts—such as which end was up, where the cross-sections should go, and how to draw flake scars. The book is now long out of print, but her influence has greatly improved the quality and accuracy of artifact illustrations everywhere.

Fort Burgwin Becomes SMU-in-Taos |
(1964–1976, 2004)

CHAPTER 17

There were no new research activities at Fort Burgwin in 1964 other than Herb Dick's work reporting his excavations at Picuris and the work of the Nubian project staffers who had moved to Fort Burgwin to write their reports. Even so, the fort was not intellectually dead. We issued three long-overdue publications: *Taos Adobes,* an innovative architectural study of Spanish Colonial domestic architecture by Bainbridge Bunting, Jean Lee Booth, and William R. Sims, Jr.; *The Reconstruction of Past Environments* by James J. Hester and James Schoenwetter; and *Contributions to the Prehistory of Nubia,* which I assembled.

When I joined the faculty at SMU I had agreed that the university administration would take the overhead funds from my NSF grants. The overhead money on the Nubian project had been going to the Museum of New Mexico while I was in Santa Fe. However, the overhead funds for the Llano Estacado project had been going to Fort Burgwin. I had to replace that money if the fort was going to survive; the income from the endowment was not enough.

My solution was to encourage universities with field schools in the area to use Fort Burgwin as a base. We charged their students room and board at a rate higher than our cost, but within the means of the field schools. There was an obvious need for this service. Soon, field schools from as far east as North Carolina and Georgia and as far west as California and as far north as Wyoming were requesting work space, housing, and food service at Fort Burgwin. Most of them were geology field schools, but there were also painting classes and writers' workshops. We were soon full to capacity, and although I refused for a long time to admit it, Fort Burgwin was no longer a research center. It had become a campus for student instruction.

I was never able to accumulate a surplus I could use to develop more facilities at the fort. We needed more office space and a secure place to store the collections.

The board had frequently suggested that I take a salary, and I had always declined, citing our precarious financial position. In 1966 they again asked me to budget a salary for myself, and this time I agreed to budget two thousand dollars a month for two months, but after the board meeting I decided this four thousand dollars could go a long ways toward the new facilities we most needed—more office and secure storage space. I decided rather than accepting my salary I'd spend it putting up the walls of the stable area on the east side of the enlisted men's quarters.

I began the construction without discussing my plans with the board. Perhaps I thought they would've said no. It was my money and I thought I could spend it any way I wanted. I bought the adobe bricks I needed and had them delivered. With the assistance of the custodian, Ben Gonzales, and two other men hired for that purpose, we put in the steel-reinforced foundation. The adobe bricks were laid, the concrete bond beam poured, and the vigas were placed. At that point I'd spent my four thousand dollars. The walls were up, but there was no roof, and no windows or doors.

In late August, at the next meeting of the board, I said, "In your absence I contributed four thousand dollars to the fort. You authorized that amount for my salary, but I used the money to put up the walls of the stable area that adjoins the enlisted men's quarters. My money ran out before I was able to put on the roof. Without a roof the walls will be damaged this coming winter by the rain and snow." After a pause, I continued. "The roof will cost two thousand dollars. Do any of you have any idea where we might get the money for the roof?"

There was stunned silence for a long moment. Lewis MacNaughton began to laugh and said, "Well, Fred, you have a lot of brass, but I really respect your willingness to invest your own money where you believe it is needed. I'll give you the two thousand dollars. Can you roof the building before you return to Dallas?" He pulled out his checkbook, wrote out the check, and handed it to me. No one else on the board said a word. I moved on to the next item on the agenda.

Fort Burgwin never did pay me a salary while I was director. My salary came from my home institution, Texas Tech at first, for running the two field schools. For several summers after that, my salary came from two NSF grants. The budget in both grants covered my summer salary while I was doing research on the Llano Estacado.

Almost immediately after I joined the faculty at SMU in 1964, I began informal discussions with Dean Claude Albritton about how Fort Burgwin might become a part of SMU. I realized that if Fort Burgwin were to survive, it needed an association with a strong academic institution where leadership and responsibility could be shared. I was worried about what might happen to Fort Burgwin if something should happen to me. Who would carry it on?

There seemed to be many advantages both to the fort and an academic institution for such a merger. As part of a demonstration that the fort could be useful to the university, I began encouraging members of the SMU faculty to offer summer classes there. The faculty who responded conducted classes at the fort in art, archaeology, creative writing, and geology.

By 1967, the negotiations for the merger of Fort Burgwin and SMU involved Dean Albritton, Jack Brandenburg (who was then president of the Fort Burgwin board), President Willis Tate of SMU, and me. Albritton and I drafted a negotiating statement outlining the assets and needs of Fort Burgwin and the intellectual contributions the fort could make to SMU. We included a budget with a financial statement of expected income and expenditures should Fort Burgwin Research Center become a part of the university. We forecast a deficit of around ten to fifteen thousand dollars a year.

I knew that in order for the merger to be approved by the Fort Burgwin board, there would have to be some improvement in the facilities on the Fort Burgwin campus. Two items were critical to the board of trustees: new dormitory space to house at least twenty students, and completion of the stables area for additional office and laboratory space. At this point, the stables area consisted of the adobe walls I had erected in 1963 with the salary I gave back to the fort. Though it had been roofed at the end of that summer with the funds from Lewis MacNaughton, there were no floors, no doors, no windows, no partitions.

As the negotiations neared a conclusion, Tate said the university would be responsible for those two items, but it was going to be my job to find the money for them. I said I would try to find the money. I thought the NSF would help with a facilities grant to finish the stables, but I had no idea where I could get the money to build a dormitory.

The merger was signed on June 30, 1968. One of the first things Dean Albritton did after the agreement was signed was set up a cost center for Fort Burgwin, using a slightly more generous version of the budget we had submitted to Tate during the negotiations. For the first time, I was to be paid as the director of Fort Burgwin for three months each summer, and there was travel money, salary for a part-time secretary, and other items.

A month after the merger was signed, I was in my office at Fort Burgwin one afternoon when David Dunn, the director of the North Carolina geology field school, came to discuss housing arrangements for his students. They had been staying in the old schoolhouse, which was in terrible shape, dirty and rat-infested. He said he had a proposal for me. He would get his university to sign a three-year contract to stay at Fort Burgwin at the present rental rate if I would agree to build a decent place where his students could sleep and work, and he had an idea of where a new dormitory might be built. I told him I knew I had to do something. I'd put it off too long. He asked me to cross the highway with him.

We walked about a hundred yards to where, in Pot Creek sawmill days, there had once been a workshop and a large Quonset hut. The Quonset hut was long gone, but its concrete block foundation still stood there, strong, complete, and four feet tall. He suggested that I build the dormitory there to take advantage of the Quonset foundation. I told him I thought that was a great idea. And I told him about my plans for the two-story wooden Swiss chalet on the site that had been Ralph Rounds's sawmill office and summer apartment. I told him that the next summer I planned to use the lower floor of the chalet as our new kitchen and dining facility and that the apartment on the upper floor would be used for faculty housing.

Later that week Dunn came to me with a layout for the new geology dorm. His plan enclosed a large open area adequate for sleeping at least thirty people. There were showers, toilets, and workplaces. It looked fine to me, and after some checking with the lumberyard in town, I determined the new dormitory could be built, using local workers, for eleven to twelve thousand dollars.

A few weeks after David returned to North Carolina, he sent me a contract promising to rent the proposed new building for three field seasons at a cost of twelve thousand dollars. I took the contract to Albritton, and he arranged for SMU to loan me the twelve thousand dollars. Beginning in the fall of 1968, and continuing through the following spring, the new dormitory was built by local labor supervised by our new custodian, Tito Archuleta, our cook Florida's husband. In June 1969, the North Carolina geology field school occupied a new, not quite completed dormitory. It took another week for the showers and partitions to be installed, but David never complained about the brief delay. The new dormitory fulfilled one of the charges President Tate gave me when he agreed to the merger with Fort Burgwin. I paid off the loan from the university to build the dormitory in three years.

In late August of 1969, I decided that while I was back in Dallas teaching there were too many things going on at the fort I didn't know about. I needed to have closer supervision of the activities there. I had been taking commercial flights when I made the trip to the fort, but these only went to Albuquerque. From there I had to rent a car, and it was a long drive to Taos from Albuquerque and back. With the limited schedule of airline flights, the trip took two days. I needed a way to get to Taos and back to Dallas in one day.

I had wanted to fly ever since I'd received nine hours of flying instruction at the college at Hays, Kansas, in 1944. For years, every time I saw a private plane overhead

I longed to be up there. Finally, I went out to the Airport Flying School at Addison Airport at the north end of Dallas and signed up for lessons. In two months I accumulated thirty hours of flight time, passed my flight test, and got my private pilot's license in October of 1969. I bought an old Cessna 172 and began flying to Taos and back, rapidly building up hours. It was fun, and I could easily make the trip in one day.

I kept the plane in a hangar I rented at Addison Airport. It was a very convenient arrangement. When I needed to go to Taos, I would get up around 5:00 A.M. and call the airport. I would ask the airport staff to take my plane out of the hangar, fill it with fuel, and have it ready to fly. I'd take off about 6:00 A.M. That old Cessna was a thirsty bird, and it didn't have long-range fuel tanks, so I always had to refill halfway, usually at Plainview, Texas. From there I flew straight to Las Vegas, New Mexico, turned northwest, went over the mountain at Mora, and came into the valley by Fort Burgwin. There I turned to the west and flew direct to the Taos airport.

I had an old pickup I left at the Taos airport, and after I parked the airplane, I'd get in the old truck and drive to Fort Burgwin, arriving between 8:30 and 9:00 A.M., Taos time. After a full day at Fort Burgwin, I returned to the Taos airport, warmed up my plane, checked the gas, and headed for Dallas. With the prevailing strong tailwinds above ten thousand feet, I easily arrived home in time for dinner.

After a few months in the Cessna 172 I accumulated two hundred hours of flying time, the required minimum to take the exam to become an instrument pilot. I took the exam and passed. A few weeks later, I partnered with my friend George Race, a pathologist at Baylor Hospital in Dallas, in buying a Cessna 182. It was a much faster aircraft, equipped with an automatic pilot, a great feature for those long trips to Taos.

Flying is expensive. SMU reimbursed me for my trips to Taos as if I had bought a round-trip air ticket to Albuquerque, rented a car, and stayed in a hotel. Even with that support, it still cost me over one hundred dollars per month to maintain the airplane, even more when I was in Egypt and didn't fly.

There were not many changes at Fort Burgwin after the merger except for a great deal of cleanup. With Buddy Bostain's sawmill finally removed from our land by order of the courts, the big area on the east side of the highway was now available. First we had to remove several hundred truckloads of trash and junk equipment from the sawmill area to the county dump. Marian Meyers obtained a federal cleanup grant for us that paid the workers. The fort supplied the truck. When the cleanup was completed, we renovated three of the best houses where the sawmill staff had lived for temporary student dormitories. We found some surplus army double-decker beds and mattresses, and we installed screens, lights, showers, hot water heaters, washbasins, and toilets. The field school students thought the housing was great.

I applied for and received an NSF grant to complete the laboratories and offices in the east and south wings of the stables area, thereby fulfilling the second of President Tate's requirements. The new wings included a secure collection storage area, four offices, an archaeology lab, and a soundproof lab for linguistic studies. I moved into one of the offices, and Marian Meyers, my part-time secretary, took the adjoining office. George Trager, the linguist who had recently joined the anthropology faculty at SMU, claimed the linguistics lab.

We moved the kitchen and dining area from the decrepit old schoolhouse to the first floor of what had been the Swiss chalet. We moved several beds and chairs and two chests of drawers upstairs for the faculty's use.

The dining area was smaller than the one in the old schoolhouse; there was room for only fifty people to eat at one time. Florida solved that problem by having two seatings three times a day. Although this solved the space problem, it put a lot of pressure on Florida and her staff, and I resolved to find funds to build a proper dining facility.

The day-to-day expenditures at Fort Burgwin were covered by the rent and meal charges the various field schools paid. It was a bargain for the field schools and for Fort Burgwin because, though the rental and food charges were modest, they were enough to keep the operation solvent with a little extra. Our major problem was the shortage of space we could offer the field schools. The old sawmill shacks were never satisfactory for a hundred or more students in residence.

One day in the late fall of 1970, a stranger knocked at my office door at SMU. He introduced himself as Fred Hoster and said he was a representative of SMU's Office of Development. He started by telling me he'd been hearing rumors about our activities at Taos, and he wanted to know more about what was going on out there.

As I began to tell him about the Fort Burgwin Research Center I could see his interest grow. I asked if he'd like to go out there with me in a Cessna 172. Hoster quickly accepted the invitation. I told him to meet me at my hangar at Addison Airport at 6:00 A.M. the next Saturday morning and gave him a sketch of the airport so he could find me. I told him that depending on the headwinds, the flight to Taos usually took three to three and a half hours, and I concluded by telling him not to drink too much coffee.

We landed at Taos airport at 8:30 A.M., Taos time. As soon as we arrived at Fort Burgwin, the beauty of the place almost overwhelmed Hoster. He saw immediately the enormous potential of the fort as a western campus for SMU. We spent the weekend, drank a few beers, cooked some steaks, and walked around the property. We looked at the buildings and discussed where we might put the new facilities I hoped to have someday. On Sunday we flew back to Dallas. As we parted, Hoster promised that he would get the board of governors of the university to see what they had at Fort Burgwin.

Fred Hoster was a good salesman. On August 14, 1971, he, the future Texas governor, Bill Clements, who was at the time chairman of the board of governors of SMU, and four other members of the board flew out in a borrowed Dresser Industries plane to spend the day at Fort Burgwin. They toured the facilities and watched some of the student activities. I cooked them a steak lunch and made them some of my special Wendorf margaritas. It was a happy luncheon. The visitors seemed impressed as we drove them back to the airport. Clements, in particular, told me he was entranced with the setting and the potential Fort Burgwin offered SMU.

During the next several months, Hoster and I met several times to discuss development ideas. Hoster saw the fort as a source of money to support a variety of programs for Fort Burgwin and the university. He proposed borrowing money to build housing and other facilities that SMU alumni could use part of the year, and students during the summer months. It was an ambitious program, and at first I favored it. As time went on, however, I became more skeptical. Hoster's plans would probably solve the financial needs of the fort, but they would change the ambiance of the valley forever. I didn't think this was in the long-term interest of the fort. However, I never expressed my reservations to Hoster.

It was almost a year later before I had an opportunity to discuss with Bill Clements my plans for new facilities at Fort Burgwin. I told him about Hoster's suggestions, but before I finished, Clements told me he was not sympathetic to the idea of bringing large groups of people onto the campus. He asked me what I wanted. It was my opportunity.

"First," I said, "we need good housing for a hundred students in small dormitories, or casitas. Second, we need a kitchen and dining facility to accommodate at least a hundred students. Third, we need roads, water, and other facilities to service the dormitory and dining facilities. Finally, I want everything to be hidden in the trees on the hillside south of the historic buildings of the fort."

Clements asked several more questions about the proposed facilities, and then asked where he could put a house for himself. We walked over to a spot I thought would make a superb building site, on a high terrace overlooking the Little Rio Grande. While we stood there he asked more questions. He thought a moment, and said, "Let's do it."

There was a hitch, of course. Several months before my conversation with Clements, the Rounds family had sold me four acres from the eighty acres they had retained that adjoined the south end of the Fort Burgwin campus. I was preparing to build a house there for myself. I had brought in (and my son Mike peeled) the vigas for the ceilings, I'd hauled in flagstone for the floors, and my son Mike had built a fence around my property. Louis Walker, a prominent architect in Santa Fe and a protégé of Frank Lloyd Wright, had drawn up preliminary plans. I also had a permit for a water well, but it had not been drilled.

When we made the decision to go ahead with the new facilities, Clements voiced a reservation. He believed it would be important to protect the investment he and the university were making by acquiring as much of the property around the south end of the Fort Burgwin campus as possible. He was concerned that someday someone could build a filling station or other inappropriate structure next to the campus. He approached Marian Meyers, who had bought about twenty acres from the Rounds's estate on the east side of the highway, just beyond the south end of the campus. She refused to sell her land to SMU or Clements. I suspect she was still angry because earlier I had been told to ask her to give up the Commanding Officer's House and move off campus.

Clements turned his attention to the remaining seventy-six acres the Rounds family owned, beyond the south end of the Fort Burgwin campus. At Clements's request, I flew to Wichita, Kansas, to see Dwight Rounds. I asked him if the family might be willing to sell those acres to the university. Because the Rounds family no longer had any interest in the Taos area, I was not surprised when he said they would sell the acreage to SMU. I returned to Dallas and called Clements; the next day he flew to Wichita and purchased the Rounds property for the university.

A few days later, as Clements and I walked around the land he had just acquired, he told me he wouldn't give the money to implement our plans unless I sold my four acres to SMU at the price I had paid for it. This came as a shock, but I could understand Clements's reasoning. When I'd bought my land, it had been adjacent to the southern boundary of the fort's property, but now with the purchase of the Rounds acreage, my land was near the middle of the campus.

I suggested a swap of my land for four acres at the northern or eastern edge of the campus, somewhere I would be out of the way. But Clements refused, saying he didn't want any SMU faculty to own houses here. I had devoted years to developing Fort Burgwin and wasn't just any member of the faculty. My initial reaction was to reject Clements's demand that I sell. I knew, however, that he would be investing several million dollars in Fort Burgwin and that in all likelihood he offered the only opportunity I would ever have to achieve my long-held goals for Fort Burgwin. I swallowed hard, and agreed to sell my four acres to the university the following week.

Our first step was to select an architect for the major building project Clements had agreed to finance. I suggested Louis Walker, the architect who'd drawn up the plans for my house. Walker had designed many distinctive houses in Santa Fe and Los Alamos. On several occasions he and his family had visited my family at Fort Burgwin, and at least once I had taken him around the proposed building area and told him about my plans for the new student housing at Fort Burgwin.

At my request, Walker came to the fort and met with Clements and me. We walked around the proposed construction site, and he outlined a design plan that was attractive to both Clements and me. Clements asked Walker to go ahead and draw up preliminary plans. A few weeks later the plans were approved with only minor changes.

It was a year after Clements had said, "Let's do it" before all the arrangements were complete and work could begin. At Clements's request, I was in charge of the construction, but the university sent Ed Hoffman, one of their construction staff, to help. Hoffman took care of building the roads, ordering supplies, and installing a 100,000-gallon water tank on top of the hill behind where the casitas were to be located. He arranged for the cleaning and testing of two deepwater wells that the Pot Creek sawmill had drilled in the early 1950s, but never used. He had the water lines and temporary electrical service put in place. In addition, he ordered the windows and doors, their frames, roof vigas, insulation, lumber, nails, and other materials, and arranged for their delivery at the times we expected to need them. All of this was done by mid-May 1973. My job was to oversee the construction of the ten casitas.

A week before construction began, Clements and I met with the Fort Burgwin board and showed them the construction plans for their approval. I had shown the plans to the board at their previous meeting, but I'd failed to get a formal motion of approval, causing two members to object because the board had not given their prior formal approval. It was my mistake, and it hurt my relationship with the board at a critical moment. Despite the objections of Lavender and Meyers, they grudgingly approved the plans to build the new dormitories and the kitchen-dining facility.

When the roads and services were completed, with the advice of the custodian, Tito Archuleta, I hired sixty local men. We began working on the casitas in late May. Originally, I had planned for ten casitas, but in the area we selected there were only eight good sites. Thus, for two of the larger plots we joined two casitas at the ends, but kept separate entrances, toilet/shower facilities, and fireplaces. Each of the doubled casitas provided space for twenty students. We had ten casitas, and as planned, dormitory space for a hundred students.

The construction site was about a half-mile south of the Fort Burgwin historic buildings, on the west side of the Little Rio Grande Creek, on a gently sloping hillside thickly wooded with piñon and juniper. Louis Walker had tucked each casita among the trees so they could not be seen from the highway. He took care to avoid any unnecessary cutting of trees.

Walker staked the positions of the windows and doors for each of the casitas, and supervised the placement of the batter boards that marked the level of the concrete floors. Tito and I organized a Henry Ford–type assembly line. We started with two casitas, setting the batter boards, excavating the foundation trenches, and leveling the dirt inside the structure. The plumbers and electricians followed and set the plumbing and electrical rough-ins. Experienced crews ordered, delivered, and finished the concrete. The two starting crews moved to other casitas and worked until all ten floors had been poured and finished. When the concrete in the first two houses had set, we had the adobe bricks delivered. Door frames were put in place and blocked upright. To guide the adobe layers, we marked the position of each door and window on the floor with chalk. Then we began laying the adobe bricks. Tito and I were there as the adobe bricks were laid at each house. Tito and I closely followed the construction at every stage and sometimes carried adobe bricks ourselves when a crew fell behind.

We hired Carmen Velarde, an elderly local woman who specialized in fireplaces, to construct the fireplace in each casita. She was widely known for her beautiful work. She started when the walls of the first casita were up. She worked fast and was able to keep up with the adobe layers and finished the fireplace in each building as they installed the vigas.

When the adobe walls reached the right height, the crew built a wooden frame at the top of the wall so a concrete-and-steel bond beam could be poured. Workers placed reinforcing steel in the frame and, using buckets, placed the concrete for the beam in the frame. When that had set, another team came in and set and blocked the roof vigas in place. At the same time two teams of electricians installed the conduits for the electrical lines and wall boxes. Electricians installed boxes in the ceilings and wired them as soon as the ceiling boards were nailed in place.

After the roofing crews nailed down the ceiling boards, they placed the insulation, and finally, nailed down the roofing deck. When the deck was on, commercial roofers came in to set the drainage canals and install a tar-and-gravel roof. One of the final jobs I had to do was to arrange with Kit Carson Electrical Cooperative to install underground electrical service to each casita and the dining hall. This time there was no problem with missing green tags.

The entire building process went well until about half of the casitas were under construction. My crew was made up of local Hispanic laborers, who were all great workers. The only problem we had began when two "gringos" showed up and asked if they could have a job. Tito didn't want them, but I asked him to hire the two men anyway. "Don't be so prejudiced," I said.

Two days later Tito came rushing to my house at noon while I was having lunch, yelling, "The men are on strike. They want more money." I grabbed my checkbook and payroll records and went to the work site, where I found the workers milling around with hostile expressions on their faces. I asked someone in the group, "What's going on?"

He said, "We want more money."

Tito found a chair, and I got up on it so everyone could see me, and I said, "I have no authority to raise your pay. The pay scale is set in Dallas. I'm not sure anyone back there will change it. They know your wages are 10 percent higher than the highest local wage being paid for this kind of work. Please reconsider what you're doing. I know there's no other work for you anywhere else in the county."

Then I said, "Let's quit for today. I'll pay each one of you what I owe you up to noon today. When you get home talk this over with your family. If you change your minds, be here at 7:00 A.M. tomorrow and you'll still have a job. If you're not here at 7:00 A.M., I'll hire someone else."

Tito found a table and brought it to me. I told the men to form a line so I could pay them. I got out the payroll records, my checkbook, and a pen. As each man came up, I shook his hand and said, "I very much enjoyed working with you. I hope you'll return tomorrow." Then I handed him his check.

Meanwhile, Tito's wife, Florida, got on the phone trying to reach the men's wives or girlfriends or mothers, to tell them what happened. She reminded them that this was the best pay in the county, and that there were no other jobs anywhere around Taos. I suspect that most of the men stopped at a local bar, cashed their checks, had a beer or two, and then went home.

Tito never said a word to me about my decision to hire the two gringos, for which I was grateful. Several of the men had told him the gringos were union agitators who'd urged the men to strike. Tito then got on the phone and called all the people he knew who needed a job, telling them to be at our workplace before 7:00 A.M. tomorrow.

The next morning I drove to the work site a little before 7:00 A.M., where I found a crowd of over a hundred men milling around. I was apprehensive until I saw they were smiling. I got out of the car and told everyone what I'd promised the men the day before. I asked each of the old crew present to check their names off on Tito's list and go to work. Every man had returned—except the two gringos. I asked, "Who was the first man here this morning?" A man held up his hand. "You're hired," I said. Then I asked, "Who was the second man?" I hired him, too. I thanked all those who'd come and asked them to give Tito their names. "If more men are ever needed I'll hire from that list," I promised.

Two weeks later, as I was nailing ceiling boards to the vigas on one of the last casitas, the two gringos had the temerity to come by to ask for their jobs back. I told them replacements had already been hired. Then I asked Tito to escort the two gentlemen off the premises. But they left in a hurry before he could get to them.

All of the casitas were completed—roofs, electrical service, the bathrooms tiled, flagstone floors laid, and doors and windows installed by mid-August, only ten weeks after we began. Each building was plastered on the interior and stuccoed on the exterior. All that remained was to bring in furniture, and that was on order.

At the dedication the following June of 1974, SMU awarded an honorary doctorate to Bill Clements. One of the reporters who covered the dedication described the beautiful kitchen-dining facility Louis Walker designed as "Frank Lloyd Wright in northern New Mexico." Walker is a genius. The kitchen-dining building was far beyond my experience as a builder, so a commercial contractor who began working soon after we finished the casitas constructed it.

The construction of the casitas and dining hall transformed Fort Burgwin. Equal to any facilities available on the Dallas campus, the new buildings ensured that Fort Burgwin was ready to become "SMU-in-Taos." One of the first things we did was stop hosting outside field schools. Only SMU-sponsored activities directed by a member of the SMU faculty would be accepted here.

There were a few problems when we began to hold regular classes during the summer at Fort Burgwin. Initially, we were unable to recruit enough students to cover the cost of the classes, and the budget deficit grew alarmingly. When we finally did enroll enough students, a problem emerged because of the disparity between the students enrolled in field schools, who put in long days of physical labor and received six units of credit for six weeks' work, and those who attended regular classes, who met for three hours of lectures each week and received three hours of credit. I was unable to persuade the instructors of those classes to increase the effort they required of their students. It seemed that many of the faculty looked on their time at Fort Burgwin as a summer vacation. It took two years to work out a fair solution. Today, thirty years later, they are still making adjustments.

In the summer of 1976, twenty years after Rounds and I started the Fort Burgwin Research Center, I decided to resign as its director. My decision to resign as director was occasioned by an offer I received from Owen Henderson and Russ Morrison, two Dallas businessmen with a great interest in archaeology who would later go with me to Bir Sahara East and Bir Tarfawi, to fund an endowed chair for me at SMU—provided I would quit my administrative jobs, the chairmanship of the anthropology department and the directorship of Fort Burgwin. They wanted me to focus on research and writing. It was an attractive offer and I agreed. The university agreed as well, and in a few months part of the endowment was sent to the university. (Despite their pledges, the rest of the money was never given, unfortunately, although the university honored my professorship as if all of the endowment monies were in place.)

Another important factor in my decision to leave the directorship of Fort Burgwin was the exciting new body of information about the prehistory of the Egyptian Western Desert we were uncovering. The archaeology in the desert had captured my intellectual curiosity. When I resigned as director of Fort Burgwin, I tried to stay away from Taos for twenty years, but my affection for the fort kept drawing me back. As compensation for the forced sale of my four acres, SMU offered to sell me four acres up Pot Creek. I bought the land at its appraised value, seven times more than I received from the university when I sold them my original four acres. Another thing I had to give up was my airplane. Since I was no longer director of Fort Burgwin, SMU would not help cover the cost of operating my airplane. George Race and I sold our plane, and George bought a new Cessna 172. I still miss flying.

It was a good time to change. SMU-in-Taos was fully operational. All of the new facilities I had planned and helped build were in place. I was exhausted by the construction of the casitas, my marriage to Peta was coming apart because of my long absences, and I no longer enjoyed managing the SMU-in-Taos campus. My family and I had enjoyed some of the best years of our lives at Fort Burgwin, and for many years it was our only real home, but the time had come to move on.

I did build a beautiful adobe house on a Pleistocene terrace adjacent to the creek. Clements had opposed my buying the four acres, but later we became close friends again, and we still occasionally socialize, both in Dallas and in Taos. I think he was pleased when he saw that I didn't build a shack.

The construction of the casitas and dining hall did not end the commitment and generosity of Bill and Rita Clements to Fort Burgwin. They showed their emotional tie to Fort Burgwin by building a beautiful home on the site Bill and I had selected for him that first day. It overlooks the Little Rio Grande Creek, not far from the casitas and the Fort Burgwin campus. In addition to giving many scholarships to help students attend SMU-in-Taos, the Clementses also provided the money to build or restore several major buildings, including the reconstruction of the old hospital at Fort Burgwin, to be used as an archaeology laboratory and collection storage area. They also underwrote the construction of three duplexes for faculty and guest housing. The Clementses have also induced several of their friends to help with the development of Fort Burgwin, resulting in an endowed lecture series, an outstanding annual musical performance, and an auditorium frequently used for lectures, musical performances, and art shows. I'm sure Ralph Rounds would be pleased at the way the fort has turned out.

In 2004 Clements and his wife Rita, along with two anonymous donors, gave SMU two million dollars to build a library and a state-of-the-art computer center on the Fort Burgwin campus. They kept part of their plan secret from me until the last moment of the dedication ceremony, when Clements, in front of more than two hundred guests, announced that this complex was named the "Fred Wendorf Information Commons." Then they uncovered two large bronze plaques describing the long friendship between Rounds and myself. It's the greatest honor I've ever received.

Fort Burgwin is an extraordinary place that was created and sustained because many generous people have experienced its magic and fostered its growth. For me, it was a lot of hard work, but it has been gratifying to be part of the evolution of Cantonment Burgwin into SMU-in-Taos. It could not have happened without the foresight of Ralph Rounds, Bill and Rita Clements, and their friends.

Jebel Sahaba and Earliest Warfare |
(1964–1967)

CHAPTER 18

S hiner and the rest of the staff continued active, large-scale fieldwork and laboratory analyses into the fall of 1964 when I was teaching classes at SMU. I was in the field mostly in Sudan, but also for a brief period in Egypt in the spring of 1965. I tried to work with each of the field teams. One of the best projects I saw during this time was that of Romuald (Roman) Schild and his Polish/Egyptian team. They had dug an enormous trench, in places more than eight feet deep, through the Arkin aggradational beach. The trench exposed the earliest Final Pleistocene site known in the area. While I was admiring the trench, Schild showed me his superb stratigraphic drawing of that trench. Schild's group was doing exceptionally high-quality research, some of the best I had seen in the Aswan Reservoir.

My group's last major excavation in the Aswan Reservoir occurred in late February and March of 1965 when Shiner, Marks, and I (on my off semester) excavated a potentially important graveyard about two miles north of Wadi Halfa and about half a mile east of the Nile. The graveyard was in a small valley, open on the west, but bound on the north by a prominent hill known as Jebel Sahaba, and enclosed on the east and south by a series of smaller inselbergs, or jebels. The graveyard was on the almost flat pediment at the foot of one of those small jebels.

Solecki and his team had discovered the Jebel Sahaba graveyard during their survey of the Wadi Halfa area in 1961, when members of his team found three fragmentary human burials there. The partial skeletons had been taken to Columbia University, but never studied. They were eventually turned over to me, and I passed them on to our physical anthropologist, John Anderson, to be studied. Tony Marks, then a graduate student at Columbia, and a member of our 1963–1965 Wadi Halfa staff, had participated in the discovery of these skeletons.

One day near the end of our 1965 season, Tony and I were working together at a Khormusan site he planned to include in his report on that late Middle Paleolithic entity. When we finished the Khormusan site, Tony mentioned the earlier find of the three partial skeletons at Jebel Sahaba. He thought there might be more burials at that locality. Tony told me he wanted to do a little more work at a Mousterian site a few miles from Jebel Sahaba, and he didn't need me to help him. I asked him to take me to the jebel and leave me there with a couple of laborers until he finished his work. Before he returned, the workers and I had exposed six burials. I had no idea how large the graveyard would be, but I knew I needed help, because the skeletons looked old and interesting.

That night I asked Joel and Tony to stop what they were doing and join me in excavating the remaining burials. We began the excavations at Jebel Sahaba at the end of the season, when we had already spent most of the money budgeted for labor. By selling a bottle of scotch and one of our spare tires to the Finnish expedition, which was also working in the reservoir that spring, we raised enough money to hire six laborers to work an additional two weeks.

The Sahaba graveyard contained fifty-eight well-preserved complete and partial skeletons, including those of eleven infants and children and forty-seven adults, of whom twenty were females, twenty males, and seven of indeterminate sex. The most interesting feature of the burials was the clear and unmistakable evidence that at least half, and perhaps all, of the bones in the Sahaba graveyard were from individuals who had died violently. There is a high probability that this graveyard is the result of organized warfare. If so, it is the earliest known evidence of organized warfare anywhere in the world.

Although violent death is indicated for a few isolated Upper Paleolithic burials in Western Europe, dating between 35,000 and 24,000 years ago, these do not indicate warfare. These older instances were single skeletons with a point or two embedded in the bones. It seems likely that these scattered cases record individual revenge killings or murders, but not warfare, as the term is generally used.

Prior to the Mesolithic and Neolithic, evidence for any kind of conflict is rare in the archaeological record. This paucity of evidence for intensive conflict has led some archaeologists to suggest that the first true warfare began after around 10,000 years ago and was the result of competition for the limited land suitable for cultivation. According to this view, the first warfare did not occur until after the beginning of agriculture and the establishment of settled villages. The early conflict at Jebel Sahaba, however, occurred much earlier than agriculture in the Nile Valley or anywhere else, and the evidence of conflict at Jebel Sahaba seems to have nothing to do with settled villages.

Why are there almost no signs of conflict, and no evidence at all of intensive, organized conflict, during the tens of thousands of years Paleolithic people were present in Africa and Europe? Why did it suddenly appear in the Nubian Nile Valley at least 3,000 years before there were traces of organized conflict in Southwest Asia and Europe? Was there something different about the Nubian environment and/or the kinds of societies present that fostered the emergence of intensive conflict? Was the resulting conflict true warfare?

The Late Paleolithic societies in Nubia were hunters and gatherers, so a useful place to consider why warfare developed in Nubia is to look at modern hunters and gatherers. Fortunately, there is an excellent study of warfare by R. C. Kelly, who examined many modern surviving hunting and gathering societies *(Warless Societies and the Origin of War)*. He reviewed the literature of more than one hundred hunting and gathering groups that are no longer functioning. Kelly noted that some of these hunters and gatherers were warlike and conducted organized attacks on their neighbors. Among the majority of the societies he studied, however, there were occasional individual conflicts, but no evidence of organized conflict or anything that might be identified as warfare.

Kelly observed that all of these non-warlike hunting and gathering groups had simple, bilateral kinship systems that recognized relationship on both the mother's and father's side, but limited a person's kin group to individuals living in the same residential group. Such an arrangement restricts the opportunity for recruiting others who might cooperate in raids on neighboring groups. These peaceful bands lacked political leaders who would control residential units beyond where they lived. Leadership in such peaceful hunting and gathering groups tends to be informal and impermanent.

Kelly's studies also showed that warlike hunting and gathering societies have more complex social arrangements with unilateral kinship systems extending across several residential bands. That is, they trace kinship beyond the residential unit in either the mother's or the father's line, but not both. The advantage of these extended, unilateral kin-relationships is that it enables individuals to have close relatives in several residential groups. These groups with unilateral kinship systems often have political systems with some control across several residential communities. Kelly could not determine which came first, warfare or the unilateral kinship system and extended political control, but he suggested that both warfare and the accompanying social/political system probably developed together.

So, what is the evidence for conflict and probable warfare at Jebel Sahaba? There were over a hundred flaked stone artifacts embedded in the bones of twenty-four of the burials and in probable association with two others. These artifacts included six stone chips that were found embedded in the bones of five skeletons when they were cleaned in the laboratory. In addition, over seventy similar artifacts were recovered from the fill around the skeletons; many probably had been associated with the skeletons, but were not found until the screening of the back-dirt. I found no artifacts in the first six skeletons I excavated because I was not looking at them as carefully as I should have. But I found them in the seventh. Although the direct association of these screened artifacts could not be confirmed, it is significant that there was no evidence of a nearby settlement from which these artifacts could have been derived. None of these were "grave goods" in the sense of materials left with the deceased for use in later life. They were parts of projectiles and other weapons that, in most instances, had been directly responsible for the death of the individual. The few possible exceptions were several scrapers and cores we recovered that might have been in pouches placed next to the body when it was buried.

A variety of tool types is represented among the artifacts recovered with the skeletons. Almost half were unretouched flakes and chips, some of them naturally pointed, but most were only small pieces with sharp edges that in most analyses would be classified as debris, not tools. Yet many of these pieces were recovered in positions where their use as parts of weapons is irrefutable; they were embedded in long bones, inside skulls, within chest and pelvic cavities, and in vertebra columns. Of the eleven children up to age twelve, three had pieces embedded between the skull and the cervical vertebra, execution-style.

Several of the adult burials displayed clear evidence of vicious fighting. One example is a group of four individuals buried together, two old males, an adult female, and an infant. The group had a total of thirty embedded lithic pieces, five with the female, eight in one male, and seventeen in the other male. The pelvic/pubic area seems to have been a favorite target. Multiple wounds there probably represent overkill and human "pincushioning" of a fallen enemy who is already dead or dying, and would seem to indicate the joint participation by a group of attackers, each member of the party throwing a spear or arrow into the fallen enemy, thus communicating their anger, strength, and power.

With only a few exceptions, most of the Sahaba skeletons had been carefully buried on their left sides, heads to the east, facing south. Their hands were placed near their faces, their knees flexed, with their heels near the buttocks. This probably indicates that survivors buried the dead.

All of the skeletons were modern *Homo sapiens,* resembling, but not identical to, those of the so-called Cro-Magnon type in Europe and the Mechta variety from the

Maghreb in Northeast Africa, all of which are dated to about the same time. These groups share robust skeletal frames, long crania, short, broad faces, well-developed brow ridges, and low rectangular orbits. The Sahaba skeletons, however, have more pronounced mid-facial projection in the area of the mouth, with large mandibles and strong muscle attachments, particularly in males.·

Since it is located above the highest flood levels of the Late Pleistocene Nile, the Jebel Sahaba graveyard has no strong stratigraphic evidence indicating its age. There is, however, a single radiocarbon age determination of 13,740 radiocarbon years old obtained from collagen extracted from Burial 43. Another indication of a Final Pleistocene age for the burials is the associated artifacts. All of the retouched tools from the graveyard are closely similar to those recovered from sites assigned to the Qadan, an entity known in the Nile Valley from many localities in the vicinity of the Second Cataract, and northward from there to Wadi Kubbaniya, about six miles north of the First Cataract at Aswan, Egypt. The Qadan is not well dated, but there are several associated radiocarbon dates ranging from 14,500 to 12,000 years ago, with most dates and the stratigraphic evidence suggesting that many of the Qadan occupations were near the recent end of that range.

Disturbance of earlier burials by later ones is strong evidence that the violent deaths at Jebel Sahaba did not occur in a single battle, but represent several conflicts over a period of time. Additional evidence of sustained violence is found in the healed or almost healed "parry fractures" of the lower arms on six of the Sahaba burials, two of which did not have embedded artifacts. Although parry fractures can happen accidentally, perhaps in a bad fall, or playing at stick fighting, the most likely cause for the broken arms in this situation is from blocking a blow. This evidence would suggest that conflict was not a rare event, but may have been a routine part of life during the period the Sahaba graveyard was in use.

What happened at Jebel Sahaba? The high frequency of women and children in the graveyard was almost surely a result of raids on habitations where family members were gathered, indicating that the attackers were a group who took vengeance on an offending enemy group. The evidence suggests that these burials represent a series of attacks by a group or groups on an enemy settlement. The goal of the attacks was not to attack and kill a specific individual of an enemy group, but to kill any and all members of that enemy group, regardless of sex or age. The Sahaba burials document a pattern of behavior different from individual revenge killings.

What does this tell us about the Qadan social system? If Kelly is correct, the evidence indicates the Qadan had a belief system that tied several residential units together, a unilateral kinship system extending beyond the residential unit, and/or leadership, either political or religious, that influenced or controlled several residential units. It is difficult to test this hypothesis in the archaeological record, but the existence of three large Qadan graveyards suggests that the social or political system of the Qadan involved more than one residential unit.

Earlier burials in Nubia and Upper Egypt are not numerous, but those that exist are different from those at Jebel Sahaba. The earlier ones occur either as single individuals, or in one instance, as a group of three skeletons, not necessarily contemporaneous. Around 14,000 to 13,000 years ago, a new group, which we named the Qadan, appeared suddenly in the Nile Valley in the area between the First and Second Cataracts. With the presence of the new group there was a change from single burials to a new style of burial in which the bodies were put in large graveyards. We excavated two of these, and the University of Colorado group, one of the North American groups studying prehistoric sites in the Aswan Reservoir, excavated a third.

The two other large graveyards are of the same age and archaeological association as Jebel Sahaba, and both Tushka and Halfa West were on the west bank. Physically, the Halfa West and Tushka skeletons are closely similar to those from Jebel Sahaba, and are assigned to the same physical type. Neither of the other graveyards, however, revealed evidence of warfare.

Some of the Qadan living sites were large, and the limited available data suggest that there was a wide range of settlement sizes. The larger sites may represent reuse of the same locality over several years. It seems likely that the large graveyards were not simply the result of larger settlements, but developed because several residential units were bound together into a larger social body that buried their dead in a common graveyard. The ethnographic record indicates that the presence of several of these larger, more strongly controlled social/political/religious entities provided the structure needed for the emergence of organized warfare along the Nile in Upper Nubia. Why did warfare occur along the Nile, and why did it occur then? These questions remain unanswered, but they deserve careful study, because they may provide a better understanding of the origin of warfare itself.

In the fall of 1965, the National Science Foundation convened a working conference on the prehistory of the Aswan Reservoir at Lake Como in northern Italy. In addition to Al Spaulding, who organized the meeting and represented the NSF, those in attendance included senior Egyptian and Sudanese antiquities officials and senior scientists of the four North American expeditions: University of Colorado, Yale University, University of Toronto, and our group from SMU. The purpose was to develop cooperation among the groups. To date there had been almost no cooperation, except between Colorado and us. We were encouraged to exchange information about the results then available.

Even before I got to Lake Como I had decided to offer as little information as possible. I told Spaulding that we were not yet far enough along in our analyses to share the results. Of course that was not true, but after all, the heads of the Yale and Toronto expeditions had written those terrible letters about me in 1962 claiming I was incompetent, among other things. Why should I offer them any help now? I could not forgive them for stating that there were no sites in the reservoir, and for urging that no money be allocated to study sites even if any should be found. Their actions caused others who might have joined us to withdraw, and almost surely caused many prehistoric sites to go unstudied. So, as far as I was concerned, the Lake Como meeting was unproductive, except for the auspicious beginning of the multinational group of archaeologists I would work with for the next forty years.

It was at the Lake Como meeting that most of us in my group decided to continue our research into the prehistory of the Nile Valley. It was here we adopted the name "Combined Prehistoric Expedition," which reflected the international diversity of the scientists and other staff, and the fact that there were three main sponsors of the work: the Egyptian Geological Survey, the Polish Academy of Sciences, and Southern Methodist University. Over drinks one evening we decided that Shiner, with Marks, Chmielewski, and de Heinzelin, would move southward in Sudan toward the headwaters of the Nile, while Schild, Said, Issawi, and I would work in Egypt, from north of the reservoir to the Mediterranean.

I had not been close to Schild or his work at Arkin in 1963–1965 because he worked across the river from me during most of that time and we rarely visited each other's sites. I had, however, noticed that Schild was an unusually gifted archaeologist. Consequently, I was pleased when he decided to stay with my group and work in Egypt.

After the excavations at Jebel Sahaba, except for two brief sessions, one in Egypt, the other in Sudan, the Aswan project was over. The first brief project, conducted in the fall of 1965, after the Lake Como meeting, lasted four weeks and focused on the sites at Tushka. I had been concerned that our previous excavations had been inadequate, and I wanted to recover collections from the largely ignored, silt-covered occupations along the border of the embayment. The silt was probably deposited during the Final Paleolithic seasonal floods, but there were no dates to support this assumption. Among the unusual features I wanted to restudy were the numerous grinding stones we found scattered over the site, presumably left by the last occupants of the area. I also wanted to determine the relationship, if any, between the settlements around seasonal ponds in the adjacent dune field and those along the adjacent shore of the embayment. The recovery of a larger sample of animal remains and charcoal samples for radiocarbon dating was also an important goal. Accompanying me at Tushka were Claude Albritton; Rushdi Said; Bahay Issawi; Ron Wetherington, an archaeologist at SMU who wanted some experience in Egypt; Bill Hootkins, a high school student whose father was a friend of mine; Bob Slaughter, an SMU paleontologist; an Egyptian antiquities inspector; a cook; a servant; and a dozen Bedouin workers.

It was a long, hot drive from Aswan. We put up the kitchen and dining tents first. While the cook was organizing dinner and the sleeping tents were erected, I had everyone go sit in the dining tent to get out of the sun. I brought out a bottle of cold beer for each of us. Bob Slaughter emptied his in one big gulp, set it down, and asked for another. I told him that there was only enough beer for one bottle per person per day. To which Bob replied, "This field trip is going to be hell!"

Most of the sites in the Wadi Tushka area consisted of tight clusters of Qadan artifacts, including numerous grinding stones and many bones of large mammals, almost entirely wild cattle, with a few gazelle and hartebeest mixed in. There were numerous fish bones near the base of the silts or slightly worked into the top of the underlying windblown sands.

We dug a total of ten sites during our four weeks at Tushka. Five were associated with the carbonate-encrusted mounds that had once been the lowest hollows or swales in a dune field along the edge of a wide, shallow channel that had contained water during seasonal floods. We assumed that the low swales between the dune crests had collected seepage water during the floods and that this water remained for some period after the flood receded. Seepage water in the dunes is probably why some of the Qadan groups stayed on long after the flood had receded and left so many artifacts. Whatever the reason, the dune areas around the seepage ponds were rich in artifacts, cattle bones, and other animal remains.

The second brief session was Marks's one-man effort in January 1967. Of three weeks' duration, it was just long enough for him to complete the excavation of the graveyard at Jebel Sahaba. He recovered eight more burials.

Figure 1. Fred Wendorf at 20. Taken December 10, 1944, the day before he boarded the troop ship SS *Argentina* bound for Italy with the 10th Mountain Division. *Courtesy of Fred Wendorf. Photographer unknown.*

Figure 2. Fred's mother, Margaret Hall Wendorf, about age 22. *Courtesy of Fred Wendorf. Photo by Gentry Photographers, Dallas.*

Figure 3. Fred's father, Denver Fred Wendorf, about age 33. *Courtesy of Fred Wendorf. Photo by Bachrach Photographers, address unknown.*

Figure 4. Fred Wendorf at Hays, Kansas, in flight jacket ready for flight school, just before he was ordered to return to the infantry in May 1943. *Courtesy of Fred Wendorf. Photographer unknown.*

Figure 5. Fred Wendorf and Jess Nusbaum discuss a burial and associated pottery found during the first pipeline project. *Courtesy of Fred Wendorf. Photo by Mashek and Ziegler, photographers, Phoenix, Arizona.*

Figure 6. View of Los Cerros Mojinos (LA2569), a partially excavated site with a mixture of adobe and jacal walls. Twenty miles west of Las Lunas, New Mexico, the site was an archaeological salvage effort prior to the bringing in of construction equipment and pipe to the right-of-way. Tom Cummings, in charge of the excavations, at right. George Cattanach (at left with drafting board) assisted Cummings. *Photo by Fred Wendorf.*

Figure 7. View of the blowout where the Midland skull was found. At left, Fred Wendorf examines fossil bones partially exposed in the white sand in the bottom of the blowout. *Courtesy of Fred Wendorf. Photographer unknown.*

Figure 8. Nancy (holding Mike) and Fred Wendorf (holding Carl) in front of their home on Arcady Street in Santa Fe, July 1, 1954. *Courtesy of Fred Wendorf. Photographer unknown.*

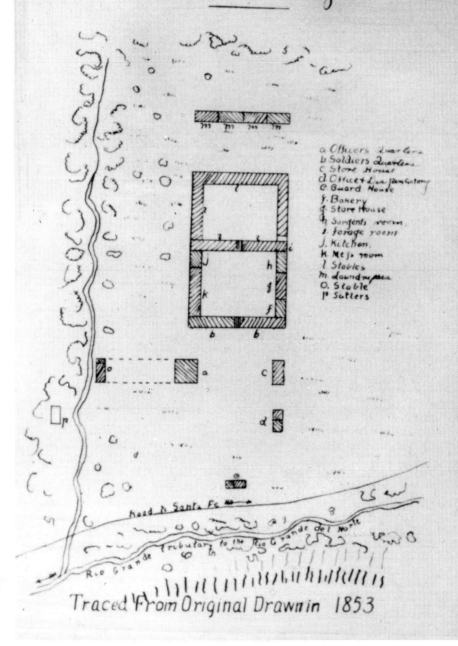

E

Cantonment Burgwin

a Officers Quarters
b Soldiers Quarters
c Stone House
d Office + Sm Jan Gatory
e Guard House
f Bakery
g Store House
h Sargents room
i Forage room
j Kitchen
k Mess room
l Stables
m Laundresses
o Stable
p Sutlers

Road to Santa Fe

Rio Grande Tributary to the Rio Grande del Norte

Rio Grande

Traced From Original Drawn in 1853

Figure 9. Colonel Mansfield's map of Cantonment Burgwin, drawn in 1853.
Courtesy of SMU-in-Taos.

Figure 10. W. W. Anderson's drawing of Cantonment Burgwin looking down the valley of the Little Rio Grande. Note the buildings on the floor of the valley in the middle distance. More than two hundred soldiers and officers were posted to the cantonment when this drawing was made. *Picture courtesy of Mrs. Virginia S. White, daughter of W. W. Anderson, and her family and heirs in Sumter, South Carolina.*

Figure 11. Drawing based on Anderson's sketch of Cantonment Burgwin (by an unknown staff artist at the Museum of New Mexico Laboratory of Anthropology). *Courtesy of SMU-in-Taos.*

Figure 12. Excavations of the enlisted men's quarters at Cantonment Burgwin, looking northwest, with the bakery oven in the corner. Note the wall traces of vertical logs set in deep trenches. Compare with Mansfield map, Figure 9. *Photo by Fred Wendorf.*

Figure 13. Looking east toward the reconstructed enlisted men's quarters at Cantonment Burgwin, 1960. The original building probably housed forty to forty-four men. *Photo by Fred Wendorf.*

Figure 14. Excavations at Pot Creek Pueblo, 1960. The basins and center post roof supports occur in most rooms. *Photo by Fred Wendorf.*

Figure 15. Excavation of a deep pit house at Site TA-20. Note the burials on the floor and the rocks on top of the skeletons (evidence of hostilities?). *Photo by Fred Wendorf.*

Figure 16. My four older children. From left to right: Michael, Gail, Carl, and Cindy. May 1963. *Photo by Fred Wendorf.*

Figure 17. Street scene in Wadi Halfa, Sudan. Our field headquarters is the white house on the right.
Photo by Fred Wendorf.

Figure 18. Richard Daugherty (left) and Genevieve Guichard (at right in distance) discover a rich, partially exposed Late Paleolithic site near Wadi Halfa. Note the animal bones and stone artifacts on the surface.
Photo by Fred Wendorf.

Figure 19. Eide Mariff, our Bedouin guide, helps excavate a Late Paleolithic burial at Tushka. *Photo by Fred Wendorf.*

Figure 20. Mary Beth Stokes and Nadia Mustapha sort artifacts at the lab at the field headquarters in Wadi Halfa. *Photo by Fred Wendorf.*

Figure 21. Anthony Marks points to a Late Paleolithic hearth dug into older sediments containing artifacts from a Late Middle Paleolithic Khormusan occupation. *Photo by Fred Wendorf.*

Figure 22. Site 440 in the Khor Musa, a deeply buried Middle Paleolithic locality, estimated to date between 100,000 to 130,000 years ago, with two occupation horizons in the fossil dune below a thick deposit of silts. Joel Shiner and Jean de Heinzelin (at left) discuss the complex stratigraphy. *Photo by Fred Wendorf.*

Figure 23. Jim Phillips points to the contact between a thick bed of dune sand at the base and underlying pond sediments. Site E-71-K12 near Esna. *Photo by Fred Wendorf.*

Figure 24. Claude Albritton (left), Rushdi Said (center), and Fred Wendorf (right) discuss the stratigraphy of the Nile sediments in the Fayum Depression. *Courtesy of Fred Wendorf. Photograper unknown.*

Figure 25. Romuald Schild classifies some of the hand axes recovered from a spring vent near Dakhla, Egypt. *Photo by Fred Wendorf.*

Figure 26. Peta and Fred Wendorf with children, Kelly (next to Peta) and Scott (next to Fred), at Gademotta, Ethiopia, in 1972. Note the excavations beyond the vehicle. *Courtesy of Fred Wendorf. Photographer unknown.*

Figure 27. Frank Servello excavating the depression at Site ETH-72-8B at Gademotta. The basin may be a hut; if so, it is among the earliest structures known. *Photo by Fred Wendorf.*

Figure 28. The Bodo skull, about 600,000 years old, found October 15, 1976, on the Kalb/Wendorf Ethiopian project to the Middle Awash. Originally thought to be *Homo erectus;* physical anthropologists have since classified it as "Archaic *Homo sapiens." Photo courtesy of Jon Kalb. Photographer unknown.*

Figure 29. Bahay Issawi supervises refueling the Russian Jeeps at Bir Sahara in February 1973. *Photo by Fred Wendorf.*

Figure 30. Ducks feeding at Bir Sahara East camp (in 1973) while cook watches from kitchen tent. Note water drums at left behind ducks. *Photo by Fred Wendorf.*

Figure 31. Crew at Bir Sahara East in 1973. Bedouin workers are seated; scientists are standing. *Courtesy of Fred Wendorf. Photographer unknown.*

Figure 32. Achilles Gautier, paleontologist, studies the large faunal remains found at Bir Tarfawi during 1974 season. *Photo by Fred Wendorf.*

Figure 33. Fuel stop in the desert on the return from Bir Sahara East in 1973. Russ Morrison and Vance Haynes (at right). *Photo by Fred Wendorf.*

Figure 34. Gail, Fred's daughter, project illustrator. Probably taken in 1990 at Nabta. *Photo by Fred Wendorf.*

Figure 35. Anne Attebury after the windstorm at Kharga in March 1967. *Photo by Fred Wendorf.*

Figure 36. View across Wadi Kubbaniya looking south. Note excavations beside the vehicle near center-left edge; several larger excavations near the right edge (white areas on floor of wadi). *Photo by Fred Wendorf.*

Figure 37. Screening sediment at Wadi Kubbaniya for carbonized edible plant remains. *Photo by Fred Wendorf.*

Figure 38. Angela Close at Wadi Kubbaniya classifies retouched stone tools and records their attributes on coding forms for later computer analysis. *Photo by Fred Wendorf.*

Figure 39. Surveyor and camp manager Ali Mazhar maps the stratigraphy in Wadi Kubbaniya. With Romuald Schild, he took 14,000 measurements, creating one of the most detailed maps of Pleistocene deposits ever made. *Photo by Fred Wendorf.*

Figure 40. Hanna Wieckowska, Polish archaeologist, examines a Late Paleolithic hearth area in Wadi Kubbaniya. *Photo by Fred Wendorf.*

Figure 41. Polydura Baker washes and screens sediment. Beside her is a Bedouin worker. Sandy Davis, a volunteer from Dallas, sits by the large screen. *Photo by Fred Wendorf.*

Figure 42. Herb Mosca, as a graduate student, points to the contact between playa sediments; the dark brown silts at the top buried an old dune on which huts were built and storage pits and water wells were dug. *Photo by Fred Wendorf.*

Figure 43. Excavations of an Early Neolithic hut floor dating between 8,050 and 7,900 years ago at Site E-75-6 in Nabta Playa. Halina Krolik and Romuald Schild examine the stratigraphy of the site, which was excavated in alternate quadrants. Note the saucerlike depressions in the exposed area of the hut floor, many of which were filled with ash and carbonized edible plant remains. *Photo by Fred Wendorf.*

Figure 44. Nieves Zedeño holds part of an open bowl with rocker-stamped design motif from an Al Jerar Early Neolithic occupation, dating between 7,800 and 7,300 years ago. Found in a storage pit at Nabta Playa. *Photo by Fred Wendorf.*

Figure 45. Completed casita dormitory at Fort Burgwin, ready for student occupants, August 1973.
Photo by Fred Wendorf.

Figure 46. View of area two miles north of Nabta basin; Kit Nelson and another student look for more sites.
Photo by Christy Bednar.

Figure 47. At Nabta Playa, Fred Wendorf examines a large stone partially buried in playa sediments (part of a megalithic alignment almost a km long). *Courtesy of Fred Wendorf. Photographer unknown.*

Figure 48. Romuald Schild examines an alignment of stones at Nabta, most of which can be refit into larger blocks in a megalithic alignment. *Photo by Fred Wendorf.*

Figure 49. Looking south across the Calendar Circle at Nabta. *Photo by Christy Bednar.*

Figure 50. Three unexcavated "Complex Structures" at Nabta. These may anticipate the large stone structures of Pharaonic Egypt. Marlin Downey in the center; Fred Wendorf and Romuald Schild at right; Marea Downey almost hidden beside Schild. *Photo by Christy Bednar.*

Figure 51. View of the pit at Nabta after the surface architecture was removed and a large shaped stone was exposed. *Photo by Fred Wendorf.*

Figure 52. The shaped stone, estimated to weigh five tons, found in the pit of the "Complex Structure" at Nabta. *Photo by Fred Wendorf.*

Figure 53. Camp at Nabta sited inside the arc of a large dune, 2006 field season. *Photo by Christy Bednar.*

The naming of the Fred Wendorf Information Commons commemorates a longstanding friendship and collaboration between Dr. Wendorf and Governor William P. Clements Jr. In 1971, at the suggestion of Dr. Wendorf, Governor Clements, then Chairman of SMU's Board of Trustees, realized the historic significance of the Fort Burgwin property and the important role it could play in SMU's academic programs. The resulting creation of the SMU-in-Taos campus provides SMU with a unique academic resource that contributes to the study and preservation of a prehistoric Pueblo and enriches SMU programs in Southwest studies as well as other academic offerings.

Dr. Fred Wendorf, Henderson-Morrison Distinguished Professor of Anthropology, joined the University in 1964. He was the founding faculty member of SMU's highly respected Department of Anthropology. Dr. Wendorf is an internationally recognized scholar as well as an outstanding researcher and teacher. He is respected for his many highly significant contributions to the archaeology of the Southwest and of Egypt. In 1987, his contributions in archaeology were recognized with his induction as a Fellow of the National Academy of Sciences.

Governor William P. Clements Jr. began his relationship with SMU in the mid-1930s as an undergraduate engineering student. He later served several...

Figure 54. Christy Bednar and Fred Wendorf stand beside the bronze plaque commemorating the dedication of the "Fred Wendorf Information Commons" at Fort Burgwin shortly after the opening ceremony in July 2004. *Courtesy of Christy Bednar. Photographer unknown.*

Figure 55. Fred Wendorf admires the laboratory/storage area for the Wendorf collection at the British Museum, London. *Photo by Christy Bednar.*

Wendorf Pottery Collection

Figure 56. Fred Wendorf lectures supporters of the Crow Canyon Archaeological Center during a visit to Nabta, February 2004. *Courtesy of Fred Wendorf. Photographer unknown.*

Excavations in the Nile Valley and Camp Life |
(1967–1969)

CHAPTER 19

D uring the final work in the Aswan Reservoir we'd become aware that we'd found numerous milling stones and hand stones in several of the Late Paleolithic sites we had excavated. We thought the grinding stones may have been used in processing cereals, either wild or domestic. At about the same time, we observed a gloss we mistakenly identified as "sickle sheen" on some of the small stone tools. And then a few months later, a pollen expert incorrectly identified barley pollen in some of our samples. Most of these "discoveries," in fact, all but the milling stones and hand stones, were later shown to be false. However, at the time we had moved north of Aswan, they were the major reason I believed that cereals may have been growing in the Egyptian Nile Valley during the Late Pleistocene. This was the reason I gave the NSF for proposing in 1966 a two-year test of that hypothesis involving both surveys and test excavations. I assumed, largely on the basis of Vignard's 1920s studies at Kom Ombo and our discoveries at Wadi Halfa and Tushka, that there'd be many Late Paleolithic sites in the Nile Valley north of Aswan. The proposal to the NSF was approved, and in January of 1967 we began surveying downstream from Aswan with hopes we might find evidence for the early use of wheat and barley, perhaps even cultivation.

Issawi set up a camp about fifteen miles north and a little west of Aswan on a sand sheet in the desert well back from the Nile. The Aswan camp was much like others Issawi had put up for us, consisting of a kitchen tent, a dining tent, a store tent, two or three tents for driver/mechanics, two for Biseri (our cook) and the servants (known as *sufraggis*), three or four tents for the Bedouin workers, and a tent for each scientist. We averaged between eight and ten scientists, including Said, Issawi, and our antiquities inspector, for a total of thirty men. It was an impressive camp of twenty or more tents, each containing a bed and mattress and an Egyptian pillow (the hardest thing

I have ever put my head on this side of a rock). We had sheets and two, sometimes three, wool blankets. In the desert beyond the Nile it sometimes fell below freezing at night.

The equipment in each tent included a water can, washbasin, kerosene lantern, and a wooden box for clothes and valuables. Some of us had a small table and chair. To create a camp like this cost between seventy-five and a hundred thousand dollars, not counting the vehicles. At first we borrowed tents from the Egyptian Geological Survey, but at the end of the 1967 project, we began to buy our own tents as funds allowed.

In many respects the camps were not different from the many geological survey camps set up all over the deserts of Egypt. In those camps, tents were arranged much like ours, in one or two straight lines, with the kitchen and servants' tents in the middle. In our camp the driver/mechanics were next to the cook's tent, and far out in the same direction were the tents for the Bedouin workers. The scientists' tents extended out from the dining tent in a long line in the opposite direction, with the tents for the most senior people (Schild and me) at the far end. The camp manager had his tent near the cooking/dining area, which allowed him to keep track of things, to get an early cup of tea each morning, and to keep up with the latest gossip. Geological survey camps were usually set up for a year or longer; ours sometimes had to be moved at least once during a field season; thus we had no permanent or elaborate fixtures. It is worth noting that both the geological survey and our group had a firm rule: no driving through the camp. A vehicle would leave tracks and break the crust on the sand that keeps it from blowing around in a high wind.

Biseri, our superb cook from Wadi Halfa, ran the kitchen those first years. Later, we employed a series of excellent cooks who had retired from the geological survey. These men were used to living and working in the desert and cooking on the simple equipment we had. Our food was clean, plentiful, varied, and properly prepared. We never contracted any food-borne diseases. The menu did not cater to American tastes, but was Egyptian, and when we were far from any source of supply, our Egyptian cook leaned on dried foods: peas, beans, okra, potatoes, turnips, and the like. The cook would usually start a vegetable garden by throwing the used dishwater every day over the plants he sowed. He would begin to harvest about two weeks before we were scheduled to return to civilization. When fresh food was available nearby, the cook always served tomatoes and several kinds of greens.

We ate heartily because we worked hard. When the camp was far from the work site, there were only two main meals. One was a breakfast of lentil soup, or *ta'miyya* (fried ground chickpeas), or *ful* (slow-cooked beans with spices). Dinner, the other, consisted of macaroni, potatoes, or rice, peas; carrots, sometimes okra or spinach; and rarely meat, fish, or chicken, prepared with savory sauces.

One of our cooks liked to serve mashed potatoes in a pile he shaped like a sitting rooster, with a head and neck, using peas for eyes, a small carrot for a beak, and a strip of carrot as a cock's comb. We often had Jell-O for dessert, but on special evenings there might be a cake, or a crème caramel if there were eggs. For those working far from camp, the noon meal was skimpier, consisting of a piece of fruit, usually an orange, a can of sardines (or a can or two of tuna if the field party was large), and some dried, hard *baladi* (country) bread. The graduate students referred to our camp and its food as the "Sahara Hilton." The tasty food, plus the hard, interesting work, including the opportunity to make new contributions to knowledge, kept the students coming back.

At the Aswan camp we returned to the practice I'd initiated in Sudanese Nubia. The staff always included two or three senior graduate students. We assumed the students would identify a problem that interested them that they could use for their dissertations. There were two such students on the Aswan staff for the 1967 field season: Jim Phillips, an SMU graduate student working as my lab assistant, and a graduate student from Columbia University, David Lubell.

When we arrived in Cairo before proceeding to Aswan, I asked both of them to go shopping for several items we would need in camp: notebooks, paper, carbon paper, pencils, pens, drawing instruments, grid paper, a roll of drafting paper, a roll of tracing paper, string, and other things for recording our archaeological research. When I gave them the list, I also gave them money and told them not to forget to get a receipt. If they forgot, I might make them pay for it. Phillips asked where they'd find all this stuff, and I told them to start at Secretary Street. He asked where that was, and I said it was up toward Opera Square. When they returned later that day, arms full of packages and pockets full of receipts, they'd learned how to get around in downtown Cairo. Thus began one of our best traditions—involving everyone in every aspect of our research and camp life.

For many years the Bedouin workers made our bread at the same time they made theirs, in the evening after work. We provided the flour. They made unleavened bread, which they rolled out like a large tortilla on a flat, round iron sheet (probably using the top of a water or fuel barrel) with a low fire underneath. To thin and shape the bread they used one or two hard, round, smooth sticks from an acacia tree that grew near their home at Esna. The roller-stick was about a half to three-quarters of an inch in diameter and eighteen inches long. They used the stick to flip the bread so it would thin evenly and cook on both sides. When freshly cooked, the bread was tender and delicious. A day or so later it got hard and difficult to eat unless it was first moistened with water.

Most of the Bedouins were hard workers, and several made an effort to learn English. I liked all of them, even the lazy ones. My Arabic was never good; it consisted of two hundred words I wrote on note cards and carried around with me to study every day. The Bedouins frequently invited us foreigners to have tea with them in the evening. All of the scientists would attend. They served a strong, dark brew, about half sugar. Some evenings they entertained us with Bedouin dances, with one or two of the men dressed as women. They would sing songs and urge us to participate. One of their favorite ditties was translated to me as "The Women of Esna." None of the other Egyptians would sing the song.

Photographs, particularly the Polaroid pictures that take only a minute to develop, enchanted the Bedouins. Near the end of the field season I always saved a packet of Polaroid film to take a picture of everyone in camp to give to all the members of the group. The Bedouins and everyone else would gather by the vehicles to receive their picture. For the occasion the Bedouins wore clean *gallabiyas* (gowns), pulling back their sleeves to show us their wristwatches. Displaying their watches was a way to show others how wealthy they were. It was a happy occasion for everyone.

The most important difference between our camps and those of the geological survey was in the beverages we drank. Muslims do not drink alcohol. We foreigners, however, consumed respectable quantities of beer and wine, and sometimes, stronger spirits. Each evening, about 6:00 P.M., after everyone had washed up and made their notes, we'd gather in the dining tent for roasted peanuts and beer. Beer sold for about thirty piasters a liter bottle, and it was good, the equivalent of many European beers—as well it should have been, since the brewers of Stella beer in Belgium provided the formula for it. The only problem was that when we bought beer we had to exchange an empty bottle to get a full one, and Issawi had to do a lot of scouring around to find sufficient empties to get enough beer to last a season.

We tried to divide the beer and wine from each bottle evenly, but that didn't work. Breakage of glassware in transport resulted in several sizes being used for both beer and wine, and disputes over who got the most were frequent. I decided to buy a large plastic measuring cup when I was next in a town. An elaborate ritual soon developed. We elected Schild to pour. All of us watched closely as Schild first determined if the bottle contained a full liter (many did not). Then he calculated when half the bottle had been dispensed, filling each with the same amount. After the first measure, he poured the second half, also equally. The pouring ceremony was never taken too seriously. It provided a pleasant break after the monotony and hard work of the day.

During these glorious days we also had wine with dinner. Our ration for wine was two bottles for the entire table at dinner. Sometimes it was Omar Khay-yam Red, sometimes Cleopatra White. Neither was a great wine, but in the desert we couldn't be too selective. Local Egyptian wines were all that were available at our price. We purchased both the beer and the wine at liquor stores in Cairo and brought them to camp with the other supplies.

The small quantities of beer and wine we consumed never caused a problem, in camp or elsewhere. We had been out in the bright sun, often with bitter cold, high winds, and blowing sand for over eight hours, and the alcohol was just enough to relax us so we could enjoy the evening and face the next day.

I sometimes wondered what our auditors at the university who looked at my receipts (in Arabic, but carefully translated) every year must have thought. They must have been even more puzzling to the federal auditors. The camp managers always bought the alcohol, along with the food. The beer receipts usually read "140 bottles of fooding materials"; wine receipts read "70 bottles of fooding materials." Alcohol was against regulations and I'm sure no one was fooled. The auditors most probably thought if we were crazy enough to go out in the middle of the Sahara for eight to ten weeks, then a little liquid refreshment shouldn't be denied.

My students and I tried to arrive in Cairo on January 2nd or 3rd for the field season. Issawi often met our plane. He would see us to our hotel, the Garden City House, a small pension near downtown about two hundred yards from the American embassy. The staff came to know us well, greeted us with smiles and hugs. It was not a fancy place. The mattresses were filled with something hard, probably camel's hair, but the hotel was convenient and clean, and we could get a room and two meals for twenty dollars a night. I always reserved a room with a bath, and that, plus meals, cost twenty-five dollars a night. The Polish members of our group usually arrived two or three days later. I gave everyone a per diem large enough to cover the hotel plus a bit more to cover the third meal and a beer.

Without enthusiasm (we hated the smog and traffic), we would spend a week in Cairo getting supplies, confirming the arrangements for travel to the field, meeting antiquities and other Egyptian officials, and getting permits. We would take an overnight train if we were working near Aswan, and go from there to our camp. If not, our drivers would take us directly to camp. The day after our arrival we unpacked our equipment and were prepared to work the next day. Most of the time when I was director of the expedition we spent eight weeks in the field. It was a hard eight weeks:

seven days a week without a break. A few times we worked for ten weeks, but that was our limit. After that "camp fever" affected us all. When we returned to Cairo we'd spend another week in the Garden City House. We had to examine the collections, and after the "partition" (one for us, one for the Egyptians), we had to pack the pieces given to us and make arrangements for their shipment. After that, those of us still in Cairo would have a party at a nearby restaurant with good food and plenty of wine while we talked over the results of the field season. It was a good life.

Apparently I didn't learn a thing from the tragedy of my divorce from Nancy, because I left Peta and Kelly alone in 1967 while I went off to Africa for a long field season along the west bank north of Aswan. This was my pattern even after the birth of my youngest son, Scott, who was born in 1968. It was not until 1972 that my family was again able to join me, this time in Ethiopia.

I found once again that my long absences were taking a toll, and Peta and I had many arguments about the enforced estrangement my job was causing us. In my defense, I don't think Peta, Kelly, and Scott would have been happy in a tent that is hot during the day and icy cold at night; it was different from living in a house in Wadi Halfa. And we worked all day, seven days a week, and my family would have seen little of me. Such was my rationalization. Schild and I briefly considered renting a house in Aswan and bringing our wives and children out so we could visit them each weekend, but both Peta and Krystyna Schild rejected the idea, knowing they would not be happy alone all week in Aswan. It was also a bad idea for our work, since we had a crew who worked seven days a week. None of the men would have been happy sitting in a tent for the two days a week we went home to our families in Aswan.

The budget for the 1967 field season included funds for two new pickups. Following Issawi's recommendation, I bought two two-wheel-drive Ford pickups. We had two battered Ford pickups we'd used during the work in the Egyptian portion of the Aswan Reservoir, and I borrowed a lorry from the Egyptian Geological Survey. Using three of the four pickups (the fourth was needed to get water for the camp), the first thing we did on January 10, 1967, was drive to Wadi Kubbaniya, the first wadi on the west bank north of Aswan, about six miles. As soon as we drove into the wadi, we saw that it contained numerous rich Late and Final Paleolithic sites. Most of these sites were embedded in dunes and silts on the floor of the wadi. We saw numerous grinding stones scattered over the surface or partially buried in the dunes.

We made our first mistake when we decided not to work at Kubbaniya that field season. We stupidly thought the whole Nile Valley must be filled with Paleolithic sites. We needed to continue our survey down the Nile, and since the Kubbaniya sites were not threatened, we decided to leave them and excavate there the following year. But a war intervened, and it was fifteen years later, in 1977, before we could return.

Kubbaniya was where one of my favorite graduate students, Jim Phillips, learned an important lesson useful to all of us. It was Phillips's first season in the field with us, a hot mid-morning, and he was thirsty. He reached for one of the cloth water bags hanging on the front of one of the pickups, and disregarding the warnings of the driver and workmen who gathered around, he took a big drink, and hung the bag back where it had been. The men had been trying to tell Jim that the water was not potable. It had come from the Nile and was to be used for the truck radiator.

That night, about 2:00 A.M., as I often do, I went out to the latrine. I saw a light in the far distance, to the north. It was moving parallel with the river a good quarter-mile from camp. The light passed in front of me a similar distance, too far to see what or who it was. The light kept moving and went on off to the south, about a quarter-mile from where I was standing. Then the light started back, but this time it passed about a hundred yards in front of me. I recognized it was Jim Phillips carrying a lantern.

"Jim," I called, "what're you doing out here?" He gave a big cry of relief and came running toward me. He had been sick with diarrhea and had taken a lantern to find a place away from camp; he'd become disoriented, and couldn't find his way back to camp. He had been walking for almost two hours, he said. He was dehydrated and ill. I roused Biseri and a servant or two, and we got Jim back to his tent, gave him some good water and antidiarrhea medicine, and put him to bed.

Phillips's experience provided several important lessons for all of us: Never drink water whose source is unknown to you. Listen when an Egyptian worker warns you about anything; he feels a strong responsibility to take care of you. Stay close to camp. If you take a lantern, set it on the ground next to your tent before walking into the desert. Light will reflect off the white tent walls so the camp tents will be visible from a considerable distance. A good flashlight is even better because it will throw light farther than a lantern and make it even easier to find camp.

Downstream about fifty miles from Wadi Kubbaniya, in the next large embayment known as El Kilh, we found another group of Late and Final Paleolithic sites in a planned reclamation area that was soon to be developed. Some forty miles farther downstream, just north of Esna, we discovered another large embayment with numerous Late and Final Paleolithic sites in an area already under reclamation. We decided to split the team and have a small group return to El Kilh to begin excavations there, while the rest of the group would begin excavating those sites in the Esna embayment that had not been destroyed. Most of the reclamation in the Esna area had been confined to leveling the silts and excavating large trenches to carry irrigation water.

Consequently, the numerous sites in the sandy areas between the silts were essentially undamaged. Several different lithic industries were represented at both El Kilh and

Map 4. Map of the area in Egypt from Wadi Kubbaniya in the south to Qena in the north. Filled circles indicate Late Paleolithic sites excavated by the Combined Prehistoric Expedition. Clusters of sites occurred near Qena (1968), Deir Fakhuri (1967), Idfu (1967), Wadi Kubbaniya (1978; 1981–1984), and Wadi Abu Suberia in the south. Drafted by Chris and Cheryl Hill.

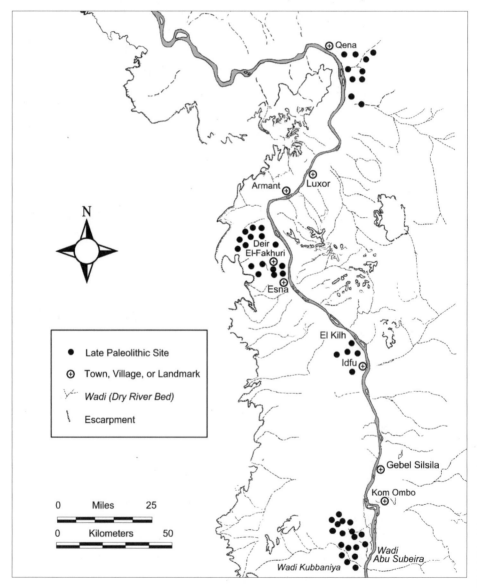

Esna. Only one was closely similar to those we excavated near Wadi Halfa. The exception was a Sebilian assemblage at El Kilh.

At this stage of our investigations we were looking for evidence of cereal use, possibly cultivation, and we noted that there were many grinding stones in these sites near Esna, particularly those of an entity we named Isnan, stratigraphically one of the most recent industries in the area. It was from one of these Isnan sites we collected sediment samples containing pollen, which was at first incorrectly identified as barley.

In 1968 and again in 1969 we continued our downstream surveys and small-scale excavations. Achilles Gautier, a distinguished paleontologist from Belgium, joined our field team in 1968. Gautier had been analyzing our collections of animal remains from our early days in Nubia, but he had never been in the field with us.

Another new member of our group in 1968 was Vance Haynes. I had known him years ago as an air force lieutenant at Sandia Base in Albuquerque. His father was the commanding general of Sheppard Air Force Base in Wichita Falls, Texas, and Vance often came by my office at the Laboratory of Anthropology in Santa Fe to talk with me about Early Man sites in the area. Now he is a highly regarded Pleistocene geologist with a special interest in Early Man in the New World. He had come with us to Egypt to help with radiocarbon dating and to broaden his experience.

The third new member of our group in 1968 was Bob Dubois, a specialist in archeomagnetic dating from the University of Oklahoma. I had high hopes that between Vance and Bob's skills, we would get some consistent dates for the archaeology we would excavate, but the results were mostly disappointing.

We did a survey of the west bank from the Temple of Dandara to a few miles north of Luxor. We found several sites on the west bank, but all were heavily deflated, so we moved to the east bank, to the Dishna embayment. There we found and excavated several sites of the Isnan industry, and two more that were Sebilian. Stratigraphically, all were embedded in silts deposited near the end of the Late Pleistocene. Several of the excavated sites yielded promising dates.

It was during this 1968 field season that I realized Schild and I complemented each other with different skills and interests. When we came to a promising new spot, Schild would walk around the whole area to gain an initial impression of different sedimentary units present and their relative ages. Then he would have a group of workers dig a series of long trenches to determine the stratigraphic relationships recorded in the sediments. This occupied much of his time at each locality. Meanwhile, I looked for archaeological sites, evaluating them for possible excavation, then selected the first sites to be excavated. There was constant communication between us and other members of the field team. I believe this complementary, rather than

competitive, association has been the major element in our successful working relationship. I thought that he needed me, and I *knew* I needed him.

The 1968 field season had been a long one and there was more to come. We were
working north of Luxor when I decided we needed a weekend in a good hotel. There
were no tourists in Egypt that year because of the Egyptian/Israeli war in 1967, and I
was sure we could get rooms. Everyone packed a bag of clean clothes, and we got in
our pickups and drove to a felucca (small boat) landing near a train station. Everyone
jumped out of the trucks, grabbed their bags, and walked about seventy-five feet down
to where the felucca would pull in. There we sat down to wait for the boat.

Jim Phillips thought he spoke good Arabic. He had learned Hebrew in his youth
and thought Arabic wasn't so hard. Perhaps too haughty for his own good, Phillips got
out of the truck and said to his driver, "Bring my bag down to me there." He pointed.

The driver looked puzzled, because what Phillips had said to him was "Take my
bag back with you." The driver put the bag back in the pickup and drove away.

When Phillips sat down next to me I said, "Move somewhere else, Jim, I don't
want to sit next to anyone who won't carry his own bag."

With that Phillips jumped up, crying, "Bag! Bag! Where's my bag?" Ahmed Said
Hindi, our great friend and longtime antiquities inspector, grabbed Phillips and took
him up the hill where the trucks had been, the last one about a half-mile away moving
in a cloud of dust. But Jim was lucky. There was a taxi, the only taxi on the west bank
for a hundred miles. Ahmed Hindi and Phillips got in the taxi, and Ahmed told the
driver, "Follow that truck."

Our camp was about five miles from the felucca dock, and about a mile off the
road against a low scarp, behind a pile of low sand dunes. The taxi driver, not accustomed to driving in loose sand, drove into the dunes and promptly got stuck. Jim and
Ahmed jumped out and started shouting and waving their arms. The drivers were just
getting out of their trucks. They heard the noise and saw the figures jumping up and
down, and one of them said, "Isn't that Ahmed and that crazy student Jim Phillips?"
The drivers drove back to them, put Phillips, his luggage, and Ahmed Hindi in the
truck, and headed back, leaving the poor taxi driver behind. Phillips and Ahmed Hindi
got across the river on the next boat, and just as our train started moving, they raced
alongside and managed to board. The taxi was gone when we returned three days later.

In 1969 we wanted to move our operations north to the Fayum Depression. This
required a new grant proposal to the NSF. Most of the text of my proposal was a
description of what we had found in the 1967 and '68 seasons, with emphasis on the

pollen that we identified as barley, and the associated grinding stones. The rest of the proposal was drawn from Gertrude Caton-Thompson and E. W. Gardner's two-volume book *The Desert Fayum*, in which they described two entities: the one they thought the earlier, Fayum A; the other, identified as Fayum B, lacking pottery and having a bladelet technology. They regarded Fayum B as a degenerate, and later, desert group. My proposal was approved and funded at the amount requested.

After the NSF grant came through another problem emerged over our Egyptian permit. After Rushdi Said's difficult, but ultimately successful, effort to get a security permit, we went to the north side of the Fayum Depression. There, we soon found out why the security people had been so difficult. The Egyptian army was preparing to return to the Sinai after a two-year absence. As part of their training they fired artillery over our camp to a target area several miles to our north. I was fearful that a "short round" might fall into our camp. It never happened, but we were nervous in our excavations as artillery shells passed overhead.

After we dug only a few test pits, it was soon apparent that several of Caton-Thompson's "Fayum B" sites were *in situ* (she'd thought all were on the surface). We called this lithic industry Qarunian. The excavations disclosed that this Terminal Paleolithic entity was stratigraphically earlier than the "Fayum A" Neolithic, thus reversing Caton-Thompson's sequence.

The Fayum Depression contained sediments recording a complicated sequence of four episodes of lake aggradation and recession during the Holocene. We gave these lakes names, beginning with *Paleomoeris* (preserved as deepwater deposits only and estimated to date between 10,000 to 9,500 years ago. So far as we could tell, there was no associated archaeology); *Premoeris* (8,500 to 8,000 years ago, with early Qarunian); *Protomoeris* (7,500 to 7,000 years ago, with later Qarunian); and *Moeris* (6,400 to 2,300 years ago, initially with Fayum Neolithic). The water in these lakes was derived entirely from the Nile. It is highly likely that each lake event reflected a change in the level of the river.

The archaeology associated with the Premoeris and Protomoeris lake sediments, the Qarunian industry, is characterized by high frequencies of arch-backed and pointed straight-backed bladelets, notches, and denticulates, and a few geometric elements. The pointed straight-backed bladelets have truncated or retouched bases. Bone tools are present, mostly small harpoons made of modified catfish jaws.

The associated faunal remains indicate that the Qarunian economy was based on fishing. There were numerous fish bones in every site. Large-mammal hunting was also practiced to a limited extent, and the presence of grinding stones indicates some processing of plants. The Qarunian sites seem to represent seasonal fish-harvesting localities occupied during low-water periods when the fish would be concentrated in the ponds, most likely from winter to late spring.

The first true Neolithic economy, with pottery and food production, indicated by ceramics and cultivated wheat and barley and domestic animals, occurs in the Fayum around 6,400 years ago (Caton-Thompson's Fayum A), and coincides with a rising level of the Moeris Lake that was terminated by the barrage (small dam) built by Amenemhat I, around 1900 B.C. As far as lithic components are concerned, these Fayum Neolithic communities appear to have no connection with the preceding Qarunian.

As the field season in the Fayum was nearing its end in early March 1969, I decided to have a party after our successful season. I wanted to celebrate the fact that the army had stopped sending shells over our heads and that no short rounds had landed near our camp. When I mentioned my plans to Issawi he was enthusiastic and suggested we have the party in the nearby Old Kingdom temple of Kasr El-Sagha. He'd said he'd take a crew of workers and remove the accumulated sand inside. A couple of days later, Issawi said he'd get some carpets to put down in the old temple, and maybe hire a few dancing girls. The more I thought about it, the less inclined I was to approve his plans. I knew the gossips would surely hear about it, and I could envision the jokes being passed around among archaeologists everywhere. I could guess how a party like this might be received at home and at the National Science Foundation, too. So, before things went any further, I called the party off. Better for the expedition to have a squeaky-clean reputation than to be known as a bunch of party boys.

It isn't that we never had fun. Our Fayum camp was on the northwest edge of the Fayum Depression, not far from the city of Fayum, which had a liquor store with a good supply of Egyptian wines. I think each of the scientists in the camp, with the exception of Issawi, drank. This included Claude Albritton, Achilles Gautier, Rushdi Said, David Lubell, Jim Phillips, Roman Schild, and me.

Each night when everyone went to bed the servants would clean up the empty bottles and put them in a pile behind the dining tent. Near the end of the field season that pile formed a pyramid about a meter high and a meter and half in diameter. A week before the season ended, a group who had gone for more wine at the liquor store returned and told us we'd drunk up all of the store's stock of wine. There'd be no more wine for a month. No one was interested in beer or the hard stuff. Our party was over, probably just in time.

Schild, who had a well-earned reputation for never passing up a toast without a shot of good Polish vodka, told me several months later that when he went home his mother took one look at him and said, "Oh, son, you look terrible." Schild told her,

"Yes, mother, I feel so sick, I think I am going to die. I did too much partying." Then he went to bed for several days. He was hung over, but he didn't want her to know.

We closed down the camp and most of us moved to Cairo. A few, Schild, Phillips, and Lubell, went directly home. Others, including Said, Albritton, and I, were invited to a dinner party at the Nile Hilton given by Mr. and Mrs. John Dorman. He was the director of the American Research Center in Cairo. The party was to celebrate Albritton's departure for the United States later that night. When the party broke up we headed for the elevator and were joined by Nahed Sabre, a belly dancer who had just performed for us. Nahed Sabre was a good friend of Mrs. Dorman's. Mrs. Dorman made introductions all around, and then proposed a great idea. She told Nahed Sabre we were all on our way to the airport to put Albritton on the airplane for home, and asked her to join us. She accepted. Because of Nahed Sabre, who was famous in Egypt, we were allowed to go on the tarmac to put Albritton on the plane, and as he went up the stairs Nahed Sabre sent him off with a couple of "twists."

About three weeks later a mailing tube addressed to Albritton arrived at his office at SMU, and, as she was supposed to do, his secretary opened it. A large colored poster of Nahed Sabre, in all her glory and limited clothing, slipped out. The inscription at the bottom read: "For my Darling Claude With All My Love, Your Nahed Sabre."

Albritton's secretary gathered a few tacks and put the poster on the bulletin board for all to see. Albritton came in a few minutes later, saw the poster and its inscription, and ducked down to much laughter from the whole office. Word got around the university, and all day long people dropped by to give Albritton a salute and a laugh.

It was at the Fayum that we first used a new (to me) technique for locating buried occupation horizons in areas of deflated artifacts. Many of the Qarunian sites in the Fayum occurred with eroded dry lake sediments, mostly from small pools where people came to harvest fish. From the surface we could never tell the direction of the bedding of the underlying sediments. There was no way to determine the position, slope, and placement of the earlier lake pools. Sometimes there was more than one, and all had different bedding angles. These sites were usually seriously deflated, but we noted that a few fresh artifacts often occurred within this mantle of surface debris. These fresh artifacts had to have been recently exposed, or the wind and sand would have quickly blunted their flaked surfaces. The presence of unworn artifacts alerted us to the probable presence of one or more buried occupation horizons, but where and in what direction and on what plane?

To locate the buried occupation horizon (or horizons), we collected a handful of small sticks. Several of us got down on our hands and knees and crawled across the surface looking carefully at each artifact. When we found a fresh artifact we poked a little stick into the sand beside it. Then we'd stand off to the side where we could see the emplaced sticks. They usually occurred in a clear band, maybe a meter wide, across the area of wind-abraded surface artifacts. A trench dug at right angles across this line of sticks disclosed the buried occupation surface and the direction of its slope, and then we could properly excavate the rest of the site.

During 1969, the security situation became increasingly precarious in Egypt. Because of Soviet influence on Egyptian security, we were told that our group could not work anywhere in Egypt. Said, Schild, and I decided this would be a good time for us to write a book about the results of our three years' research on the prehistory of the Nile Valley. We agreed that the best time and place to write the book would be during the summer of 1970 in the mountains of northern New Mexico, at the Fort Burgwin Research Center. I had sufficient funds in my NSF and Smithsonian grants to bring both Said and Schild to Taos.

About two weeks before Said was to depart for New Mexico, he was appointed general director of the Egyptian General Organization for Mining and Mineral Research and director of the Egyptian Geological Survey. It was a position he had long sought and could not decline. After we received Said's letter, Schild and I decided to go ahead and write our portions of the book. Everything was ready; the text figures were drawn, the artifact counts completed, the results of the analyses in hand, the fauna identified. Most important, we were ready to write. Schild would dictate on the stratigraphy for a while (no one but he could read his writing), then I would write sections on the artifacts; then we'd go back to Schild until we finished our goal for the day. Both our wives, and most of my children, were with us at the research center, so we set a goal of completing at least six pages each day, before lunch, so we could take trips with our families. If we failed to reach our goal, it was back to work after lunch until the required pages were finished. I believe Roman and his wife Krystyna were with us for about eight weeks, and we worked every day, so that when they left we had a two-hundred-plus-page manuscript. There was a lot more to do before the manuscript would be ready to publish, including getting it typed and edited. Then we'd have to persuade Said, the new director of Egypt's geological survey, to find the time to write his section on the geology.

During this period of writing in New Mexico, Schild and I forged a deep friendship. We had liked each other from the beginning, and during three long seasons of joint field research, I developed the highest regard for his scholarship, his integrity, and his dedication to research. I now feel he is my brother.

••••

Looking back, I think an important reason for my success in obtaining the many grants from the NSF and the Foreign Currency Program of the Smithsonian to support my research in North Africa was the fact that most of my projects were longitudinal; that is, the research was designed to be done over a period of several years. This was clearly stated in the first proposal I submitted for a several-year project. The NSF usually only funded me for one year, but if they funded the first phase of the project they would have made a significant investment in vehicles, tents, and other equipment so that they usually wanted to continue the support, if the research was successful.

Another important factor in the success of my proposals is that I always promptly published the results of my research. I believe unpublished research not only wastes money, but also wastes archaeological resources. I share that view with most staff members of every organization that has supported my research. If someone has had an earlier grant or two from a foundation, but has not provided a report on what was learned, I doubt if another proposal would be favorably received.

I think another, perhaps more important, factor that supported my research funding is that from the beginning of my work in Africa I always included Egyptian and Polish colleagues as full participants. This may have been more significant during those periods when there was friction between the American government and Egypt during the time of Nasser, or America and communist Poland, and perhaps some bureaucrat might have wanted a show of friendship. This governmental friction never surfaced in our work or in my personal relationships with my Egyptian and Polish colleagues.

National Science Foundation Science Departmental Development Award for SMU
(1969–1973)

CHAPTER 20

A s part of the *Sputnik* reaction, around 1963 Congress directed the NSF to develop a five-year Science Departmental Development Program to enhance graduate studies in the sciences by making awards to selected departments of $250,000. Most of these awards went to the "hard" sciences, although a few went to sociology, psychology, and economics departments. No anthropology department had yet received an award. In 1969 the NSF announced there was to be one more round of awards in their Science Departmental Development Program, and SMU decided to enter the contest. I assumed the university administration would select one of the long-established departments to apply for the grant, such as geology, statistics, or economics. I was so sure that anthropology would not be asked to compete that I didn't even send the provost a letter expressing an interest.

One day Neil McFarland called me and asked if I'd be interested in competing for this Science Departmental Grant. He said that the university had decided that the anthropology department was more likely than any other to be successful, and he asked me to begin preparing a proposal.

I immediately got the departmental faculty together, told them the news, and asked for their suggestions. If awarded, the grant would be for $250,000 over three years, to be spent for new faculty, graduate student stipends, and equipment. The grant would be "front-end loaded," with most of the money to be spent in the first two years for faculty salaries. The university would pick up all faculty salaries in the third year. We didn't need any additional equipment; we had gotten everything we needed with the new Heroy Building.

There was general agreement that a significant portion should go for graduate student stipends, but we couldn't agree about what new faculty to propose. We spent several days discussing which specialties should be represented before we agreed on six new positions: a physical anthropologist with an interest in fossil man, two social anthropologists interested in applied anthropology, a linguist, a prehistorian with interest in Sub-Saharan Africa, and a geoarchaeologist (who would be assigned to the geology department). I already had Vance Haynes in mind for the latter position.

I had no idea how many departments were competing with us, and no one ever told me. The guide provided by the NSF did not tell me how many departments would be considered. It did tell me that the goal was to enhance the science faculties, the quality of the graduate students, and the equipment needed for research. With these points in mind I wrote the proposal. The university approved it and submitted it to a special office in the NSF for evaluation and review.

Several months later I was asked to go to Washington to meet the staff member, a sociologist by training, who was reviewing our proposal. He told me he was not favorably inclined toward our proposal because of the way we'd structured the new faculty. He went on to say that our proposed new faculty was too academically oriented and not sufficiently devoted to applied research. He thought it highly unlikely a proposal with that emphasis would be supported.

I returned to Dallas depressed. About three weeks later my sociologist evaluator called again to say that he wanted me to come back to Washington to meet with him again. He wanted to suggest some changes that would make the proposal more acceptable.

Near the end of my second visit, after I'd agreed to the changes he wanted, he told me that Congressman Earl Cabell of Dallas, a ranking member of the subcommittee on appropriations for the NSF, had called to find out the status of the SMU proposal. Cabell told the director of the NSF he had a special interest in that proposal, adding that he wanted to be kept informed. He may have read about the proposal in reports he received from the NSF, or perhaps someone (not I, and I do not know who) may have talked to him and asked for his help.

I made one concession I regret. The fossil man specialist was changed to a physical anthropologist with interest in modern populations. Only then would my sociology friend approve the proposal. A few days later we got the grant.

At the time the grant was awarded, we had grown slowly to a faculty of eleven, with thirty graduate students; now suddenly there were to be seventeen full-time faculty and more than fifty graduate students. It took considerable thought and effort to integrate all of them into the department.

On the whole, we made good choices with regard to the new faculty and students, but neither of the two new social anthropologists stayed long. Both told me they disliked Dallas. Both obtained good appointments at major universities (one at Columbia, the other at Berkeley). To replace them, in 1973 we hired Ben Wallace and Robert Van Kemper, both applied social anthropologists, who are still active and at SMU. Van Kemper is the current chair of the department. There were two new physical anthropologists, but one of them left when he didn't get tenure. Laddy Novak remained. In 1972 we hired Garth Sampson, an archaeologist with interests in southern Africa and the application of science to archaeology. Sampson stayed with us, too, and retired in June 2007.

I may have made a mistake in placing Vance Haynes in the geology department. He left after three years. Haynes had received the same arrangement with the administration I had when I came to SMU; that is, he was to teach one semester and do research the remainder of the year. Vance was very active while he was at SMU. He taught Quaternary geology and Paleoindian geology. At Bill Heroy's request he established the radiocarbon dating laboratory at SMU and hired Herbert Haas as coprincipal investigator. But Vance's wife, Taffy, was not happy. She didn't like Dallas and loved Tucson. It wasn't long until he received an offer from the University of Arizona, and Vance accepted it. Could I have persuaded him to stay?

The Science Departmental Development Grant made it possible for me to bring distinguished visiting professors for two- and three-year appointments to the faculty. Joel Shiner directed our field school at Fort Burgwin, but we needed someone with a stronger interest in Southwestern archaeology. My first distinguished visitor appointment was Erik Reed, who had recently retired from the National Park Service as the regional archaeologist in the Southwest. He joined the SMU faculty in the fall of 1971. He was widely regarded as one of the most important theoretical archaeologists working in the American Southwest. Unfortunately, Erik was at SMU only a year when he became ill and had to return to Santa Fe. I was sorry to lose him because his interests in archaeological theory filled a void in our faculty.

My next distinguished visitor appointment was J. O. Brew, my former professor at Harvard, who had just retired as the director of the Peabody Museum. He came in the fall of 1972 and left in the spring of 1976.

In 1973 George Trager, an internationally prominent scholar in anthropological linguistics, asked if I could find jobs at SMU for him and his wife Felicia (who had a PhD in linguistics). I went to friends at the English department and asked if they would like to have Trager and his wife half-time in their department. If so, I planned to hire both of them half-time for the anthropology department. There was an immediate, positive response. They wanted George Trager to teach a course in their department. He was appointed full professor with tenure, and Felicia, assistant professor, without tenure. She taught linguistic anthropology in our department, but wasn't popular with the students and some of the faculty. Three years later George asked me to put Felicia up for promotion with tenure. I groaned.

"I can't do that," I told him. "She'd never make it through the faculty, and even if she did, the dean would probably veto it." It wasn't long before George told me they were leaving. Felicia had found a job in Illinois. She died a year later, and George went to California to be near his sons. He was a great scholar and a good friend. It was a personal loss when they left.

During this interval when everything seemed to be going so well, with a new building and several exciting new faculty members, I encouraged the many amateur archaeologists in the Dallas–Fort Worth area to develop an archaeological society that would invite speakers and have formal programs, either as part of the Dallas Archaeological Society or as a new group. The old Dallas group, with its keen interest in digging, was not interested. A new group was formed, which initiated a lively roster of programs. One of the most memorable of those programs was when Donald Crabtree of Idaho came to speak. Crabtree was a famous flint knapper, someone who flakes flint and makes artifacts using only those techniques that were known to aboriginal people.

When the Crabtree lecture was announced, there was a lot of interest. He would draw a large crowd. It was to be the first program of the new archaeology society.

One of the graduate students in the department then was Fekri Hassan, who had been a student of Rushdi Said's at Cairo University. Said had encouraged him to come to SMU for his doctorate. He'd spent most of the 1968 season with us along the Nile, and it was obvious that Said had trained him well in geology. Hassan came to Dallas with his new wife, Affifa. Fekri spoke and wrote excellent English, but Affifa's English was poor. When they arrived, Hassan had ten dollars in his pocket. After some scrounging by the other students, they soon had everything they needed for a small apartment. I found them a suitable apartment near SMU and arranged for him to receive a fellowship so they could pay the rent and buy food. I confess I had mixed feelings: were they courageous to make such a profound leap with so few resources, or were they foolish? Maybe both, but I soon realized that Hassan was a very bright graduate student.

A few weeks prior to the Crabtree lecture, Fekri and Affifa Hassan came to me and offered to cook and serve an Egyptian dinner to everyone who attended the lecture. They asked if it would be possible to charge a small fee for the dinner to cover the cost of the food. I agreed and gave them a little more to pay them something for their efforts. With the help of two women graduate students, Affifa cooked and Fekri and several other graduate students served.

The dinner was a great success. They rented big, long tables and over 100 chairs. The seminar room at the Heroy Building was full; there were about 150 paid diners. Crabtree gave a great talk, showed a movie, and demonstrated how to flake flint. The new archaeological society was off and running.

Affifa worked hard on her English, and for almost a year she waited tables in the nearby Hilton Hotel café. Coming from a sheltered Muslim background, she had a difficult time wearing the revealing uniform required there, but she did, and she made enough money to achieve her goals. Her English improved, she enrolled as a geochemistry graduate student in the geology department, and in three years got her PhD under Vance's supervision.

She and Hassan are now divorced. She lives in the Washington area and works as a geochemist for the Department of the Interior. Hassan is now the emeritus Petri Professor of Archaeology at the University of London, one of the most distinguished chairs in archaeology in the world.

Ethiopia Beckons |
(1971–1973)

CHAPTER 21

With our research shut down in Egypt, I decided to shift our operations elsewhere. I considered several areas where my students and I might work profitably, but I thought Ethiopia was the most promising. In 1970, Joel Shiner and Tony Marks had worked in the upper Atbara in eastern Sudan, near the border of Ethiopia, where they found many sites. In Ethiopia, the upper end of the Atbara is known as the Tekaze River. I wrote a proposal requesting funds for a one-year survey of the Tekaze Valley. The NSF awarded me the amount requested. In the winter of 1971, supported by the new NSF grant, I took eight graduate students to Ethiopia. I had hoped Schild would join us, but he had a prior commitment.

Addis Ababa in 1971 was a small city. Most of the government buildings, including the museum, were clustered in the downtown area. There were several hotels, but only one, the Hilton, could be rated as excellent. The roads and important streets were paved, but there was not much traffic. The city was clean and most of the people were well dressed. Only a few peasants wore native dress. The few Europeans in the city were mostly Italians. There weren't many beggars, although we would see some in the big market. Some had open smallpox sores, and some bore signs of leprosy. On the highway leaving the city, the cultural break was sharp. The houses and the people were so primitive I felt as if I had moved back in time 4,000 years.

I was on my way to the Tekaze Valley to set up a field headquarters when a passenger on the plane I was taking from Addis Ababa to Tekaze asked where I was going. When I said the Tekaze Valley, he asked if I knew that war between Eritrea and Ethiopia had just erupted in the Tekaze. I did not. The U.S. embassy staff had told me nothing about the war when I had been in the scientific attaché's office the day before. Didn't they know?

I got off the plane at the next stop, the medieval capital of Gondar, not far from Lake Tana and the headwaters of the Blue Nile. I had left the students at the small hotel where all of us had been staying in Addis with instructions to stay near the hotel until I called them. I reached Fekri Hassan on my first try.

I said, "I'm in Gondar. There's a war underway in the Tekaze Valley. Tell everyone about it. I want everybody to join me in Gondar. This looks like a good area for us to work, and we sure as hell can't go to the Tekaze Valley." Five students flew to Gondar the next day; three others came in our new Land Cruiser pickup, arriving three days later.

After we began our survey, we soon learned that for miles around Gondar there was nothing but fields that had been intensively cultivated for a long, long time. Any archaeology had long ago been destroyed. As soon as we realized this, I ordered all of us back to Addis Ababa. It was not a promising beginning for our research in Ethiopia.

I was at loose ends in Addis for a few days trying to decide what to do next. I called the office of the minister of culture and asked if I could come by for a visit. He invited me to come right over.

He was a tall, slim, good-looking man in his late forties. He asked if I would come have a drink with him at his home later that afternoon. He told me there'd be four other guests, three ladies and an Italian movie producer. We chatted for a while about my recent misadventure of almost landing in a war zone, and I asked him where I might go to look for an archaeological project.

"I think I'd go to the Central Rift Valley," he said. "The roads are good there, and there are lots of obsidian exposures. There might be some interesting archaeology, but I don't know any particular area where you might work." We finished our small talk, and I agreed to join him and his guests.

His home was a large apartment in one of the best residential areas in Addis. It was simply furnished, modern, and beautiful. On entering, the first thing I saw was his impressive collection of Ethiopian silver crosses, some in frames and others simply mounted on the walls of his living room. With his arms out he swept around the room, saying, "They came from all over Ethiopia, and each region has its own style."

I was drawn to the beautifully decorated crosses from Lalabella, an area where there were many churches carved out of sandstone bedrock. I vowed to buy Peta one of those beautiful Lalabella crosses.

In a few minutes the other guests arrived. The three women were young, slim, and beautiful, with the high rounded foreheads of Ethiopia's aristocracy. The movie producer was a middle-aged Italian who spoke no English. He devoted his time to two of the beautiful young ladies. The other, the prettiest, I thought, spoke English well, but seemed to be more than friendly with the minister. I thought I was the "odd man out," and so after I finished my drink, I thanked the minister and prepared to take my leave.

"But you must not leave," he said. "We are going to the crown prince's house for dinner. I have told him about you and he is expecting you."

There were about thirty people at the crown prince's house, as well as an orchestra. The crown prince was behind the bar mixing drinks. As he fixed mine, we talked, and I learned that he had attended Cornell University in New York.

A long table had been set with golden plates for dinner. I discovered I was seated next to the young woman who was so friendly with the minister. He was somewhere else, and I thought maybe he expected me to look after his girlfriend. The young lady and I chatted, and since the orchestra was playing good dance music, I asked her if she would like to dance. She was light on her feet and had obviously received a lot of ballet training. The pretty lady did not seem to mind my injured right arm, which had never given me a problem while dancing.

To open the conversation, I asked her if she had a job. "No, I do not do anything. I'm a princess. Don't you know the crown prince is my brother?" I was so startled I couldn't speak. Thoughts kept running through my mind: "What would the Ethiopians do to a foreigner if they thought he was having an affair with one of their princesses?" I was sure it would not be pleasant. I don't think I said another word to the princess the rest of the evening. She might have been offended, but I'm not *that* much of a risk taker.

A few days after the dinner I decided to take the minister's suggestion and look at the Central Rift Valley, the most pronounced topographic feature cutting through the center of Ethiopia. It is a gigantic tectonic trench from thirty to sixty miles wide, with five large lakes in the floor of the valley. A paved highway extends down the center of the Rift Valley, from Addis Ababa to Shashemene in southern Ethiopia.

The largest body of water in the basin, the second from the north as you drive down the valley, is known as Lake Ziway. It is about seventy miles southeast of Addis. My plan was to scout the area, and if possible, find some sites. Leaving the students in Addis Ababa, I recruited an antiquities inspector, and we drove down the highway through the lake district. As I entered the town of Ziway, on the southwest side of Lake Ziway, I noticed an unusually large hill about a mile west of the highway. I could see a steep, almost vertical scarp on its south side. I also saw a trail from the highway toward the hill, so I turned off and drove to its base. The antiquities inspector and I got out of the truck and started climbing. I soon saw many Middle Paleolithic obsidian artifacts on the surface. Higher up, I noted several places where artifacts were weathering out of a fine-grained colluvium broken by lenses of interbedded airborne volcanic ash. The colluvium and ash comprised most of the upper part of the hill. The top part of the hill was known as Gademotta, and another, more eroded lower section to the

Map 5. Map of Northeast Africa showing the relationship between Ethiopia, Sudan, and Egypt. Lake Ziway, where the Combined Prehistoric Expedition excavated six Middle Stone Age sites in 1972–1973, is about a hundred miles southeast of Addis Ababa. Also shown is Lake Tana, where the CPE did an initial survey, finding no interesting sites. Drafted by Chris and Cheryl Hill.

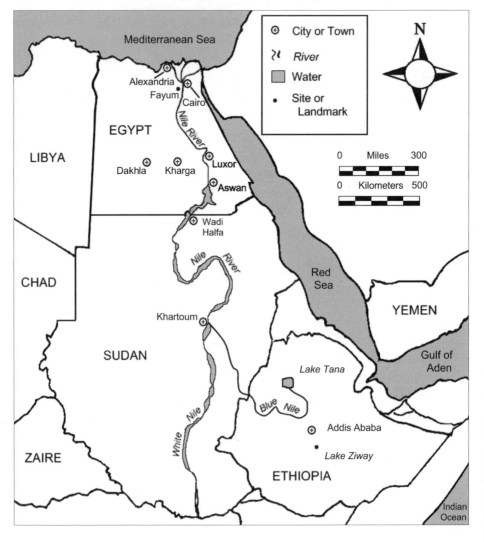

northeast was called Kulkuletti. Middle Paleolithic artifacts were embedded in the sediments of both hills. I decided this locality would require a major effort. I wanted to save as much money as possible for the next year. Thus, when I returned to Addis, I terminated the field season, and the students and I returned home.

As soon as I reached Dallas I wrote a proposal describing what I had seen at Lake Ziway and requested support for two years, beginning in January 1972. In the fall of 1971 I received a large NSF grant to work at Lake Ziway.

In early January 1972, I returned to Ziway with Schild and Hanna Wieckowska, an excellent artifact illustrator and an experienced Polish archaeologist on her first trip to East Africa, along with five graduate students from SMU: Gerald Humphreys, Lewis MacNaughton, Tom Ryan, Frank Servello, and Nancy Singleton. The group included three geologists: Claude Albritton, Bob Laury (also at SMU), and Vance Haynes, my close friend who had by this time moved on to the University of Arizona. Albritton's teenage son, Claude, was also with us. The group remained in Addis Ababa for two days while I went to Ziway with our antiquities inspector. We rented rooms for everyone at a local hotel, the Beckly Mola, where the owner agreed to serve meals to the group at a good price.

A few weeks later, Peta and our two young children, Kelly (now eight) and Scott (four), joined us. I was waiting for them at the airport, but I had become ill with diarrhea. Schild and I had gotten careless and split a papaya that hadn't been properly washed. Both of us were ill, I more than he. I had rented adjoining rooms for Peta and the children at the Addis Hilton, so I went to bed the minute we got to the hotel. It took a couple of days before I could get up and welcome my family properly. Once we left Addis and got back to Ziway, however, I rapidly improved and was soon off to work at Gademotta and Kulkuletti. The children were well behaved, but they ran everywhere around the hotel, keeping Peta busy. It wasn't long before I agreed that the children could spend their days at Gademotta watching the students and me work. The laborers enjoyed Kelly and Scott, and they helped Peta look after them.

I thought everything was safe at Ziway, but on his own initiative, Beckly Mola, the owner of the hotel, hired a big, tall man with a long spear to guard my children at night. As Beckly Mola told me, he wanted to be sure they were safe. Thinking back, I realize I should have been concerned as well about the several troops of baboons that ranged on the flat at the foot of the small mountain where we worked. Fortunately, nothing untoward happened.

The Middle Paleolithic archaeology at Gademotta and Kulkuletti was interesting and potentially more important to East African prehistory than we had imagined when we began working. The hill was a collapsed caldera, and there was a long sequence of Middle Paleolithic occupations preserved in the sediments on the surviving slopes of the mountain. There had once been a large lake around the foot of the volcano, and there is evidence of an earlier lake higher up on the slopes near where we were working. We did extensive and detailed excavations at six sites, four at Gademotta and two at Kulkuletti, all embedded in the colluvium with several impressive deep soils, sandstone layers, and beds of airborne volcanic ash, both above and below the archaeological horizons. We dated three of the ash layers. The stratigraphically earliest Middle Stone Age locality at Gademotta was under a fossil soil and an ash bed dated by Potassium/Argon analyses to 235,000 years old. Two ash beds at Kulkuletti gave ages of 181,000 (lower bed) and 149,000 years old (upper bed).

The oldest site in the sequence is ETH-72-8B. The numerous artifacts recovered from the site occur as a lens that extends to the edges of a concavity or basin. Since there was no entry or exit for water, the depression was almost surely dug by man. The basin was probably used for a hut, and judging by the density of the artifacts in the basin, it was used for a considerable period of time. Over nine thousand artifacts were recovered from the concavity. The basin is circular, 24 feet in diameter, and 12 inches deep, too large for a nuclear family, but suitable for an extended family. Although huts occur in Middle Paleolithic sites on the Russian Plain, they are not common, and this one may be much older than those, or any other dwelling known.

These Potassium/Argon age determinations came as a surprise to most archaeologists working in Africa, because at that time the Middle Stone Age was generally thought to begin around 40,000 years ago, on the basis of several radiocarbon dates on charcoal that may not have been adequately pretreated.

Recently, those two ash beds have been shown to be even older. Using a more precise dating technique identified as $^{40}Ar/^{39}Ar$, Leah E. Morgan and Paul Renne of the Geochronology Laboratory at the University of California at Berkeley sampled and redated three of the previously dated ash beds in the Ziway sequence. The oldest dated ash bed, Unit 25 in the our stratigraphy, yielded an age of 278,000 ±3,000 years old. This ash bed overlies Site ETH-72-8B, which earlier had given a Potassium/Argon date of 235,000 ±5,000 years. Unit 7 in our stratigraphy at Gademotta (and correlated stratigraphy with Unit 25 at Gademotta) dated 280,000 ±8,000 years ago; an ash fill in an erosion channel, Unit 11 in our stratigraphy, dated 183,000 ±10,000 years.

These new $^{40}Ar/^{39}Ar$ dates place the oldest Middle Stone Age site at Gademotta within the range of the oldest dated MSA sites in East Africa (Kapthurin, in Kenya).

Another interesting feature we noted was the remarkable cultural integrity of the assemblages, both vertically and horizontally, in the fine-grained colluvium in which they were enclosed. Many pieces could be refitted, including resharpening spalls that had been removed from the distal (pointed) ends of several of the Mousterian Points and Converging Sidescrapers. These resharpening spalls clearly established, at least in these localities, that many, if not all, of these points did not function as projectile tips, but as knives. Some of them had been used, resharpened, reused again, resharpened once more, then reused a third time before being discarded on the occupation floor among the edge-dulled resharpening spalls. Had we not been collecting and closely examining every piece of obsidian, even the smallest chips, we would have missed the refits on the Mousterian Points. The wear on the edges of these spalls was clear evidence that they were resharpening spalls.

It remains to be seen whether Mousterian Points found at other Ethiopian localities served a similar function, or if they were used as projectile tips. The discovery of refits that demonstrate that they were used as knives is largely ignored in the Middle Paleolithic literature. Archaeologists for a long time have assumed that Mousterian Points were tips for spears used to kill large animals. This view will not change quickly. It is part of the archaeologist's lore that these people were great hunters, and they may well have been, but not necessarily with Mousterian Points.

Most of our workmen came from a village about ten miles west of where we were excavating. One day I told Gerald Humphreys, the field director, that the crew seemed to have grown and that we had all the workers we could use. Later that day, Schild and I were looking at the obsidian quarry outcrop on an adjacent hill when I noticed a man crawling on his stomach toward me. It was clear he was begging. With some effort I got the man to stand up while I sent for our antiquities inspector, who spoke Oromo (the language of the village). The inspector told me the man was begging for a job. I looked at him cringing before me, thought about what I had just told Humphreys, and then asked the inspector to tell Humphreys to put the man to work. I got more than a little ribbing from Humphreys at lunch, but I never became accustomed to the overwhelming poverty of the people who lived around us.

About midway into the field season I received word that on the following Sunday the headman of the village where most of our workers lived was going to give a special party for all of us, including my wife and children. We dressed up and drove up to the village, guided by one of our workers who lived there. The village leader met us carrying a rifle and leading a beautiful white horse with an elaborately decorated saddle and bridle. We had tea and he spoke a few words I didn't understand. The antiquities inspector translated.

The headman said, "I know this foreigner does not understand what I have done for him, but tell him I have made him my blood brother. Now no one will bother or harm him, his family, or any of his students because if ever they do I am obligated to take blood vengeance upon them."

I had not expected his gift, and I was deeply moved. I thanked him profusely, saying, "I will be eternally grateful to you for the steps you have taken to protect my associates, my family, and me. I greatly appreciate what you have done for us. It gives all of us a sense of security. We will always remember you, your people, and your warm hospitality."

After my words were translated for him, he let Kelly ride his horse around the yard. She was so thrilled she couldn't stop smiling. Not long ago I showed Kelly a picture I took of her riding that horse. She told me that ride was the high point of her stay in Ethiopia. It was for me, too.

At the end of the excavations at Gademotta there was a lot of washing of artifacts, classifying, and recording to be done. Humphreys asked if he could do an additional survey for sites in the area. In particular, he wanted to find and excavate one or two Late Stone Age localities he could use for his dissertation. I agreed and he soon began excavating at two Late Stone Age sites.

On my return from Ethiopia in 1971, I stopped at Cairo at the request of Bahay Issawi. He wanted the Combined Prehistoric Expedition to return to Egypt because, as he explained to me, we were doing good science and were a stimulus to others in the Egyptian Geological Survey. If I'd agree, he felt sure he could get us a permit to work somewhere in Egypt. I told him we had to keep working in Ethiopia for at least a year, maybe two. But I missed all our friends in Egypt, so I agreed to try to get another grant from the NSF for work there, provided he would first obtain an agreement from Egyptian security officials about a safe place for us to work.

A few weeks later Issawi went to a high-ranking security officer he knew and told him he wanted our group to return to Egypt because we were a great asset to Egypt and had many friends there. He added that he wanted us to study prehistoric archaeology with the geological survey.

After further discussion, the officer walked over to the wall, where there was a large map of Egypt, pointed at the center of the desert area west of Kharga, and said, "Put the foreigners here; there is nothing secret anywhere in this part of Egypt."

Issawi reported that he had a permit for us to begin work in 1972 in the desert area extending across west-central Egypt, from Kharga to Dakhla and on to Abu Mingar. As soon as his information reached me, I wrote a proposal to the NSF requesting additional funds to work in the Egyptian Sahara. Since almost nothing was known about the Paleolithic archaeology west of Kharga, most of my proposal was devoted to a summary of Caton-Thompson's work at the spring vents near Kharga. There were still two more field seasons to be completed at Gademotta (1972 and 1973), and for those two years I received two NSF grants each year, one for Egypt, the other for Ethiopia. It was a full schedule, but a productive period.

After we returned to Dallas, Jim Gallagher, one of our senior graduate students, asked if he and his wife could go with us to Ethiopia for the 1973 field season. They wanted to study modern stoneworking in Ethiopia. If their results justified, they planned to stay in Ethiopia for several months after the other students and I left. I thought it was a good plan, and so I told him he could use the project's vehicle after we left.

In January 1973 Schild and I returned to Gademotta for a brief field season to recheck the stratigraphy and dig two more Middle Stone Age sites. Gallagher and his wife began collecting obsidian artifacts at a nearby outcrop. They soon noticed several freshly struck obsidian blades that had hair on the edges. After watching the quarry for several days, they confirmed that men from backcountry villages had left the blades with hair on them. The men walked to the "big city" of Ziway from the countryside and would stop, shave their faces with sharp new blades, and then enter the town. This supported the Gallaghers' assumption that stone tool manufacturing might still be going on in some of these isolated villages. They decided to find out as soon as I left and could use our vehicle.

It was true. They soon found an isolated backcountry village that specialized in leatherworking. The people there were still making and using obsidian tools, in particular, the scrapers to prepare cowhides. They inserted the scrapers into a wooden handle, and when the stone edge became dull, they removed the scraper from the haft and resharpened it by flaking the working edge. Sometimes they abandoned the stone bit when it was still long; other times they kept using and resharpening it until the bit was short. This was something new: the typology of the scrapers depended on how long the scrapers were used, not on some template in the stone knapper's mind. It made a great dissertation.

Protecting Historic Shipwrecks
(1969–1988)

CHAPTER 22

A rchaeology of all kinds interests me, and I was able to do a very different kind of archaeology when I became involved with the furor over old shipwrecks off the Texas coast. In the summer of 1969, Texas newspapers were filled with stories about a group of treasure hunters from Indiana who were reported to be looting a Spanish ship off the Texas coast. According to the stories, the ship had been wrecked off Padre Island in 1554. It was thought that three Spanish ships all loaded with silver coins and other treasure had been wrecked during a storm. The presence of these shipwrecks and their approximate locations had been widely known among the beach people of Padre Island for many years. Spanish coins of the right age and style had been found on the beach for decades, but no one had taken much interest in the ships or their contents before the arrival of the Indiana treasure hunters.

The state land commissioner believed he had authority to administer the coastal lands, and it was reported that he had given a permit to the treasure hunters. Some members of the state legislature intimated that the commissioner was favoring the treasure hunters, and may even have received money from them. Tempers were hot, resulting in fistfights on the floor of the legislature. But later in the summer of 1969, when passions had cooled, the legislature passed, and Governor Preston Smith signed, one of the best laws in the country to protect antiquities on state land. The bill included shipwrecks within Texas territorial waters, and it authorized a Texas Antiquities Committee to administer the new law. In November of 1969, the governor appointed Curry Holden and me as citizen members of the committee. Curry had been my boss the two years I'd spent in Lubbock at Texas Tech. He was a friend of the governor's, and I suspect Curry asked him to appoint me. The other five members were *ex officio* state officials: the state archaeologist, the state land commissioner, the director of the Texas State Historical Commission, the head of the Department of Fish and Wildlife, and the director of the Texas State Museum. To my surprise, I was elected chairman.

Shortly after we were appointed, Governor Smith asked the committee to meet at his office. It was a friendly gathering, and as it broke up, the governor looked at each of us in turn and said, "As soon as you can, go down to the coast and clean up that mess."

He didn't, however, offer any money with which to do this cleaning up. As chairman, I knew I had to organize a project to locate the Spanish treasure ships, including the one the Indiana group was looting, as well as any other old shipwrecks in the vicinity of Padre Island.

When I got back to SMU, I went to see Albritton to discuss the problem with him. He heard me out and said we needed to talk with Gene McDermott, one of the founders of Texas Instruments, who would be interested because he was a geophysicist and a major benefactor of the university. He said he'd make an appointment with McDermott and told me in the meantime to write a brief proposal with a budget.

As I envisioned it, the project would require the rental of a cesium magnetometer, a dive boat, two theodolites, and a crew of twelve—two to run the magnetometer, four to handle the theodolites, and six divers, two of whom would be experienced dive masters. I estimated the work would take two months. While I worked on the proposal, I called George Race, who had briefly considered studying for a PhD in SMU's anthropology department. Instead of anthropology, he wisely decided to stay with medicine. He was chief of pathology at Baylor Hospital and co-owner with me of the Cessna 182. Race owned a large house on Padre Island. I told him about the project and asked him if we could use his house for two months starting June 1, 1970. Race said we could have the house for two months, rent-free. I thanked him, then finished the text and budget for the proposal. My estimated cost for the project, even with free housing, was $25,000.

Our meeting with McDermott was brief. After Albritton introduced me, I handed McDermott the proposal. He read both the text and the budget. He smiled and said, "This sounds like an interesting project. I wish I could go with you. The cesium magnetometer is exactly what you need to find those ships."

"Yes," I said. "I've been told the treasure hunters used one to find the ship they're looting."

"I'll give you the $25,000 you need. To whom should I make the check?"

"To Southern Methodist University," I answered with a smile. Without another word, he wrote out the check and handed it to me; I thanked him and we left.

It occurred to me that I didn't know how to scuba dive, surely a necessary skill for this project. Later that afternoon, I went to a local dive shop near SMU. Fortunately, the owner was in, and I explained my problem to him. He thought for a moment and said, "If you'll commit to spending every evening for a month learning how to scuba dive, I'll find five or six scuba instructors who'll take turns teaching you. At the end of the month you'll take a test. If you pass, you'll be a certified scuba diver. We'll do this without charge, just to help out with your project."

I took him up on his offer, though it wasn't easy trying to swim with only one usable arm. Even more difficult was removing and putting on the equipment under water, but eventually I was successful. During the final test in the pool, I was able to do everything the instructors required except swimming five laps in the time allotted. I managed to do it on my third try, and they gave me my certificate. Although not nearly as skilled as the other divers, I was able to take my turn diving with the other men when we got to Padre Island.

We began work on June 1, 1970, and after two weeks of searching with the magnetometer we found a large magnetic anomaly on June 15, 1970. The scuba divers confirmed it was the Spanish treasure ship the Indiana group had been looting. The discovery brought a lot of favorable publicity to our project. We found and brought up a small cannon and a few other items, all with television cameras and reporters present to record the event. At the next meeting of the Texas legislature the legislators appropriated $250,000 for the Texas State Historical Commission, the estimated cost of completing the excavation of the Spanish ship, raising it to the surface, cleaning, and preserving it.

Despite my war-wounded right arm, I enjoyed scuba diving, and for a year I even taught a class on underwater archaeology in the anthropology department, at some small lakes a few miles north of Dallas. I taught the students how to make a grid, take notes underwater, and recover objects found on the bottom of the lakes. I had to admit, however, that I would never be a good underwater archaeologist, and I turned the class over to Joel Shiner, who was a highly skilled scuba diver, as well as a good archaeologist. He taught the course until he retired from SMU in 1986.

After the successful project on the coast, the antiquities committee voted to ask the Texas attorney general to recover the material the Indiana group had taken from the 1554 Spanish ship, and to sue them if necessary. The Indiana treasure hunters were cooperative, but they refused to surrender their loot without compensation from the state. The case went to the Texas Supreme Court, and then to the federal courts, but Texas always lost, usually by a five-to-four vote. Eventually, the state bought the collection, but I don't remember how much it paid.

One of the people who attended these court sessions year after year with me was Joe McKnight, a law professor at SMU. One day, in the spring of 1984, at the Fifth Circuit Court of Appeals in New Orleans, McKnight and I were watching the proceedings. Texas lost once again, in a five-to-four decision.

As we left the courthouse, Joe said, "Fred, you'll never win so long as historic shipwrecks are under Admiralty Law, which, as you know, simply says, 'finders keepers.'"

As we walked along, I asked, "Is there a way to remove historic shipwrecks from Admiralty Law?"

"It would take an act of Congress," he answered.

"As a favor to me, will you draft a bill that would do this?" I asked.

"Sure," he said. "I can have it for you in about two weeks, but it'll be difficult to get Congress to pass the bill."

Joe kept his word. In two weeks he gave me a draft of a bill that he assured me would protect historic shipwrecks and survive a court challenge. I immediately called my friend and stockbroker, Garry Weber, a former Dallas County judge and a widely respected Democratic politician. I knew he was interested in old shipwrecks. I asked him to have lunch with me and told him what I wanted to talk about.

Garry asked to include Duncan Boeckman, a prominent Republican with an interest in archaeology, in our lunch meeting. The three of us met about a week later. I outlined the problem and gave each of them a copy of Joe McKnight's draft. Both Weber and Boeckman said they thought it was a great idea. Weber said he would contact the speaker of the House, Jim Wright, and ask him to sponsor the bill in the House. Boeckman said he would contact Senator John Tower and see if he would introduce it in the Senate. They suggested that I go to Washington as soon as possible to discuss the bill personally with Wright and Tower. I made appointments with both men and went to Washington.

First I went to the speaker's chambers. The House was in session, but his staff called him out to meet with me for a few minutes. After preliminary greetings, he said, "Dr. Wendorf, I've read the draft of the bill to protect historic shipwrecks that Garry Weber sent to me, and I've selected the committee to prepare the bill and hold hearings. This should go quickly. I don't foresee any problems, but I'll ask my staff to keep you informed if any should develop. I assume you've begun alerting your colleagues about the bill and urging them to write their congressmen asking them to support it?" I told him that I'd been calling my colleagues, and that I thought there'd be many letters in support of this bill.

From Speaker Wright's office I went to see Senator John Tower. He was in his office and was expecting me. He said, "I've heard from Duncan Boeckman that he strongly supports your efforts to preserve historic shipwrecks. I also think it's a great idea and long overdue. I'll give your bill my full support. I won't make any moves, however, until the House has acted. That should be in three or four months. I understand you have the backing of Speaker Wright." I assured him we did and that soon there'd be letters to members of the Senate and the House from many amateur archaeologists who supported our efforts, as well as from my professional colleagues.

When I returned from Washington I sought the help of the Society for American Archaeology, the Archaeological Institute of America, and the American Anthropological Association. All agreed to help by contacting their members. I urged my archaeologist friends to write to their senators and congressmen asking them to support the Historic Shipwreck Bill. Probably the most important help I received came from the many amateur archaeological societies I contacted to ask for their assistance. They were so responsive that their letters and telephone calls probably reached every member of Congress.

About six months after I met with Speaker Wright, the bill passed the House. In the Senate, however, there were problems. Senator Paula Hawkins from Florida put a personal "hold" on the bill. Tower went to see her and told her that he would soon retire and he wanted the Historic Shipwreck Bill to be his final legislative action. Still she refused to release her hold. She would not tell him why she objected to the bill, but some have suggested that she was influenced by some treasure hunters among her constituents. As expected, she was defeated at the next election. Senator John Tower, however, never saw the shipwreck bill become law. He was killed in a plane crash several months after he retired.

Part of the reason the Historic Shipwreck Bill went so smoothly through Congress prior to Senator Hawkins's action was because potential opponents, such as treasure hunters, scuba divers, and sport fishermen, all of whom might have been adversely affected, did not have time to get organized. The delay resulting from Senator Hawkins's action gave many of these groups an opportunity to express their concerns to their congressmen. The most volatile were the treasure hunters. I had a couple of debates over saving historic shipwrecks with one of the treasure hunters before a Senate subcommittee chaired by Senator Orrin Hatch. During these debates I got strong and effective support from George Bass, head of the underwater research group at Texas A&M University. I didn't find out how Senator Hatch voted when the shipwreck bill came before the Senate, but at the hearings Hatch gave me the impression he was among the opposition.

On March 26, 1987, three years after Senator Tower and Speaker Wright first introduced the legislation to protect historic shipwrecks, Senator Bill Bradley introduced the bill again in the Senate under a new title: "Abandoned Shipwreck Act of 1987."

Opposition came from a few professional treasure hunters and, at first, from some of the sport divers who felt the legislation would restrict their access to wrecks. Although I was no longer a scuba diver, I understood their concern, and at my urging compromises were subsequently made with the sport divers, and the revised bill (S-858) received the endorsement of the major sport divers' associations, as well as the Scuba Equipment Manufacturers Association, the State Historical Preservation Officers, and every major national archaeological association. Although I wrote letters and spoke at two hearings, most of this support came as a result of Loretta Neumann's lobbying efforts. The Society for American Archaeology and the Society for Historical Archaeology had recently hired her as a lobbyist. She was effective, and she joined us at just the right moment. The Senate passed Bill S-858 on December 19, 1987.

On March 29, 1988, the revised Historic Shipwreck Bill came up for a vote in the House under special rules, but it fell six votes short of the two-thirds majority needed. After a recess, on April 13, 1988, the bill came up for another vote and was approved.

Even after the bill passed the House there were some tense moments. As the Republicans were passing into the chamber to vote, Benny Keel, the senior archaeologist in the Department of the Interior, was standing in the hall. Keel overheard Representative Newt Gingrich say as he passed out notes to his Republican colleagues, "The Abandoned Shipwreck Bill is the speaker's bill. Don't vote for it."

When the voting was over, Benny Keel heard Gingrich say to his group as they passed by him, "Well, we lost that one, but tomorrow I'll go to the White House and ask the president to veto it."

Keel immediately called me and told me about Gingrich's threat and asked if I could help. At first I was at a loss, but then I remembered that I had an influential friend in California who was a close friend of President and Mrs. Reagan. I knew my friend was interested in protecting historic shipwrecks and had even offered to help if I ever needed it. I called her, told her the problem, and asked her to help if she could. She said she would, right away.

I can't reveal her name, at least not yet, and I don't know for sure what role, if any, she may have played in the final decision, but the next day President Reagan signed the bill. It became law on April 28, 1988, and is known as Public Law Number 100-298, with a short title of "Abandoned Shipwreck Act of 1987." The bill had passed the Senate in 1987, thus the date in the title. Since its passage, the Abandoned Shipwreck Act has twice been challenged in the courts. On both occasions the challengers lost.

The passage of the Historic Shipwreck Bill was only partially the result of my efforts. It took the active support of hundreds of interested people. The fact that the Historic Shipwreck Bill was sponsored by the Democratic speaker of the House and a leading Republican in the Senate was an important factor in the broad bipartisan endorsement the bill received. For that I am grateful to Garry Weber and Duncan Boeckman, as well as Senator John Tower and Speaker Jim Wright.

Treasure hunters no longer pillage the many wrecks along our coasts. Trained professionals now supervise the excavation of historic shipwrecks, and the recovered artifacts are preserved and placed in museums where everyone, not just a few, can enjoy them. More important to me, these ships are treated like any other archaeological resource; the maps and records of the excavations are preserved, so it is possible for scholars to study them to determine where and in what arrangement the artifacts were found, how and where the ship was built, what cargo it was carrying, and what life was like on board ship. These ships represent moments frozen in time. It is only in this feature that they differ from most archaeological sites on land, and they deserve the same or greater protection.

Dakhla Oasis and Egypt's Western Desert |
(1971–1972)

CHAPTER 23

The longest field season Schild and I had in Ethiopia started right after Christmas in 1971 and continued until late March of 1972. Even then we weren't through. When the fieldwork in Ethiopia ended, Peta and the children went to England to stay with her mother until I could join them about six weeks later. Then Schild and I, with three graduate students, Tom Ryan and Frank Servello, both of whom had been with us at Gademotta, and J. Lech, a Polish archaeologist who joined us for this trip, all went to Cairo and from there with Issawi and the small group of men he had assembled to help us, to Kharga and Dakhla. At Dakhla we found and excavated two fossil spring vents that together yielded over a thousand Late Acheulean hand axes. Servello, Ryan, and Lech dug the spring vents, and all three were hard workers.

Although it was interesting, our study of the vents did not result in a major contribution to knowledge because the original distribution pattern of the hand axes on the living surface around the spring had been destroyed long ago, probably long before 70,000 years ago, and therefore could not be analyzed. Nevertheless, the hand axes were useful data. The collection was large, typologically diverse, and represented the use of the springs over a long interval of time.

Were these axes gifts to the god of the springs, as some suggested? I doubt it. Schild offered the most likely explanation: groups who lived near the spring used and discarded the hand axes. The spring pool expanded and contracted as rainfall increased and declined, and the water and gravity carried a few hand axes toward the spring vent every year. This process was repeated many, many times over the life of the spring, perhaps longer than a thousand years. While the spring was active, various groups may have made hundreds of visits, each visit adding a few more hand axes.

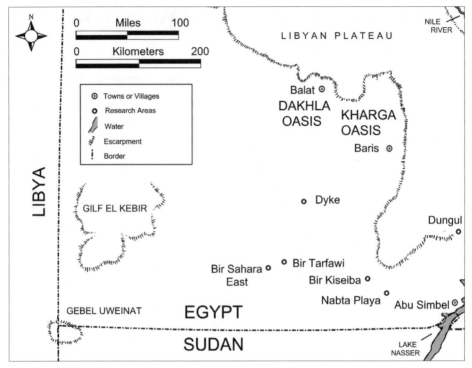

Map 6. Southwestern Egypt. Excavations by the Combined Prehistoric Expedition at Balat in the
Dakhla Oasis (1972); the Dyke area (1972); Bir Sahara East and Bir Tarfawi (1973–1974; 1986–1988);
Bir Kiseiba (1979–1980); Kharga Oasis (1966); and Nabta (first surveyed in 1974,
and excavated in 1975, 1977, 1990–present). Drafted by Chris and Cheryl Hill.

Despite our disappointment at not finding an Acheulean living surface, Schild and I did a small book on our Dakhla research, *The Prehistory of Dakhla Oasis and Adjacent Desert*.

That season Dakhla was surprisingly hot in April and May. There were frequent sandstorms, and the flies were terrible. We decided to give up on Dakhla before we had done an adequate survey of the area, even before we knew where we might work next.

From the time we arrived in Dakhla in early April, Issawi had urged Schild and me to take a trip with him toward the southwest, across the desert to Bir Tarfawi and Bir Sahara, two unoccupied wells located in adjacent large, shallow basins. A few months earlier, on a trip to the Gilf Kebir, a high plateau in far southwestern Egypt, Issawi had seen lake sediments in both the Tarfawi and Sahara basins. He thought one or both might contain archaeology. So Issawi, Schild, and I, along with Biseri our cook, a driver, and three workmen, traveled across the desert in two vehicles, a small lorry and a pickup. Guided by Issawi's compass, we traveled about three hundred miles across an area devoid of tracks or any sign of life. At that time the only road was a rough gravel/asphalt track going west from Kharga to Dakhla and on to Farafra. There was no road going south from Kharga/Dakhla, except the camel trail of the Darb el Arbain, marked by hundreds of camel skeletons in a belt nearly a mile wide. It was a forlorn, open, sandy, and rocky landscape. Because Issawi knew the way, we left Eide Mariff in camp with the rest of the workers, along with Ryan and Servello.

When we reached the two wells we made an exciting discovery. The lake sediments in both basins contained numerous clusters of lithic artifacts that recorded a sequence of Middle Paleolithic occupations. In some localities the artifacts occurred with numerous bones of large animals. We immediately decided to make these basins the focus of our research in the Sahara for the next several years. We would begin in 1973, assuming, of course, that I could get a grant from the NSF.

Although Issawi had always referred to the two basins as Bir Sahara and Bir Tarfawi, and our Bedouin workers always called this depression "Bir Sahara," I soon learned that Bir Sahara was the wrong name. Soon after we began working there Vance Haynes informed me that Bir Sahara was the name of a well that H. J. L. Beadnell, a British geologist, drilled in 1927. This drilled well was about nine miles southwest of the depression we had been calling Bir Sahara. So, to differentiate between the two, I changed the name of our basin on our maps to "Bir Sahara East."

On the way back to Dakhla after our brief visit to the Tarfawi/Sahara East basins, we found a small, interesting cluster of Middle Paleolithic artifacts. They were a long way from any surface water, and there was no trace of a basin where seasonal water might have collected. The presence of artifacts in such a locality indicated the area once had been much wetter than we had previously assumed or that wind deflation could have destroyed all traces of a small basin, had one existed. We laid a grid over the area where the artifacts occurred, plotted all the artifacts on a map, and collected them for later study.

Several dozen miles farther north we found traces of yet another settlement in a shallow basin where water could persist for some time after rains. It had three long, oval hutlike features outlined with slabs that had fallen over. We dug a small trench and recovered a collection of stone artifacts dominated by elongated scalene triangles with small short sides.

After Schild finished his stratigraphic study at the small basin, we moved north again, following our tracks. Suddenly we saw a brown "wall" in front of us, thousands of feet high. A sandstorm was bearing down on us from the northwest. We immediately stopped the vehicles and threw up two tents as fast as we could. We put our bedding inside, and gave the tent stakes one more pounding. We positioned the vehicles so they would be partly sheltered, with the motors and windshields facing away from the wind, their rears pointed into the wind, to give some protection to our little camp.

Schild and I took a few bottles of wine into our tent, so we were ready when the storm hit. It blew all day and most of the night. The wind made the center tent pole jump up and down so violently I was sure it would break. Schild and I took turns trying to hold the pole down. I'm not sure if the wine helped much in the effort, but at least our tent didn't blow down. When the storm was at its peak, we heard a scratching at the door. We opened it a crack, and there was Biseri bringing us food, carefully covered.

The storm finally blew itself out early the next morning. Shortly after dawn we repacked everything and headed to the main camp, apprehensive about what we might find. As we feared, when the camp came into view we could see that several tents had blown down, including the dining tent and a workers' tent. We soon learned that all of the workers had gathered in one tent to wait out the storm, and that a horned viper had come in, too. There was a great scramble as the workers tried to get out of the tent away from the snake. The tent fell down as they pulled the pegs out scrambling to escape. The snake had the tent to itself until after the storm passed.

Schild and I were the only real losers in that storm. We had spent most of the two weeks before we went to Bir Tarfawi classifying and measuring the thousand-plus hand axes we recovered from the excavated spring vents at Dakhla. While we were doing this we were besieged by millions of flies. For relief from the flies, we had taken over the dining tent, where we could put up mosquito netting. We gathered every can of fly spray we could buy in Dakhla, but flies still got in, mostly when the servants brought clean dishes in from the dishwashing. Their clothes were covered with flies, and most of these stayed with us in the dining tent when the servants left. We'd stop work and spray like mad. Then we'd get back to work until the next person came in carrying a load of flies. We finished the measurement and description of all of the hand axes the day before we left for Bir Tarfawi, and I'd put the paper record, about fifty pages, in the pocket of the dining tent. It was there when the storm hit and the dining tent blew down. All the papers in the pocket went south to Sudan. There was nothing left; we had to redo the analyses, still plagued with all those flies.

I intended to join Peta and the children in England so we could spend the month of May seeing the Lake District and other points of interest. When I arrived in Cairo to meet with Issawi to go to Dakhla, I found several messages from my secretary at SMU saying my bank had advised her that my account was overdrawn. She urged me to return to Dallas immediately. I couldn't understand what had happened, since I had left plenty of money in the account, and the university business office was to deposit my check each month, which should have been more than enough to cover the checks I had left with my secretary in ready-to-mail envelopes to pay the mortgage and other routine bills. I sent urgent telegrams to Albritton and the manager of the university business office, but got no response. When I returned to Cairo from Dakhla there was still no answer. I called Peta and told her I had to go home as soon as I could get a flight, and asked her to return, too.

When I arrived in Dallas I went immediately to the bank and found out that there had been no deposit to my account since the end of December. The bank, however, had covered all my checks, almost $6,000 in all, at no cost to me. I thanked the bank officer profusely, then went over to the university business office and found the chief clerk. I demanded to know why I was not being paid. He told me I was not in the budget. I reminded him that I was a tenured professor with a contract and that there was even money in my Ethiopian project budget to pay me.

With that his face lit up. "Ah," he said, "I forgot about that. I'll determine exactly what we owe you and immediately draft a check."

I got my check from the business office and went to the bank, deposited it, and settled up with the bank's business office. I thanked the staff again for their exceptional service.

I went in to see Albritton and raised a little hell with him. He said, "Oh, I got your telegram, but I didn't know there was a problem."

About a month later, when the audit of the university books was completed, I received a call from SMU's business manager and then one from Albritton, both telling me that in their haste they had overpaid me by $1,000.00, and asking me to write them a check for that amount. I said no and hung up on each of them. The next week I was summoned to Provost Neil McFarland's office. McFarland is a fine man and a great scholar, and I have always been fond of him. He told me he'd heard about the $1,000 overpayment and my refusal to repay the university. I told him I had refused, then I gave him the whole story, including my five months of fieldwork in Ethiopia and the Egyptian desert without being paid. I told him I thought the university owed me a great deal more than $1,000 for my trouble and expense, including the loss of my family's much anticipated vacation in England. I ended by saying he should make sure this sort of thing never happened again.

McFarland smiled and said, "Would you accept the $1,000 as a bonus?"

One good thing came out of this unfortunate situation: almost immediately the university changed the accounting system so that from then on the appropriate salary payments were always made whether the faculty or staff member was in Dallas or Timbuktu.

There was another point I did not raise with McFarland: the loss of the vacation in the Lake District had an adverse effect on my marriage with Peta. We had been apart too long for both of us. I was trying not to face the painful reality that another marital rupture was brewing. There was so much interesting archaeology to be done that I was easily distracted from my family's growing distress.

Bir Sahara East and Bir Tarfawi |
(1972–1974)

CHAPTER 24

With my financial difficulties at the SMU business office resolved, I began writing a two-year NSF grant proposal to work at Bir Sahara East and Bir Tarfawi. Our brief inspection of the two basins in 1972 had confirmed the presence of many rich Middle Paleolithic localities, with abundant megafauna embedded in the permanent lake deposits of both basins. It was clear that long stratigraphic sequences were present in both basins. I submitted the proposal late in June of 1972, and the grant was awarded that November.

But doing archaeology in the middle of the Western Desert of Egypt could be intimidating; it was for me when I first went out there. Today it is no longer the desert it was when we first ventured onto the sand in 1972. Then it was a huge, pristine area seemingly devoid of life, and I loved it, even though I knew it could be dangerous. In recent years there have been many changes, not all of them positive. Vandals have burned the palm trees and some of the other vegetation in the oases. The Egyptian army has established several military posts in the area, and the sense of pristine isolation is gone. When we first crossed the desert in 1972, good drinking water was available by digging shallow wells at several of the birs. Ten years later the army or its contractors had contaminated all of them. As a consequence, we now have to bring our drinking water from Abu Simbel, or obtain it from one of the drilled wells that supply water to the new farms in an area now known as East Uweinat, near the Libyan and Sudanese borders.

Although I grumble about the changes in the desert the Egyptian army made, I admit there were three important positive developments. One of these was the paved road the army built that goes from Abu Simbel west to East Uweinat, ending about sixty miles from the Libyan border. A second improvement was the new paved road from

Dakhla going south past Bir Tarfawi to East Uweinat. The army maintains both roads, and now travel is much easier and faster. The third improvement was the water wells the army drilled at East Uweinat and at several other areas in the Western Desert. These wells make up for the desecration of the old water holes, unless the Egyptian government someday decides to abandon the farms and plug the drilled wells at East Uweinat.

In 1972, before we had the results of our Potassium/Argon age measurements for Middle Stone Age occupations at Gademotta and Kulkuletti, the prevailing view of the time depth for the Middle Paleolithic in Africa was less than 50,000 years, and probably no older than 40,000 years ago. It was generally held that the wettest period in the Sahara was between 20,000 and 30,000 years ago, based on many radiocarbon dates of that age on carbonates and snail shells from permanent lake deposits in several parts of the Sahara. I wrote the proposal based on those assumptions. I emphasized the fact that we expected to date the lakes in our two basins using radiocarbon measurements on carbonates, shells, and bone. There were no volcanic deposits in the area; thus the dating methods we employed in Ethiopia were not available.

We eventually learned that neither carbonates nor snail shells were suitable for radiocarbon dating because both dead and modern carbon move freely in and out, making age measurements on those materials unreliable. It took a long time for most geologists and archaeologists to accept the fact that the lakes in the desert are much older, and for years they published papers about the "pluvial" events contemporary with glacial advances. The reality is just the opposite: wet events in the Sahara approximately correlate with warm Interglacials or Interstadials, and episodes of aridity and deflation coincide with global periods of cold temperatures and periods of glacial advance. But we didn't learn that until several years later.

In addition to the dating, I highlighted the opportunity to examine the evident rich and varied animal remains we saw in association with the sites, and the opportunity for studying the Middle Paleolithic food economy in the Eastern Sahara and its changes through time. Because of differences in a few stone artifacts (mostly the presence of large, bifacially flaked leaf-shaped points, known as "foliates," on the surface at Tarfawi), I suggested the two basins might not be contemporary, with Tarfawi being later.

In early January of 1973, we were at Bir Tarfawi, about 260 miles from the Nile Valley, the closest place to civilization. I was apprehensive, but I kept my worries to myself. Fortunately, there were no accidents and we had most everything we needed. (This is a good place to mention that we work in the desert in the winter because it is easier to add warm clothing and be able to work when the temperature is below freezing than it is to live and work during the summer, when the temperature in the desert often reaches 140°F or more.)

In 1973 and again in 1974 the Egyptian Geological Survey provided us a fleet of eleven vehicles, including one large truck and several small ones, two fuel tankers, and four Jeeps. In addition, we had our two Ford pickups. The crew included thirteen geological survey driver/mechanics to drive and maintain the vehicles, sixteen Bedouin workers, the usual contingent of cooks and servants, and twelve scientists, two of whom, Vance Haynes and Peter Mehringher, hoped to recover fossil pollen from the lake deposits. Other scientists were Rushdi Said, the director of the geological survey; Bahay Issawi, surveyor and camp manager; Romuald Schild and Michal Kobusiewicz from the Polish Academy of Sciences; Tom Ryan and Scott Hayes, both graduate students from SMU; and me.

Our group also included two potential benefactors, Owen Henderson and Russ Morrison, the Dallas businessmen who partially funded my endowed professorship. They were a lot of fun in camp as well as hard workers. They were easy to get along with and took everything in stride. One particularly cold morning at Bir Sahara East (the water in my washbasin had frozen solid that night) I went into Owen and Russ's tent before breakfast and found Russ up and dressed. Owen was still in bed under his covers. I asked him if his feet were warm, and he said they were, pulling back his blankets to show me he was wearing his boots.

One of the best things Owen and Russ did for camp morale was to "publish" a camp newspaper, *The Bir Sahara Times*. It was only one page long, handwritten, and came out every morning at breakfast. It contained anecdotes about events of the previous day, some true, some made up, but the editors always embellished even the true stories for the maximum embarrassment of the persons involved. After the first issue, all of us eagerly went to breakfast to read *The Times* to find out what crazy things the editors had disclosed.

The 1973 camp was our first "all dried food" long-term camp. There were two exceptions to the dried food: a colony of 140 ducks and 1 goat. Two ducks a night would last us for ten weeks. We'd eat the goat at the celebration on the last night of camp.

The ducks were a noisy lot, but they survived the demanding trip out to what seemed to me to be the end of the world. Once in camp, the servants kept the ducks in a small tent next to the cook's tent. The ducks were allowed to roam free during the day, but they never wandered far from their tent. Each night they were put back into their tent. That first night the ducks chattered continuously and probably kept the cook awake all night. I happened to be watching early the next morning when the cook let them out to eat the scattering of feed he had put out for them, and I noted that he paid particular attention to the ducks that kept on quacking. He reached out and caught two of the noisiest ducks, and deftly cut their heads off. The next morning I watched to see if he selected the noisiest ducks again. He did. About six weeks later I happened to see his duck selection process again, and it was the same, except that none of the ducks made a sound, even when he chased and caught them.

This season Pete Mehringher, an expert in fossil pollen at Washington State University, in Pullman, Washington, was along in an unsuccessful effort to recover pollen from the lake sediments at Bir Sahara East. Mehringher was an active duck hunter back in Pullman, and he enjoyed eating duck, but not every night. At that time, air service for Pullman was limited, and when the field season was over, Mehringher left Cairo as soon as he could. His wife made the long trip to the Portland, Oregon, airport to meet his plane. On the drive from Portland to Pullman she told him that for his homecoming she had prepared his favorite meal: roast duck.

Each field season always included amusing food tales: Tom Ryan, one of the graduate students with us on the two expeditions, had complained during the first season that I had not brought enough Tabasco sauce. It was my mistake; we ran out halfway through the field season. "Don't worry about the Tabasco, Fred," Ryan said. "I'll bring us a bottle large enough to last the entire season."

Being a Louisiana boy, he got the largest bottle I had ever seen, and when we were packing to leave, he put it in his duffel bag, wrapped in several shirts and other clothing. Still, he and Herb Mosca, also a graduate student at SMU, watched the bag whenever they had to change planes. With great relief he and Mosca got to Cairo, found a taxi, and went to our hotel, the Garden City House. The bags were on the roof of the taxi. The driver climbed up and grabbed Ryan's duffel bag.

Ryan cried, "No," but the driver didn't understand. He dropped the bag to the concrete curb below. Ryan heard breaking glass, and soon Tabasco sauce was seeping out of the bag. It took two washings before Ryan could wear any of the clothes in the bag. There was no Tabasco for anyone that season.

We had a problem of sorts about our goat, too. Ryan took a liking to it. He noted that the goat was so hungry it was eating the ends of the tent ropes, even the wooden tent pegs. Since it was not being fed, Ryan began to sneak food from his plate out to the goat. Everyone in camp knew he was feeding the goat. One of his colleagues told me Ryan planned to ask me not to kill the creature, but Tom and his goat didn't have a chance. When he finally asked, I had to tell him that everyone else was looking forward to eating real meat after so much duck. Tom refused to join us for dinner that last night. For solace, I gave him a double ration of beer.

....

At the end of the 1973 field season, we decided to return to civilization by driving east across the desert to the Nile. There were no roads or tracks across this part of the desert. We were guided by Bahay Issawi's compass or by Eide Mariff's stars when we traveled at night. It was a large convoy that traveled back to Aswan and the Nile, and our progress was slow.

Late one afternoon we came into a large, unnamed dry basin. We decided to take an unplanned rest stop and have a petrol refill. Bahay calculated we were about six miles east of Jebel Nabta, a prominent, isolated hill that he had mapped several years earlier, about sixty-five miles, as the birds fly, west of Abu Simbel. As the vehicles stopped, we scattered for a relief stop, and several of us looked down and saw numerous stone artifacts and potsherds around our feet. A quick look disclosed numerous other concentrations of artifacts at several other places along the edge of the basin. It was a rich area, and I asked Tom if he would like to survey it next year. Tom said he would indeed. I told him we'd plan for him to do it the next year (1974) while the rest of us were working at Bir Sahara East and Bir Tarfawi.

The next year, several weeks before we left for Egypt, I asked Ryan if he still wanted to be left at Jebel Nabta, where we had seen several sites on our way to the Nile at the end of the previous season. He said he did. I asked him who he wanted to work with, and without hesitation he said, "Herb Mosca." He'd obviously been thinking about the project. Herb was another promising graduate student in the department who wanted to go to Egypt with us. Herb was in his mid-twenties, lean and tough, with a pleasant disposition, an ideal person for Tom Ryan to be isolated with in the desert for six weeks. Both were smart and hard workers.

Because of a serious misunderstanding between Rushdi Said and Issawi, Said decided to send Issawi to Libya to work for several years. Said was of the opinion that almost anyone could manage a camp in the Western Desert, including the organization of the complex transport of vehicles and their supplies to Bir Tarfawi. As a replacement for Issawi, and to show his low opinion of him, for our 1974 field season, Said looked for the least qualified person in the survey to be our camp manager. He selected a man who had been running a drilling rig.

Said allowed our regular guide, Eide, to accompany Issawi to Libya, and there was no one else in the survey who would admit to knowing how to get to Bir Tarfawi. The survey sent Eide's brother, Mohamed Shater, to be our guide, but despite living on the fringe of the desert for most of his life, he said he knew nothing about traveling in the desert except by camel, and nothing at all about finding Bir Tarfawi. The loss of Eide for our 1974 season was the first of many challenges to come.

I had invited my second son Mike to join us in the desert this second field season because I knew he'd wanted to be an archaeologist since his early days looking for stone artifacts and potsherds in the hills around Fort Burgwin. He said he really wanted to come to the desert with me. Peta knew how Mike felt and insisted that I take him. She even used her own money to buy him an air ticket. I wasn't surprised at Peta's gift because I knew she was very fond of Mike and knew he would appreciate her generosity.

In mid-January 1974, Mike and I and the rest of our crew assembled at Abu Simbel. We started out on what was supposed to be a long, one-day journey. We went first to Nabta, where we dropped off the two graduate students, Tom Ryan and Herb Mosca, a geological crew consisting of Vance Haynes, three young Egyptian Geological Survey geologists, a couple of workers, and a cook from the survey.

The group had a small lorry, two Russian Jeeps, a water tanker, and three tents. Tom and Herb were to do an archaeological survey, and the geologists were to make a map. In about six weeks, after their surveys and maps were completed, the group was to join us at Bir Sahara East. Not long after we left the survey group behind, we had our first sign of trouble: a broken axle on the large lorry. We were about eighteen miles west of Jebel Nabta, about ninety miles from the Nile. The motor pool had assigned us a worn-out lorry to carry our tents and other camp gear. Neither it nor the two Russian Jeeps were ready for a challenging journey.

It took a day and a half to fix the axle. We slept in our vehicles or on the sand. We had seven cases of beer, six cases of wine, several wooden crates containing ducks, and two goats. We had tried other animals such as sheep, turkeys, and chickens, but finally realized ducks and goats were the only animals that could survive a trip into the desert. When we were working in the Aswan Reservoir, we had taken a few turkeys with us, but as soon as they were let out of the cages, they took one look around, put their heads on the ground, and died. The problem with goats is that they have to be fed, and the cooks never seemed to remember to bring enough food for them. Both of the goats and one crate of ducks got away while we were en route to Bir Tarfawi during the two-day stop at Jebel Nabta. I'm not sure how it happened, but there was one broken duck crate on the ground when we finally left on the next, southwesterly leg of our trip to Bir Tarfawi.

Soon after the axle was repaired on the lorry, the two Jeeps broke down about twenty miles apart, before we were halfway to Bir Tarfawi. Both ran out of oil. We abandoned them until we could return to the Nile, put them on a truck, and take them back to Cairo for repair.

At the Egyptian-Sudanese border we turned due west. Someone had arranged for large laths, or stakes, to be planted every two hundred yards or so to mark our westward route along the border. The only problem was that during World War II this track had been a favorite route of the British for the movement of supplies from Wadi Halfa to Kufra, in southeast Libya. Their trucks had chewed up a mile-wide swath of the roadway.

As soon as we reached the Kufra track, our trucks began to get stuck in the churned-up, soft sand. It became a major problem when the truck with the supply of gasoline got stuck near the rear of the column. It ran on diesel and was almost empty. The truck carrying extra diesel was stuck near the head of the column. It ran on gasoline, and it, too, was low on fuel. The two trucks overheated and were soon low on water. I fumed that whoever planned this trip couldn't have made a bigger mess of things if he'd done it deliberately.

At dusk on the third day, the head of the column reached the end of the stakes and turned right to follow another line of stakes that was to guide our group northward to Bir Tarfawi. The sand was much harder, and soon the leading cars left the others behind to work their way out of the soft sand as best they could. Before long it was dark, and we lost the line of stakes. We decided we should stop and camp for one more night. It was good we did because almost immediately a cold sandstorm blew up and we lost all visibility. Mike and I dug a shallow hole beside the front tire of a large truck to shelter us from the wind. After we'd gotten comfortable in our hole, some kind soul came by and threw us a blanket. We settled down, trying to keep each other warm, and hoped to get some sleep. At one point in the night, Mike asked, "Dad, are all your field trips this difficult?"

The storm passed, and the morning of the fourth day dawned bright and clear. A truck came with news from the rest of the column: they had taken diesel fuel to the truck carrying the gasoline, and everyone had been refueled. All of the vehicles were moving forward, but there was a shortage of water. The camp manager decided that our two pickups and a Jeep should move north and find Bir Sahara East.

Before our scout group drove away, our camp manager suggested that when we found Bir Sahara East, we should dig out and clean the well there. A fourth car would follow and bring water back to the vehicles that needed it. This was a good plan, and soon all of the vehicles were in camp. The camp manager had the workers begin setting up the tents, and before dark everyone had a place to sleep. He set the camp in a good location on hard, packed sand on the east side of the depression above the well of Bir Sahara East.

We had lost three days. In the end the camp manager–driller got everything organized: no one was left behind, we had water, and the camp was functioning. The next day the entire group of scientists went to the north end of Bir Tarfawi, where in 1973 we had seen a dry lake bed with numerous large animal bones recently exposed by wind deflation. Our paleontologist, Achilles Gautier, determined that the bones included rhino, gazelle, antelope, and giant buffalo. The surface of the dry lake bed was littered with Middle Paleolithic artifacts, some of which seemed to be associated with the animal bones.

While others looked for sites in other parts of the Tarfawi basin, Gautier and I mapped the exposed fauna and the surface artifacts. Most of our previous work in 1973 concentrated on the Middle Paleolithic sites in the Sahara East basin.

Six weeks after we arrived at Bir Tarfawi/Sahara East, Rushdi Said made a surprise visit to our camp. He came with a car and driver, as is appropriate for the director of the geological survey, but it was a risky trip in only one vehicle. I was about to remind him that on long trips we always travel in two cars when he told me he was not pleased about the two abandoned Russian Jeeps he had seen on his way over. I wasn't pleased about our lack of a guide across the desert and the poor condition of the vehicles we were assigned, but after we groused a bit at each other, all was forgiven. Said had stopped off to see Tom Ryan, Herb Mosca, Vance Haynes, and the others at their camp near Jebel Nabta. Everything was going well, he said, except that their water tanker had once been used to haul gasoline, and their water tasted terrible. He also told me that our Nabta group would not join us as planned; they needed more time to complete both the archaeological and geological surveys. They wanted us to return to the Nile by way of Nabta and pick them up.

At Bir Tarfawi we worked eight weeks excavating several Middle Paleolithic sites. In addition, we tested a large spring vent with associated Final Acheulean hand axes at Bir Sahara East. The results of this work in the two basins were reported in Romuald Schild's and my *The Prehistory of an Egyptian Oasis.*

I don't recall any unusual events on the return trip to the Nile. As requested, we traveled by way of Jebel Nabta and examined several localities Ryan and Mosca thought merited additional study. Most were embedded in dunes or playa sediments. One site was particularly interesting. They had dug several test holes there, and one of these cut into a storage feature, while another yielded several large pieces of charcoal and a sherd with impressed designs on the exterior. We saved the sherd for later study, and the charcoal for radiocarbon dating.

Organizational Activities and Awards |
(1973–1996)

CHAPTER 25

As a professional archaeologist, I've always felt it was important to participate in the professional organizations that had the potential to effect policy
changes in the interest of archaeology's goals. In this chapter I'll briefly discuss my roles in these organizations and mention some of the honors that rewarded
my efforts.

In September 1972 Jane Holden Kelly (the daughter of Curry Holden, my old
boss at Texas Tech) was treasurer of the Society for American Archaeology. She called
me one day and asked if I would agree to seek election to replace her as treasurer of the
society. The SAA is the largest, most highly respected organization relating to American
archaeology, and the treasurer of that organization has considerable influence over
its activities. I learned from Jane that serious financial problems had arisen because
the society was spending more than it took in. I agreed to run, and in April of 1973 I
won the election for a term of three years, one as treasurer-elect, and two as treasurer.

At the annual meeting in April 1974, after I became treasurer, I announced to
the membership that we had a serious financial problem due in part to declining
membership and expanding expenditures. I told the members I would implement
a "tight money" policy, and with rare exceptions, I would reject all new proposals for
money. I defended my decisions before the board of trustees on financial rather than
intellectual grounds. A few times when I rejected a proposal, the applicant would go
around me and ask the membership to vote on the issue at the annual meeting. In
those cases I defended my decision to the membership on the same grounds I gave
the board of trustees. The members always supported me, but there were a few close
votes. I believed most of the members wanted fiscal responsibility, and that is what I
tried to give them.

My financial parsimony was coupled with the society's successful effort to increase the membership. As a result, at the end of my term as treasurer, the budget was not only balanced, but we had a surplus of about $250,000.

After my term as treasurer I was chosen as president-elect for one year, to be followed by a two-year term as president (1979–1981). During my term of office there were many problems between the officers of the SAA and the executive director of the much larger American Anthropological Association, which kept the SAA's account books. The problems, mostly over the management of the SAA's funds and the cost of printing and distributing our journal, *American Antiquity*, had a long history. When it was first organized, the SAA was small, and for many years the membership was less than five hundred. As the SAA grew, friction developed, partly because of the personality of the SAA's executive director, and partly because the SAA officers wanted to make their own decisions. Questions concerning where the annual meetings should be held and arrangements with the hotels were always contentious. We managed to keep harmony between the two organizations until the end of my term. Shortly after I stepped down there was a formal break, and the two societies went their separate ways, to the relief of the officers and most members of the SAA. The surplus we'd accrued gave the society a buffer it had never had before, allowing a few new initiatives, such as hiring a part-time lobbyist.

There was another issue I was unable to resolve as president. Congress had recently passed legislation that mandated archaeological investigation of any "land-disturbing" project involving federal funds, licenses, or permits. At the same time, pressure was building to have private firms, rather than universities, do salvage and preservation efforts. I anticipated that the federal bureaucracy would soon be making rules and regulations about this with little or no participation from the archaeological community. I raised the issue at my inaugural address, but there was little interest among the members. As I predicted, the rules were drafted without much participation from nongovernmental archaeologists.

In May of 1983, two years after my term ended as president of SAA, I received a call from one of the senior park service people I knew in Washington. He told me there would soon be a vacancy on the Secretary of the Interior's Advisory Board for the National Park Service, and he would like me to become a member of the board. It is a prestigious body of eight members who hold staggered four-year terms. The president of the United States appoints all of the members.

My caller asked if I had any influential friends who might suggest my name to President Reagan. The only one I could think of was Bill Clements, from my Fort Burgwin days. He was a strong Republican who had been governor of Texas (and would be again later), but was now out of office. I called Clements, and he agreed to suggest my name. A few weeks later, on July 20, 1983, I received a letter from the White House informing me of my appointment for a four-year term from July 1983 to July 1987. I am a lifelong "Yellow-Dog" Democrat, but neither Clements nor anyone else, then or before, ever asked me about my political affiliation.

I enjoyed and benefited from my participation on the Secretary of the Interior's Advisory Board for the National Park Service. All of the members, except me, were well-to-do and had influence in high places. All of us had a great interest in the National Park Service and what it does. We met at least once, sometimes twice a year, always at a national park or monument, the most interesting places one could imagine. At every meeting we were briefed, usually by the director, on the operation of the park service, its financial status, and the current problems he faced. This was followed by a summary report of the activities of the host park or monument. I learned a lot about the park system and its problems. I remain impressed with the care the rangers and other personnel take of our legacy, and how much they accomplish with the little money they receive.

After two years I was elected chairman of the advisory board. I used this opportunity to talk to the other members about my interest in archaeology, in particular, my concern for the preservation of historic shipwrecks, which I've already mentioned in Chapter 22.

Another use I made of my position as chairman was to develop interest within the park service for the preservation of the superb Art Deco buildings at Fair Park in Dallas. The city had not been consistent about the maintenance of the buildings, and they were deteriorating. I knew there was interest, mostly at city hall, in tearing down those magnificent structures. The Dallas Historical Society and all the other historical groups in the city opposed their planned destruction. The park service responded to my recommendation that the Fair Park buildings be preserved, and with the help of the local historical groups, and at the urging of the secretary's advisory board, the entire Art Deco complex was declared a National Historic Landmark in June of 1987. This assured that the complex wouldn't be destroyed. Later that year, in October, the Historic Preservation League of Dallas presented me with the Griffon Award. (Several sculptures of this fearsome creature decorate the roof edge of the old Dallas County courthouse.)

A little over a year after I stepped down from the secretary's advisory board, in October of 1988, the secretary of the interior awarded me a Distinguished Service Medal for Conservation, one of the highest awards the Department of the Interior can bestow.

••••

Since university professors often are not paid large salaries, one way our society honors such people is to give them awards. I received my first award on April 10, 1975, for my work in the Aswan Reservoir in Nubia, and at the recommendation of S. A. Huzayyin, I was elected an associate member of the Institut d'Egypt in Cairo. As far as awards are concerned, however, 1987 and 1988 were banner years for me. On April 20, 1987, I was elected to the United States National Academy of Sciences, the most prestigious award I could receive. The membership of the academy includes the most highly regarded scientists in our country, as well as the most distinguished foreign scientists who are elected as foreign associates. I secretly coveted election to the academy, but I realized that as a faculty member in a small university without a strong research record, I was not a likely candidate. For several years prior to my election, Jimmy Griffin, a member of the academy, had asked me to send him a copy of my most recent vita and a statement about my research accomplishments, but he avoided telling me why he wanted them. The academy insists that candidates must not know when they are being considered for membership. My friends honored that stipulation, probably because my election was by no means assured. Even if I were to be supported by all of the anthropologists in the anthropology section, the entire academy membership makes the final decision by secret ballot.

Once Griffin said to me, "Maybe next year." I knew he was up to something, and I thought—hoped—it might be the national academy. Later, two other friends in the academy told me separately, "This year, Fred." Finally, in April of 1987, during the annual meeting of the academy, I received a group phone call from Frank Hole, Jack Roberts, and Jimmy Griffin, three of my closest friends in the organization, who congratulated me on my election to the national academy.

I was so elated I was speechless. The *Dallas Morning News* called for a statement and found me at the airport waiting to board a flight to attend a meeting. I expressed my surprise and gratitude to those who'd worked so hard for my election. Twenty years later my election to the national academy is still one of the highlights of my life.

In March of 1988, a year after I left the Secretary of Interior's Advisory Board for the National Park Service, Ellen Herscher, a staff coordinator at the American Association of Museums, recommended me for the Cultural Properties Advisory Committee, a new group housed in the State Department charged with the responsibility to assist in the implementation of recent legislation to restrict the importation of antique cultural properties, such as archaeological artifacts, pottery, sculptures, paintings, and other old works of art. This new legislation was in response to UNESCO actions restricting the movement and sale of cultural properties without the permission of the country of origin. On April 26, 1988, President Reagan appointed me to the advisory committee.

At the first meeting I noted that I was the only member who was an archaeologist, a field sure to have a lot of business before such a board. Several of the members were art dealers; others were heads of museums, mostly art museums. Even at the first meeting it was clear that a few of the art dealers were not enthusiastic about the goals of the cultural properties legislation. The discussions were amiable, but sometimes sharp.

The Cultural Properties Board, unlike the Secretary of the Interior's Advisory Board, was openly political. One of the first things the staff did was to ask each member their political affiliation. When I said I was a Democrat, I saw displeasure on the young staff member's face. The appointments to the board were for four years, but in order to have staggered terms the staff decided to assign different term lengths for this first group of board members. I was not surprised when I was among those to receive a two-year term.

Under the terms of the legislation no action could be taken until a petition came from a country requesting the American government's assistance in stopping the importation of their cultural material into the United States. A formal application listing the endangered cultural properties had to be submitted and agreements signed before U.S. Customs could take action and seize the illegally imported material. It sounds cumbersome, and at first it was, partly because the antiquities authorities in almost every country failed to understand the need for the red tape. They were suspicious of our intentions, but after a few countries signed agreements, and there were some well-publicized recoveries of cultural materials by U.S. Customs, the resistance declined.

I used my contacts in Egypt to help start initial negotiations there, but I didn't feel I was useful as a member of the board. When my two years were up in 1989, I was ready to return to my research in Africa.

My last professional activity, other than continuing to excavate in Egypt and minor surveying in Sudan, was with the Society of Professional Archaeologists (SOPA). In the fall of 1992, Larry Banks, the senior archaeologist in the Army Corps of Engineers and president of SOPA, came to my office at SMU and asked if I'd object if he entered my name as a candidate for president of SOPA.

I said I'd be honored and pleased, and thanked him for considering me. I'd been a member since the first days of SOPA, but I'd never held an office in the society. I asked him the size of the membership. He told me there were about 450 members at that time.

"Why so few?" I asked. "That's not enough to be an effective organization. With all the salvage archaeology today and the increase in faculty teaching archaeology in universities and colleges, there must be between 4,000 and 5,000 professional archaeologists in the United States."

"I think many archaeologists are leery of the authority SOPA has to impose professional standards on our membership," Banks said. I replied, "But the standards aren't different from those of the Society for American Archaeology. Why're they concerned?" "Because SOPA has the power to investigate and impose penalties. SAA does not," he said.

I asked if he'd favor merging SOPA with SAA. "I think it would be the best thing possible for American archaeology," he responded. "But I believe there'd be strong opposition among many members of SOPA, and probably SAA."

In the spring of 1993, I became president-elect of SOPA for a two-year term, then president for two more years. During my first year as president I made several efforts to increase the membership in the society, with little success. I knew the small membership limited its ability to have a significant role in monitoring archaeological methods and standards. If you weren't a member of SOPA, you could do completely irresponsible archaeology without penalty. It was rare, but I had heard of a few instances of gross misbehavior that brought discredit to archaeology.

I began discussing a possible merger with SAA with individual members of the SOPA board and with some of the more influential members at large. At the beginning of my last year as president in 1996, the issue was well enough understood that the SOPA board voted to open negotiations with officers of SAA. The formula both groups eventually accepted was this: SOPA would cease to exist; at the same time SAA would create a separate professional entity within SAA that would adopt the same standards SOPA previously used. The new professional entity would have the same enforcement powers that existed in SOPA.

We brought the formula to both boards for their approval, and then submitted it to the membership of both organizations. The debate was sharp, sometimes hot, but in the end both memberships overwhelmingly approved the proposal. SOPA went out of business as I ended my term as president. Almost all SOPA members joined the new professional entity of the SAA, and so did many SAA members doing contract archaeological surveys and preservation.

Human Settlement in the Eastern | Sahara during the Holocene
(1975–1976)

CHAPTER 26

In the field, at about the same time I was serving as treasurer of the SAA, we were intensifying our studies of the Holocene in the Egyptian desert. The Holocene is the period after the last glacial event, the modern climatic period that began around 10,000 years ago and continues to today. Although we excavated several early and middle Holocene sites during our work in the Aswan Reservoir, the Holocene had not been one of our major interests while we were surveying and testing sites downstream from Aswan. It wasn't until we reached the Fayum Depression and its remarkable sites, ranging in age from early to late Holocene, that we again made a major effort to study the Holocene archaeology in the desert.

We had often seen traces of Holocene-age archaeology as we traveled across the desert, but many of them were so wind-deflated they held little interest. Also, the discovery of a rich sequence of Middle Paleolithic sites at Bir Sahara East and Bir Tarfawi in 1972 had diverted our attention away from the Holocene.

It wasn't until 1975 that we began a serious effort to study the Holocene-age human settlements in the Eastern Sahara. We began that effort at Nabta Playa, the large basin we had found accidentally in 1973, where Tom Ryan and Herb Mosca had spent eight weeks surveying in 1974 and had recorded several Early and Late Neolithic sites embedded in playa sediments.

While everyone else began working on the sites in the Nabta basin, Roman and I planned that at the beginning of the 1975 field season we would do something different: we would go exploring. A group consisting of Schild, Said, Vance Haynes, and me, with our guide, Eide Mariff, and three other drivers from the Egyptian Geological Survey, would leave Nabta for a week to do a survey of the area at the far western edge of Egypt, along the foot of the Gilf Kebir, a massive block of sandstone extending from the southern edge of the Great Sand Sea in northwestern Egypt to just north of the Sudan border in the south. The Gilf was 600 to 900 feet high, with steep, nearly vertical scarps on all sides, and an almost flat top. The western edge of the Gilf lies in Egypt, but barely; it's only a few miles east of the Egyptian-Libyan border. Egyptians rarely visited the site.

We planned to go to the southeastern edge of the Gilf and search some of the valleys known to cut back into the Gilf in that area. Ralph Bagnold and a group of young British army officers had surveyed some of the Gilf in the 1930s and found and studied several archaeological sites there. We wanted to determine if there was enough archaeology to justify a major project.

Vance Haynes had first worked with the Combined Prehistoric Expedition in 1968, near Dandara, and had been with us in 1973 and 1974 at Bir Sahara East and Bir Tarfawi. He preferred to do his geology on a broader scale than those of us of the CPE. We typically hunkered down in one area and studied it in detail, sometimes for several field seasons. Vance sought more independence. He applied for and received a National Geographic Society grant to purchase three Volkswagen 181s, affection-ately known as "Volkswagen Things." They were light, fuel-efficient, and reasonably sturdy. Vance arranged to show up at Nabta with his three "Things," a small Egyptian Geological Survey lorry, and an extra driver shortly after we arrived in camp. Schild and I would be joining forces with him for a survey in the Gilf.

After two or three days of tinkering with the motors on his "Things," Vance announced he was ready to go. He had a well-deserved, but not entirely accurate, reputation among those who worked with him in the Sahara for spending more time tuning and fixing his vehicles than he did doing geology. On the other hand, his numerous important publications show otherwise.

We loaded the "Things" with three small tents, purchased especially for this trip, along with a jerry can of water and canteens for each person, into each vehicle. We each also got a five-gallon can of gasoline and two boxes of dried food. One of the "Things" carried a small kerosene stove. The small lorry carried extra fuel for the "Things" and extra water and food for everyone. When we left, the lorry had two driv-ers. One had come with Vance and joined the first driver in the lorry. Our group was large enough for two people to ride in each "Thing," so we took turns driving, except for Schild, who couldn't drive. He and I were in one car, Vance and Eide in a second, and Said and the other driver in the third.

We left the Nabta camp early one morning in the second week of January and drove to Bir Sahara East, where we had our first meal of dried food. The dried meat tasted like cardboard. We put up the tents, refueled each vehicle, and went to bed.

Schild and I were still hungry, but we didn't complain, even though we regretted not bringing so much as a candy bar. The next morning our small convoy left Bir Sahara East and traveled slightly north of west, driving through rough country. At the end of the day we reached the point where we planned to leave the lorry behind. We refilled our vehicles and canteens and parked the lorry on top of a prominent hill. The two drivers were to wait there with it for our return, which we expected to be in three or four days. As we drove away we turned to the southwest, through more of the same rough country.

Soon, however, we noted impressions left in the hard-packed sand by a tracked vehicle. The impressions were clearly visible. We were able to follow them for several hours, but then lost them completely in an area of sandstone and shale. It is likely that the tracks had been left by a 1917 British army patrol that went into the area of the Gilf with a tracked vehicle to check on the reported presence of the Senusi, a tribe living in eastern Libya, near Kufra. They were known to be unfriendly to Egypt and the British.

As a diversion from life in Cairo, Bagnold and several other British officers stationed there began exploring the Western Desert in the 1930s. He and his Long Range Desert Group were in the area again during World War II, when they raided Germans and Italians behind the lines. Neither in the 1930s nor 1940s did Bagnold use tracked vehicles. In the 1930s they drove specially fitted Ford pickups, and in World War II they had Jeeps and Bedford trucks. It seemed likely the tracked vehicle we were following dated back to World War I. This is a good illustration of how disturbances of the hard-packed sandy desert surface can be visible for many years. In general, in the areas of flat sand sheets that characterize much of this desert, the wind arranges sand grains by size into numerous small patterns that persist through a long period of time, until there is a change in the climate, or a person or vehicle disturbs the patterns, or the area is covered by a modern sand dune.

Soon after we lost the old tracks, we saw the massive vertical wall of the Gilf Kebir in front of us. We worked our way south along the scarp and explored its southeastern section. We discovered an entrance to Wadi Bakht, one of the two large valleys that drain the east and southeast sides of the Gilf. As we drove up the north side of the wadi we could see an old dune that had once blocked drainage out of the valley. Soon, though, the surface sand grew soft. We stopped and got out of the cars and walked up the wadi. We saw numerous Neolithic artifacts, mostly Middle Neolithic and Late Neolithic, on the surface leading to the dune dam and on the deflated pond sediments beyond. We spent several hours in the area around the dam and drew a profile of the lake sediments exposed in the cut through the dune. It was this cut that had drained the lake. We also collected several ostrich eggshells from the pond sediments, enough for a radiocarbon date.

We could see a patch of soft sand on the south side of the wadi, so we shouted warnings to Said and Eide Mariff. They didn't hear us and continued to drive their "Thing" up the south side, and promptly got stuck in the soft sand. Schild and I went on with our artifact collecting while the others went to help Said and Eide Mariff. It took an hour's digging and pushing to extract the vehicle. When they got it out, Said drove his car out of the valley, where he waited for the rest of us to join him. I think he was spooked by the experience. I was, too. We were far removed from any help, and it was no place to get stuck or have a breakdown with such limited resources on hand. We decided to be more careful as we drove after that.

Bagnold's group reported in the *Geographical Journal* in 1939 in an article titled "An Expedition to Gilf Kebir and Uweinat, 1938" that they had found and collected an assemblage of Late or Final Acheulean hand axes on the surface of a long alluvial slope near the southeast corner of the Gilf. O. H. Myers, a trained prehistorian, made the collection. After our incident in the first valley we had no interest in searching for more valleys, so Schild and I went to see if we could locate where Myers had found the hand axes. When we got near the spot he'd described about two miles east of the Gilf scarp, we could see Myers's trenches, as well as many nails still embedded in the sediment of the alluvial fan. These nails marked the grid Myers had used to map the distribution of the hand axes.

Late that afternoon, we moved several miles north and found a place close to the wall of the Gilf. It was sheltered from the wind, and we camped there for the night. Two days later we were back with the lorry, and a day after that we were at Nabta. The Gilf didn't seem promising for archaeology. It was far from sources of water and other supplies, and most of the archaeology we saw in Wadi Bakht had been deflated. We decided to work elsewhere.

We had first noticed the Nabta basin and its potential importance when we stopped there to refuel on the way back from a long field season at Bir Sahara East/Bir Tarfawi in 1973. It was in this basin Tom Ryan and Herb Mosca had identified several promising sites. At one of these, they dug two small holes near the center of the site. In the first hole they cut into the side of a storage pit; the other yielded several pieces of charcoal and a potsherd decorated on the exterior with impressed rocker-stamped designs. When we returned to Dallas, we submitted the charcoal from their pit for radiocarbon dating. It yielded the surprising date of 8,000 years old. When that date came in, I looked at the potsherd, and then back at the date, and decided Tom and

Herb were having some fun with me by claiming they found a highly decorated potsherd in this Early Neolithic site. The sherd came from a small, deep, well-made bowl decorated with complex, rocker-stamped, comb-impressed designs. That sherd was different from the earliest known pottery in the Egyptian Nile Valley. It was unlike any I had seen in the valley, or from the Levant. If it was really 8,000 years old, then it was 1,600 years older than the Fayum Neolithic pottery, the oldest known along the Nile, or elsewhere in Egypt. How to explain that? Tom and Herb knew I was skeptical, and they could have been angry, but they were not. However, they remained firm in their insistence that the charcoal was associated with the potsherd.

In the summer of 1974 I submitted a proposal to the NSF requesting funds for a one-year grant to excavate several sites at Nabta Playa. In the proposal I pointed out the antiquity and significance of the Nabta rocker-stamped pottery, the numerous grinding stones on the surface of several of the sites Ryan and Mosca recorded, and the presence of storage pits, all of which suggested the possibility that we might find charred cereal grains. The proposal was approved for the amount requested. Everyone was intrigued by the possibility of wild cereals during the Late Paleolithic along the Nile, but most wanted to see the actual seeds.

In January of 1975, when we returned to Nabta to begin a systematic study of the Holocene archaeology there, one of the first places I wanted to examine was the site where Tom and Herb had found the potsherd.

Sadly, Ryan was not with us when we returned to Nabta. He had taken a job as an archaeologist with the U.S. Army Corps of Engineers and abandoned his plans for a graduate degree. Herb Mosca took us to find the spot. As we walked toward the site, we could still see traces of the small pit that had yielded the interesting sherd and charcoal. Schild, Mosca, and I made a careful search of the nearby surface and found two more similarly impressed sherds. We decided to excavate part of the site.

I asked Michal Kobusiewicz, an experienced Polish archaeologist, to direct the excavations, with Mosca as his assistant. As the excavations progressed we exposed several hut floors and storage pits. Some of the hut floors yielded a few sherds of rocker-impressed pottery similar to the sherd from the initial pit and those found on the surface. We knew we'd found something important with this pottery, but we found no charred cereals.

At the end of that 1975 field season, we submitted several samples of charcoal from the house floors and nearby storage pits for radiocarbon dating. The dates ranged in age from 8,050 to 7,600 years ago. With these new dates and associated potsherds, I had to admit that well-made, rocker-impressed pottery was much older in the Western Desert than I had previously believed. It was also evident that this

Saharan pottery was different from the oldest pottery in the Fayum Neolithic, where we'd worked in 1969. It was older than the Fayum pottery by at least 1,600 years. The evidence led me to begin thinking that pottery was present in the Eastern Sahara well before it was known in the Nile Valley.

We worked at Nabta Playa for eight weeks. Water for our camp had to be brought across the desert from Abu Simbel, some sixty miles to the east "as the crow flies." Once or twice a week two people in a pickup carrying a specially made water container would leave camp at daybreak and head east. When they arrived in Abu Simbel, one man would buy fresh vegetables, and sometimes fish or meat, for the camp. While one man purchased the food, the driver filled the water container no more than three-quarters full at the pump station where filtered and treated water was available for a small fee. The container held a ton of water, but this was too heavy for our pickup. It was a strain for the vehicle to carry even three-quarters of a ton. Water would slosh out during the trip, and we needed the water. After a quick lunch and a cup of tea, they drove north from Abu Simbel about five miles on the highway, then turned due west. There were no roads or trails, just rocky, sandy desert. With a fully loaded truck, it took five hours to reach our camp. They usually arrived after dark, around 8:00 P.M.

Because water was so difficult to obtain, we were careful with it. It was there I developed the "three-beaker bath," a cleansing technique I still employ whenever I'm in camp. Others probably also use it, with minor variations.

Each day, as soon as we returned from the field, everyone headed for his or her tent and a bath. If I had put my water can in the sun outside my tent before we left in the morning, I would have a warm bath. Occasionally I would forget, and the bath would be a cold one. Even on the coldest day, if I left the container outside, the sun would heat the water to a comfortable temperature.

Each tent had a plastic dishpan about two feet in diameter for use as a bathtub. First, I removed all my clothes, no matter how cold the day. Stooping over the bathtub, I wet my hair, just enough for shampoo to lather. Then, I took a beaker and slowly poured water over my head. Sometimes it took two beakers of water to rinse the soapsuds. With a washcloth I used the "clean" soapy water to wash my face, neck, arms, and legs. Then I squatted in the tub to wash my "best bits." I used a second or third beaker to rinse off the soapy water, starting at my face and on down. I'd step out of the tub, wrap a towel around me before I got too cold, sit on a chair I'd placed near the washbasin, and wash my feet. Using the soapy water in the tub, followed by a half beaker of clean water, I would rinse off. Total water used: three, maybe three and a half beakers. I was not truly clean, of course, but I was "camp clean." It didn't matter too much, since we all smelled alike.

One time after a ten-week stay in the desert we went to Cairo and rented rooms at my favorite cheap hotel, the Garden City House. I had a room and bath with a shower in the tub. I got in the tub, turned on the shower and began washing my body, starting at the top and going down. Halfway through I looked down. The bottom of the tub was covered with sand and dirt, which, despite my daily bath, had accumulated during the long field season.

In order to have a better idea of the variation in the Neolithic in the Western Desert, Schild and I decided we needed to sample other areas where Holocene sites had been reported, or where on one of our surveys we had seen what appeared to be sites of that age. So, when I returned to Dallas in March of 1975, I began preparing a one-year proposal to work at Kharga. The first section of the proposal outlined the results of our 1975 season at Nabta, followed by a discussion of our goals, including our desire to investigate the diversity in the Neolithic of the Sahara and establish the chronology of the Neolithic sequence.

In the proposal, I drew heavily on the magnificent book by Gertrude Caton-Thompson describing her 1930s work at Kharga. She had excavated several spring vents and studied their associated artifacts. The sites ranged in age from Late Acheulean through several phases of Middle Paleolithic, including a spectacular Aterian locality (a Middle Paleolithic entity with a unique stone toolkit widely known in the Central and Western Sahara and coastal Maghreb). Caton-Thompson's group also studied several localities they identified as "Peasant Neolithic." I knew from their discussion that several other spring vents were present, but these hadn't been studied. I proposed to focus on these unstudied sites and whatever Neolithic entities we could find.

The only deficiency in Caton-Thompson's data that I was aware of lay in the small sample sizes she was able to recover from some of the Middle Paleolithic entities. These small samples had frustrated our efforts to make a close comparison between her Middle Paleolithic results and ours from Bir Tarfawi and Bir Sahara East. As in the Fayum, at Kharga we would be walking in Caton-Thompson's footprints.

I applied for and received a new NSF grant for the 1976 season at Kharga. The grant included funds for two new 1976 Land Rover pickups, which I bought in England and had shipped to Alexandria the following January. Upon their arrival, Said cleared them through customs. With a second driver, he took them to Cairo, and then to Kharga, where we took charge of them.

We had a new camp manager, Mohamed Hinnawi, a gentle, soft-spoken senior geologist of the Egyptian Geological Survey. Those who worked with us in 1976 remember Hinnawi best for the care he took with our money. He booked us on the cheapest bus he could find going from Cairo to Kharga, complete with goats, small children, and more passengers than seats. He refused to buy what he considered was "too much toilet paper." When we ran out at the end of the third week in camp, he could find no toilet paper in Kharga. As a substitute he bought a large supply of a purple decorative paper that will forever be known as "Hinnawi Crepe."

Among the 1976 staff was Anne Attebury, a graduate student at SMU, the first unmarried woman staff member ever permitted in a geological survey camp. It was Said who changed the rules. Attebury was a pretty young woman, and she got a lot of attention from the young geologists and Egyptian Antiquities Organization person-nel. One of the latter made a pass at her within his first half hour in camp. I repri-manded him, but Anne was unruffled and went on with her work.

Because of a head cold, Attebury had more problems than most with Hinnawi's toilet paper. She quickly went through her own supply of Kleenex tissues and her share of the initial supply of toilet paper. For most of the field season she had only Hinnawi Crepe.

Attebury was an excellent archaeologist, slow and careful. She excavated two spring mounds with associated Late Neolithic archaeology. After several days of dig-ging, however, it was clear to both of us that the sediments in both spring mounds were hopelessly mixed. I moved her to two other Late Neolithic sites at the edge of what had been spring-fed ponds. The associated pottery in both sites was plain, smoothed, but not burnished, unlike the Neolithic rocker-stamped pottery we had found at Nabta.

While Anne was excavating the two spring ponds, I found and excavated a Mid-dle Paleolithic "Aterian" living surface embedded under a thin horizon of carbon-ates, a residue that evaporates in spring waters that covered the occupation surface. I was particularly interested in this site because most of the Aterian flakes and cores had been made on thin flint tablets available within 50 feet of the occupation. This proximity resulted in a lithic raw material economy significantly different from those we recovered from Bir Tarfawi and Bir Sahara East, where the lithic raw material had come from quarries several miles distant, near the edge of the Tarfawi depression.

Most of the initial preparation of the Middle Paleolithic cores at Tarfawi occurred at the distant quarries. From there the core blocks were taken to the shores of the Sahara/Tarfawi lakes, where they were shaped and initially exploited. There the tool-makers removed from the cores and left numerous atypical or failed Levallois flakes.

The numerous Middle Paleolithic sites along the shores of the Sahara/Tarfawi lakes functioned, for the most part, as secondary workshops. In contrast, the lithic assemblage at the Aterian site I dug at Kharga had high frequencies of early workshop and core preparation debris and numerous finished tools. These frequencies indicate that the initial preparation of the cores, the removal of blanks, and the shaping of the tools all occurred at this locality.

I walked around and looked at the artifacts still present on the surface of several other Middle Paleolithic sites Caton-Thompson had excavated at Kharga. All of them contained high frequencies of early workshop debris. This was a casual observation on my part, and may have been biased by selection due to Caton-Thompson's surface collecting, or that of later visitors. But the Kharga sites I examined seemed to have a lithic structure different from that in our Middle Paleolithic sites in the beaches and in the drying lake sediments at Bir Tarfawi and Bir Sahara East. I concluded that the differences were a reflection of the proximity of good tabular flint at the Kharga sites, and a result of the longer distances the quartzitic sandstone had to be carried at Bir Tarfawi and Bir Sahara East.

During the first week, 200 yards from our Kharga camp, I found a small, dense surface concentration containing numerous elongated scalene triangles. When Schild arrived a week or so after the others had begun their excavations, he and I together, using a plane table, grid paper, and a sharp pencil, mapped the position of every artifact by type on the surface of the "scalene triangle site." This technique is known as scatter patterning. We dug a few stratigraphic trenches, but all of the archaeology lay on the cemented surface; we recovered just a few pieces from the carbonate-cemented silt immediately below the surface.

A sad event occurred at Kharga that may be useful to others who are fortunate enough to work in the Sahara. Herb Mosca, one of my best senior graduate students, had almost finished his PhD dissertation, a significant part of which was an analysis of a large Late Neolithic site at Kharga. Near the end of the season he was doing a final check and had everything laid out on his bed, including maps, tables, and charts.

As dinnertime approached, I was looking at the sky because I didn't like the feel in the air; it was too quiet and hot. I stopped by Herb's tent and suggested that he might want to put everything away in his wooden box before he came to dinner. Herb forgot my warning and left everything on his bed when he left for the dining tent.

A sandstorm with high northwest winds hit without warning an hour or so later, near the end of the meal. The wind was as strong as anything I'd seen before in the desert. Our camp was in a soft, sandy area, not well protected from winds in any direction. Almost immediately most of the tents in camp, including Herb's, were blown down, and everything in them not properly protected was blown away.

The next morning most of us not engaged in putting the camp back together searched everywhere for Herb's manuscript and maps. The largest piece we found was about the size of a half dollar. Herb was desolate.

With computer technology and "backing up your data," a loss such as Mosca's would probably be rare today. After that storm I became more aware of such dangers and always cautioned the students and the staff to take appropriate precautions, even when the air is clear and calm.

While we were excavating at Kharga, Vance Haynes and Pete Mehringher, with a geologist from the geological survey and a driver/mechanic, came by our camp on the way back from a long survey in northern Sudan. Before they reached our camp, they had stopped briefly in an area east of Bir Kiseiba and found many archaeological sites. They urged us to examine the area, too.

After Haynes and his group left for Cairo and home, Hinnawi, Schild, and I made a one-day survey of the Bir Kiseiba area, and, as Haynes had reported, we found many sites in the area extending from eight to twenty miles east of Kiseiba. We had more good fortune when Hinnawi saw the sites near Kiseiba, because he remembered other playas with archaeological sites like these in an area south of the Bir. We decided to work in the Kiseiba area as soon as possible.

For me personally, 1975–1976 were terrible years. In 1975, Angela Close, a graduate student of Charles McBurney's at Cambridge University, had asked me, on his behalf, to serve on her dissertation examination committee. Angela, a Briton, had spent a semester at SMU studying some of our collections from Nubia, and she had used the data in her dissertation. When I agreed to sit on her committee, she sent me a copy of her dissertation. It was an excellent, innovative, and well-written thesis. She compared several North African Late Paleolithic lithic assemblages from Algeria and Libya with others in the Nile Valley. She identified several stylistic attributes present on some lithic tools, but absent on others, and used statistics on the frequencies of these attributes to measure the social distance between the various sites that were otherwise closely similar lithic assemblages. It was a new way to look at flaked stone artifacts.

I traveled to Cambridge, and after her successful defense of her dissertation, Angela went with me to see Stonehenge. While we were there we became romantically involved. She was beautiful and young. I fell hopelessly in love with her and stupidly thought Peta wouldn't find out about this indiscretion.

When I returned to Dallas, I began to plan how I might bring Angela to SMU so she could work with me and we could continue our relationship. I had a collection of five closely related sites near Esna that looked ideal for her statistical technique. With the help of Senator John Tower, and using that proposed study, I got her a "green card" so she could come to the States and work.

Two days before she arrived in Dallas, Peta was showing Kelly and Scott how a passport works. She got out my passport from my study and saw that I had been in England several days longer than I had told her. She knew immediately that I had been with Angela. She may have been alerted by my decision to bring Angela to Dallas. I think women have a sixth sense about things like that. As soon as I got home that evening she confronted me, and I confessed.

I was in turmoil; I still loved Peta, but I was unable to control my feelings for Angela. Peta would have forgiven me if I had sent Angela back to England. Her love and trust might not have been the same as before, but we could have saved our marriage. I was torn; I loved Peta and wanted to save our marriage, but I couldn't find the strength to send Angela home. I moved to an apartment and tried to concentrate on my work.

Three months later I finally mustered the strength to ask Peta to forgive me and give our marriage another chance. I called her and told her I wanted to see her. She brought me into the kitchen, but before I could say anything, she excused herself and left the room. I looked down, and there on the kitchen counter in front of me was a love letter she was writing to a man who lived in another state. When she came back, I said, "I guess it's too late."

She nodded and said, "Yes, I'm truly sorry." I doubt if it was an accident she'd left the letter where I could see it.

Three months later, in January 1976, I left for Egypt and Kharga Oasis, where the expedition was to spend eight weeks in camp. While I was there, Said brought me a letter from Peta. He gave it to me at the dinner table, and I opened it, thinking it might be a letter of reconciliation. But she wanted a divorce. I was so shocked I had to leave the table.

In April of 1976, a few days after I returned from Egypt, she asked me to drive her to the courthouse to finalize the divorce. We had been married twelve years. After the divorce I tried one more time to reconcile with Peta, just before I was going to Europe to attend a meeting of the International Union of Prehistoric and Protohistoric Sciences. This time I pleaded with her to let me come home. I told her that if she said yes, I wouldn't go to Europe. Again she refused.

While I was in Europe at the conference I asked Angela to marry me. She said yes. After the meeting in France, we went to her home in Kettlewell, a small village in the hill country of Yorkshire. We were married at the county clerk's office in Skipton, a market town about fifteen miles from Kettlewell.

When we returned to Dallas I went immediately to see Peta because I didn't want her to hear from someone else that Angela and I were married. She opened the door, but before I could say a word, she said, "Oh, Fred, I'm so glad you're back. Please come back home." "Oh, God, Peta," I said. "Angela and I were just married in England. I'm so sorry."

How could we have had so many near misses? I left Peta, got in my car, and cried for a long time before I could drive away. I knew I was being punished for being weak and foolish. I vowed that I would never do anything that would ruin my marriage with Angela.

My divorce and marriage to Angela were terrible for my young children, Kelly and Scott. Scott was only eight. Several months later Peta married a man who had a ranch in New Mexico. Scott and Kelly soon left their University Park schools and moved to New Mexico with their mother and new stepfather.

Kelly was twelve when Peta and I divorced, and may have been better prepared for the changes in her life. In New Mexico, Kelly became a star athlete in track. She could outrun many of the boys and all of the girls on the track team, to the great embarrassment of the boys.

It was also a difficult time for me. Peta told me I could always come to New Mexico and visit the children, but she would only let them stay with me for a month in the summer. The month in the summer was not enough; I could feel both of them drifting away from me.

When Peta and I were divorced, my four oldest children from my first marriage were either adults or almost adults. The oldest, Carl, had graduated from the University of Arizona and was working in Tucson as an electrical engineer. Mike and Gail were in college; Cindy was in high school in Bisbee, where Nancy had relocated after our divorce to be near her mother.

In 1977 Mike graduated from the University of Arizona with a BA degree in anthropology. After graduation, he came to stay with Angela and me in our apartment while he decided what he wanted to do with his life. At the end of the summer Mike told me he'd decided he wanted to be an archaeologist. He ultimately chose to attend the University of California at Berkeley, which at the time had one of the best archaeology programs in the country.

In September of 1965 Gail enrolled in the School of Arts at SMU, but after only one semester at SMU she left for Riverside, California, to join the man she wanted to marry. She promised me she would get a college degree, and a few months after they married she enrolled in a special major in archaeological illustration in the art program at California State University in Los Angeles, and received her BA in 1978. She told me she was not happy at SMU, but I suspect it was the romance beckoning in California, not the social life at SMU, which caused her to leave.

When I married Angela, Cindy was sixteen. She never accepted Angela, and when she graduated from high school she declined to come to SMU, even though as my daughter she would have had free tuition. She enrolled at the University of Arizona and received her BA degree in psychology. After graduation, for several years she worked in Bisbee as social worker for the state.

I called each of my children at least once a month to let them know I was think-ing of them, and to be sure they were well and happy. I also made it a point to visit each one a couple times a year. Even so, I couldn't help but feel they thought I had abandoned them.

The Middle Awash and Bodo Man
(1975–1980)

CHAPTER 27

As it turned out, when the 1973 field season at Gademotta ended (described in Chapter 20), I was not through in Ethiopia. Jon Kalb, a Texas geologist who had been working in the Awash Basin with Donald Johanson of "Lucy" fame, had had a major disagreement with him. Kalb had obtained a license to study a large area in the Middle Awash south of the area where Lucy had been found and was looking for an archaeologist to work with him at his new site.

In the fall of 1975 Kalb came to see me in Dallas. He told me he had found several Acheulean and Middle Stone Age living sites in the Middle Awash with fauna, as well as several single large animal kills or scavenge/butchery localities. Kalb's description was impressive. He asked me to join him, but I was reluctant to seek an NSF grant on the basis of Kalb's descriptions alone, so I decided to ask two of my graduate students to go to Ethiopia, work with Kalb, and survey the area covered by his permit. The first to join Kalb in the Middle Awash was Herb Mosca. I arranged for him to go to Ethiopia with me after the 1976 excavations at Kharga Oasis and stay on for several weeks after I left. I expected Mosca to stay six weeks with Kalb, but he stayed for nine months. When he returned to Dallas, Herb told me he was giving up archaeology and would study for a master's degree in geology. He eventually became an oil geologist, and a successful one.

The second student I sent to work with Kalb was Bill Singleton. I arranged for him to join Kalb in January of 1977, after Mosca left. He and his wife had been working for several months in Zimbabwe. I planned to visit them in the Middle Awash Valley after the excavations at Wadi Kubbaniya. I hoped to visit the most important sites and decide if a large project was justified. If it was, I would leave Singleton to continue the survey while I prepared a proposal to the NSF. At the same time I would write a second major proposal to the NSF to support our research at Wadi Kubbaniya in Egypt. That project was to begin in January 1978.

Meanwhile, I needed to find ten thousand dollars to cover Mosca's and Singleton's expenses. I went first to Owen Henderson and Russ Morrison, who earlier had been with me to the Middle Awash and had seen the rich archaeology there. They wrote a check for five thousand dollars. I told them there was a good chance that the survey party might make a major discovery, and if so, I asked if they would consent to being identified in the news story. They both said no.

I then asked Bill DeSanders, a Dallas Cadillac dealer who had an interest in my work, for his support. He, too, sent me a check for five thousand dollars. I asked DeSanders if he would object to being identified as a benefactor of the project, and he said he had no objection.

Within a few weeks of my departure from Ethiopia in 1978, Kalb called me in Dallas to tell me that an Ethiopian student in the survey party had found a human cranium with most of the face intact except the lower jaw. It was found in the Middle Awash, at a place known as Bodo. The skullcap was broken into many pieces, but was restorable. On the basis of the preserved face, Jon thought it might be a progressive *Homo erectus,* a type of human known to be present in southern and eastern Africa around 700,000 years ago.

He asked if I wanted to come to Addis for the press announcement with the minister of culture. I told him to go ahead without me. I waited a couple of days, thinking the find had been announced in Addis Ababa, and I then told a reporter from the *Dallas Morning News* about the find. Unfortunately, my story came out the day before the find was announced in Addis. The minister was not pleased, but Kalb managed to smooth things over.

The Bodo cranium turned out to be the oldest known archaic *Homo sapiens.* The fauna with it were dated around 600,000 years old. Bodo was an important find, but its discovery brought trouble. I have been told that Johanson thought Kalb was a CIA agent. Johanson went to the Ethiopian minister and told him of his concern. The minister knew of the bad blood between the two men and didn't take the allegation seriously. However, a few months later, Glynn Isaac, an archaeologist at the University of California at Berkeley, heard the rumors that Kalb *was* a CIA agent. Isaac was a member of the NSF panel reviewing my two latest proposals, and at the next meeting of the NSF panel he brought up the matter of Kalb and the CIA.

Nancy Gonzales, the NSF staff member who was chairing the meeting, was so disturbed by the allegation that she called me in Dallas that day and asked me if I was coming to the annual meeting of the Society for American Archaeology to be held later that week in Washington. I said I was coming the next day. She requested that I meet with her as soon as possible. I left early the next day for Washington and went immediately to her office.

The first thing Gonzales asked was if Kalb or I were CIA agents. I laughed at her question and said, "I'm not, and I've never had anything to do with the CIA. Furthermore, I seriously doubt if Kalb is an agent. He doesn't act like one. I know some people in Africa I think could be CIA agents, since they are always hanging around the politicians. Such people would never go into the hellhole of the Afar Depression or the Middle Awash, drink hippo water, and fight mosquitoes for four to six months at a time. No way."

"Where does he get his money?" she asked. I replied, "Kalb receives modest funds from a small foundation in Connecticut." She smiled and said, "I believe you, Fred. But just to be sure, I'm going to the State Department and the CIA tomorrow and ask them if Kalb is one of their agents." "Oh, for Christ sakes, Nancy, don't do that; it will only stir things up," I said.

But she insisted. Then she changed the subject and said, "The panel has approved both of your proposals, but I'll only approve one, either the proposal for the Middle Awash, or the one for Wadi Kubbaniya. Which do you want?"

"That's easy," I said. "Only crazy people want to work in the Middle Awash; it's hot and miserable there. Besides, I have a promising project at Wadi Kubbaniya. If I can have only one, that's the proposal I want you to fund."

Later that day I ran into Glynn Isaac at the meetings. He told me that at the NSF panel meeting he had brought up the issue about the CIA. He asked me if I was a CIA agent. I answered him as I had Gonzales. "Thanks, Fred. I just had to ask," he said. "Glynn," I said, "We have to be careful about rumors like this. They might get an innocent person killed."

Since the Soviets were by then running Ethiopia, I was not surprised that in mid-1978 the head of the Department of Public Security expelled Kalb from Ethiopia. As it was later described to me, the meeting between Kalb and Ethiopia's minister of culture went something like this: "Jon, I had dismissed Johanson's story about you and the CIA, but I've just been informed that an official at the National Science Foundation has been asking the U.S. State Department and the CIA if you're one of their agents." Jon and his family were ordered to leave Ethiopia within a week, even though they had lived in the country for seven and a half years. Shortly thereafter, the minister terminated all archaeological and human paleontological research in Ethiopia for ten years.

In 1993 the editor of the *American Journal of Physical Anthropology* called to ask me to review Robert Bell's book *Impure Science*. The first chapter concerned the Kalb-Johanson problem. After describing the incident, I went on to say that I found Johanson's accusation to be ludicrous because "No CIA agent would go out into the hellhole of the Middle Awash for months on end, traveling in a beat-up Land Rover, sleeping on the ground, with no one to talk to but a couple of graduate students and an Afar guide. What would he have reported? That the water tasted like hippo urine?"

Return to Nabta Playa and Bir Kiseiba
(1977, 1978–1980)

CHAPTER 28

B y 1977, Angela Close went with us every year to the Egyptian Sahara. Charles McBurney, at Cambridge University, had trained her to be a good archaeologist. She was, in addition, skilled in mathematics and statistics. She was an excellent writer and editor, as well as remarkably bright and hardworking. Despite being shy and reserved, she quickly became a valuable member of our field and laboratory team.

A large group of scientists participated in the 1977 field season at Nabta. These included Mohamed Hinnawi, our camp manager the previous year at Kharga; his boss, Rushdi Said, president of the Egyptian Geological Survey; Romuald Schild, Michal Kobusiewicz, and Hanna Wieckowska, all archaeologists from the Polish Academy of Sciences; Vance Haynes, a geologist from the University of Arizona; Nabil El Hadidi, a botanist from the University of Cairo; Ahmed Said Hindi, antiquities inspector for the Egyptian Antiquities Organization; and Anne Attebury, Angela Close, Kimball Banks, and me from SMU.

Before we went into the field, Kimball Banks managed to draw attention to himself while we were still in Cairo. Despite my warning to avoid the perfume shops in the Souk (a fabulous market in Cairo where you can buy everything), a perfume salesman had trapped him, and he had bought a large bottle of strong perfume. He put it in his coat pocket and somehow it broke.

He and I were to have lunch with Said at a nice café in downtown Cairo. I arrived first, and when Banks came in there was no need from him to tell me what happened. Those seated near us abandoned their tables and moved elsewhere. You could smell him across the room. When Said arrived, he sat down next to Banks. A moment later he identified the source of the potent smell and moved next to me. I suggested to

Banks that maybe he should go to the restroom to see if he could wash off some of the perfume. "I've already tried that," he said. I responded, "Try again."

When he left the table, Said whispered to me, "I didn't know he was that kind of fellow." I broke out laughing and said, "He's not. I understand he has a full scorecard."

But when Banks returned, Said, nevertheless, kept well away from him.

In 1977 we focused on the Neolithic sites at Nabta and those in two nearby playa basins. The work included major excavations at two sites: one, the Early Neolithic village where Tom and Herb had found the 8,000-year-old potsherd; and the other, a younger settlement with two rich horizons, a Middle Neolithic, at what we thought was the base, and a Late Neolithic above that. We also dug two additional Neolithic sites. In one of them the tool group was dominated by elegant, long, thin lunates, and the other had long stemmed points lightly retouched at the distal end. We were unable to place either of the sites in chronological sequence because we were confused by the stratigraphy in the basin. Nabil El Hadidi, our botanist, asked what plant remains I expected to find. I told him I hoped we'd find cereals, possibly barley or even wheat. I pointed out all the grinding stones scattered over the surface and said people were using them to grind some kind of grain, and I bet it was barley. I mentioned a Polish expert in fossil pollen who had identified barley pollen at one of our Late Paleolithic sites near Esna.

A few days later Hadidi announced that he had indeed recovered several grains of barley from a storage pit in the site we were excavating, the site with several radiocarbon dates around 8,000 years ago. Later that week he announced another discovery: seeds of both wheat and barley at a second, slightly later site, dating about 7,000 years old, across the basin from his first find. It was a spectacular discovery: the oldest known barley and wheat in Egypt. We thought it explained the numerous grinding stones and large storage pits that occurred at both sites. The next day Hadidi left to return to Cairo, but before leaving he said he'd clean the seeds carefully and show them to us when we got to Cairo.

In spite of the enormous scope of our excavations and the numerous stratigraphic trenches we dug, we were unable to decipher the complex stratigraphy the sediments in Nabta Playa presented. Although we were still confused by the stratigraphy, after the end of this field season, Schild and I coauthored our first synthesis of the prehistory in the Eastern Sahara, titled *The Prehistory of the Eastern Sahara.*

We had, without any discussion, adopted an understanding that when Schild wrote most of a manuscript for publication, he would be the senior author, and when I wrote most of the manuscript, I would be the senior author. I believe this arrangement began when Schild sent me a draft of the manuscript for *The Prehistory of Dakhla Oasis* and he'd listed me as senior author even though I had little to do with writing the manuscript. I wrote back and told Schild to put himself as senior author with me as second author. About this same time we adopted another policy without talking about it. We decided neither of us would publish anything on our field work together without the other being listed as coauthor. These arrangements have worked well for both of us.

This was Kimball Banks's first season in the Sahara, although he had spent several years digging in the American Southwest. He was a graduate student at SMU, about twenty-seven years old, and full of fun. He looked and dressed like a cowboy. He wore a large felt hat, handlebar mustache, boots, jeans, and a wide leather belt. He drove a pickup, and I liked him a lot.

We were having trouble with both of our Land Rovers. The low-octane Egyptian gasoline caused them to "diesel." After a long, hot drive, when they were turned off, both would continue running for several minutes. Banks told me he knew how to stop the dieseling. I told him to go ahead and fix them.

He borrowed a few tools from the driver-mechanics and went to work. The mechanics watched, but they kept looking at me and shaking their heads. When Banks decided the Land Rovers were fixed, he got in one, started the motor, and tried to drive off. It barely moved. He got in the second Land Rover and tried it. Same thing.

"Come on, Kim, let's get a cup of tea and let the mechanics retune them," I said. A half hour later they were ready to roll, but still dieseling. That was the last time Banks ever claimed to be a mechanic.

Bir Kiseiba is a desert well that, until recently, was a source of good water about three feet below the surface. Generations of Bedouin camel herders and traders before us had used it. They followed the Darb el Arbain (Road of Forty Days), which ran from Esna and Kharga to Bir Kiseiba, and from there to El Fasher in western Sudan and beyond into Central Africa. The *bir* is at the eastern edge and near the foot of the northeast-trending Kiseiba Scarp, a nearly vertical cliff from 300 to 600 feet high in the Kiseiba area. Farther east the Kiseiba Scarp blends into the Eocene Scarp, a nearly vertical cliff 1,500 feet high that marks the abrupt northern boundary of the warm tans and browns of the Nabta/Kiseiba lowlands and separates them from the gloomy, gray highlands of the Eocene Plateau to the north.

Our camp manager in 1979 at Bir Kiseiba was the easygoing Mohammed Hinnawi, who had been with us at Kharga (1976), Nabta Playa (1977), and the first season at Wadi Kubbaniya (1978). With Issawi, he had mapped the Holocene playas in this area and knew the Kiseiba area well. He took us to several playas he thought were likely to contain archaeology.

Hinnawi picked a much better campsite than we'd had at Kharga. He placed the tents on hard-packed sand near two large, nearly adjoining jebels, about six miles northeast of Bir Kiseiba. They were easily seen from a great distance in any direction, and thus easy to find when we were coming home late in the afternoon from a distant survey.

Beginning about two miles east of the twin jebels and continuing in a west-to-east direction for another twenty miles was an extensive pediment that sloped to the south, away from the Kiseiba Scarp. At its foot was a large bedrock basin with several subbasins. Most of the basins had been deflated to Paleocene bedrock, but here and there the landscape offered some protection against the wind for the softer Holocene playa sediments in the subbasins. Often archaeology was embedded in these playa deposits. The archaeology frequently included material from several typological entities, but the most frequent sites were what we called El Nabta and Al Jerar Early Neolithic, both of which had storage pits and shallow huts, like those at Nabta. In a few places, still earlier Neolithic sites occurred within the pediment deposits overlooking the deflated basins. We excavated several of these earlier Neolithic sites, including two Michal Kobusiewicz and Hanna Wieckowska had dug. Kimball Banks cleared what may have been an El Nabta pit house, some sort of rectangular, subsurface feature. In the same general area Kobusiewicz excavated a rich El Nabta site with an earlier occupation stratified below it.

Our fieldwork at Bir Kiseiba provided significant new data suggesting a complex Holocene climatic sequence for the region. But perhaps the most exciting new find in these excavations was the evidence that domestic cattle had been present at several excavated localities dating before 9,000 years ago. The consistent, but rare, presence of cattle bones suggested that cattle had been an important component of the desert economy, possibly a source of milk and blood, both of which modern cattle pastoralists in East Africa drink.

Rare ceramics also occurred in several of these earliest Neolithic sites dating before 9,000 years ago. This new information from the Kiseiba sites and the stratigraphic observations on the sequence of sediments in the playas enabled us to publish our first synthesis of the Neolithic in the Egyptian Sahara. Schild, Close, and I assembled and edited the study, which was titled *Cattle Keepers of the Eastern Sahara: The Neolithic of Bir Kiseiba*.

At a meeting with Hal Williams, my dean at SMU, shortly after *Cattle Keepers* was published, Williams gently criticized me for publishing the book in-house. He told me that it would have had more impact if a commercial press had published it.

"I know, Hal," I said, "but it would take two years to line up a commercial press and another year or more to get it printed and distributed. By publishing the work here, the information will reach my colleagues and the NSF within a year. Since the NSF will soon review my next grant application, I believe it pays to be prompt in showing what you learned with their money."

At the end of our first season at Kiseiba, Mohammed Hinnawi was promoted to an office job in Cairo. Rushdi Said assigned Ali Mazhar, another senior geologist at the survey, to be our camp manager in 1980.

Ali Mazhar is, if you don't cross him, a pleasant man. He runs a tight, efficient camp. Those who enjoyed the pleasures of mealtime at our camp after Mazhar came on board will tell you that their strongest impression came from Ali Mazhar. Though the food was always great, and the cook was every man's hero, it is Ali Mazhar everyone remembers.

Food handling operations in camp occurred in two tents. First, the square dining tent, which was about fifteen feet on the side, with a doorway at one end and a long table set up in the center, which could seat ten comfortably, twelve if necessary. About thirty feet away was the second, the cook tent, which was also square, perhaps eighteen feet on a side, with a butane cookstove, an oven, and several small kerosene stoves for emergencies if the butane was exhausted. Boxes of cooking gear lined the margin of the cook tent. Food preparation and cooking occurred there, and the dishes were washed and air-dried there. Two *sufraggis* worked in the kitchen, except when they were sweeping the dining tent, setting the table, carrying water, or sweeping the dust out of our sleeping tents.

Ali always sat by the door of the dining tent. Because the cook tent was noisy, with people talking and the stove hissing, it was difficult for us to get the *sufraggis'* attention. Ali had a loud voice, and when he yelled, *Yasser!* or *Mohamed!* everyone in the dining tent jumped. Immediately, Yasser or Mohamed would come through the doorway, wide-eyed and ready to do whatever Ali wanted. It was a pleasure to witness such efficiency.

Ali decided to go to Bir Kiseiba by way of Kharga rather than going west from Aswan and Abu Simbel. He put all of us foreigners on a fast bus from Cairo (there were no goats on this one). Once we arrived in Kharga, we stayed at the geological survey rest house until Ali was ready to move south. We had to wait because the antiquities inspector was coming separately to Kharga from Assuit.

I was with Ali at Kharga on a cold day in January of 1980, waiting for the bus from Assuit to arrive. The bus was late, of course. When it came, Ali waited by the door until a tall, good-looking young man got off. He wore a suit and thin shoes, and carried a small briefcase. Ali knew at once he was our new antiquities inspector, and he walked up to him and asked if he was Atiya Radwan. The young man nodded yes, so Ali asked if he had any more luggage. No, the young man replied.

Ali pointed to a building across the square. "Go into that building. Find a bed and go to sleep. We will wake you at 5:00 A.M. tomorrow, and feed you breakfast. We leave for our camp at 6:00 A.M." He turned away muttering to himself and to me, "Why do they send these boys to us without heavy coats or good shoes? Don't they know it is cold in the desert?"

The next morning Ali was waiting when Atiya came out. He told Atiya to follow him to one of our pickups. In Arabic, he said, "Get in. You will be riding in this vehicle." Atiya could speak some English, enough to get by in most camps. When he got into the pickup cab two people were already there who were speaking a language he had never heard before. They ignored Atiya, because they thought he spoke only Arabic.

Our small convoy of four pickups started up and headed south. The large lorry had delivered our tents and other equipment to the camp a week before, and our Bedouin workers had already erected the camp. After a few miles there was no more road, just sand. Ali used his compass to go directly south, and we arrived at our camp about 10:00 P.M., long after dark. Someone called for Atiya, took him to his tent, and, in Arabic, told him that inside his tent he would find a bed, mattress, blankets, a washbasin, water can, and a kerosene lantern. Atiya went to bed confident that he was among civilized people who spoke Arabic, and that they would guide him to the mosque and the cinema tomorrow.

Atiya got up early, eager to see this new "city" where he was to live for two, maybe three months. He opened the tent flap and stepped out, but saw only sand in all directions. When he looked again and saw the other tents and beyond them nothing but more sand, he broke down and cried, saying, "Oh, what have I done to be punished this way?"

A few minutes later I came by Atiya's tent to ask him to go with me to see the sites where we would be digging. Atiya refused, saying he was too sick. I asked one of the graduate students to loan me a couple of *Playboy* magazines; I went back and gave them to Atiya. I said, "Here's something to read. I hope you feel better tomorrow."

The next day he was ready to go to the field in his thin shoes and light suit jacket. I knew he was cold, but I had nothing to give him. Despite the cold, he became interested in our work. Not many days passed before he asked me to teach him how to do prehistoric archaeology.

Our evaluation of the kind of Neolithic societies present in the desert more than 9,000 years ago was based in large part on the early pottery and the domestic cattle in the Sahara. Our ideas were controversial, of course. The presence of both pottery and cattle has important implications for our understanding of how Neolithic people lived in the Eastern Sahara and the nature of the Neolithic society that eventually developed in the Western Desert of Egypt.

The few known Final Paleolithic sites along the Nile with radiocarbon dates between 10,000 and 7,500 years ago have an economy with a strong emphasis on fishing and hunting large animals, particularly wild cattle, hartebeest, and gazelle. Except in the Fayum, no sites are known that date between 7,500 and 6,400 years ago. We assume people were there, but we know nothing about them. There is no evidence for the presence of pottery or domestic cattle before 6,400 years ago, unless we accept the use of cattle skulls as head markers on several of the burials at Tushka as evidence of domestication. I do not.

When it comes to pottery, the Nile data are in strong contrast with those from contemporary Early Neolithic sites in the desert. Almost all desert sites have yielded occasional sherds of well-made pottery decorated with closely packed rocker-stamped designs on the exterior. None of the sites has yielded enough sherds to make one restorable vessel, suggesting that whoever dropped the pot picked up most of the pieces. The sherds we find are those few that were missed. This may indicate that the pottery, or the designs on the pots, had religious significance, but there is no other evidence to support that suggestion.

When we first published the evidence for early pottery recovered from sites of the Adam Early Neolithic, there was considerable skepticism, in part because the sherds were not numerous in any of these sites, and because the Adam sherds were so much older than pottery in the Levant, then thought to be the intellectual source of pottery in Africa. That dispute, however, was short-lived, because by the mid-1980s there were several sites with a lot of similar or more complex pottery in northern Niger, with dates similar to those from the Adam sites in Egypt. These Niger sites are adjacent to now dry, but once permanent, lakes.

The high technical quality of El Adam pottery, the skill used in executing the complex decorative motifs, and its presence in a wide band across North Africa from Khartoum westward to northern Niger before 9,000 radiocarbon years ago suggest that pottery-making was not a recent craft that developed after the onset of the first Holocene rains in the Sahara.

I think it likely that hunter-gatherers living somewhere in the present-day Sahelian zone of North Africa invented pottery with rocker-stamped decorations, and that they began making this pottery while the southern Sahara was still hyperarid and unoccupied. It seems likely that in the Final Pleistocene or earliest Holocene, as the monsoons strengthened and the first rains came into the desert, some of these early pottery-using groups moved northward with the rains. If the Niger dates are correct, the first settlers in the Sahara were not the Adam Early Neolithic cattle herders in the Egyptian Sahara, who seem to have been seasonal visitors anyway, but were the hunter-gatherers who occupied those early pottery-rich sites located around the then permanent lakes in northern Niger.

One interesting feature of El Adam, and the subsequent El Ghorab Early Neolithic, is that there are no indications they dug water wells. This, and the fact that in the Nabta/Kiseiba area the only available water was seasonal and present in the playas for only a few months after the summer rains, strongly suggest that these earliest Holocene occupants must have been seasonal groups who brought their small herds into the area to graze and then took their cattle elsewhere before the playas were completely dry. Their dry season homes were possibly along the Nile in the Wadi Halfa area, or farther south in central Sudan, where there was permanent water. There are almost no data to support either of these hypotheses, but the absence of pottery and domestic cattle in the Wadi Halfa collections leads me to favor the Sudanese option, despite the paucity of data for this time period in the modern Sahelian zone.

The most important El Adam Early Neolithic site we excavated is about fifteen miles southeast of Bir Kiseiba, where there is a large basin we named El Adam Playa ("The Bone Playa") because of the numerous faunal remains we found there. Most of these bones were from one site where they were either on a recently deflated surface or slightly embedded in the upper part of the playa silts. The bones were clustered at the edge of a large El Adam Early Neolithic settlement. Charcoal from this site yielded several dates ranging from 9,800 to 8,900 radiocarbon years ago, or around 1,000 to 1,800 years older than Tom Ryan and Herb Mosca's Early Neolithic site at Nabta. The excavations at the large El Adam site produced several sherds of well-made pottery with closely packed rocker-stamped designs, generally similar to the pottery Tom and Herb found at Nabta, but with different design motifs.

El Adam is the oldest Early Neolithic entity thus far identified in the Egyptian Sahara. It also occurs at several sites in the Nabta basin, at El Kortein Playa, about nine miles north of Nabta, and at El Gebel el Baid Playa, about twenty-two miles north of Nabta.

The earliest known El Adam Early Neolithic sites were occupied some time after the initial onset of the Final Pleistocene/earliest Holocene wet intervals in the desert. At both El Adam and El Gebel el Baid Playas, the Adam Early Neolithic playa sediments occur above beds of playa sands and silty-sands from 15 to 18 feet thick. These underlying sediments may represent the first runoff that deposited weathered small rock fragments and sand in closed basins after the long period of aridity that coincided with the long Last Glacial period of hyperaridity. There are no known sites associated with these earliest playa deposits.

The excavations at El Adam Playa yielded a rich collection of faunal remains, mostly hare and gazelle, but also many bones of cattle. Achilles Gautier identified the cattle as domestic, in part because of the slightly smaller size of Saharan cattle compared to wild cattle in the Nile Valley, but more confidently on ecological grounds. He noted there was no permanent water anywhere in this area at this time, and cattle need to drink every day or every other day to survive. Gautier also observed that the archaeological faunal assemblage is not a natural one. Except for the cattle, all of the other fauna are small, limited to two kinds of gazelle, hares, a few foxes, and other small carnivores. There are no intermediate-sized animals such as hartebeest that should also be present if the cattle were wild. Along with wild cattle, hartebeest were major prey animals in the Late and Final Paleolithic in the Nile Valley.

Gautier's conclusion that domestic cattle were present at several Saharan Early Neolithic sites, dating as early as 9,500 to 9,800 radiocarbon years ago, was highly controversial. Some critics suggested that the cattle bones were probably not associated with the excavated sites, although they occurred at almost every excavated Early Neolithic site in the Kiseiba/Nabta area. Others implied that the dates must be wrong, even though the dates are derived from charcoal from several different sites. After all, critics said, the earliest domestic cattle in Southwest Asia are dated no earlier than 8,000 to 8,500 years ago, and the Saharan cattle had to be later. "Why?" I asked, but no one could answer me.

Although Gautier in 1980 (in his appendix to the *Prehistory of the Eastern Sahara*) first discussed his conclusion that the early Holocene cattle in the Eastern Sahara were domestic, it was four years later, in our book *Cattle Keepers of the Eastern Sahara*, that he (plus Schild, Close, and I) made cattle domestication a major issue by emphasizing that domestic cattle were present in the desert as early as 9,500, possibly 9,800, years ago. It was also in *Cattle Keepers* that we pointed to the evidence for pottery in these earliest Holocene settlements, long before there was pottery in the Nile Valley sites, and probably earlier than pottery appeared in the Levant.

Both of these issues in *Cattle Keepers* provoked disbelief from many European archaeozoologists and archaeologists who firmly believed everything had originated in Southwest Asia or the Levant. As a consequence, Schild, Close, and I spent a lot of time writing articles defending our positions on both the pottery and cattle issues.

Objections to the early dates for domestic cattle in Kiseiba have not completely disappeared, but in my opinion, the doubters are wrong. The data in favor of Gautier's conclusion of domestic status for these cattle remain strong. His conclusions are supported by the ecology of the early Holocene in the Eastern Sahara, the biological needs of cattle, and the structure of the faunal assemblages. There is also evidence, though Gautier doesn't mention it, from the study of linguistic chronologies. Words related to "cattle keeping" are old in northeastern African languages, particularly among those groups still living in the Sudanese Sahara and adjacent Chad.

What may be the final blow to the arguments of the anti-domestic-cattle group are the results of several studies of mitochondrial DNA (mtDNA) in modern North African, East African, and Near Eastern, European, and Indian cattle. These genetic studies have shown that the African and Near Eastern/European cattle have different DNA patterns and have been separate populations for between 25,000 and 180,000 years. (See a recent paper on this topic by O. Hanotte and others. For the interested reader, many of the earlier mtDNA studies of African cattle are cited there.)

The cattle remains in El Adam sites are always limited to a few specimens. This bothers some critics, but it is what one would expect if, as among most modern African cattle pastoralists, cattle were rarely killed for meat, but rather for important ceremonial occasions, such as a death, marriage, or when the summer rains fail.

In an area near the excavated El Adam sites, Kobusiewicz dug a large El Nabta site with many storage pits. To determine the extent of the storage pits, he had his crew sweep an area 50 yards wide and 75 yards long. To everyone's surprise, the sweeping exposed the outlines of several large "walk-in" wells, some of which had what appeared to be watering basins off to one side. We had time to test only one of the wells, which was over 6 feet deep and 15 feet in diameter with steep vertical sides, except in one shallower area where there may have been steps down to the water.

The discoveries of well-made pottery and domestic cattle in the sites of the Adam Early Neolithic were a revelation to me. From that point on I saw the Early Neolithic people in the desert in a different light: I saw them as a creative, relatively sophisticated people, participants in a cultural system that had little or no relationship to that found among contemporaneous hunters and fishermen, or later Neolithic groups living in the Nile Valley.

The desert groups had a sophisticated ceramic tradition at least 3,000 years ahead of comparable ceramic production in the Nile Valley of Egypt and northern Sudan. They were participating in the domestication of one of the most economically important animals native to Northeast Africa. Along the way, as I've already said, they developed their own tradition, in which the cattle were valued as symbols of wealth and power and were not eaten except on important ceremonial occasions, a tradition still followed by many African cattle pastoralists today.

Two thousand years later, around 8,000 years ago, the groups living in the

Kiseiba/Nabta desert introduced a settlement system different from that represented by the small seasonal groups who had previously lived in the area. The new people occupied large villages and collected and stored a wide range of edible wild plant foods for later consumption. They placed their villages in the lower parts of almost every large basin in the Nabta/Kiseiba area. They dug large, deep wells so they could have water in the dry season for themselves and their cattle. Their villages were seasonally flooded, but as soon as the floodwaters receded, they rebuilt and reoccupied their huts, often in the same place. This suggests some emotional tie to a place and, possibly, ownership of that spot.

Our 1980 field season at Bir Kiseiba was ten weeks long and very demanding. We placed the camp about twelve miles east of Bir Kiseiba, to be closer to where most of the people were working. Unfortunately, some thoughtless camel herder who watered his animals at the spring eye had contaminated the water at Bir Kiseiba, so at first our drivers had to haul water from Bir Abu Hussein, above the scarp, about twelve miles north of Bir Kiseiba.

Two weeks into the season Eide Mariff found another, smaller spring less than a mile from our camp. The water was drinkable, but barely. It had a lot of minerals in it, but since it was all we had, we used it for washing and for drinking, too. After the first week of using Bir Eide water, however, Ali Mazhar decided he'd had enough. He sent a driver with several empty five-gallon water cans to Bir Abu Hussein to bring back water for tea and coffee. We also used it for drinking water. The driver made that run every week until we closed camp.

We departed our 1980 camp in mid-March, amid the usual confusion. Workers broke down our tents as soon as we moved our luggage and other baggage outside. Boxes of cooking equipment, stoves, ovens, dishes, and the boxes of excavation supplies and equipment were the first things loaded onto the large lorry, followed by our metal beds, placed vertically so as to form a six-foot-high frame around the bed of the lorry. Our mattresses and any stray boxes followed. The tents and tent floors were next, creating a huge pile of canvas on top of the lorry. Several ropes criss-crossing the pile of tents and mattresses tied everything down. The Bedouins who could not find a place in one of the pickups or beside Eide in the lorry climbed on top of the tents, grabbed a good rope, and hung on.

When everything was tied to Eide's satisfaction, he checked the Land Cruiser, a recent gift from Atlantic Richfield, and our four pickups, their beds filled with crates of food, wooden boxes containing blankets, our luggage, and sleeping bags. With a signal to the other drivers to follow, Eide took off toward the Nile, 160 miles away. I had asked Eide to take us by one other well about thirty miles to the east, but he evidently didn't understand me and headed off on a line about forty-five degrees off where I wanted to go. I finally caught up with him and persuaded him to go in the direction I wanted. This little episode led Angela to compose a song she sang for us on the way to the Nile. It became the theme song for the Combined Prehistoric Expedition. For many years we sang it at least once during the evening "Happy Hour." More than anything else, it conveys the spirit of our group, or perhaps our desperation:

Eide Must Be Stuck in the Sand
by Angela E. Close

We left for Aswan about eight in the morning.
Before we left camp we had plenty of warning
Our trip might be long, for while we were still warming
Our engine, Eide must be stuck in the sand.

Refrain:
Oh dear, where can the lorry be?
Dear, dear, where can the lorry be?
Oh dear, where can the lorry be?
Eide must be stuck in the sand.

He set off from camp with a load of the workers.
They all rode the lorry, it looked like a circus.
They're most of them good men, but some of them shirkers,
And all of them men of Eide's band.

The road went due south but to Fred's consternation
He saw Eide go west at the wrong elevation.
He stopped him and after a small altercation
All travel by that road was banned.

We came to Bir Nakhlai and there we debated
The problems of lorries, the whiles that we waited.
We couldn't have helped them, but oh how we hated
To think of Eide stuck in the sand.

We came to Site 6 and we all had our lunches.
The grasses were growing in clumps and in bunches.
And finally, Wendorf had one of his hunches
That Eide must be stuck in the sand.

The wind was so bad as it blew past the Rover,
We fled to the vehicles and had to take cover,
But we knew that our group was really in clover,
For poor Eide was stuck in the sand.

We thought of them digging with sand in their faces
While duck-pens and tents disappeared without traces
For gypsum will never provide a good basis
For driving straight out of the sand.

Daoud was sent back and he found that the trouble
Was not with the driver, but rather the puddle
Of fuel that leaked twixt the rocks and the rubble
The diesel-tank lay in the sand.

And so, friends, we come to the end of my story
Of going to Aswan and losing the lorry.
If I have misled you, I truly am sorry
For Eide never sticks in the sand.

Final refrain:
Oh dear, where can the lorry be?
Dear, dear, where can the lorry be?
Oh dear, where can the lorry be?
Eide never sticks in the sand.

Wadi Kubbaniya
(1978, 1981–1984)

CHAPTER 29

Wadi Kubbaniya is the most important surviving Late and Final Paleolithic archaeological locality in Egypt. At one time, there may have been other areas containing equally important Late Paleolithic archaeological remains, but if so, those sites have been destroyed. Most of this destruction took place in the past fifty years, since the completion of the New High Dam at Aswan and after Egypt began reclaiming vast areas of the Low Desert on both sides of the Nile north of Aswan. The final blow came in 1992 when the Egyptian government offered free title to anyone who would cultivate any unused land. Kubbaniya was made an archaeological preserve in 1984, but today it is seriously threatened and may even be destroyed by the time you read this. With Egypt's rapidly increasing population, there is enormous pressure to cultivate every part of the country where water is available. Until now, the Egyptian Antiquities Organization officials have protected Kubbaniya, but it is doubtful they can do so much longer.

At the end of the 1977 field season at Nabta Playa, I was told that security restrictions that had prevented our working at the rich and highly promising Late Paleolithic sites at Wadi Kubbaniya had been lifted. I immediately applied for a permit. We had failed to take advantage of an opportunity to excavate there when we had first seen the area in 1967, and I was determined not to lose it again. We had, in the meantime, found some important sites at Bir Kiseiba that we needed to study before they were destroyed by wind deflation, so we compromised by going first to Wadi Kubbaniya for one season to test the sites and plan for an extended project there, and going back to the desert for two field seasons to excavate several important Early Neolithic sites in the vicinity of Bir Kiseiba.

We excavated at Kubbaniya for five field seasons. The first excavations were in 1978, after which we skipped two years to finish what we had started at Bir Kiseiba. We returned to Kubbaniya for four more years starting in 1981 and continuing until the spring of 1984. The NSF, on a year-to-year basis, funded all these excavations.

Kubbaniya is probably the largest wadi in Egypt that enters the Nile from the west, draining much of the area west of the Nile from south of Aswan, north almost to Idfu, and from the foot of the Eocene Plateau to the Nile Valley, an area of over a thousand square miles. Kubbaniya enters the Nile floodplain about six miles north of Aswan, with a mouth about a mile wide. It is flanked on both the north and south sides by vertical sandstone cliffs more than six hundred feet high. During the Holocene wet intervals, the wadi may have carried occasional washes, but there is no indication that it was a permanent stream. Before that, during the Late and Final Paleolithic, and during the Late Middle Paleolithic Khormusan, except for river floods, the wadi was completely dry, and there is no evidence of rain in the desert.

At Kubbaniya, we were able to sort out the complicated history of the Late Pleistocene Nile. There are large remnants of two suites of silts of Late Pleistocene age that filled the Nile Valley at different times. The silts filled up to 96 feet above the modern floodplain at Wadi Halfa, and 75 feet above the floodplain at Aswan. One of these bodies of silt is associated with Late Middle Paleolithic archaeology; the other occurs with Late Paleolithic. Without the archaeology, the radiocarbon dates, and thermoluminescence (TL) measurements, the Pleistocene stratigraphy would have been difficult to sort out. The silts in the two events of aggradation are closely similar in color, texture, and mineralogy.

It is likely that changes in global climate were the fundamental causes of both the Middle Paleolithic and Late Paleolithic episodes of valley filling. Intervals of colder global temperatures that produced glacial advances at higher latitudes were particularly important. The colder climate had a profound impact on the landscape, on the amount of rainfall in the highland headwater areas of the Nile in East Africa, and on the amount of sediment the floodwater carried during the seasonal rains. Although the precise way this process functioned is not well understood, the generally accepted model of Nile behavior during the Late Pleistocene is as follows: Cold temperatures are associated with a reduction in the size and strength of the summer monsoon rains. With less rainfall in East and Tropical Africa, there was a decreased flow in the Nile. During the period of the Late Paleolithic Alluviation, dunes seem to have blocked the White Nile, with its headwaters in the Central African highlands. As a consequence, during the Late Paleolithic the White Nile played no role in the downstream sedimentation of the Nile. There are no data on the White Nile during the Middle Paleolithic Nile Alluviation, but since the downstream results were similar, I would expect conditions were not different from those during the Late Paleolithic.

Reduced temperatures during the glacial periods of the Late Pleistocene caused the tree line in Ethiopia and Kenya to fall more than 3,000 feet below that of today. The cold significantly reduced the plant cover in the highlands, creating large open areas. The accompanying frost action created small fractured rocks and fine particles littering the barren surfaces in the highlands.

So far as we can tell, there was no rainfall in the Nile Valley in Egypt and Sudan at this time. Meanwhile, the highlands of East Africa, while also dry, had limited rains during the early part of the summers. In Ethiopia, at the headwaters of the Blue Nile, these rains brought floodwaters laden with silts and other sediments into the main channel of the Nile. As the slope decreased and the velocity of the water declined downstream, the coarse particles were the first to be dropped to the streambed, with the finer particles being deposited farther downstream. As a result, the silt accumulation was higher toward the south and gradually declined toward the north, as can be seen in the area around Wadi Halfa, where silt deposition during both the Middle Paleolithic and the Late Paleolithic Alluviations reached an elevation slightly more than 96 feet above the modern floodplain; at Kubbaniya, they were about 75 feet, and about 60 feet at Esna. They continue to drop going north until the Qena Bend; there they disappear below the modern floodplain. The decline in silt accumulation north of Aswan may have been due to the effect of the 200-to-300-feet reduction in sea level in the Mediterranean during the glacial maxima.

The silts of the earlier Nile Alluviation, or "valley filling," associated with Late Middle Paleolithic archaeology, either Khormusan or something similar, have several thermoluminescence age measurements that indicate the Middle Paleolithic Nile Alluviation began before 60,000 years ago and ended around 40,000 to 45,000 years ago. This episode of valley filling most likely correlates with the period of glacial advance in Eurasia that is recorded in the ocean cores as Oxygen Isotope Stage 4.

An interval of downcutting separates the Middle Paleolithic and Late Paleolithic Nile Alluviations, but this event has not been well studied, and the timing and depth of the downcutting are unknown. Presumably, it is associated with the warmer interval of Oxygen Isotope Stage 3, when there was a significant retreat of the glaciers in the higher latitudes of Eurasia and North America. These phenomena are discussed in more detail in Schild's and my paper, "The Late Pleistocene Nile in Wadi Kubbaniya."

In contrast to the limited dates available for the Middle Paleolithic Nile Alluviation, the age of the Late Paleolithic event is firmly established by a large suite of radiocarbon measurements on charcoal from dozens of sites up and down the Nile, including Wadi Kubbaniya. The earliest known sites associated with the Late Paleolithic Alluviation are believed to date between 30,000 and 23,000 years ago. The latest sites are around 12,500–12,000 years ago. These most recent dates correlate with a time when summer rains greatly expanded in East and Tropical Africa, causing the White Nile to break through the dune barrier in southern Sudan, producing high floods in the Nile downstream in Sudan and Egypt around 12,500 radiocarbon years ago. The earliest rains, just pre-Holocene, in East Africa, Egypt, and the Western Desert probably occurred at this time.

During the intervals of both the Late Middle Paleolithic and the Late Paleolithic Nile Alluviations, the deserts of Egypt and Sudan were hyperarid, and the only available water was in the Nile Valley. And that's where the people were. The river at that time was different from the massive stream of today. It was a relatively small, meandering, and aggrading river, with a flow estimated to have been only 20% that of today. Seasonal floods brought floodwaters into the mouths of the dry streambeds of the embayments on both sides of the river and deposited silt on their floors.

Since it was also dry and barren beyond the river, water tables were lower than today. Deflation formed basins in areas of softer sediments, and numerous sand dunes developed in the desert and the Low Desert near the Nile. At Wadi Kubbaniya, massive dunes accumulated on the upland behind the scarp bordering the north side of the wadi, and some of these drifted over the scarp. Around 23,000 years ago, the deposition of silts in the valley continued to build up until seasonal floods were able to invade the wadi and deposit water and silt over the dune-covered wadi floor. Soon plants, sustained by the water, began to grow on the sandy/silty floor, and phytogenic dunes rapidly formed around the plants. The following winter/spring was dry, and the winds brought more sand, then the next summer more silt and more plants, a process that was repeated over and over for thousands of years. These seasonal floods brought more than water and silt; they brought numerous fish to spawn along the margins of the floodplain, where Late Paleolithic fishermen caught them in great numbers.

When we returned to Kubbaniya in 1978 we strongly believed we would find charred grains of wild barley and wheat. Instead, we had a most embarrassing experience. The problem might never have been detected had the tandem linear accelerator not become available to us when it did. A sample of charcoal from a buried hearth we had excavated in 1978 had been dated by radiocarbon to about 17,000 years ago. A few weeks later our botanist, Nabil El Hadidi, reported in a letter to me that in the same hearth there were several carbonized seeds of barley. We accepted the association as genuine, and we published several articles and a book based on this discovery. The book was *Loaves and Fishes: The Prehistory of Wadi Kubbaniya*.

After I selected the title for the book, I worried that some people at SMU might think the title was blasphemous. I was, after all, a professor at Southern *Methodist* University, and I'd had some experience with Methodist fundamentalists in my own family. I didn't want to embarrass the administration, so I decided to discuss the proposed title with Joseph Quillin, dean of the Perkins School of Theology at SMU. I made an appointment with him, and when I got to his office I told him about the work at Wadi Kubbaniya, the finding of the grains of cereal and the numerous fish bones, and asked him if he or any members of his faculty would be offended if I called the book *Loaves and Fishes*. "Why would we?" he asked. That ended our discussion.

I was beginning to have some uncomfortable doubts about the status of the barley Hadidi found, so I decided to obtain additional botanical assistance. I went to the Institute of Archaeology at the University of London to discuss the problem with Gordon Hillman, a highly regarded botanist who specialized in Southwest Asian domestic and wild plant foods. One of the questions I hoped he would resolve was whether the Kubbaniya seeds were wild or domestic. I brought with me several pictures of the Kubbaniya seeds, as well as pictures of the barley recovered from the Early Neolithic site at Nabta, and showed them to Hillman. He immediately identified all of them as domestic and explained the identifying characteristics of domestic barley to me. Why had no other botanist, including those who had seen only the pictures, but especially those who'd also examined the seeds, not been able to tell me that the seeds were domestic? The domestic status of the barley seeds made it highly unlikely that they were in true association with the Late Paleolithic occupation at Kubbaniya: wild barley, possibly, but domestic, no. There were also problems with the Nabta barley; the seeds were too old to be domestic in Egypt, but only 1,600 years too old, and thus possibly associated.

My meeting with Hillman occurred in late 1980, as we were preparing to return to Kubbaniya the following January. We planned to make extensive excavations at several sites on the floor of the wadi. I told Hillman about our plans and persuaded him to join us at Kubbaniya in February.

Hadidi had identified one of the most frequently charred plant remains recovered at the Wadi Kubbaniya sites as chickpeas, a Southwestern Asian domestic plant. The chickpeas were so abundant and recovered from so many different sites that the possibility of later mixture seemed remote. Thus, before the accelerator dated the cereals, the chickpeas had served to reinforce the conclusion in our minds that the seeds of barley and wheat were in true association with the Late Paleolithic.

By early January we had the camp set up, and the full staff was present and excavating, except for Schild, who had been delayed in Warsaw with administrative problems. We continued to find more chickpeas.

I had to return to Cairo on the day Schild was scheduled to arrive late at night. I booked a double room for us at the Garden City House, the Combined Prehistoric Expedition's informal base in Cairo. Schild arrived about 2:00 A.M. and awakened me when he came in. I had been dreaming, and in my too-vivid dream Hillman had just arrived, and when I showed him some of the chickpeas, he said, "Fred, these aren't chickpeas; they are baggy waggy nuts."

Schild blanched when I told him about the dream. "Oh Fred, what're we going to do if they're 'baggy waggy nuts'?" Neither of us slept well the remainder of that night.

A week later Hillman arrived on the back of a donkey a boy was leading from the nearby village of Kubbaniya. His was the most memorable and colorful arrival ever in our camp. As soon as he stowed his baggage in his tent, I got out several of the chickpeas we had recovered from our sites and showed them to him. He examined them closely under a hand lens, then under our low-power microscope.

Hillman said, "Fred, these aren't chickpeas, but tubers of *Cyperus*, commonly known as nut grass. They were widely eaten in North Africa until a few years ago. Because they contain a volatile toxin and are high in fiber, before they can be eaten, they must be roasted to remove the toxin, then ground to break up the fibers." Hillman looked at the rest of our charred botanical remains. It seemed Hadidi had incorrectly identified almost all of them.

Later that spring, unfortunately after the publication of *Loaves and Fishes*, I took the Kubbaniya seeds to the accelerator laboratory at the University of Arizona, where four of them were dated. Every seed was only 5,000 years old. They probably had come from some late Predynastic site. I was acutely embarrassed, and as quickly as possible, we published an article in *Science* retracting our earlier claims of a Late Paleolithic antiquity for the seeds.

Initially, I had trouble getting *Science* to retract the article. The assistant editor said it was not significant. I was dumbfounded, but I wrote a letter to the editor explaining that they had highlighted the initial story of the barley on the cover of *Science* and that all of us had a responsibility to correct the record. He published our retraction in the next issue.

We now realize that from the beginning we were not as skeptical of the barley as we should have been. In part, our error occurred because barley seeds were exactly what we expected to find as a result of the presence of "sickle sheen" on some of our retouched tools, and the reports of barley pollen and wheat rust spores in some of our sediment samples. Even after we published the retraction of our earlier claims, I received letters from archaeologists in the United States and overseas urging me not to accept the accelerator dates, because our earlier claims were a closer fit to their own ideas. To each I responded, "No. I'm sorry, but I made a mistake."

••••

In spite of, or because of, the embarrassing episode of the barley and wheat, we made a special effort to recover carbonized plant remains. The sites in Wadi Kubbaniya yielded some of our most important data on the Late Paleolithic food economy and diet in the Nile Valley. Numerous Late Paleolithic occupations, representing seven different lithic entities, occur with sediments of the Late Paleolithic Alluviation at Wadi Kubbaniya. There is also a large suite of radiocarbon measurements on charcoal between 21,000 and 12,000 years ago associated with the Late Paleolithic sites in the wadi. These dates and the other data summarized below can be found in *The Prehistory of Wadi Kubbaniya*, Volumes 2 and 3, mentioned above.

The Middle Paleolithic is not well represented at Wadi Kubbaniya. The best evidence indicating use of the area at that time is from one locality near the mouth of the wadi where a poor, Late Middle Paleolithic "Khormusan-like" assemblage occurred in sands near the top of the Middle Paleolithic Alluviation. It differs from most Middle Paleolithic complexes in having a strong emphasis on the gougelike tools, or burins, normally a characteristic tool-type of the Upper and Late Paleolithic.

We recovered no fauna at the Khormusan-like site at Wadi Kubbaniya. There are also no absolute radiocarbon dates for the Khormusan sites we excavated near Wadi Halfa; they're all infinite, and the most recent is more than 41,000 years old. A series of eight thermoluminescence dates on sediments from the Middle Paleolithic Nile Alluviation at Wadi Kubbaniya provides a better basis for the age estimate of the Khormusan-like site at Wadi Kubbaniya. The series places those sediments between 45,000 and 61,000 years ago, indicating a date for the Khormusan there of around 50,000 years ago.

Late Paleolithic sites at Kubbaniya were clustered in two areas. The largest group was about a mile upstream from the mouth of the wadi, where an extensive block of alternating sand and silt layers was preserved. Angela Close excavated part of a large site with many occupation horizons embedded in the sand/silt deposit. Nearby, Hanna Wieckowska, assisted by Halina Krolik, dug another large, stratified site downstream from Close. Both were rich sites with numerous artifacts and fish bones.

The other important area at Kubbaniya was about three hundred yards from the wadi mouth. Here, another large block of silt was preserved, and several Late Paleolithic sites were embedded in the upper part of these silts. I asked Michal Kobusiewicz, who was assisted by one of my advanced graduate students, Christy Bednar, to direct the excavations there. Christy was then in her mid-thirties, tall, slim, and good-looking. She was smart as could be and a hard worker. The faculty regarded her as the brightest student in our department.

It was Christy's first project with me, and she knew nothing about Paleolithic stone typology. Kobusiewicz was with the Polish Academy of Sciences, stationed at Posnan, in western Poland, in an area known as Wielkopolska. In the evenings he often entertained us in camp by pretending to identify the area where our "halva" (sweet, a confection made of sesame seeds) was grown. He was also identified as the culprit, the "halva-mouse," who raided our supply in the evening after everyone had gone to bed. Of course, he denied this repeatedly. He told us great stories about Wielkopolska, particularly of his hunts for wild boar and bear. So vivid were his stories that even today I am not sure if the hunts were real or the fruits of his imagination. Kobusiewicz was the perfect person to supervise Bednar. He was regarded as a great teacher and knew more about lithic typology than anyone in camp, except possibly Schild.

Most of the seven different lithic entities at Kubbaniya also occur in the Wadi Halfa area of northern Sudan, or at Ballana in southernmost Egypt, and in a few cases in the embayments farther north that we'd tested in the 1967 and 1968 field seasons. In part because of the confusion the erroneous radiocarbon dates from the excavated sites near Wadi Halfa caused, we had no idea as to relative ages and stratigraphic positions of many of these industries prior to our work at Kubbaniya. To us they appeared to be jumbled.

At Kubbaniya, at last, it was possible to straighten out the confusion, which we did by digging many stratigraphic pits and trenches, establishing the true relative stratigraphic position of every depositional unit in the wadi and relating each site to the proper unit. With these data, and for the first time, we determined the stratigraphic position of almost every cultural entity in the wadi.

The characteristic tools in all of the Late Paleolithic entities at Kubbaniya, except for the Sebilian, are made on small bladelets (less than 5 cm long) or microblades (less than 3 cm long), usually with retouch or "backing" on one lateral edge. (A tool is said to be "backed" when the retouch is vertical to the plane of the piece and removes a small part of that edge. If the retouch does not remove a recognizable portion of the edge, or is irregular, it is just called retouch. The position and amount of backing vary among the industries and help distinguish one industry from another.)

All of these lithic industries had been dated elsewhere, but as I've said, some of the previous dates are controversial. Except for the three earliest and the latest entities, there are no radiocarbon dates for the remaining industries at Kubbaniya; however, the others can be placed within the local stratigraphic sequence. This is important, because the Kubbaniya stratigraphy offers the best evidence available for the relative ages of some of these lithic entities. The sites represent almost all of the post–Kubbaniyan Late Paleolithic entities known in Upper Egypt and Nubia. Some of them, such as the Qadan, are known at many sites south of Kubbaniya, in Sudanese and Egyptian Nubia, while others, such as the Afian and Isnan, occur frequently farther to the north in Upper Egypt. These overlaps in distributions suggest that Wadi Kubbaniya may have been near a shifting cultural boundary during the later part of the Late Paleolithic.

The earliest Late Paleolithic occupations in the wadi occur at three localities that share an Idfuan-like toolkit with almost equal numbers of four classes of tools, of which the most interesting are the steeply retouched bladelets and double-backed perforators (with points at both the distal and proximal ends). Several radiocarbon dates from these sites suggest that this Idfuan-like occupation at Kubbaniya began before 21,000 years ago, and lasted until about 19,500 years ago.

The fauna from these Idfuan-like sites include numerous fish bones, mostly small tilapia, harvested after the seasonal flood at cutoff basins and pools the retreating water left. Several burned pits occur near these cutoff basins. They may have been used for drying fish. In addition, there are numerous bird bones, mostly from ducks and geese of species that today are winter visitors to Egypt. Both the fish and the birds indicate that these Idfuan-like sites were occupied in the fall to winter months.

The only other known localities with a similar lithic industry are the three Idfuan sites near Esna we excavated in 1967. The associated radiocarbon dates there are about the same, as well. The absence of Idfuan sites south of Kubbaniya indicates that the wadi was probably at or near the southern boundary of the Idfuan area of occupation.

Among the more interesting discoveries at Wadi Kubbaniya was a human burial, probably contemporary with the early Late Paleolithic Idfuan, but possibly slightly later. There are no dates associated with the skeleton, but the stratigraphy at the burial site is interesting. The burial was near the mouth of the wadi, in a pit dug into the Sand Sheet, the highest and latest preserved sediment in the area assigned to the Middle Paleolithic Nile Alluviation.

The body had been buried facedown, in an extended position. The fill of the grave-pit consisted entirely of sands from the Sand Sheet, with no traces of silt. When we first discovered it, the heavily mineralized skeleton was encased in a block of calcareous rock formed by the concentration of calcium carbonate within the grave-pit. When we saw the carbonate block we thought the skeleton might be Middle Paleolithic.

The best clues to the age of the skeleton, however, were the two lightly retouched bladelets found in the abdominal cavity of the skeleton. They tie the skeleton to the early Late Paleolithic. The next strong clue was geological, based on the absence of silt in the grave-pit. Since the Late Paleolithic Alluviation had covered the burial with a thick bed of silt by about 20,000 years ago, the grave-pit must have been dug before that date, because it could not have been dug through the silts and into the Sand Sheet and then refilled without including at least traces of the silt. The firmly cemented matrix that encased the burial is also important. This cementation requires abundant lime-rich waters, such as those that covered the site during the Late Paleolithic Alluviation, from about 21,000 to 12,500 years ago, but not since. Thus the skeleton cannot be of Holocene age, and is probably more than 20,000 years old, but less than 25,000 years old because elsewhere groups of that age were using distinctive, large, retouched blades.

The skeleton is that of a young adult male, physically similar to those found at Jebel Sahaba, near Wadi Halfa, Sudan, and at Tushka in southern Egypt. He is a modern *Homo sapiens,* but more rugged and with a more pronounced projection in the mid-facial area. I sometimes facetiously say, "He could eat corn through a picket fence."

In addition to the retouched bladelets in the abdomen, there was a healed fractured bone in the left lower arm, and a partially healed wound with a tip of a point in his left upper arm. These and the bladelets, as well as other evidence of conflict at Jebel Sahaba, suggest that hostility was a recurring feature along the Nile during the Late Paleolithic. Unlike Jebel Sahaba, however, the Kubbaniya skeleton does not support the presence of organized warfare. The wounds could have resulted from a conflict between two individuals.

The most interesting and numerous of the Late Paleolithic entities at Wadi Kubbaniya is the one we called the Kubbaniyan, twelve sites of which we excavated and studied in detail. We dated ten of them using radiocarbon. Most of the Kubbaniyan occupations were embedded within phytogenic dunes, where they occurred between alternating lenses of windblown sand and Nile silts with abundant charcoal and other occupation debris. This depositional process resulted in an unusual preservation of organic remains. The numerous radiocarbon dates on charcoal for the Kubbaniyan place the occupation as beginning between 19,000 and 19,500 years ago and ending about 17,000 years ago. There is no evidence for a connection with the Idfuan, the preceding early Late Paleolithic entity.

With an economic system that involved the intensive use of seasonally abundant foods, from fish to birds to marshland tubers, the Kubbaniyan groups exploited the wadi for most of the year. In summer, at the onset of the flood, they took large quantities of spawning catfish that had moved to the edge of the floodplain to leave their eggs where they would hatch and the fingerlings could eat the submerged vegetation. Several thousand fish bones, most of which were adult tilapia and a few eels, were recovered from our excavations in the dune area. The size of the harvest was so great that some of the fish may have been dried for later consumption. In early fall, as the flood receded, the fish harvest began again at the cutoff pools the retreating flood left. Here the people caught mostly small, yearling fish, and a few adult tilapia, but in such quantities that they dug pits, possibly to dry the fish.

In the fall and winter, they harvested and processed numerous wetland tubers by roasting and grinding. All of the Kubbaniyan sites in the wadi had numerous, well-made upper and lower grinding stones. The floral remains include ten varieties of tubers and soft vegetable tissues, of which nut-grass tubers were the most common, followed by club-rush and fern and seven other varieties not yet identified. There were also seeds of chamomile, asparagus, club-rush, aniseed, and water lily. All of these plants were part of the diet. Many of the seeds were recovered from human coprolites.

During the fall, winter, and early spring they hunted migratory birds, mostly ducks and geese. They hunted large mammals, hartebeest, gazelle, wild cattle, and an occasional hippo, but these were not major components of the diet. It seems that most of the large-animal hunting occurred during the highest point of the flood, when the animals would've been pushed to the edge of the floodplain, where they were more vulnerable. There are only two periods when the wadi may not have been used much: at the height of the flood, when the sites were underwater, and during the low-water period, from April to late June, when water was probably available only in the deepest part of the valley.

Kubbaniyan flaked stone artifacts are simple and homogenous, dominated by one or two types of tools. In the early Kubbaniyan, Ouchtata bladelets with weak retouch often represent over 80 percent of the retouched tools. In the later Kubbaniyan sites, however, the Ouchtata retouched bladelets are less frequent and are replaced by scaled pieces (a flake with flat, bifacial flaking on both ends, and sometimes on both lateral edges). The abundance of scaled pieces in the later sites is thought to indicate an emphasis on a new activity, not well identified, possibly woodworking. Other interesting tools in the Kubbaniyan include burins, often struck on large, flat Levallois flakes made of flint. There are no flint outcrops near Wadi Kubbaniya. The flint may have been imported from the Esna area, sixty miles downstream, where good flint is abundant.

The Kubbaniyan entity is unknown farther south of Kubbaniya, but several sites are known at Esna and El Kilh, suggesting a northern distribution, despite the resemblance to the contemporary Halfan found near Wadi Halfa and at Ballana. The Halfan raw material was small chert and agate pebbles; the Kubbaniyan used larger pebbles, probably accounting for the differences in the size of the tools the two groups used. Both made many bladelets, but the Halfan also have the distinctive Halfa cores and Halfa Flakes missing in the Kubbaniyan.

Four other later Late Paleolithic entities occur at Wadi Kubbaniya. One group is found with a massive dune that had partially closed the wadi. The other three came after 13,000 years ago, when the massive dune blocked the wadi, changing the ecology forever. As a result, Kubbaniya was no longer such an attractive place for settlement. The sites were smaller and briefly occupied, and the people left fewer artifacts. By 12,000 years ago, the last of the Late Paleolithic groups had disappeared from the wadi.

One of the last of these, the Sebilian, presumably of southern origin, is closely similar to those Sebilian sites excavated near Wadi Halfa. The Sebilian was present at least as far north as the Dishna Plain, near the Qena Bend. At Kubbaniya the people used large flakes, often produced by Levallois technology made on quartzitic sandstone, as at Wadi Halfa. The Sebilian has no known local antecedents. It appears the group occupied an area for a time, and then they disappeared. The small cluster of quartzitic sandstone Sebilian artifacts at Wadi Kubbaniya cannot be placed precisely in the Kubbaniyan stratigraphic sequence, except the cluster dates after the massive dune on which it was dropped.

Another late group at Kubbaniya is the Qadan, one of the most common Late Paleolithic lithic industries in the Nile Valley between the Second Cataract and Tushka in southern Egypt. We found only one Qadan site at Wadi Kubbaniya, and it is unknown farther north. At Kubbaniya, the Qadan site is associated with the high beach of a seepage lake behind the sand-and-silt dam that closed the wadi, and dates shortly after the dune blocked the wadi.

Despite the numerous Qadan sites we've excavated, that entity is not well dated. The stratigraphic evidence suggests that the Qadan and Sebilian are about the same age, with the Sebilian perhaps slightly older. The available radiocarbon dates for Qadan, however, include one of 15,100 years ago on charcoal, another of 13,740 years ago on collagen from Burial 43 at Jebel Sahaba, and one of 14,500 years ago on charcoal from Tushka.

At Kubbaniya I worked with a superb team of European and American specialists and prehistorians, the largest staff since I began working in Nubia. Besides Schild and me, twenty-nine scientists participated: two paleontologists, six botanists, three geologists, one statistician, one analytical chemist, two antiquities inspectors, and fourteen archaeologists. Among the archaeologists four were from Poland, one from France, one from Sudan, and ten from the United States. Of the Americans, eight were my graduate students at SMU. They were not all there at the same time, but here I've listed them as if they were. Only three completed their PhDs: Kimball Banks, Christopher Hill, and Phillip Volkman. The others left archaeology: Christy Bednar, James Bennett, Henry Kenny, Brenda Scoggins, and Bill Singleton. I was and remain disappointed that they didn't continue their studies. All of them did great work at Kubbaniya.

Schild was outstanding. He was responsible for the microstratigraphic work in the wadi. He supervised the hand coring of countless boreholes, most of them exceeding 18 feet in depth. He drew most of the cross-sections, too. With Ali Mazhar, our camp manager, geologist, and surveyor, Schild made a remarkable map of the Late Pleistocene sediments in the wadi. By such careful work he was able to decipher the complex stratigraphy in the wadi. It is a classic study rarely equaled anywhere in the world.

Herb Haas, the director of the radiocarbon laboratory at SMU, was largely responsible for the success of our efforts to date our sites at Kubbaniya using radiocarbon measurements. Haas was a Swiss national with all of the best qualities of scientists of his home country: he was cautious, precise, hardworking, and determined. On the basis of results of competitions among several radiocarbon laboratories worldwide, the Haas laboratory was judged to be one of three of the most precise and dependable in the world. Until the laboratory was closed a few years ago, in an unfortunate budget-cutting move, all of our radiocarbon samples were processed in the Haas laboratory.

Despite the diversity of the archaeological entities excavated at Wadi Kubbaniya, and the intensity of our work, we found time for fun. When we began working at Kubbaniya in 1981, Stella beer, the focus of our alcoholic libations during our early years in Egypt, was relatively cheap. Some of us also brought in our allotment of one bottle of vodka or scotch, which we shared with the others during the predinner "Happy Hours." The bottles never lasted beyond the night they were opened, so we began to examine the cheap, locally made beverages available in the rare liquor shops in Cairo and other cities.

One of them, "WHITE CAT, BETTER THAN DRY GIN," we consumed in some quantity, mostly because it was inexpensive. It was terrible. If you shook it, "little fishes" could be seen floating around in the bottle. Cut with canned fruit juice, it became drinkable. No one ever went blind drinking it, although there were a few bad hangovers.

One who had her share of hangovers was Brenda Scoggins, a senior archaeology graduate student who was a medical technician in Dallas. During Brenda's second field season at Wadi Kubbaniya, we celebrated Schild's "Name Day," a Polish tradition honoring the saint with the same name. Schild brought a bottle of good Polish vodka to the camp in anticipation. Equally shared among ten of us, the bottle provided a nice glow. After dinner, Scoggins decided we needed more celebration and brought out a bottle of White Cat she had bought in Cairo. Veterans of previous evenings with

We love making fun of CPE "regulars." In this cartoon Achilles Gautier teases Sandy Davis, a frequent volunteer/guest from Dallas who always brought a camp shower. Hard-core CPE'ers love to talk about the famous Wendorf edict: If you can't do it on three liters a day, it doesn't need to be done.

Our "tame" paleontologist Achilles Gautier is not only a world-renowned archaeobiologist, but also a talented cartoonist. During the 1999 field season at Nabta Playa, he spoofed himself, Fred, and Roman Schild (with hammer) as the camp prepared to celebrate Roman's Name Day.

White Cat decided not to participate. Scoggins was tipsy when she toddled off to her tent. We later learned that she tripped as she entered and hit her head against the center tent pole, then against her wooden box.

The next morning when she came to breakfast she looked as though she had lost a vicious fight: both eyes were bloodshot and bright red. She had a black eye and bruises over much of her face. It was a working day and Scoggins had a crew of six workers who were to dig a series of stratigraphic trenches to look for buried occupation horizons. It was windy that day with lots of blowing sand, but Scoggins managed to get her men to the work area and started them off. Then she went to a nearby shallow trench, upwind from the blowing sand. She placed herself so she could watch the men work. An hour or so later when I went to see how she was doing, I found the men snickering at Scoggins's appearance. Only the top of her head from her nose up was visible. Scoggins was watching us with bright red eyes that looked like headlights.

There were two graduate students on the staff of the expedition, as in most field seasons. The one who had been with us the previous field season was the "senior graduate student." The other, known as the "junior graduate student," had special responsibilities. He or she was to keep track of the beer and wine consumption and inform me if there was a shortage. The junior graduate student was to open the wine in the evening before dinner, but the distribution of the wine was Schild's job.

In 1983 the junior graduate student was Christy Bednar. She was unusual in that she was several years older than the other students and had more money than most of them. One day she discovered there wasn't enough beer to last until the end of the project. Instead of coming to me (she knew me well enough to know I would probably decline to buy more beer), she gave Ali Mazhar, our camp manager, some money herself and asked him to buy the beer.

Nineteen eighty-three was the memorable year Schild decided he'd learn to drive. In Poland at the time, most people did not; they used public transportation or walked. We had two 1976 Land Rover pickups that had seen several years of good service, and I suggested he could learn on one of them. Schild chose one, and after a few minutes of instruction about how to start the engine, use the clutch to change the gears, stop and steer, he headed west alone, up the sand-filled wadi. Fearing he might get stuck in the soft sand on the floor of the wadi and have to be rescued by our workers, who would undoubtedly laugh at him, he drove the vehicle at a fairly good speed in a lower gear than necessary, resulting in considerable noise.

On this occasion, Scoggins was in one of the toilets—a wooden box with a twelve-inch-diameter hole in the top where you sat—surrounded by a long sheet of canvas about six feet wide, attached to five poles arranged so as to give some privacy. She didn't pay much attention to the noise up the wadi until it grew louder—and closer. When she peeked out of the curtain, she saw a Land Rover coming straight at her with surprising speed. She fled the toilet, trousers around her knees, just ahead of Schild's Land Rover as it brushed the edge of the toilet.

Near the end of the season I decided to complete the archaeological survey of the north side of the wadi, near its mouth. It was an extensive sandy area where I had seen several sites, mostly deflated. I asked Christy Bednar to take a couple of workers and map the area, locate all the sites on the map, and identify the entity each represented. I watched her for a couple of days as she used a compass and tape trying to make a map. It was a big job, probably more than she could do in the time available, and I asked her if she could use some help. She said she did.

We soon had a grid staked out over the area and defined the limits of most of the sites on the map. When I saw I was no longer needed, I left her to finish. She did a superb job. A few days later I used her notes to write a report of the survey. It was published, with her map, in the third volume of the Kubbaniya series of books, under both of our names.

A few weeks after we returned from Egypt, Christy came to my office to tell me she was dropping out of graduate school. She was probably my best student, but she was divorced and had three young children to support. She had taken a job in the development department of KERA, a public radio and television station in Dallas. In the months that followed she sometimes came by and brought me some map files or other items she had found when her father closed his petroleum consulting office. Once she and her parents invited me to a fancy dinner at the Petroleum Club in Dallas. We stayed friends, though I rarely saw her.

Dagdag Safsaf and Bir Misaha
(1985)

CHAPTER 30

W hile we were working at Wadi Kubbaniya in 1981–1984, the Egyptian General Petroleum Company (GPC) had developed an experimental farm about twenty miles south of Bir Sahara East. They built an asphalt road from Dakhla Oasis south to the farm and beyond to the Sudan border, and an east-west road from near Bir Kiseiba to Bir Sahara East. They drilled water wells and built a landing strip about five miles north of the farm. The army established a post at the junction of the two roads, about a mile north of Bir Sahara East.

After completing our work at Wadi Kubbaniya in 1984, we returned to the Western Desert in early January 1985 to do an archaeological survey of a large area of sand sheet west of Bir Kiseiba, near the Gilf Kebir. We were interested in the relationship, if any, between the buried channels discovered in 1982 by ground-penetrating radar on the space shuttle and archaeological settlements, particularly those of Holocene age, that is, less than 10,000 years old.

Initially, our camp was set up near Bir Safsaf. The water at Bir Safsaf could be used for washing, but it contained too much carbonate and other minerals to be potable. Ali Mazhar, our camp manager, found it necessary to bring water for drinking and tea from the drilled well at the General Petroleum Company experimental farm, about thirty miles south of Bir Tarfawi. He set our camp inside the arc of the largest dune in the Bir Safsaf area. The dune protected our camp from the wind, and could be seen from a great distance, making it a useful guide to camp when we returned late in the evening.

On the first day of our survey we found a large cluster of fifteen deflated stone-filled hearths and numerous associated lithic artifacts dominated by elongated scalene triangles with small, short sides, a characteristic tool of El Ghorab Early Neolithic.

One of the members of our staff that year was Abbas Mohamed, a Sudanese prehistorian who had received his PhD from Cambridge University. Abbas suggested we name the area Dagdag Safsaf, because of the rough track we followed into the wadi basin. As Abbas explained to me, Dagdag means "rough" or "corrugated" in Sudanese Arabic.

Our new Ghorab site was near the mouth of a shallow wadi that drained an area of low hills to the east and ran northwest toward Bir Safsaf. We were unable to recover charcoal from any of the hearths, and there was no way we could date the site precisely. Other El Ghorab settlements in the area around Bir Kiseiba and Nabta Playa we dated to between 8,600 and 8,300 years ago, and the Dagdag site probably falls somewhere in that range. The deflation had destroyed any faunal remains that might have been present. Nothing was preserved except stone artifacts.

After mapping the hearths, we dug a couple of trenches near the floor of the wadi and, surprisingly, discovered two separate, buried Acheulean horizons. The lower was in a gravel bed about 2.5 to 3 feet below the surface. The upper horizon was enclosed within playa silts that overlay the gravel bed. The associated hand axes in both horizons were stream-worn and not in the position where prehistoric people left them hundreds of thousands of years ago. Clearly of different ages, the hand axes in the lower horizon were crudely made and could be classified as Early or, possibly, Middle Acheulean, while those in the upper horizon were much more finely made and typologically Late Acheulean.

In 1983 NASA had discovered features resembling river channels on a recent space shuttle flight. These channels were first observed when ground-penetrating radar on the shuttle was used to photograph the desert surface of northern Sudan and adjacent Egypt. A group of several U.S. Geological Survey (USGS) geologists, with Vance Haynes and an independent archaeologist, that was studying these radar channels published a paper suggesting that they had been flowing streams during the Neolithic. I seriously doubted that interpretation. I was convinced that had there been permanent water in those channels during the Holocene, there would have been many archaeological sites nearby. My experience in that part of the desert led me to believe that such sites did not exist in the area of the radar channels.

Schild and I believe these radar channels are very old, perhaps pre-Pleistocene. We have noted that the Early or Middle Pleistocene stream system evident on the Landstat images is sometimes inset within the radar channels, and is thus earlier than the Neolithic.

Angela and I decided to do a controlled test of the USGS hypothesis by surveying an area where there were many radar channels and compare the frequency of archaeological sites in that area with that found in a similar area outside the channels. We expected the test to show us where the greatest density of archaeological sites occurred: along the channels, or in a similar area of sand sheet where there were no channels.

Using a radar photograph of the area near Bir Safsaf the USGS provided, we laid a grid over a rectangular area with many braided radar channels, and over a similar area nearby with no channels. In both areas the surface was open and clear with no vegetation. Any cluster of artifacts could be seen for several hundred yards, a single rock from 50 yards or more. Guided by previously placed survey flags, Angela and I, plus a driver, drove the Jeep in straight lines back and forth at 100-yard intervals across both areas and plotted on a map every archaeological site we found. In addition, we identified the probable entity represented, its age, and the artifact density. We recorded all of this for each archaeological occurrence.

The archaeological density in the two areas was very different. We found many more sites on the nonchannel sand sheet. This was the opposite of what you would expect if the radar channels had held water in the Holocene.

When the work at Dagdag Safsaf was complete we moved our camp farther to the southwest, south of the General Petroleum Company experimental farms. We wanted to be near the GPC farms to be close to good water, and near the Egyptian/Sudanese border, where the ground-penetrating radar on the space shuttle had indicated the presence of several large channels buried under the sand.

One of our first discoveries in the new area was an assemblage of Late Acheulean hand axes partially buried near the gently sloping crest at the edge of a small basin. The hand axes were fresh and, as we sometimes describe stone tools with unworn or un-wind-abraded flake scars, "sharp enough to cut your hand."

Anticipating the discovery of an undisturbed Acheulean living surface, Schild and I carefully uncovered and plotted the orientations of the numerous buried hand axes. Suddenly, Schild said, "Fred, look at the alignment of the hand axes we've just uncovered. All of them are pointing in the same direction. That's clear evidence they're not in their primary position, but have been washed down this slope." We reluctantly finished excavating, mapping, and collecting the remaining Late Acheulean hand axes, but our excitement was gone.

Next, we decided to survey the area along the border to the west toward the well H. J. L. Beadnell dug in 1927 that he named Bir Misaha (the "Survey Well"). We had no trouble finding it, because there was a pile of abandoned equipment nearby. The well, however, had been deliberately filled with sand (by the British in World War II perhaps) and was no longer usable.

We were unable to find any interesting archaeological sites nearby, but we did find a large British World War II camp, complete with tents, now rotted, blown down, and sand-covered, many beer and wine bottles, and tobacco tins. It was easy to identify the officers' quarters because that was where we found all the wine bottles. We assumed that the enlisted men lived in the tents where most of the beer bottles were concentrated.

I'm not as well informed as I should be on British army movements in southern Egypt during World War II, but I know that in late 1943 British forces moved from Wadi Halfa in northern Sudan toward Kufra, where there was an Italian base in southern Libya. At the same time the French began to advance from Chad toward Kufra. Together the British and the French took Kufra and drove the Italians from southern Libya. The camp we discovered may have been a supply depot for that assault.

Our curiosity satisfied, we drove north about a hundred miles to Bir Tarfawi to excavate a trench where we had found deeply buried ostrich eggshell fragments during our work there in 1974.

When we'd worked at Sahara East and Tarfawi in 1973–1974, and for several years afterwards, chronology seemed an insoluble problem. In 1984 Vance Haynes offered a promising solution to the dating of sites that are more than 40,000 years old. He called to tell me Gifford Miller of the University of Colorado was working on the development of a new dating technique using ostrich eggshells. Vance urged me to contact Miller. I called Miller that day and offered to try to find him some old eggshells; he agreed to try to date them. To fulfill my pledge, we moved to Bir Tarfawi for a short stay in early March of 1985.

The first night we were at Tarfawi, the early March weather was so cold that the water in our washbasins froze solid. We were so surprised at the cold that everyone in camp stayed in bed that morning until the cook and his helpers began to stir and brought us coffee. I don't know how cold it was; no one had a thermometer, but it was the coldest night I've ever experienced in the more than thirty winters I've spent in the Eastern Sahara.

The new trench at Bir Tarfawi yielded several more fragments of eggshells from near the bottom of the lake deposits. I sent them to Miller, who immediately began processing the samples. The results indicated considerable age, but the dates were only relative.

However, Henry Schwarcz, of the University of Toronto gave the eggshells an absolute chronology. Schwarcz did a uranium-series analysis of another group of eggshell fragments we had collected from the same deep trench at Tarfawi. The preliminary results indicated an age of slightly more than 100,000 years old.

The new techniques were indeed promising, and the questions in Schild's and my mind about the stratigraphy in the Tarfawi and Sahara East basins justified our planning a major new effort at these basins. We planned to return to the Tarfawi/Sahara basins the following year (1986), if I could persuade the NSF to give me a grant.

Return to Bir Sahara East and Bir Tarfawi |
(1986–1989)

CHAPTER 31

Based on Miller and Schwarcz's promising results on dating ostrich eggshells that I discussed in the previous chapter, I submitted a grant proposal to the National Science Foundation for a four-year project at Bir Sahara East and Bir Tarfawi, beginning in January 1986. The grant was awarded, but for one year only. A few weeks later I discussed the problem with the NSF program director for anthropology, who suggested that I prepare a summary of our progress and a new budget each year after the field season and submit it for the advisory panel's consideration. With that important encouragement, we were ready to roll.

For internal political reasons, in 1986 the Egyptian Geological Survey decided not to work with foreign expeditions. But with Issawi's help, it was arranged for the General Petroleum Company (GPC) to sponsor our work at Tarfawi and Sahara East. The company had set up an experimental farm some twenty miles south of Bir Tarfawi and had drilled a well to provide water for their staff and to irrigate their farming areas. The agreement called for GPC to loan us a surveyor who would create an accurate map. They would also provide water for the camp. This agreement was important to us: For the first time we would be able to have precise elevations of the groundwater in the two basins. Use of the water well at the farm was another essential, because the army had polluted the well at Bir Sahara East.

We made the decision to return to Tarfawi because by that time we realized that the Middle Paleolithic sites at Tarfawi and Sahara East were exceptional. When we started work in the desert in 1973, we had not known how unusual it was to find Middle Paleolithic sites in such large numbers, undisturbed, with associated fauna. We supposed that the desert contained many similar features of this age with abundant archaeology. But as we came to know the desert, we realized there were no other basins like Bir Tarfawi and Bir Sahara East in Egypt, or in northern Sudan. Nowhere else in the world would we be able to find such a concentration of well-preserved Middle Paleolithic sites. The Bir Tarfawi and Bir Sahara East depressions were, and still are, unique.

Before we began working, Schild, Close, and I agreed on the approaches we would take, and equally importantly, the approaches we would not take. We were not interested in traditional studies that emphasize the definition of Middle Paleolithic cultural units. We wanted to focus on research that would contribute to our understanding of Middle Paleolithic behavior and its environmental context by identifying the settings in which the sites occurred and establishing the functions of the various settings through analysis of the lithic technology, tool typology, and associated fauna. We planned to excavate at least one site in each identified setting in each lake event to see if there had been a change through time.

A key element in our study was the analysis of the lithic artifacts, including the sometimes-ignored chips and lithic debris, which the French often refer to as "deb-itage." We would attempt to determine the nature of the manufacturing activities that occurred at each site, what was brought into them, what kinds of artifacts were produced there, and what became of them (if they were used and abandoned there, or if they were taken elsewhere). With this approach we hoped to glean information on the kinds of activities that occurred at each site, the patterns of tool curation, and the nature of the settlement system in which the site functioned. The key elements of our plan had been the focus of my proposal to the NSF.

At an early stage of our research we discovered several interesting characteristics of our Middle Paleolithic sites in the Sahara East and Tarfawi basins: (1) regardless of their chronological position, sites in similar settings tended to contain the same kinds of artifacts in similar frequencies; (2) sites in different settings had different artifact frequencies; and (3) these patterns persisted throughout the long Middle Paleolithic sequence in both depressions, a period of more than 100,000 years. To us, it was clear evidence that Middle Paleolithic people had an established, patterned set of behaviors in the Tarfawi/Sahara East landscape.

One of the clearest expressions of this patterned behavior was the way the people used artifacts in their lithic economy. They used the quarries, most of which were located at the eastern edge of the Tarfawi depression, only for the extraction and initial shaping of fist-sized stone blocks. They carried these partially shaped blocks to the shores of the lakes, and there shaped them by flaking into Levallois cores. Many Middle Paleolithic groups in Africa, Southwest Asia, and Europe utilized this

Levallois technique. The goal was to prepare a core so that large, thin, wide flakes could be removed. These Levallois flakes were "blanks" they could retouch into a variety of tools.

At Tarfawi, after being carried to the edge of the lake or playa pond, the unfinished cores were shaped and initially exploited at secondary workshops. Most of the cores found at the lakeshore sites were either broken or exhausted. Many of the good cores had been taken elsewhere or had been used up. The retouched tools in these lakeside secondary workshops were almost all large flakes with one or more sawlike edges, or denticulates. Their function is not well known; they may have been used to process plants. We wondered why they were concentrated on the beaches. Other pieces in the beach sites included many unretouched Levallois flakes that seem to have been failed Levallois pieces abandoned as unusable.

In contrast, the sites on dry lake beds were rarely used as secondary workshops, and the tools we found there were mostly sidescrapers and retouched Mousterian Points, with few sawlike tools. Most of the sites on the dry lake beds had numerous bones of large mammals, including rhinos, extinct buffalo, extinct camel, and several varieties of gazelles and antelopes, some of which were in positions suggesting an association with the archaeology. We could not tell if the skeletons of the dry lake bed sites were scavenged animals that died in a catastrophic drought, or animals that had gathered at a drying lake bed and were killed. Many of the animals may have died on the dry lake bed without human participation.

It seemed likely to me that neither the lakeshore nor the lake bed localities were used as night camps, because of the threat from large carnivores. Today, in Sahelian and tropical areas, people stay away from lake and stream shores at night because of large nocturnal predators. Although we searched for them, we were unable to find any night camps where, we speculated, most of the final exploitation of the Levallois cores had occurred. I think they were probably located on higher ground, beyond the edge of the basins, well back from the water. If so, the Middle Paleolithic night camps were almost certainly destroyed by the extensive deflation of the upland landscapes that occurred after the Last Interglacial.

A major reason we returned to Tarfawi and Bir Sahara East in 1986 was the hope that recently developed dating techniques would yield consistent absolute ages for the periods when lakes existed in the basins. If we could determine absolute ages we could compare the sequences of lakes in the basins with dated oceanic events and determine the relationship between the two phenomena. Another priority was to obtain better data on the stratigraphic sequences in the two basins. Only in stratigraphy were we truly successful. Our efforts to obtain consistent, precise dates for the lake events had only limited success, despite employing a variety of techniques on several kinds of materials.

We assembled a great field crew for this project. Besides Schild, Close, and me, there were five archaeologists, two paleontologists (one for the big animals, one for the birds, mice, and other small animals), and three geochemists (two for dating, one for carbonates). Several more geochemists dated samples, but did not go into the field.

Two others, Chris Hill and Halina Krolik (both veterans of the Wadi Kubbaniya project), stayed for the three seasons of the project with Schild, Close, and me. In addition to excavating several key sites, Chris Hill, one of the brightest and most hardworking graduate students I've ever had, initiated the first use (by us) of stable isotopes for determining past environments. He also drafted most of the maps and diagrams we used in our book on the work at Sahara East and Tarfawi.

When evaluated on the basis of the stratigraphy in the basins, four of the dating techniques yielded results that provided us with a useful chronology for the Middle Paleolithic wet periods in the two basins. But no technique provided the precision we needed for close comparison with the oceanic sequence, which was our ultimate goal.

Tarfawi and Sahara East are only six miles apart, and today their water tables are at the same level. On the basis of the elevation of the lake beds, the magnitude of the lacustrine episodes, and the results of the various age determinations, Schild and I believe that the Middle Paleolithic lakes in the two basins were simultaneous responses to changes in the local environment. We correlated the two stratigraphic sequences based on that assumption.

As I noted earlier, the age measurements from four techniques were compared with the stratigraphic position of the dated samples. These dates lead us to believe the sequence of five periods of Middle Paleolithic lakes and the early playa occurred between 250,000 and 65,000 years ago. The five warm periods of lakes were separated by periods of cold, aridity, erosion, and deflation. The lake episodes appear to have an approximate correlation with the oceanic Oxygen Isotope Stages assigned to Interglacials and their subphases.

The Middle Paleolithic sites at Tarfawi and Sahara East occur in four different settings: lake shorelines, ranging from marsh deposits to high-energy beaches; dry lake bottoms; a seasonal playa; and a sand sheet. The sites along shorelines were the most numerous, occurring in every lake interval, including the Middle Paleolithic Playa. Many of these shoreline localities were repeatedly occupied, resulting in a dense mass of lithic artifacts. The lithic assemblages in all of the shoreline sites have similar characteristics, strongly indicating that they functioned as secondary workshops, mostly for the preparation and exploitation of Levallois cores.

It is interesting to note that the adaptation represented by the sites along the shorelines, as reflected in the stone tool assemblages, remained essentially unchanged through all of the lake and playa events at Tarfawi/Sahara. This suggests it is highly likely that this was not an adaptation by a single group who came when it was wet, abandoned the area when it became dry, and repeatedly returned when the rains returned. We reject that idea because of the long interval of hyperaridity that separated each period of permanent lakes. The region was almost certainly abandoned during these dry intervals. It seems likely to us that this adaptation was present at least across most of the Saharan/Sahelian zone and was utilized by many different societies.

One of the Middle Paleolithic sites embedded in a "deepwater dry lake bottom" had a thin cover of later-drying lake sediments over the occupation horizon. This site was unique. It had everything—a lot of workshop debris, abundant faunal remains, and many retouched points and sidescrapers. There were also a few flakes with saw-tooth edges and many unretouched Levallois flakes, mostly seemingly failed attempts to produce Levallois points. Apparently this site functioned much like the beach sites, and was used as a secondary workshop for exploiting Levallois cores. Like the other dry, deepwater localities, it was a place for processing meat. It was the only site of this type we excavated.

Animal remains were abundant at a few sites in both basins, mostly large mammals. There were also crocodiles, turtles, and fish in the two earlier lake phases in the Tarfawi basin. The fish included several species found today only in the Nile, the Niger River, and Lake Chad. Some of these fish, such as the Nile perch, require deep, permanent water. This suggests that on at least two occasions there were water connections between the Tarfawi depression and either the Nile, the Niger, or Lake Chad, but as yet we cannot determine which of these was the source of the fish.

I still doubt that the radar channels we examined near Bir Safsaf had permanent water during the Holocene, but I have changed my mind as to the role of those channels during the Last Interglacial and still earlier Middle Pleistocene wet intervals. The fish remains require a distant water connection, so those channels must have been flowing rivers during some of the wet intervals of the Last Interglacial and possibly before.

The mice and other small mammals and bird remains from Bir Tarfawi provided another detailed data set on the environment at the time the lakes existed. Among the forms present were several species whose modern distributions are limited to Tropical Africa, in areas at least 900 miles to the south, where the landscape is a savanna or wooded savanna. Several species today are confined to areas with rainfall of 500 mil-limeters per year or more.

Three long seasons in 1986, 1987, and 1988 at Tarfawi/Sahara East continued the pattern that characterized almost all of the CPE research after we left the Aswan Reservoir. Once we found an area with a lot of sites and well-preserved associated stratigraphy, we tended to work there for several seasons, sometimes taking a break of a year or more to search for other promising areas. Breaks in long periods of research are useful, for they provide time to reconsider and evaluate the results of the ini-tial research. In three instances, one of which was at Tarfawi/Sahara East, we took a break, then returned to a locality and did additional work that significantly revised our earlier conclusions. In the absence of wars and problems with permits, we would have spent more time at Esna and the Fayum, but we might never have known about Gademotta in Ethiopia.

The archaeological and paleoenvironmental data we recovered, the results of our dating efforts, and the major conclusions that resulted from our research at Tarfawi and Sahara East we reported in a hefty volume titled *Egypt during the Last Interglacial: The Middle Paleolithic of Bir Tarfawi and Bir Sahara East.*

Beginning between 60,000 and 65,000 years ago, after the final moist pulsation of the Last Interglacial, the climate of the Western Desert became hyperarid. The last of the lakes disappeared, possibly with the onset of the cold temperatures of Oxygen Isotope Stage 4. The larger animals and humans abandoned the area, and eventually it became a lifeless desert until around 11,000 radiocarbon years ago, when there is evidence of rain for the first time in almost 50,000 years.

According to my memory, the 1988 season was the only time the expedition brought too much beer. We had carefully calculated the number of bottles needed for the time we'd be in camp, but we closed the camp a week early. The GPC told us they would have space for all of the scientists on the next plane, which Ali Mazhar wanted us to take. For him it would be an easier trip to Esna to store the equipment if he did not have to bother with the foreigners. All of the camp equipment made it to our store at Esna; the extra case of beer did not.

We needed one more season at Bir Sahara East to complete the excavations and to collect the additional samples for dating that were scheduled for that basin. However, my request to the NSF for funding to support a fourth field season at Sahara East/Tarfawi was denied. I am not sure why we did not receive the money, but I cannot complain. I have been told that I have received far more NSF grants than anyone else.

In this instance, the rejection of my proposal may have saved my life. In late February of 1989, a few days after my return to Dallas from a brief survey of Wadi Qena, my urologist called to report that I had rapidly growing prostate cancer. I was operated on just in time. As any man who has had radical prostate surgery knows, it changes your life forever—not as much as the battle wound I received when I was twenty years old, but enough.

Surveys in Northern Sudan and Other Projects
(1989–1990, 1994)

CHAPTER 32

I n October of 1989, three months before we began our 1990 survey and excavation program at Nabta, I asked Bahay Issawi to write to the Sudanese Geological Survey and ask if they would help us conduct a three-week survey across the Sahara from El Fasher in the south to Merga in the north. After some discussion, mostly about how much I would pay them, the Sudanese survey agreed. They assigned Schafe, one of their senior geologists, and a clerk and two drivers to go with us. They also agreed to loan us three tents and other camping equipment, a small lorry, and a Jeep. On January 1, 1990, Issawi, Schild, Close, and I flew from Cairo to Khartoum. The next day we completed final arrangements with the geological survey. A week later the Jeep and the truck with the equipment and several barrels of fuel for the northward trip left Khartoum for El Fasher, supposedly a three-week trip. Two weeks later our group, including Schafe, caught a flight for El Fasher.

On arriving at the completely empty El Fasher airport, we got a ride into town on an army truck and reported to the local military officials. They immediately suggested we go back to the airport and stay there until our truck arrived. El Fasher was built around a small lake that was swarming with mosquitoes. The town was in the midst of a malaria epidemic. We bought some fruit and other food at the market, and the military returned us to the airport.

I remembered tales about El Fasher airport Joel Shiner had told us. He was a pilot during World War II and had landed there one time while ferrying an aircraft from Brazil across the Atlantic via Africa, India, and over the "Hump" into China. Shiner had described it as a "nice little airport, clean and well managed." He would not have recognized the place in 1990. It was filthy; all the toilets were clogged and had not worked for many years. One old barracks building housed metal cots with dirty cotton mattresses. We selected the five cleanest beds and gathered them into three rooms, where we set up our quarters to await the arrival of our truck and Jeep.

We waited and we waited, and still no vehicles came. We read, we talked about the project ahead, and we went for short walks, careful to stay within sight of the airport. Finally, three weeks after we arrived in El Fasher, and five weeks after the vehicles left Khartoum, they arrived.

The drivers told us they had barely made it. They were out of fuel; even the spare barrels of fuel for our trip north were empty. Schafe told us he was sure they had sold most of it. I should have terminated the project then and left the men to find their own way back to Khartoum, but Schafe was embarrassed. He went to the local military commander and persuaded him to sell us the fuel we needed. Two days later we drove north, leaving El Fasher heading toward Millet, the next town, about forty-five miles north.

It took us two days to reach Millet. Between them, the two vehicles had several flat tires that had to be repaired, and the drivers refused to drive more than four hours a day. They started the day about 8:00 A.M. with coffee. About 9:30 A.M. they would stop for an hour to have breakfast that included hot tea, for which they had to build a fire. At noon they stopped for another hour to have lunch, again with hot tea, and finally, after driving two hours after lunch, they stopped again. "No more driving," they said and began to set up camp. Each day was like that, and Bahay was furious. He tried to persuade the men to eat less and drive more, but they refused, saying their union would not permit it. Schafe tried to reason with them, but they would not listen.

On the morning of our third day out, we drove into the town of Millet, our first destination. The town was known to be smugglers' headquarters. The houses were made of grass and sorghum stalks, but almost every one had a TV antenna on the roof and a TV receiver inside. We wondered if the TV receivers could be used, and I believe they were, somehow, even though we were hundreds of miles from the nearest broadcasting stations in Khartoum and Libya.

You could buy almost anything in the market in Millet: from expensive English soaps to heavy wool sweaters, perfumes, toilet bowls, and bathtubs. The drivers and the clerk abandoned the vehicles and headed to the market, not to be seen again for three hours. When they came back they were all struggling under big bundles. The clerk was particularly pleased with his purchase of a heavy wool sweater to take to his mother in Khartoum. I asked him when she could wear it, and he said in the winter when it's cold in Khartoum. I was amazed because it was over 100°F every day we were in Khartoum, and it was January.

Where had all these goods come from? From Libya, is all they would tell us. I assume it was some form of "foreign aid" from Libya to Sudan, because a convoy of several huge, powerful eighteen-wheeler trucks came in while we were there. They stopped beyond the outskirts of the town, unloaded their cargos, and then headed back across the desert to Libya for another load. In this way they avoided Sudanese customs. It is a mystery how these goods got from this little town to where they might be used. I suspect buyers came to Millet, selected what they wanted, paid for the merchandise, and had it trucked to Khartoum and other big Sudanese cities.

With the bargain-loving crew finally back, we headed north, following a little-used trail, until we came to Malha Crater, a huge cone, an extinct volcano with a lake inside the caldera. We decided to drive to the top, following a track up the side of the cone to the rim. Far inside the volcano we could see many people filling water cans on the shore of the lake and others carrying water containers, following trails up to the rim. It was a surrealistic and primitive scene. We turned around and away from the Malha Crater and continued driving north toward the Sahara.

From time to time throughout this trip, we stopped and looked at archaeological sites. All of them were late. At the edges of almost all these sites there were one or more piles of slag from smelting iron. We saw no prehistoric sites, but we didn't spend much time looking for them. I noted that all of the wadis we crossed were still aggrading. I knew it would be difficult to find buried sites along these wadis.

The day after we visited Malha Crater, we skirted another village, where people were hauling water out of a deep, hand-dug well. We saw a large leather bucket on a long rope being dropped to the water at the bottom of the well. When it was filled, a camel pulled the bucket out of the hole to the top of the well. There the water spilled onto a trough and from there into a pool where several cattle and a few small livestock were drinking. At some distance from the pool several herds of cattle and small livestock awaited their turn to drink.

Issawi asked some of the local people standing around how long they would bring up water from the well, and he was told they worked all day and night, as long as the water was needed. The activity at the Malha Crater and the well told us water was scarce in this region.

From the well we drove north following a small track through open acacia woodlands. On the east side we skirted an area of highlands known as the Madub Mountains. Throughout the drive north we occasionally saw people, who were always friendly, and we often stopped so Issawi could visit with them. He wanted to find out the local price of cattle.

The next morning, after we had driven about two hours, we came to a valley in which there was a small, dispersed village of at least a dozen round houses built of driftwood and branches. The houses were scattered along both banks of a shallow wadi. There were also several cultivated fields, some of which had scraps of sorghum stalks still standing.

Each of the houses had an open door facing east, and sometimes a window on the same side. There were no other openings. The open doorways and windows made it easy for us to look inside. We noted that the houses were fully equipped with tools and pottery vessels of several sizes. Most of the pots were decorated with what appeared to be comb-impressed designs similar to those we'd found on our Early Neolithic pottery at Nabta and Kiseiba. The village appeared to be abandoned, but before long several boys showed up to look us over and to make sure we didn't take anything.

Although shy at first, the boys eventually came close enough for Issawi to talk to them. We learned that the people in this village belonged to the Madub, a mixed pastoralist/farming group who, with their cattle and goats, lived in the nearby Madub Mountains in the winter. They had permanent water there. This explained why there were no adults in the village. The boys told Issawi that when the summer rains began, the people returned to the village to plant their sorghum fields.

Proceeding north, our little caravan the next day moved through the open acacia woodlands. We came to a nice open area and decided to stop for lunch. We had finished eating and were about to return to the vehicles when a man rode up on a beautiful white racing camel. He had an Arab's facial features and dark skin. He was not tall, but he looked lean and tough. His glance was contemptuous as he looked first at our drivers who were still having lunch, and then at us.

Issawi invited him to join us, and after the usual polite greetings, our visitor got down from his camel and asked Issawi, "How many wives do you have?" Bahay responded, "Only one." Our visitor looked at Bahay with surprise. He said, "You don't look sick or poor; why don't you have more wives?" Bahay shrugged and smiled. "Don't need them," he said.

Our visitor then looked at Angela, and asked, "Whose wife is she?" Bahay pointed to me. The man said something Bahay did not translate, but I suspect it wasn't approving. His look told me that I did not impress him. "I have three wives, and I will soon have a fourth," he announced. "She is young and pretty. I am rich and I can have any woman I want." He looked around again, said good-bye to Issawi, mounted his camel, and rode off in the direction he had come from, no doubt to check on his wives.

As we continued north, the trees got farther and farther apart, and soon we entered what I call "the land of upside-down trees." Someone had cut down all the trees near the margin of the open woodlands and desert grasslands. Here, in this ecotone, almost all of the acacia trees had been cut down, their trunks trimmed of their branches and hauled away, to be made into charcoal and sold. The next high wind would roll the remaining trunkless branches onto their tops—thus my term, upside-down trees. I pity the people who live in this area when the next drought comes. The soil will blow away because there will be nothing to hold the dirt, and the desert will grow larger and larger until the tree cutting is stopped.

We turned around and drove a few hundred yards back inside the still-uncut open acacia woodlands to spend the night. The next morning we loaded up and headed north again. As we passed the last upside-down trees, we saw ahead of us an enormous open landscape of tall bunch grass, and beyond that, short bunch grass, and in the far distance, a blanket of seemingly endless sand.

A few minutes later, less than a mile from the last tree, our Jeep came to a halt and the driver announced, "Something is wrong with this car. I cannot go any farther." The lorry pulled up behind us and that driver also announced that something was wrong with his truck, too. "I will have to turn around and go back," he said. Of course, they had planned this. There was nothing wrong with either vehicle. The drivers were afraid to enter the desert.

Schafe shouted at them, Issawi cursed them, and I yelled at them, but they refused to go into the desert. I could not help but contrast the difference between our Sudanese drivers and our Egyptian drivers, who would drive all day and, if necessary, all night and go anywhere we asked them to go. We had no choice but to turn around and head back to El Fasher. Now there was no four hours a day restriction on driving. We were back in El Fasher by the end of the second day. Close, Issawi, Schild, Schafe, and I took the plane back to Khartoum the next morning. We left the two drivers and the clerk to find their own way back.

Once in Khartoum, Schafe filed a report with the director of the survey about what happened. It wasn't long until the director called me into his office. He was embarrassed and offered his profound apologies. He also gave me a full refund of the money I'd paid to the survey for the rental of the vehicles, the fuel, and the wages of those who had come with us. I still had to buy the round-trip airfares from Cairo, and to El Fasher, but there was nothing I could do about that. Besides, it had been a great experience, although not one I would like to repeat. I hope the old Arab, his white camel, his four wives, and his many cows survived the next drought.

Despite the experience on the El Fasher trip, I decided to make one more effort to see if we could find Early Neolithic sites in northern Sudan for comparison with the material from our sites at Nabta Playa and Bir Kiseiba. Before the beginning of the 1994 field season at Nabta, I decided to make another trip the first week in January into Sudan, this time from the north, from Bir Misaha on the Egyptian/Sudanese boundary to the saltwater lake of Merga, about three hundred miles to the south. We had Eide Mariff again as guide and driver, and one of our regular Egyptian drivers. Bahay Issawi was also with us, as well as Angela, but Roman could not come to Egypt until later. Angela and I had Sudanese visas, just in case we encountered a border patrol.

We had no difficulties on the trip down, and when we arrived in the vicinity of Merga, Eide selected a campsite three miles east of the lake on a bluff where he could see anyone who might be in the area. He found good drinking water a few feet below the surface in a small valley a half-mile from camp.

We began our survey by going east about twenty miles from our camp. We soon entered a small basin that had a large stone building near the center, probably somewhere between 750 and 1,000 years old. The building had from thirty to forty rooms around the periphery. Three hundred yards north of the stone structure, near the edge of the playa sediments, we found numerous bones of several large animals. The lower leg bones on one of the large animals were standing upright, embedded in the playa sediment. Nearby, at least one other animal appeared to have been partially butchered. We found a few flakes, possibly butchering tools, around the bones. A few feet away we found two sherds of rocker-stamped pottery, similar to the pottery we'd found in sites of the Jerar Early Neolithic. Both sherds were still embedded in the playa sediment. Since we did not have a permit to excavate, we left everything undisturbed.

We next turned our attention to the area west of Merga, between the lake and the Chad border. I noted that Eide seemed uneasy, but he wouldn't say why. When I asked what was bothering him, instead of answering he said, "Let's break camp after breakfast and put everything in the back of the trucks." That was enough for me. We immediately broke camp.

We went northwest from camp about twenty miles, and found a shallow, sand-filled drainage. We turned south to follow it downstream, and almost immediately we noted burned rocks at the edge of the channel. We found several stone tools associated with the hearth, unlike any of the lithic artifacts we'd found at Nabta and Bir Kiseiba.

Continuing our survey and following the channel to the south, we went a mile or two when Eide stopped the car and jumped out to look at some large tire tracks of several large trucks, so recent that sand was still falling inside them. Around the truck tracks were the footprints of men who were walking, possibly to reduce the load in the trucks while they crossed the wadi. We didn't need to see more; we hastily got back in our vehicles, did a 180-degree turn, and got away from there as quickly as we could. A few hours later we were back in Egypt.

We don't know who was in those trucks. They may have been from the Sudanese army. Even though we had visas, it was possible the army could've forced us to enter and exit Sudan through a regular point of entry, maybe El Fasher. The other, a more unpleasant, possibility was that the trucks and men belonged to the Chad rebels, who were known to come to Merga for water occasionally. The rebels would probably have robbed, raped, or shot us, maybe all three.

A few weeks after we returned from the trip to Merga in northern Sudan, Eide paid me an enormous compliment. He invited me to meet his two wives. I went with him to the gate of his compound, where he asked me to wait. He went inside and brought both wives to the gate. He introduced me to both of them, the older wife first, then the second. I thanked Eide and his wives, and then, in English, he said, "Thank you, Fred," and indicated that I could leave.

New Excavations at Nabta Playa | and Correcting Mistakes
(1990–2001)

CHAPTER 33

After our experience with the plant remains at Wadi Kubbaniya, Schild and I decided that we needed to investigate the barley and wheat found at Nabta Playa. We were worried that the cereals were not in true association with the two sites where they were found. Part of the basis for our concern was that the cereals were 1,600 years older than the earliest known wheat and barley elsewhere in Egypt. So we decided to return to Nabta as soon as we could. That turned out to be in January of 1990. In addition to examining where the cereals were found, we wanted to recheck the stratigraphy near Bir Kiseiba and at El Kortein Playa. We suspected that we had made a mistake with the stratigraphy of the "Kortein Early Neolithic." We could examine both assumptions at one time.

When we arrived at Nabta in January 1990, our first efforts were to examine the exact places Hadidi had found barley and wheat in 1977. We would try to find more cereals. The first sample with barley we had taken was from the fill of a large, deep, bell-shaped storage pit exposed in the wall of a long stratigraphic trench we had dug across Site E-75-6. In the months we were elsewhere, the trench had filled with wind-blown sand. We began removing this loose sand as soon as our camp was set up.

To help with the plant identifications, the field staff this year included Krystyna Wasylikowa, a senior Polish botanist from Krakow. She had a lot of experience with wheat and barley seeds. As she and I watched the sand being removed from the trench, the outline of the pit soon became clearly visible, as was a small cutout in the fill of the pit that marked the spot where Hadidi had taken the barley sample. As we emptied the pit to collect more samples, some windblown charred plant remains and bits of charcoal got caught in a small, shallow crevice in front of the spot where Wasylikowa and I were standing. She reached down and scooped up a small handful of the carbonized material. As she looked at the palm of her hand, she exclaimed, "My God, look at all the seeds."

Wasylikowa did not identify the seeds for me; they were of no value to us because we did not know where they came from. She did say that none was barley. We emptied the remaining fill of the storage pit, put the dirt in plastic bags, and took the bags to the lab tent, where she sorted each bag under a magnifying glass. She found hundreds of charred plant remains. None was barley.

The second locality, which we'd identified as Site E-75-8, was the other place barley and wheat reportedly had been recovered. This site is part of an extensive settlement (3,000 feet long and 900 feet wide) where in 1975 and 1977 we had dug a long trench 6 feet deep across the highest part of the site, exposing Late and Final Neolithic horizons on the top, and below that a Middle Neolithic horizon resting on a bed of windblown sand more than 6 feet deep. Assuming the thick bed of sand was the base of the occupation at the site, we thought the earliest occupation was of Middle Neolithic age. We were wrong; several years later we discovered a still earlier Neolithic occupation 12 feet below the surface. But it was the upper part of the trench that was of interest: were the cereals in true association with the site?

In locating where Hadidi had taken his sample at E-75-8, one of our Bedouin workers who had assisted Hadidi in collecting the sample was of great help to us. The worker looked at the trench face and quickly pointed to a small cavity in the wall, about 16 inches in diameter and 8 inches deep. "Here," he said. "This is where I took the samples for the plant man."

We took a large sample of dirt around the place Hadidi had collected his sample and gave it to Wasylikowa. She reported that there were no plant remains in it. There were many grinding stones on the surface and throughout the sandy sediment of the site, but our subsequent sampling in many different parts of E-75-8 failed to recover more plant remains. Presumably, the absence of seeds is due to poor preservation.

We cannot be sure that Hadidi deliberately enriched our sample with barley and wheat at Kubbaniya. A much stronger case can be made, however, with regard to the barley and wheat he found at the two sites at Nabta. In the subsequent extensive excavations during the 1990 season we recovered literally tens of thousands of charred edible plant remains at Site E-75-6, but none was barley or wheat. As at Kubbaniya, I believe Hadidi wanted to give us what we expected to find, perhaps in a naïve attempt to be helpful, or perhaps to bring a little glory to himself. No one will ever know, but he paid a price. From that time on, archaeologists and botanists shunned him, and Wasylikowa publicly criticized him at an international botanical meeting. To punish him I added his name as a coauthor of the retraction article we later published in *Science*.

After we resolved the problem of the barley and wheat at Nabta, we moved to El Kortein Playa, where we reexamined the stratigraphic sequence there. This small basin is about nine miles north of Nabta. As we feared, it was soon evident that we had made a mistake in the stratigraphy in the Kortein basin: we'd failed to see the clear evidence that our "El Kortein Early Neolithic" was a mixture of two entities. The hearth that had yielded charcoal dating 8,840 years old and the straight-backed pointed bladelets we found near that hearth were from a small El Adam occupation. The nearby stemmed points and storage pits, on the other hand, had come from a late Early Neolithic entity we had named Al Jerar, which dated between 7,800 and 7,300 years ago. Schild and I removed the Kortein from all of our subsequent summaries of the sequence of Neolithic industries in the Western Desert.

Although in 1990 we had planned to be at Nabta for a single season, we quickly realized we would need to spend many more field seasons in the area. The most compelling reason for continuing to work at Nabta was the abundant and diverse plant remains Wasylikowa found at Site E-75-6. We knew a large sample of plant remains would be useful in gaining a better understanding of the Early Neolithic food economy and the past environment in that area. And we knew that the Holocene climatic sequence was much more complex and interesting than we had previously thought. We began to see strong evidence for a surprisingly complex social-ceremonial system among the hunter-gatherer-pastoralists living in the Nabta basin. These developments were providing exciting new information that has led us to continue working at Nabta up to today. If the CPE is permitted to do so, the group will continue to work there for many more years.

The new stratigraphic data we recently acquired from the Nabta/Kiseiba area have led Schild and me to propose a new chronological/cultural terminology for this area. In our new scheme, we term the dry periods "Arid Phases" and the humid intervals "Interphases." We have defined seven cultural entities, each of which coincided with a specific Humid Interphase. We also named the period with the greatest precipitation the "Holocene Climatic Maximum," an interval that lasted about 800 years (8,100 to 7,300 years ago). During this time we estimated the rainfall to be around 200 mm per year.

The evidence suggests that the arid phases that intervened between the humid interphases began abruptly and were so harsh the entire area was quickly abandoned. When the rains returned, the people returned to the desert. Each humid interphase was slightly different from the preceding one in microenvironmental details. We think it likely that some of the cultural differences that characterize these entities in the various interphases may reflect adaptations to the changes in the environment. In some instances, however, new populations may be represented. We discuss this in detail in Schild's and my "Conclusions" in our book *Holocene Settlement of the Egyptian Sahara*, Volume 1, *The Archaeology of Nabta Playa*.

After we completed the excavations in the Bir Kiseiba area, Schild, Close, and I had many discussions about the lifestyle of these cattle herders and where they came from. We agreed that the sites of these two earliest entities, El Adam and El Ghorab, represented small groups who lived in the area seasonally, probably during and a few months after the summer rains. When the water in the playas began to disappear, they were forced to move to a place where there was permanent water. There was no evidence that any of these earliest groups dug wells, and yet their sites contain rare bones of cattle, and cattle need water at least every other day. These sites also contained occasional sherds of pottery. In our discussions, there were two obvious possibilities about the source of these early cattle herders.

The first was the Nile Valley. The stone artifacts Schild recovered during the Nubian campaign (1963–1964) from several Arkinian sites near Wadi Halfa, particularly the straight-backed bladelets and blades, were similar to those in the Adam Early Neolithic. These resemblances could not be dismissed, but to me the Nile seemed unlikely because all of the cattle bones found in the sites at Arkin have been rechecked and are still identified as wild. Also, the Nile sites did not contain pottery.

The other possibility was central Sudan. Permanent surface water exists there today at about the latitude of Khartoum and west and south of there, but no one knows anything about the early Holocene archaeology in that area.

Kit Nelson, one of my graduate students, studied the ceramics we had recovered from the Neolithic entities in the Western Desert. She based her PhD dissertation at SMU on her analyses of this pottery, and particularly on those sherds from the sites near Nabta and Bir Kiseiba. She also drew on Maria Gatto's supporting analyses. A graduate student at the University of Naples in Italy, Gatto was also on our staff. Nelson published the two sets of data in *Holocene Settlement of the Egyptian Sahara*, Volume 2, *The Pottery of Nabta Playa*.

Kit Nelson was in her mid-twenties when she joined our expedition. She had a quick mind and was full of energy. She was easygoing and a delightful person to have in camp. She spent five seasons with the expedition at Nabta and was a superb excavator.

Maria Gatto was our other ceramic specialist. She was then in her early thirties. She spent two seasons with us at Nabta and was a careful excavator and a highly competent, strongly motivated archaeologist.

Nelson insists that all of the pottery in the Early Neolithic sites at Nabta and Bir Kiseiba was locally made. She may be right, but in my opinion the first locally made pottery was that which she and Gatto found in sites of the Jerar Early Neolithic, which dates between 7,800 and 7,300 years ago. Jerar is the only Early Neolithic entity with abundant pottery, and it is the earliest with "failed" and unfinished pottery. In my opinion, the pottery in the Adam, Ghorab, and Nabta entities (dating between 9,500 and 7,800 years ago) was made elsewhere and brought into the area by the early cattle pastoralists.

We made an important discovery during our work in Nabta in the early 1990s: the enormous collection of 20,000 identifiable plant remains, the largest collection of plant remains recovered from any early Holocene site in North Africa. Most of this huge collection came from the two most recent Early Neolithic entities, which we named El Nabta and Al Jerar. A large suite of radiocarbon measurements dating from 8,050 to 7,300 years ago is associated with the sites where most of the plant remains were recovered. Most of these sites are large, with many hut floors, large storage pits, and deep walk-in wells. These villages reflect a new economic/settlement system that first appeared at Nabta and Kiseiba during the late Early Neolithic.

Halina Krolik and Romuald Schild supervised the excavation of Site E-75-6, the most important site of this period. They cleared fifteen hut floors (more were present, but not excavated). Each hut had at least one, sometimes several, hearths. In addition, there were many small, bowl-shaped depressions filled with ash and, sometimes, with many charred plant remains.

The carbonized plants from E-75-6 represent 130 different taxa including trees, bushes, grasses, sedges, legumes, fruit stones, and tubers. Seventeen are identified to species level, and 21 others are classified to genus. Among these, 10 are annuals, 9 are herbaceous perennials, and 10 are trees and shrubs. Annuals were the most abundant, with several common taxa, including sorghum, which was the most common edible seed. Wasylikowa suggested that the wild sorghum might have been cultivated, because the sorghum seeds were often stored separately from other seeds. Among the perennials, two varieties of millet were abundant, with cypress tubers next in importance.

These carbonized plant remains provide our best evidence on the environment at Nabta during the Holocene Climatic Maximum. They are also the key evidence for the food economy of those late Early Neolithic groups. The numerous large storage pits and the abundant, but wild, plant remains suggest intensive seasonal collecting of wild plants. Most of this collecting must have occurred when the plants matured, for the most part, in late fall and early winter. They were then stored. It is likely that the plants were consumed during the late winter/spring, when game and other foods were scarce in the waterless desert.

The villages were always in the lower parts of the basins and must have been occupied after the summer rains had passed and the playas had dried. Since there was no surface water anywhere, to live there these people dug wells to obtain water for themselves and their cattle. All of the excavated sites of the Nabta and Jerar entities have several large, deep water-wells. In the two older entities, the Adam and the Ghorab cattle herders, there are no known wells.

We have proposed that this economic/settlement system of intensive collecting and storage may have occurred because these groups could not move from the Nabta/Kiseiba area to a locality where other food could be gathered/obtained seasonally during the dry period. We suggested that hostile neighbors or an unsuitable surrounding landscape might have confined or limited their movement.

In addition to Wasylikowa and two of her assistants, another botanist, Hala Barakat, the daughter of two famous Egyptian physicists, assisted us. Barakat identified all our wood charcoal from Nabta and the surrounding basins and used the charcoal data for her PhD dissertation at a university in France. Some of the charcoal came from trees of species that today grow far to the south in Sudan, and others found today only along the Nile.

There is another interesting bit of data concerning the Jerar entity. In 1964, during the Aswan Reservoir campaign, Joel Shiner excavated several small, dense sites along the Nubian Nile near Wadi Halfa. Because of the similarities in pottery, he called them "Khartoum Related." The sites were in an area that now Lake Nasser covers, but in 1964 we had brought the collections from these sites to Dallas and stored them at SMU.

While she was on a trip to Dallas in 1999, Maria Gatto asked to see the collection of pottery from Shiner's Khartoum Related sites. After she examined the collection she informed me that Shiner's pottery was closely similar in all features to that recovered from the Al Jerar sites in the Nabta/Kiseiba area. The question is, do Shiner's sites represent trading groups who came to the Nile, or were they refugees who moved to the Nile to escape the hyperarid desert that terminated the Jerar occupation? Either interpretation may be correct, but if Al Jerar trading groups occupied these sites, they were clearly late. Among the stone artifacts found there were several "wide lunates," a characteristic tool of the later Ghanam Middle Neolithic, but unknown in the Jerar.

After the severe drought that ended the Jerar occupation that began a little after 7,300 years ago, local rainfall returned to Nabta around 7,150–7,100 years ago. There was, however, much less rainfall than during any of the previous humid interphases. Even so, the rains were enough to bring a new group into the Nabta/Kiseiba area. We call this entity the Ghanam Middle Neolithic. There are only five modest Middle Neolithic sites known in the entire Nabta/Kiseiba area, indicating a population considerably smaller than during the Nabta and Al Jerar Early Neolithic. The ten radiocarbon dates associated with the Ghanam Middle Neolithic range from 7,100 to 6,600 years ago.

Although no plant remains have been recovered at any of these Middle Neolithic sites, they all have many grinding stones and large, deep, bell-shaped storage pits, like those in the Nabta and Jerar settlements. The inhabitants dug many deep water-wells where they could obtain perched water close to the surface, which suggests to me that these Middle Neolithic people probably followed the same economic/settlement system as the Nabta/Jerar, and intensively gathered plant foods and stored them for later consumption.

The new Ghanam group also brought the first domestic sheep and goats to the Western Desert. We assume, but cannot document, a herding technology different from that employed with the cattle. But how the people blended cattle and sheep/goat herding remains a mystery. They also introduced a new style of rocker-stamped pottery vaguely similar to the pottery in Al Jerar, but with important differences: there are new design motifs; they used thicker-walled vessels that are often not as well made; and they frequently smudged, but did not polish, the interiors of bowls.

A short, but intense, interval of aridity marks the end of the Middle Neolithic occupation in the Nabta area. The overlying sediments containing Late Neolithic artifacts record the return of the rains around 6,500 years ago.

These Late and Final Neolithic sites contain several important new features. Among these new elements is a ceramic technology radically different from the previous entities. Instead of vessels made of unrefined playa clay decorated with rocker-stamped or rough textured exteriors, the new pottery has thin vessel walls and was made with a highly refined clay that fired bright red in an oxidizing atmosphere. These red vessels also had sparse, fine temper. The most frequent vessel forms in this new ceramic tradition are deep bowls and tall beaker-shapes with rounded bases. While most of the pottery is smoothed on the surface, some is burnished on both the interiors and exteriors, and sometimes there is a highly burnished red slip on the exterior. By at least 6,000 years ago, and probably before, the ceramic assemblages included red pottery that was fired in a controlled atmosphere, using a technique that often produced "black-topped" rims and smudged and burnished interiors. It is unlikely that this new ceramic technology was developed in the Western Desert of

Egypt. There are no evident preliminary steps and no precursors; it appears suddenly and full-blown in the earliest Late Neolithic sites in the desert.

Ultimately, the intellectual source for this red pottery was probably the southern Levant, where similar red/brown-colored, slipped, and polished pottery is widely known from an even earlier date. The Nile Valley would seem to be a likely intermediate source, but the earliest radiocarbon dates for similar pottery in the Nile Valley are too late for them to be a source for the Late Neolithic at Nabta. Farther south, near the Second Cataract, the oldest similar black-and-red pottery was found at Site DIW-50, but that site is too late to be a source for the Late Neolithic pottery in the desert. Its origin remains a mystery.

The Final Neolithic saw the appearance of pottery made from clays quarried from the local Qussier member of the Nubian Formation. These primary clays contain abundant flakes of shale-like biotite that look like temper, but are not. This Qussier clay fires to a light gray to grayish yellow color. The vessels usually have smoothed interior and exterior surfaces, but the exterior is sometimes decorated with incised hatching or tightly packed impressions. Some of these Qussier pots were almost certainly locally made at Nabta.

The majority of the lithic debitage in the Late and Final Neolithic sites consists of unretouched quartz flakes, so numerous it seems likely they served as expedient tools. The retouched tool assemblages are often made on imported flint, occasionally using local chert and quartz crystal. A characteristic tool is a scraper made on "side-blow flakes," often found in caches, with unretouched blanks and initially shaped pieces.

These new features in the stone artifacts and the new ceramic technology strongly suggest that the Late Neolithic people at Nabta were not the descendants of the Ghanam Middle Neolithic people who had abandoned the area only a hundred years earlier.

In May of 2000, the SMU administration decided it did not want the expense and responsibility of caring for my Nubian artifact collection, and asked me to find a suitable home for it. Almost immediately, Dr. Vivian Davies, Keeper of Ancient Egypt and Sudan at the British Museum, called me from London and asked if I would be interested in placing the collection in the British Museum, which is one of the finest museums in the world. I was delighted at this opportunity, because I knew the collection would be properly cared for, would not be discarded, and because of London's central location, would be available to scholars everywhere. A few weeks after my discussion with Davies, skilled packers were sent from London to evaluate the collection and its special packing needs, and in September of 2001, the artifacts, maps, notes, slides, photographs, negatives, computer printouts—an estimated 6,000,000 pieces—were shipped to the British Museum. The museum honored me greatly by officially christening the collection "The Fred Wendorf Collection of Egyptian and Sudanese Prehistory" and placing my name on the wall that honors hundreds of benefactors of the British Museum, going back to George III.

CHAPTER 34

B eginning in the 1990 field season, we had begun to recognize unusual stone constructions in and around the Nabta basin. The first of these unusual features we discovered was an alignment of large, crudely shaped stones, some of them weighing several tons. Other exotic features seemed at first to be only piles of large stones. One of these piles covered a chamber with a complete, articulated cow. Still other stone piles contained disarticulated parts of cows and sheep/goats. Another group had arrangements of very large upright stones forming ovals in which even larger stones occupied the centers. Before the ovals were constructed, the inhabitants had dug large pits to expose a tablerock some 6 to 10 feet below the surface. The buried tablerock was often shaped. Finally, they refilled the pits and erected the surface architecture above the filled pit. Another interesting feature is a circle made of small slabs, which seems to have been a crude solar calendar.

These structures evidently represent several different kinds of functions, most probably ceremonial. Associated archaeology and radiocarbon dates place the construction of some of the structures as early as 6,450 years ago, while the most recent date as late as 4,800 years ago. All of these exotic structures seem to be Late Neolithic and Final Neolithic phenomena.

We were surprised to find these large-stone features, and I confess it took us several years of working at Nabta before we began to focus on them and study them in detail. I believe they are the physical expression of a complex ritual system. Because of the human effort required for prolonged periods of time to erect some of the larger features, it seems likely they were a part of a religion-based, socio-political system that an elite class conceived, supervised, and managed.

••••

In 1977, during our second field season at Nabta, we had mapped as bedrock outcrops several piles of broken quartzitic sandstone blocks about 300 yards east of the largest site in the Nabta basin, E-75-8. The piles were of various sizes and formed an irregular line from southwest to northeast. Schild and I were so certain they were bedrock that Schild even plotted one of the stone piles as bedrock on one of his profiles published in our 1980 book, *The Prehistory of the Eastern Sahara*.

In February of 1990 I was excavating a group of houses and storage pits at a deflated area below the hill where the line of "bedrock outcrops" was located. Late in the morning I took a break and walked up to the top of the adjacent hill about 200 yards away. I noticed two clusters of unusually large quartzitic sandstone blocks, and nearby a large, unbroken oval rock of the same material. The rock was about 10 feet long, 8 feet wide, and 2.5 feet thick. It was tilted to one side with one end partially buried. It seemed a good place to rest and contemplate the world.

While leaning on the rock I made a few kicks at the ground with my heavy field shoes. I was surprised to note that I was kicking up playa silts, so I got up and walked around the rock making a few more kicks. I went over to the two nearby clusters of large broken blocks and decided that the broken pieces had come from two different large, shaped rocks. When reassembled, these rocks would be larger than the one I had been using for a leaning post. It was one of those "eureka" moments.

I went back to the site where I had been working, collected my two workers and their tools, and returned to the top of the hill. I had them dig a deep pit beside the stone I had leaned against. They found nothing but playa silts until, at a depth of 7 feet below the surface, they found a thin layer of windblown sand resting on bedrock—real bedrock. In the sand they found several sherds of late (Al Jerar) Early Neolithic pottery, as well as a few pieces of flaked flint. I looked around, and in an irregular line going generally south, and at about 130-feet intervals, were eight other clusters of broken large rocks, most of them smaller than the first two rock piles, but otherwise similar. That afternoon, and all the next day, I had my men dig pits down to bedrock beside every pile of rocks. At the bottom of most of the pits was more Al Jerar cultural material, indicating that the buried portion of this late Early Neolithic settlement extended for more than 3,000 feet in a general north-south direction. For most of this area the occupation horizon was covered by 6 to 8 feet of playa deposits. I knew those rocks had not floated to where I'd found them; people had to have brought them there.

That evening when I told Schild what I'd discovered, he was skeptical. The next day he took some workers, cleaned every one of my pits, and got down in each one, looking at the playa sediments, the underlying dune sand, and the bedrock. Only then did he agree that the big stones were not bedrock, but formed a "megalithic alignment."

A year later, in 1991, we were discussing the discovery of our large stone alignment when we began to wonder if it pointed to Polaris, the polar star. At that time we didn't know that the polar star moves around the sky through time and was not anywhere near true north 6,000 years ago, our estimated age for the alignment that evening. After some discussion, we decided to use our flashlights to find out. I would drive up to the alignment and drop someone off by each pile of rocks, and then I'd have all of them turn on the lights together to see if they aligned with Polaris.

At this point, someone suggested that such a ceremonial event needed to be sanctified by the sacrifice of a virgin. Pretty Nieves Zedeño, a native of Ecuador, and a senior graduate student at SMU, volunteered. "I'll be the virgin, and I'm going to my tent to get an appropriate dress." The rest of us brought our flashlights and gathered around the Land Cruiser. When Nieves returned she was dressed in a flimsy white negligee. She got on the roof of the car, lay down on the baggage rack, and held on tight. The rest of us found seats in the Land Cruiser.

I was driving, and as we headed toward the megalithic alignment a few hundred yards away, I stopped every 500 feet or so to shout, "Check on the virgin." Schild would jump out and yell, "Check on the virgin," and get back in the car.

Meanwhile, the young and innocent Wagdi Naim Labib, our antiquities inspector, whispered worriedly to Applegate, "What are they going to do with Nieves?" Each time Applegate, one of our graduate students, whispered back, "They're going to sacrifice her."

When we got to the north end of the alignment, I turned south down the alignment. One person got out by each pile of rocks with his or her flashlight, until I reached the end of the line. I honked my horn and all the flashlights went on at once. I looked down the line of lights and then looked up to see if the lights pointed toward Polaris. The alignment was nowhere near the pole star.

Disappointed, but wiser, we got back in the car and returned to the dining tent. From there everyone went to their tents, except Wagdi, who stopped Applegate and asked, "What's going to happen to Nieves?" Alex said, "Nothing," and headed off to bed, leaving poor Wagdi more confused than ever. And nothing did happen to Nieves, who enjoyed the fun as much as the rest of us did. We liked Wagdi, and he was an excellent inspector, but at the beginning of the following field season, he asked to be sent to some other expedition—*any* other expedition.

In subsequent field seasons I identified at least one, possibly two, other irregular megalithic alignments on the western side of the Nabta Playa. Most of these stones were lying on the surface, and many of them were broken. At least two of the stones had been shaped into an anthropomorphic outline. Later, when reconstructing some of the broken stones, Schild discovered that several more of the megalithic rocks, including at least one large stone and several smaller ones, had been shaped into anthropomorphic outlines. I assumed that the alignments had once been straight, and that the irregularities were due to the shifting of the stones as wind removed some of the playa under and around them.

One day during the 1992 field season, Nieves Zedeño recognized another unique feature of the megaliths. She took me to look at a circle about 12 feet in diameter made of small, upright stone slabs. I'd seen this stone circle before, but dismissed it as a later hut base and had given it no more thought. Zedeño pointed out that there were four pairs of longer and narrower, upright stones she called "gates." She also noted that two pairs of the gates were aligned north-south and that the other two pairs of gates were aligned from southwest to northeast. "About 70 degrees east of north," she said.

"Could that second alignment point to the position of the summer solstice sunrise?" she asked. I didn't know, but it was a great idea. Even so, it took me several years to find the answer to her question.

In 1994, two years after Zedeño found what we now think was an early solar calendar, Alex Applegate asked me to come with him to look at a pile of rocks in the floor of the wadi that entered the Nabta basin from the north. When we got to the rock pile, he pointed out that it contained rocks from several outcrops of different colors, and for this reason people must have put the stones there. I told him I thought the stones might cover the grave of some leader of the Nabta people and asked him to dig it carefully.

The pile of rocks formed a large conical mound about 20 feet in diameter and 4 feet high, half of which was buried below wadi sediments. When Applegate removed the rocks he discovered that they covered an oval pit about 6 feet long, 3 feet wide, and 2 feet deep. It had a thick, C-shaped collar of clay and gravel surrounding it on three sides. The pit had been roofed with sticks covered with white clay. When I saw the clay collar and the traces of the roof I thought, *"This must be the tomb of a local leader."*

When Applegate cleaned the pit, however, he discovered the articulated skeleton of a young adult cow. "Oh, hell," I said, disappointed. "It's nothing but a cow."

It took some time, but eventually I realized that the cow was very important to these people. A young adult cow would have been a significant offering for Late Neolithic pastoralists, representing a considerable sacrifice of wealth. It might indicate the presence of a "cow cult." A piece of a stick from the roof yielded a radiocarbon date of 6,450 years old—1,000 years before there is evidence of a similar cow cult in the Predynastic era of the Nile Valley.

Later in the same 1994 season, Applegate dug another rock pile 100 yards to the southwest from the first rock pile, next to the low quartzite ridge that borders the wadi on the west side. This pile lacked a chamber, but contained the disarticulated remains of three cows and one sheep/goat placed among the rocks.

In 1996 and 1997 Applegate and another graduate student excavated seven other stone tumuli in the same general area, along the rocky ledge that bordered the wadi on the west side. All of them lacked chambers, but, like Applegate's second tumulus, they contained, in total, the disarticulated bones of seven cattle and two sheep/goats scattered among the rocks.

In the same area, we found an extended human skeleton missing its skull, covered with a low mound of stones. There were no skull fragments nearby. Had the head been removed as part of a human sacrifice?

One afternoon in late February, near the end of the 1994 field season, Schild, Angela, and I were standing by our vehicles discussing the cow burial. "I wonder where they buried their leaders," I mused. Schild's gaze was off in the distance where, about a mile south, there was a hill on which a line of rocks could be seen. I glanced over where he was looking as he said, "I mapped those rocks as bedrock, but let's go look at them again."

Angela went with Schild, and I followed in my Land Cruiser. The hill was a large remnant of playa silt on which there were many clusters of large stones. Most were arranged in the same general pattern, which consisted of an oval made of medium-sized rocks, many of them roughly shaped, standing upright, slightly embedded in the playa silts. The ovals surrounded at least one, sometimes two, and in one instance three, very large, roughly shaped rectangular rocks lying horizontally in the center. The ovals ranged from 20 to 30 feet in outside diameter. All of the stones were of hard, dark brown quartzitic sandstone. The playa surface around the clusters was littered with small and large flakes of the same sandstone, indicating that some of the rock shaping had occurred nearby.

The long axis of the ovals, and the large stone(s) inside them, were aligned slightly west of north and slightly east of south. There were about thirty of these clusters on this playa remnant, including one interlocking group of eight smaller cluster units. Groups of scattered large stones also occurred at both the northern and southern ends of the site. They may have been stockpiles of unused blocks, or they may once have been similar large stone clusters torn apart and scattered for religious or political reasons.

Eventually, we found three more groups of large stone clusters. One was at the south end of the playa, the second group on the east side of the basin. The third was a group of four clusters on a playa remnant 200 yards east of our first group. Schild and I agree that people built them, but we do not know why, or when.

As we walked around the group of thirty rock clusters, I decided to excavate some of these large stone features as soon as possible. The big rocks were too large to be moved by three or four men; I needed a mechanism and some heavy rope to lift the stones. We were almost at the end of our field season, and if these clusters marked elite burials I would need time and money.

Before leaving Nabta in 1994, I had looked over the stones comprising what we later called Structures A and B, about 50 yards apart. I planned that Halina Krolik and I would excavate both of the rock clusters at the same time. I would do Structure A; she would do B. Some of the stones were so large that I decided we would need help moving them away from the area to be excavated. The budget called for only twelve workers. Somehow we had to lift the rocks so the twelve men could drag them away.

Ali Mazhar suggested a tripod. He thought he could have one made at a machine shop in Aswan. In January of 1995, when we assembled at the start of the season, the tripod was ready. The legs of the tripod were about 12 feet long, made of 4-inch-diameter steel water pipe. Each leg was attached to a hinge so the legs could be moved around. The other faces of the hinges were welded to a small steel platform with a hook welded to the bottom to attach the block and tackle. Each leg of the tripod rested on a flat plate at the end to keep it from digging into the dirt.

Ali bought 50 feet of heavy rope, about 20 feet of strong chains, and a block and tackle adequate to lift up to 3 tons. Some of our rocks looked to be well over 3 tons, but this is all we had to move them.

I was convinced the large stone clusters were graves, probably elite graves. If that assumption was correct, our crew should be able to excavate five or six burials in a field season. I made my research plan accordingly.

As it turned out, the excavation of five clusters in one season was much too ambitious. Because of the large, deep pits under the surface architecture, we excavated only two of these large stone clusters in their entirety. We tested another and mapped a fourth. We made several boreholes, too. It took our entire scientific staff and labor crew two seasons to complete these excavations, representing an investment of slightly more than two hundred thousand dollars. I sometimes mention that figure when someone suggests we should excavate more of these clusters of big stones.

We call these large clusters of stones "Complex Structures" because they have both subsurface and surface components. They are important because they provide clues to the character of the societies that erected them. Someone had to plan and design them and supervise the work. It took a lot of people to make and place them.

As planned, our first excavations were done simultaneously at two of the largest rock clusters, Complex Structures A and B. The first task was to move the large stones lying horizontally in the center of the ring of smaller upright stones. Since the rings of smaller stones define the edges of the structures, we had to shift several of the peripheral stones out of the way to provide a route for the men to carry the excavated dirt to where screens were set up. Even some of the smaller stones weighed more than 100 pounds and took two to three men to move them.

The initial excavations in each of the selected large rock features were in an area 9 feet square in the center of the oval area defined by the peripheral ring rocks. At first, all digging was done with trowels to a depth of 18 inches below the surface. Both excavations failed to find any trace of human remains. The first 12 inches were soft and sandy. Below that it became firmly cemented playa clay and silty-clay, with deep, sand-filled desiccation cracks. At 18 inches I had the men stop screening and switch to large picks and hoelike tools known as *torreas*.

Believing there would be a burial chamber at the bottom of the pit, the men continued to dig carefully through the hard playa sediments. As they dug, they found occasional slabs, flakes, and one or two large blocks of quartzitic sandstone buried in the hard clay. These indicated a large pit had been dug there and later refilled.

Imagine our excitement when at a depth of about 3 feet below the surface we exposed the smoothed top edge of a large, shaped stone with a headlike extension at one end. As we removed the sediment from around this shaped rock, we realized it weighed over 3 tons, maybe even 5 tons. How could we lift it out of the pit with our 3-ton pulley?

Everyone was excited, but we'd found the large, shaped rock just before lunch, and we had to take a break. When we returned to the site, the men cleaned most of the dirt from around the shaped stone. Excitement kept building, reaching a peak when we discovered that stone slabs had been placed to hold the sculpture upright, and that the "head" was oriented slightly west of north, the same orientation as the surface structure. The workers and I were sure the sculpture covered a burial of some powerful, rich chief.

The men brought out the tripod and set the legs so they rested on the surface on three sides of the pit. Then they attached the block and tackle to the hook at the top and shifted the legs until the hook was directly over the shaped stone. Using boards to protect the surface of the sculpture from abrasion, they attached one end of the heavy rope to the block and tackle; they passed the other end three times through a hole dug in the playa under the shaped stone and then through the pulley on the block and tackle. Then they began to pull. They pulled and pulled, but the stone did not budge. By this time it was late. Annoyed and frustrated, we returned to camp for dinner.

Later that evening there was a loud discussion among the men in the workers' camp. Ali Mazhar told me it was a "dousha," almost a quarrel. The next morning the leader of the workers came to Ali Mazhar just before work started and said in Arabic, "We're going to move that rock this morning." And they did.

First, they removed the sediment from around the stone, including all but a small amount from under the base of the rock. With the tripod and tackle placed over it, they raised the stone an inch or two, and with another rope they pulled it toward the edge of the pit a few inches and set it down. They repeated this procedure several times, each time moving the tripod where it would help them move the rock until they were almost against the pit wall. Then they raised the stone a few inches, put dirt and rocks under it, set it down, and repeated the process over and over until most of the pit was refilled and the base of the shaped stone was near the surface. Using ropes, they pulled the shaped stone out of the pit and set it upright. I got behind it and someone took my picture.

The sculptured stone was made of hard, dense quartzitic sandstone, about 7.5 feet long, 5 feet high, and 2 feet thick. It had a flat, smooth, almost polished, top. One side was convex and had been shaped by pecking. At one end was a fanlike projection that might represent a head. There were several cut marks and grooves at the other end, placed to control the flakes that were used to shape that end. The other side and base were both irregular and unshaped. When viewed from the worked side, the stone bore a vague resemblance to an animal, I thought perhaps a cow.

It weighed well over 5 tons, according to a mining engineer who visited our camp later that day. We kept the men out of the pit when the stone was being moved, for safety, but the tripod and the 3-ton block and tackle did not fail us. Still looking for a fabulously rich burial, the men removed the dirt they had put back in the pit. Then they dug a foot lower. Under where the stone sculpture had been, they came down to the center of a circular rock, about 10 feet in diameter, carefully shaped around its convex edges. It, too, had a projection extending slightly west of north and was smoothed on top. I said to myself, "*This must be the tomb of a very important person.*" As I write this I can still feel my excitement.

We were at the end of our field season, however, and we still had a lot more digging to do before we could expose the area around the "tomb." There were several large rocks standing vertically over the projection at the north end. It looked as if they had been dropped there to close a vertical shaft. Could it be the entrance to the tomb? We partially back-filled the excavated area to protect it until we could return next year.

By the end of the first season we spent excavating part of two clusters of large stones, I realized that I had misjudged the effort needed to excavate these structures. We had excavated only half of two features. I decided a backhoe was what we needed. Ali Mazhar told me there was a good backhoe in the Egyptian Geological Survey equipment in Cairo. He said the survey would rent it to me for a thousand dollars a month, a reasonable price. I knew the person I needed to operate it: Eligio Aragon, or Alley Cat, as his many friends call him. A gifted backhoe operator, he lives in Peralta, New Mexico, and specializes in the excavation of archaeological sites. He is in great demand.

I called Alley Cat and asked him if he would come to Egypt the following February to help excavate some interesting sites in the desert west of Abu Simbel. He didn't know where Egypt was, much less Abu Simbel, but quickly agreed to come. I bought him a round-trip air ticket and arranged for him to come to Abu Simbel on February 1st. I would meet him at the Abu Simbel airport and bring him to camp.

Ali Mazhar called Mohamed Hinnawi, the director of the Egyptian Geological Survey, and he promised to deliver the backhoe to Nabta on February 3rd. Alley Cat arrived on schedule and I picked him up, cleared him with security, and took him to camp, a hundred miles from Abu Simbel across a landscape with nothing but sand and rock. It was the first true desert he had seen. He looked from side to side, but hardly said a word until we turned toward our camp a mile away, at the foot of a big C-shaped barchan dune. He gasped and said, "Is that where I'm going to live?" "Yes," I said. "For the next two weeks."

When the lorry with the backhoe arrived, Alley Cat, Ali Mazhar, and I got in a pickup and drove down to the highway to help with unloading the backhoe. I knew things were not going as well as I expected when the lorry driver asked to borrow the battery from my pickup to start the backhoe.

Alley Cat started the backhoe and managed to get it off the truck. He called me over and told me hydraulic fluid was dripping from the backhoe. He said the hydraulic hoses that operate the machine had been cut. He offered to see if he could drive the backhoe to the site about a mile away. He got halfway there and called me over to tell me he thought he should turn around and load the backhoe back on the lorry while there was enough hydraulic fluid. "It's junk," he said.

Meanwhile, Ali Mazhar was having a word with the lorry driver about what had happened to the backhoe. The driver said, "I do not know anything."

The driver had bruises all over his face. Ali Mazhar asked, "What happened to you? Looks like someone beat the hell out of you."

Finally the driver confessed. "I was driving through Qena [there was a minor war underway in the area around Qena between the police and members of the Muslim Brotherhood], and when I passed in front of the police station I heard a loud explosion. All the lights went out. Suddenly the police began jumping out of the windows and doors. They thought they were being bombed. I kept on driving, but the police caught up with me and pulled me from the truck and beat me. They said the explosion I heard was when I cut the main electrical cable. I guess that was when the hydraulic lines on the backhoe were cut. I am sorry."

Ali Mazhar then told him, in Arabic, "You did not load the backhoe properly, you dumb bastard. Turn this damn truck around and go back to Cairo. I will have you punished when I return at the end of the month."

After Alley Cat and I got to camp, he took me aside and said, "Don't be too disappointed, Fred. That backhoe was no good even if all of the hydraulics had been working. It was a worn-out Russian model that must have been pawned off on the unsuspecting Egyptians. It could never have dug a useful hole for you in that heavy clay. It was only good enough to bury a dead cow, but not deep."

I asked him if he wanted to go back home to New Mexico, but he said that he'd like to stay a couple of weeks and see if he could be useful. He was obviously enjoying himself. Each day he joined the Bedouin laborers and worked wherever he was needed. He would eat with us, but in the evenings he joined the Bedouin workers around their campfire, smoking and drinking tea. When his two weeks were up, I took him back to Abu Simbel and put him on the plane for Cairo and home. When he got home he was a local celebrity. A few months later he was featured in *New Mexico Magazine*, which ran an article about him and his adventures in Egypt.

The Egyptian Geological Survey didn't charge me the thousand dollars I owed for the rental of the backhoe. Even without the backhoe we started the second season at the Complex Structures full of anticipation. We quickly removed the back-dirt we had put in the pit to protect the grave(s) we were sure were present below the huge circular stone of Structure A. Euphoria was everywhere.

Two days later the back-dirt was removed, and as I was using a trowel to excavate the pit fill from the southeastern edge of the "tomb," I discovered the flat-topped stone was only an extensively shaped tablerock. "*It's bedrock, damn it. There are no burials here. What a fool you are, Fred,*" I said to myself. I threw down my trowel, struggled out of the pit, and went for a long walk, alone, cursing my stupidity.

About an hour later I came back to the excavation pit and broke the news to my colleague, Halina Krolik. She was clearing the north edge of the tablerock. At first she refused to believe it, and showed me the traces of shaping she had found on her edge. But when she saw what I had seen, she, too, threw down her trowel and almost cried.

We have since learned a good deal about how these Complex Structures were built, but we have not learned precisely when or why they were built. The same general procedure evidently was used to build all of them. The first step in their erection was to locate a tablerock buried under 6 to 10 feet of playa clays and silts. Tablerocks are thick lenses of hard stone that remain when erosion has removed the surrounding softer sediment. In our instance, we know that many years after the tablerock was formed it was buried under a thick bed of playa silts and clays deposited between 7,250 to 7,300 years ago, at the beginning of Post–Al Jerar Arid Phase. We proved this by finding Al Jerar pottery and stone tools in several areas that were covered by several feet of playa sediments. In many areas wind erosion quickly removed these silts and clays, but they were essentially intact in the areas where the Complex Structures were located.

How the inhabitants found the tablerocks is a puzzle. Perhaps when wet, the mostly clay sediment was soft enough to be penetrated by a hard stick. Or perhaps the vegetation growing on the surface above a tablerock was different from the vegetation elsewhere, thus guiding them to the locations of the tablerocks. Whatever method they used, when they found a suitable rock, they dug a large pit in the playa to expose the entire circumference and some of the softer, cemented sand below and around the tablerock. These pits were up to 16 feet in diameter at the base and from 7 to 12 feet or more deep. The removal of this fill represented a lot of man-days of effort.

In Structure B the tablerock was irregular and had been slightly modified by removing two or three flakes at the north end. The surface architecture, however, was similar to that of Structure A, except that none of the stones in the oval was upright when Krolik began her excavations.

The age of these Complex Structures is not firmly established, but we have some clues. There is a small Al Jerar Early Neolithic site stratified under the playa remnant a few meters west of where Complex Structures A and B were built. This tells us the silts and clays under the Complex Structures were deposited after 7,300 years ago, the most recent date for Al Jerar Early Neolithic. A radiocarbon date of 4,800 years ago on charcoal from Structure C probably dates the youngest of these features. There are also several radiocarbon dates between 5,700 and 5,000 years ago from nearby quarry pits that were probably the source for some of the stone in the structures. These dates place the use of the quarry pits near the beginning of Asnam Final Neolithic.

I believe Structure C, one of the eight interlocking units, was the most recent of these features. The outline of the pit dug before the placement of the surface stones of Structure C was clearly visible near the surface, an indication that there had been limited rainfall since that pit was dug. Had there been much rainfall, churning of the surrounding playa clays would have obscured the walls of the pit, as it did at Structures A and B where the pit walls were visible only near the bottom of the pits. Wetting and drying and churning of the clays, indicating considerable rainfall, had destroyed all traces of the pit walls except near the tablerock. This indicates that Complex Structures A and B are older than Structure C, but how much older remains unknown.

In 1996 I asked J. McKim Malville, a well-known astrophysicist at the University of Colorado, to determine if the megalithic alignments at Nabta had astronomical significance. I told him we had identified a stone circle we thought might be a solar calendar circle, and we had thirty-six large stone features we described as "Complex Structures." Malville agreed to join our group for three weeks during the 1997 field season.

When he arrived he proposed that my initial alignment was actually composed of three separate alignments, and that all three were like spokes on a wheel, merging at Complex Structure A, which formed the hub. He identified these three lines as A1, A2, and A3. He noted that the other two alignments I had discovered were really three. These also converged on Structure A. He called them B1, B2, and C1.

Malville later determined by calculation that C1 was aligned with the rising position of Sirius in 4820 B.C. The three A alignments were oriented toward the rising position of Dubhe, the brightest star in the Big Dipper. They were dated at 4742, 4423, and 4199 B.C. Alignments B1 and B2 he associated with the bright stars in the belt of Orion, Alnilam, and Alnitak and were dated 4176 and 3786 B.C.

Malville suggested that the most compelling case for stellar association was Alignment C because Sirius is the brightest star in the night sky, rising just ahead of the sun. There is abundant evidence of the importance of Sirius in Old Kingdom Egypt, starting with the First Dynasty, where it seems to have served as the primary calibrator of the Egyptian calendar. The C alignment, however, has the weakest archaeological support. The megaliths are extremely large, up to 15 feet on a side, down slope, and only 50 feet from a bedrock outcrop of the same quartzite. Did they reach their present position by creeping down slope with the erosion of the underlying playa? Or did the Nabta religious leaders take advantage of a suitable bedrock outcrop and move several large slabs a short distance to the positions where they wanted them? Whatever the answer will be for Alignment C, it is clear that the ceremonial life at Nabta during the Late and Final Neolithic included a strong interest in the stars and their movements across the sky.

These large stone alignments and the other large stone features caused Schild and me to begin thinking about how much human energy was required to quarry, shape, transport, and set up the huge stones, and what kind of sociopolitical system might be required to plan the projects and manage the labor to build them. We concluded that a leadership with considerable management skills and control over a group or groups of people for extended periods of time was needed. We realized that a relatively small labor force could have built the alignments over a long period of time. The number and variety of large stone constructions suggest, however, that a large labor force was used, which in turn, implies the presence of a society with at least incipient social complexity.

The discovery of the Nabta megaliths have attracted wide archaeological and popular attention. Some 1,000 years older than Stonehenge, the megaliths are the oldest astronomically aligned archaeological feature yet discovered. Our work with Malville was published in *Nature* and was the subject of articles in the *New York Times* and many other newspapers and magazines. Unfortunately, the publicity has also attracted others who began to come to Nabta and disturb the monuments, rearrange the calendar circle, build new circles, and leave offerings, such as rock crystals and plastic dolls. I've been told some damage was done by a group or groups of Europeans who believe people from outer space landed at Nabta around 16,000 years ago and would soon return. Fortunately, we have maps and a photographic record of the most important megalithic features prior to the vandalism.

Life Changes and More Archaeology |
(1992–1996)

CHAPTER 35

One morning in December 1992, Angela told me she wanted a divorce. It came as a shock to me, although I knew she'd been unhappy. She had long wanted and expected to be a member of the anthropology faculty at SMU. On several occasions I had informally discussed an appointment for her with several members of departmental faculty. I learned that she was highly regarded for her knowledge of statistics, her writing ability, and editing skills. As an adjunct member of our faculty she had taught several courses that our students gave high marks. She had an impressive publication record equivalent to or stronger than that of most members of our faculty. Still, several members of the faculty were opposed to her appointment.

It was not that the other faculty did not like her; it was the situation. They were concerned about appointing anyone to our departmental faculty who was married to one of the department's senior professors. It was a precedent they did not want to set. I told Angela what I had learned and even offered to retire, leave SMU, and go with her to another university. She did not want me to do that, and so she felt trapped.

As the years went by I think she became increasingly frustrated and unhappy. Finally, she decided she had to divorce me. She told me she knew she would never get out from under my shadow as long as we were married, and her career as an independent scholar meant more to her than our marriage. She wanted to go where she could have her own life.

I was devastated and went into a deep emotional depression, so distraught I did not want to live. At the suggestion of a close friend, I saw a psychiatrist who put me on a common antidepressant. About a month later I told him, "Now I can sit on the porch, rock, and smile while the house burns down." He said perhaps he'd given me too much of that drug. He gave me a prescription for a new antidepressant that would help my depression, but not put me out of touch with reality.

The next year, in 1993, Angela didn't go into the field. I went, but she stayed in Dallas, got an attorney, and before I left, we divided up the furniture and small items in our home. She rented an apartment near SMU and moved everything of hers there before I left for Egypt.

When I returned to Dallas I had a difficult time. Angela was still my employee, my post-doc research associate, and we worked together every day. Often I asked her to come home with me, and she would say, "Not yet, Fred, maybe next month." Issawi even came to Dallas to urge her not to divorce me.

Later that year, at a meeting with our attorneys, she told me she'd insist on going with me to Egypt for the 1994 field season. I didn't think I could endure that, but she made it a requirement in the divorce papers, so I coped. The papers were filed, and eventually we went separately to the field camp in Egypt. Our divorce became final in early January of 1994, on the first day we were in camp. We had been married almost seventeen years.

When we both got settled in our tents, I went to her and asked, "Are you sure you want to do this?" "Yes," she answered. I turned away, angry for the first time, determined to have nothing more to do with her.

After that field season she got a job at a university in Ohio, but soon left there for the University of Washington in Seattle, where she is now a tenured full professor. We see each other sometimes at meetings, and once I took her to dinner, but both the love and pain were gone.

Nineteen ninety-three had been a long year, but in late November things began to improve in my personal life. David Freidel and his wife, Carolyn Sargent, two of my closest friends in the anthropology department, invited me to dinner and asked if I would mind if my former graduate student Christy Bednar joined us. To which I responded, "I'd like very much to see Christy again." We had a pleasant evening with Carolyn and David, and Christy and I began seeing each other the next day.

At the beginning of January of 1994, just before I was to leave for the field season in Egypt, my daughter Cindy came to Dallas to live with me while she attended SMU as a graduate student in psychology. Before I left, she met Christy and they became friends. About two weeks after my departure, Cindy collapsed with a massive episode of multiple sclerosis. Alone, in a strange city and nearly helpless, Cindy called Christy and asked for her help. Christy was then working as the director of development for Hockaday, a prominent girls' school in Dallas. She immediately went to her home, gathered what she needed, including her dog, and moved into my house so she could be with Cindy at night and on weekends. A few days later Christy sent me a letter telling me what had happened to Cindy and what she had done to help her. Christy assured me that she'd look after Cindy until I returned, and then she would move back to her house.

It took about two weeks for Christy's letter to reach me, but as soon as I received it I got a driver and the Land Cruiser and we drove across the roadless desert to Abu Simbel, about sixty miles from our camp. There was a good hotel in Abu Simbel with a telephone I could use to call Dallas. Of course, it was the middle of the night in Dallas, but Christy answered the phone. I asked her about Cindy, and she told me that Cindy was still very ill, and that she would stay with her until I returned.

My feelings for Christy suddenly struck me, and I said, "You don't have to leave, Christy; just put your slippers under my bed." To which she replied, "But I don't have any slippers, Fred." When I asked, "What size do you wear?" she told me. The next day I sent a telegram to my secretary at SMU and asked her to order from L. L. Bean a pair of fur-lined slippers in Christy's size and have them sent air mail to Christy at my home address. They arrived in late February, a week or so before I returned to Dallas. Christy met my plane, and after looking into her eyes and giving her a big hug and kiss, the first thing I said was "Where are your slippers?"

She responded, "Under your bed, Fred."

One night in April of 1994 a large tornado struck my Queen Anne–style Victorian house in Lancaster, Texas, a Dallas suburb. (I had bought the old house, which had been condemned, in 1969 after my divorce from Peta. Angela and I had lived there during our marriage, despite the long commute to SMU. I had long wanted to restore an older home, and I'd had experience in renovating older structures at my earlier adobe house in Lubbock, as well as in the reconstruction work at Fort Burgwin.) On this eventful night, Christy and I were upstairs, having a drink, about 9:00 P.M. when we noticed there was a huge thunderstorm going on outside, with a lot of lightning and thunder. We went down to the glass-surrounded half landing of the circular stairs outside my bedroom to have a better view of the storm. In a few minutes we noticed the air outside had turned green. Then we saw many flashes of light, sparking from numerous electric transformers in Duncanville, the next town to the west. It was a striking, terrible sight, and almost immediately we heard a noise like the roar of a jet plane headed toward us from the west.

I had heard such a sound before, and I said, "Christy, that noise is a tornado. Come on; we need to find someplace safe." We rushed downstairs and got under the big dining room table. A few seconds after we got under the table, the tornado hit. I put my weak arm around Christy, put my good arm through the table mechanism to hold it down, and told Christy to pull her legs under the table. We were beside a chimney, and if it were to fall I wanted the table to protect us. Windows blew in, rocks slammed into the house, and trees crashed down. Foolishly, I was concerned about my library in the room next to us. The tornado seemed to take a long time to pass, though it was probably only a minute or two.

Throughout the ordeal, Christy remained calm. Right then I decided that if I were ever to marry again, she'd be the kind of woman I wanted to marry. The time wasn't right just yet, but the idea had been planted. And both of us knew we would eventually marry.

While the prospect of another marriage was brewing, I resumed my usual activities at SMU and in the field. We couldn't work at Nabta in the 1995 season because we'd made a commitment that we would devote that season to the excavation of a promising Late Paleolithic site near Esna, which expanding agricultural activity was about to destroy. We'd paid the landowner a fee to keep the site safe from cultivation until the end of March 1995; nevertheless, he had let irrigation water cover the site, dissolving the carbonate that held together most of the buried faunal remains. It was, however, an interesting site because the stratigraphy was complex, and associated cultural materials recorded an activity we had not previously studied in our 1967 field season near Esna.

At the time the site was occupied, the surrounding area had been a stabilized dune field. In the midst of the dunes there had been a seepage pond that had held water during, and probably for some time after, the seasonal flood. Numerous animals had been killed there: primarily hartebeest, wild cattle, and gazelle. The size of the animals and the skeletal elements present indicated that the animals had been killed, processed, and eaten at or near the pond.

There were many stone artifacts buried in the pond sediments and in the adjacent dune sands. They were typologically similar to those found in the early Late Paleolithic site at Wadi Kubbaniya and at several other sites near Esna (the Idfuan entity) dating between 19,500 and 21,000 years old.

Laura Longo, an Italian archaeologist who specialized in the study of use wear on stone artifacts, examined a large sample of the artifacts for traces of wear. The indicated uses included scraping skins (both wet and dry), cutting, sawing, butchering, and impacting (from use as points). Over 60% of the utilized pieces were hafted.

It was a kill-butchery-camp locality, and the first Nile Valley site we investigated where there was such a dependence on hunting large mammals. The site is important because it rounds out our knowledge of the Late Paleolithic settlement/economic system.

I and Romuald Schild, Polydura Baker, Gautier, Longo, and Amal Mohamed recorded the data from these excavations in a small booklet, *A Late Paleolithic Kill-Butchery-Camp in Upper Egypt.*

Christy and I had by this time set a date for our wedding, and in 1995 I negotiated a contract with the American Research Center in Egypt to do a salvage archaeology project in the Eastern Sinai where the Egyptians planned to build several small dams and cultivate several areas that were known to have archaeological sites. I hired Frank Eddy as field director and recruited Roman Schild, Mark Becker, and Kim Banks as archaeologists. Becker had been a graduate student in our department, but had gone to the University of Colorado at Boulder for his PhD. They found many sites, and we planned to undertake a full-scale excavation program in the spring and summer of 1996.

During the period leading up to our wedding in April of 1996, I was generally supervising the USAID-financed project, and I had to make an inspection of the work for the American Research Center in Egypt, the contracting agency for the project. Christy arranged for our wedding to take place a few days before I had to be in Sinai, which allowed us to have our honeymoon in Egypt. She knew that we'd have several days in a four-star hotel, followed by ten days of living in a tent in the Sinai. On April 27, 1996, Christy and I were married at my home in Lancaster, Texas. Over two hundred of our family and friends attended.

When Christy and I got to camp after our honeymoon we had a great welcoming. I never found out how they arranged it, but on our arrival our tent was decorated with signs, tinsel, and colored Christmas lights and ropes. Mark Becker, one of the archaeologists and a former student of mine, made us "his and her hand axes," and our draftsman, Marek Puszkarski, made "Honeymoon Tent" signs. I thought my former student Kimball Banks would short sheet our bed, but he spared us. Even so, before we got in, I tore up and remade the bed, just to make sure.

Christy and I were delighted at the attention we received. The next day I had to look at the sites the team was excavating, some of which were in rough country, and I suggested that she might like to stay in camp. Christy insisted on going with me everywhere I went, even in the rough areas where we sometimes had to walk. She was interested in the work and obviously enjoyed it. Since she'd spent a field season in Kubbaniya in 1983, she knew what to expect working with me in the desert.

On one occasion after our marriage, Mohamed Eide, one of our Bedouin workers, out of the blue said, "I think I would like to come to America." One of our archaeologists, Kit Nelson, told him that he might not like it there since he could have only one wife in the States. "Then how come Fred has four wives?" Mohamed asked. Another worker, whose name was Dawoud, said, "Yes, that's true. I have even seen one of them." Mohamed then asked, "How come only Christy gets to come to Egypt? Don't the other wives get jealous?"

Frank Eddy assembled and edited an impressive series of excavation reports for the project. He insisted on attaching my name as second author, though he did almost all of the work preparing the volume. The book is titled *An Archaeological Investigation of the Central Sinai, Egypt.*

Field Schools for Antiquities | Inspectors and Beyond

(1998 to the present)

CHAPTER 36

For at least two years, Rudolph Kuper, Fekri Hassan, and I, individually, had discussed with Gaballa A. Gaballa, the chairman of the Egyptian Antiquities Organization, the problem of his inspectors' lack of understanding of prehistoric archaeology. Most of his inspectors had no training in prehistoric archaeology, making it difficult for them to function as inspectors on expeditions doing prehistoric research.

In 1998 a crisis loomed when the Egyptian government began working on the Tushka Project, a mammoth reclamation effort that eventually extended from the west bank of the Nile to Nabta and beyond. Dr. Gaballa called for a small conference at Abu Simbel in February of that year to discuss the problems of the Tushka Project. About thirty people attended, including the following senior archaeologists: Mary McDonald, from Canada; Rudolph Kuper and Stephen Kropelin, from Germany; Fekri Hassan; Romuald Schild; Bahay Issawi; and I. Several brought two or three other members of their staffs, all of them active in the study of prehistoric archaeology in Egypt.

As the discussion began, many of those present expressed alarm over the pending loss of archaeological resources because of the Tushka Project. There was concern over how the data from that archaeology could be saved. A large amount of money would be needed, and everyone realized that outside funding for a major salvage archaeology project like that mounted for the Aswan Reservoir was unlikely. The conclusion was that if the data from the soon-to-be-destroyed sites were to be saved for the future, the salvage effort would have to be largely staffed and funded by Egyptians.

The discussion shifted to the lack of training in prehistoric archaeology among Egyptian antiquities inspectors, the group that would have to staff any salvage effort by the antiquities organization. At the close of the meeting Gaballa asked me to stay. He asked if I'd be willing to train a group of inspectors. I said I would if he'd help me and that I would organize a field school. He asked what I needed for him to do.

"Talk to USAID. See if they'll give me a grant to run a field school for your antiquities inspectors. I can't use the funds I receive from the National Science Foundation for that purpose," I said.

Instead of going to USAID, as I suggested, Gaballa went to the American ambassador. A few weeks later, shortly after I returned to Dallas, a representative from USAID called me. She told me the ambassador had asked USAID to talk to me about a field school for Egyptian antiquities inspectors. She asked me how many students and faculty would be involved, to describe what I wanted to do, and how long such a school would last. After I answered her questions, she told me how to prepare the proposal and the budget, and where to submit them. She told me she wanted me to send a proposal as soon as possible.

I submitted my proposal a few weeks later. With minor changes, it was quickly approved. I planned a six-week field school for sixteen inspectors, to be held at Nabta. It would consist of real, one-day-per-week surveys over an area extending in every direction for twenty-five miles with Nabta as the hub. The students would learn how to find, record, and evaluate prehistoric sites.

The students would learn excavation techniques by digging a stratified early Holocene site I had selected near the highway, about two miles from our camp. The students would do most of the digging under the supervision of the faculty. A few laborers would be available for moving dirt away from the excavations and digging test pits; otherwise, the students would do the digging.

In the evenings, and on days when it was too windy to excavate, the students would classify and record the artifacts they found. The faculty would give at least one lecture each week. The field school was to be high-intensity, lasting all day, and sometimes late into the evening, seven days a week, for six weeks.

Eventually, the CPE hosted two field schools devoted to training antiquities inspectors in the methods used to locate and excavate prehistoric sites. The first was held from January 2nd to February 14th, 1999. The second took place January 3rd to February 15th, 2001. Both were supported by grants from the Institute of International Education, USAID.

The first field school consisted of sixteen students and a faculty of eight, Kimball Banks, Christopher Hill, Michal Kobusiewicz, Kit Nelson, Romuald Schild, Atiya Radwan, Mansour Bouriek Radwan, and me. Bahay Issawi was the camp manager. Kit Nelson assembled and printed thirty copies of two field manuals, one for the faculty, the other for the students.

The first field school was a disaster, in large part because the students were not volunteers, as I had requested, but draftees. One of them told me he'd been picked out as he walked down the hall of his office building. According to him, his boss had spotted him in the hall and said, "You're going to a field school at Nabta to learn something about prehistory. Come into my office and I'll give you the schedule and a travel voucher. Everyone will assemble at Abu Simbel. You'll live in a dormitory and have a lot of fun."

With no idea of where Nabta was or what they were facing, few brought heavy coats to protect them from the desert cold. One of the students left after the first night. "Too cold," he said. None was prepared for the intensive training experience they were about to face.

Despite the problems with the field school, it would have been worse without Atiya Radwan's outstanding efforts. He'd spent five seasons with me as an antiquities inspector and knew what it would be like. When many of the students decided they wanted to leave, it was Radwan who persuaded them to stay and finish the training. Fifteen of them did; we lost only the student who quit after the first night.

At the end of the field school I told Radwan I wanted to hold a second field school, and I would need his help. I told him I'd do a second field school only if he was permitted to select the students and prepare them ahead of time for what life would be like in camp. I said I'd ask Ali Mazhar to be the camp manager. Radwan smiled and said he'd be glad to help.

With Gaballa's support, I submitted another proposal to USAID for the second field school. When the proposal was approved, I wrote to Gaballa and asked him to permit Atiya to select the inspectors who would attend the second field school. He agreed.

The faculty in the 2001 field school again consisted of longtime colleagues. Even those who were still graduate students had spent several field seasons with me in the desert. There were eight faculty on the second field school, two of whom, Achilles Gautier (a paleontologist) and Marek Puszkarski (a draftsman and illustrator), were part-time. The full-time faculty were Alex Applegate, Halina Krolik, Atiya Radwan, Mansour Radwan, Romuald Schild, and I. There were sixteen students. All were volunteers who knew what they were facing and were prepared to deal with life in the desert. At my insistence, one of the students was a woman. There was only one woman applicant, Heba Tallah, an antiquities inspector at Abu Simbel. It was fortunate she was included because it was the consensus of the faculty that she was the best student. She won the "Golden Trowel" awarded for her exceptional efforts. Gaballa arranged for all the students to receive additional compensation (sometimes referred to as "combat pay") while they attended the field school.

••••

During the 1998 field season, while the research at Nabta was in full swing and we were discovering all those completely unexpected megalithic alignments and other large stone constructions, I began to worry about the long-term viability of the Combined Prehistoric Expedition. We had three vehicles, all of them of 1989 or 1990 vintage. They were well worn and barely usable off the pavement. We had more than twenty tents and beds, a fully equipped kitchen, and other equipment, including an electronic theodolite and three large water tanks. Aside from the vehicles, we had everything needed for prolonged research in the desert. In addition to the vehicles, the camp represented an investment of around seventy-five to a hundred thousand dollars.

It was this equipment and the staff participants that made the Combined Prehistoric Expedition such a unique and productive endeavor. But who would lead it if something happened to me? I decided it was time for me to retire and transfer the responsibility for the expedition to my friend and colleague, Romuald Schild. He agreed to take over and assumed the directorship on March 1, 1999, at the end of the fieldwork for that year. Roman graciously insisted that I continue to participate in the expedition, and I have gone with the CPE most years for short periods, but I no longer lead any research activity.

Upon my retirement, the generous support by the NSF, so important to the expedition since 1962, was no longer available, because I had been the person responsible for directing the research and spending the money, and the NSF only funds projects run by American researchers affiliated with academic institutions. When I retired, I no longer had an academic base to receive grants and account for expenditures to the NSF. The Polish Academy of Sciences gave some money to Schild, but not enough to permit the eight- and ten-week field seasons that previously had been possible.

Several friends of the expedition in the United States decided to form a tax-exempt organization to support CPE research. They named it the Combined Prehistoric Expedition Foundation. I serve as its president, and Schild as vice president. The support thus far has assisted in the purchase of two new Toyota four-wheel-drive pickups; it has provided funds to cover the travel expenses of five American archeology graduate students to participate in the research activities of the expedition; it has purchased a solar-powered electrical system to provide lights in the kitchen, dining area, and the laboratory; and it has bought a "hardened, dust-proof" computer. In addition, the foundation has provided funds for Schild to extend the time the expedition can stay in the field to six weeks. Someday, we hope to extend the field time to eight weeks. The expedition is in good hands, and I expect it will continue to flourish for many years.

As I write this I have just turned eighty-four years old, and just like an old automobile with lots of mileage, one expects the body to show wear and tear. Mine is beginning to show its years. After the 2001 field school was completed and I returned to Dallas, I went to my urologist for a routine physical examination. The next day he called me to report that I had fast-growing malignant cells in my blood. My PSA number (prostate specific antigen) had begun to climb rapidly. He recommended that I come to his office immediately to begin chemotherapy shots. I was there within the hour, and I received my first shot. Initially the shots were once a month, but within four months there were no more traces of malignancy in my blood, and my PSA score was back down to zero. The shots were rescheduled for once every three months. Except for one period when the count went up briefly, my PSA remained zero, and there are no traces of malignancy. In the spring of 2006 the shots were scheduled at six-month intervals. Although the cancer is no longer evident, I was told that I would be taking the shots for the remainder of my life.

In June and July of 2004, Christy and I were at Fort Burgwin. I had not yet begun this book, but I was thinking about it. I was not feeling well, and from time to time I would pass a little blood in my urine. It was time for me to see my urologist again. At the beginning of August we returned to Dallas. My urologist operated on me three days later and removed several malignant tumors from my bladder. Despite the complications of these shots and operations, I have managed to go on with my life, but at a slower pace. I have written this book, which has taken me three years. The first version took me a year. Editing and entering new data took another two years.

Christy tells me she would like to see some part of the world beside Egypt. And I tell her that we will, and life will go on, as it should. My brother Roman and I are talking about one more book, and maybe we'll write it before our time runs out.

| Epilogue

W hen I meet new people and they find out I've been an archaeologist for many years, they often ask, "What was your most important (interesting, significant, valuable, or oldest) discovery." The question tells me that the person does not understand how science works. Science advances by disproving accepted dogma. Almost never does it advance because of some unique discovery. We archaeologists sometimes become excited when we find something unexpected, for example when we found the cow burials, the megalithic alignments, and the Complex Structures at Nabta, but mostly, new ideas result from long, patient work that demonstrates a widely held opinion is wrong.

This is what happened when we found and excavated numerous Paleolithic sites in Nubia, where everyone said there were no sites. It is hard to believe, but it took three years of excavation and the publication of two books before the significance of this previously unknown archaeology was widely recognized.

A similar situation existed when we found the early ceramics at Bir Kiseiba. It was firmly believed that pottery was introduced to the Sahara from the Nile Valley, and that the Nile in turn received pottery from Southwest Asia. Numerous radiocarbon dates associated with the Saharan pottery changed that. The earliest Saharan pottery is dated several thousand years older than the oldest pottery in the Nile Valley. It took many years, the excavation of a dozen or more sites, and repeated publication of the data before the antiquity of the Saharan pottery was widely accepted.

The discovery of domestic cattle, also at Bir Kiseiba, is another example of the long, careful research needed before the status of the cattle began to be accepted. These cattle are about 2,000 years earlier than the first domestic cattle in Southwest Asia, long thought to be the source of domestic cattle in Africa. Even today, some doubt our identification of the cattle bones, or our interpretation that they were domestic.

Finally, at Gademotta, we have Potassium/Argon age measurements of 235,000 years ago above a Middle Stone Age occupation surface with artifacts indicating possible "early modern behavior." Our dates are much older than the accepted age for the Middle Stone Age and modern human presence in East Africa, so they were ignored until recently. Others are finally beginning to think the Gademotta dates may be correct, but our thesis needs to be evaluated by obtaining more dates. To this I agree enthusiastically, and recently new dates have been obtained using a new, more precise technique known as Argon/Argon, which confirms that the Middle Stone Age archaeology at Gademotta is even older than we thought.

It took a lot of work by many scholars and numerous age determinations before it was generally accepted that the wet phases in the Eastern Sahara, the intervals with permanent lakes, were contemporary with Interglacials, not cold glacial events. For many years after our data were published, a few individuals continued to talk about "pluvials" and date them between 40,000 and 20,000 years ago. Sometimes I think researchers have to die before their new ideas are accepted. The truth is, science needs these conservative folk to maintain a balance between new ideas and the old ones.

Each of these examples shows what science should be; they represent advances in knowledge that displace previously held theories. Except for the Paleolithic sites in Nubia now covered by the waters of the Aswan Reservoir, each one should be examined and challenged by new excavations, new data, new dates, and new ideas. I am confident of our data, and I will defend them until I am shown they are wrong.

I haven't produced a single "most important" new body of archaeological data. I have many. Some projects had a greater impact on my understanding of the prehistory in Northeast Africa, and gave me more pleasure. In this group I include the Nubian project, including the graveyard at Jebel Sahaba; the work with the long Middle Paleolithic sequence at Bir Sahara East and Bir Tarfawi; Wadi Kubbaniya, where we sorted out the Late Paleolithic sequence in the Nile Valley; and Nabta Playa, particularly the study of the unusual features that suggest an emerging social complexity in the Late and Final Neolithic. I might also add the study of the early ceramics and the squabble over the domestic cattle at Bir Kiseiba and Nabta.

My wife, Christy, sometimes tells me I'm a risk-taker. That was true when at age twenty I volunteered for combat in Italy with the 10th Mountain Division. It cost me the use of my right arm, but I am proud that I went. I was also a risk-taker when I insisted there had to be a rich archaeological record along the Nubian Nile. Because so much money was involved, had I been wrong it would have ruined my career as an archaeologist, and might have cost me my job.

All of the examples of our archaeological discoveries that resulted in a significant modification of our understanding of the prehistory of northeastern Africa were controversial and involved risk. Each was "goring someone's ox." In every case, however, I carefully studied the data and often sought additional evidence before I made a decision. This is not being a risk-taker; it is being a scientist. I sometimes made mistakes, as in the instance of the barley at Kubbaniya and Nabta, but I was able to pursue more evidence and eventually correct my mistakes.

The CPE has allowed me the opportunity to participate in the discovery and study of the rich prehistoric heritage of Egypt, Ethiopia, and the Nubian Sudan, and to help write the many papers and books that brought Northeast African prehistory to the attention of the archaeological world. Instead of the archaeological backwater that the Nile Valley had been generally assumed to be before the expedition began working, we now realize that this area was an important contributor to our knowledge of the human past in Africa. A few of those contributions include the following discoveries:

(1) The long sequence of Middle Paleolithic localities, dating from ca. 250,000 to 65,000 years ago, and associated with permanent lakes in the Eastern Sahara, now one of the driest places on earth;

(2) A rich and diverse sequence of Late Paleolithic entities in the Late Pleistocene Nile Valley, and more than a hundred examples of their previously unknown and unique variety of humans;

(3) Jebel Sahaba, the earliest evidence of true warfare, which tempts us with clues that may help us understand the forces behind the origin of warfare;

(4) A complex and highly developed ceramic tradition that began over 9,500 years ago in the Western Desert, almost 3,000 years before pottery was known in the Nile Valley;

(5) The earliest known domestic cattle, at least 2,000 years before cattle were domesticated in Southwest Asia;

(6) The sequence of complex Neolithic entities that first appear in the Western Desert at the beginning of the early Holocene; and

(7) The mysterious alignments and large stone constructions whose functions remain elusive to us, but which tell us that a complex social system almost certainly was emerging at Nabta between 6,500 and 4,500 uncalibrated years ago.

Several of my friends have told me they believe the most important event in my life was being wounded in Italy when I was twenty years old. They say it changed me physically and emotionally, and it made me what I am today. I think they are probably right.

Eventually, I had to face the fact of my disability and force myself to do most simple things using only my left hand. I learned to anticipate some tasks, like buttoning the cuffs on my left side before I put on the shirt. I even learned to shoot a rifle and shotgun. For many months I was such a poor shot that I hunted alone to avoid being embarrassed. In time I began to improve and began to hunt with others, but I had to accept the fact that I would never again be the marksman I once was.

For many years I shook hands with my left hand, a choice that brought unwanted attention to my damaged right arm. And when I began working in Sudan and Egypt I learned that Muslims were offended when I extended my left hand. So I forced myself to use my right hand, not only with Muslims, but with everyone I met. It pleased me greatly that many people failed to notice that my right hand was different. Those who did notice would ask, "What happened to your hand?" And I would say, "It's my war souvenir." And go on.

I tried never to talk about the war and being wounded. I was not ashamed. In fact, I was rather proud that I had served as a young, twenty-year-old second lieutenant in the 10th Mountain Division, but I wanted to leave that time behind and get on with my life. My family learned about most of the events of March 3, 1945, when they read an early draft of this book.

I believe that the result of all my efforts to function and appear normal is that I became stubborn. I use that term not in the pejorative sense, but rather as "very determined." Each failure made me work harder, made me keep trying until I would eventually succeed. This stubbornness carried over into my academic and, later, my professional life. I was determined to become an archaeologist, a good, productive archaeologist.

Many of the opportunities I received after I returned to the University of Arizona and later at Harvard were efforts to help me professionally. How much of this was due to sympathy and how much was assistance to a promising student I do not know. I like to think that all of this happened because my benefactors saw some quality, some determination, that was worth rewarding. On the other hand, perhaps it was just what the medic said to me on March 3, 1945, "Lieutenant, you're one lucky son of a bitch."

| Acknowledgments

I wrote *Desert Days* for several reasons, but initially because my children, my wife Christy, and many of my friends urged me to do so. All of them at one time or another had asked me to tell the story of my life. I am, however, particularly indebted to my youngest son, Scott, who in 2004 had read a short article I had written about my forty-plus years of collaboration with my close friend, my brother, Roman Schild.

Scott stopped by my office at Southern Methodist University, stuck his head in my doorway, and said, "Dad, you have got to write the story of your life, and do it now while you still remember. And get it published; it will be of interest to many people." Before he left he made me promise to write this book.

A few days later I started writing, thinking I could finish the text in a year. I did finish a five-hundred-plus-page draft in twelve months, and I persuaded a professional editor and old friend, Barbara Miercort, to read and comment on it. She did more than that. She carefully edited the entire manuscript, making black marks on every page, and then fussed at me because I fudged the story about my personal life, my marriages and divorces. She also gave me a hard time because she knew I had presented a cleaned-up version of the Italian battlefield where as a twenty-year-old second lieutenant I was seriously wounded on March 3, 1945. Barbara made me think about things I had buried in my subconscious mind, and several times in our discussions about the manuscript her questions and comments brought tears to my eyes. And so I began writing Version Two. When I finished it a year and a half later, the manuscript needed and received attention from the senior editor at SMU Press, Kathryn Lang. Kathie was generous with her time and produced a much improved manuscript. She polished my prose and helped provide structure to the many stories and events in my narrative. When my spirits were down she encouraged me by telling how much she liked the book even as she called it "a diamond in the rough." She left the true battlefield story alone. It is the Prologue in this volume and is very different from my first version. The new one is as blunt and true as I could make it.

I have been fortunate to live an interesting life, go to strange places, do interesting work, and learn about the past. I had the freedom to do these things because of the encouragement of Claude Albritton, my dean at SMU. As a consequence of his support, I have spent many field seasons in the Egyptian Sahara, hundreds of miles from the nearest people, doing exciting archaeology about people and societies whose existence was previously unknown. For over sixty years I have worked with many leading scholars from a variety of scientific disciplines in Europe, America, and Africa, and I call many of them friends. I am particularly proud of my Egyptian, Ethiopian, and Sudanese friends who facilitated my work in their countries. An important part of that help came from the Bedouins who worked with me and taught me how to live and travel in the desert. On several occasions they kept me from harm. One of the reasons I wrote this book was to tell the story of some of our adventures together.

I have also participated in some of the most exciting archaeological projects anyone could imagine. There was the study of an 11,000-year-old Final Pleistocene partial human skeleton from West Texas, and in Egypt the discovery of previously unknown solar- and star-based ceremonial features built during the Late Neolithic. These megaliths possibly anticipated the development of social complexity in the Nile Valley. But the most exciting and interesting period in my life was from 1962 to 1965, when the expedition excavated numerous diverse and rich Paleolithic sites in the area that was covered by the Aswan Reservoir just as we were finishing our work, an area where experts insisted there was no archaeology of interest.

Most of this research was done under the auspices of the Combined Prehistoric Expedition, which I led for thirty-seven years (1962–1999). An informal organization supported by the Geological Survey of Egypt, the Polish Academy of Sciences, and Southern Methodist University, the CPE is one of the world's most productive assemblages of archaeologists, geologists, botanists, zoologists, and other earth scientists. These scientists have produced over thirty books and more than a hundred journal articles. Most of the CPE's work was devoted to the study of the prehistory of the Nile Valley and the enormous Western Desert of Egypt, but there were brief forays to the Rift Valley in central Ethiopia, Yemen, and Sinai.

Prehistoric archaeology in America today is very different from what it was when I was a graduate student, when there were only a few hundred professional archaeologists, mostly working as museum curators or faculty in one of the rare universities that offered courses in archaeology. When I received my PhD there was only one job open in archaeology, and I did not get it. Today there are over five thousand professional archaeologists in the United States, many of them employed by firms that contract to excavate, record, and preserve the cultural heritage threatened by economic development projects. I was involved in the beginning of some of the earliest efforts to preserve our threatened cultural heritage, and one of the major reasons I wanted to write this book was to tell everyone how it happened and who made it possible.

My early life as an archaeologist greatly benefited from the support of a few important people. These early mentors included Emil W. Haury, Harold S. Colton, Stanley A. Stubbs, John Otis Brew, Jesse L. Nusbaum, George Lavender, Pete Erwin, and Spike Keller. They put me on the right course to start my life as an archaeologist and challenged me to do as much as I could.

I am grateful for the strong financial support I received in the development of Fort Burgwin. Ralph M. Rounds and his family, particularly Bill and Dwight Rounds, made the Fort Burgwin Research Center possible. A few years later William P. Clements and his wife Rita provided the resources that allowed the Research Center to become "SMU-in-Taos at Fort Burgwin."

I owe a great debt to the National Science Foundation, and in particular to the anthropology program, and its director, John Yellen. His support made possible the field work and the results of the CPE's research.

Several private donors have also contributed to the success of my various endeavors. My major benefactors include Cliff and Betsy Alexander, Ned and Raynette Boshell, Mason and Barbara Brown, Marlin and Marea Downey, Jim and Judy Gibbs, Herbert and Nancy Hunt, and Cliff and Barbara Miercort.

When I moved my research to the Aswan Reservoir, Rushdi Said and Bahay Issawi introduced me to the desert and helped me overcome Egyptian red tape, while Bill Adams was a special friend in Wadi Halfa, opening all the important doors. I am grateful also to the management and staff of the Geological Survey of Egypt, in particular to Mohamed Hinnawi and Ali Mazhar for their efficient management of our camps. Ali Mazhar has been our camp manager every year beginning with 1980, and he is still going strong.

For over twenty years I benefited from the friendship and skillful assistance of my secretary at SMU, Marylee Skwirz. She cheerfully typed, corrected, and retyped each of the books and articles I wrote. She stayed with me while I struggled to learn how to use an Apple computer, and when she knew I wouldn't sink without her, she retired, just before I retired at SMU.

I wish to acknowledge the assistance I received from John Imbrie of Brown University, an infantryman in the 10th Mountain Division and today its record keeper. He helped me contact Lt. Col. Charles E. (Ed) Halstead, Jr., whom I knew as Staff Sergeant Ed Halstead, the leader of the first squad in my platoon. Two members of his squad were killed at my side. Ed stayed in the army and became an officer. He corrected my memory of the weapons we used and saved me considerable embarrassment, for which I will always be grateful. I also want to acknowledge the help I received in the early phase of this book from Wilhart Etelamaki, the leader of the second squad in my platoon. He won a Silver Star for his heroism that morning of March 3, 1945. Will died a few years ago, but he is not forgotten.

I want to thank those who have read one of the various drafts of this manuscript and have offered me the benefit of their advice and suggestions on improving the text. Excluding the editors previously thanked, in alphabetical order they are Ofer Bar-Yosef, Lewis R. Binford, Governor William Clements, William M. Finnin, Dianne Finnin, Donald Fowler, Vance Haynes, Christopher Hill, Cheryl Hill, Jon Kalb, Bennie Keel, Stuart Struever, Carl Wendorf, Gail Wendorf, Scott Wendorf, and Christopher Wolff.

I especially want to acknowledge my children, who grew up to be resilient, creative, and productive adults. I want to thank them for their forbearance during my many long absences while they were growing up. Though I was too often gone, they were never far from my heart. All are grown now, widely scattered around the world, with independent lives of their own. Scott, my youngest, lives in Dallas with his wife, Andrea, and their three children, Frances, Henry, and Miller. Scott is an intellectual property (patent) attorney who works for a major oil service company. I see them when I can, but not often enough.

My youngest daughter, Kelly, lives in Australia, where she is a successful magazine publisher. Her husband, Alok, is also a magazine publisher. They have two beautiful children, Arun and Sahaja. Kelly looks much like her mother, Peta.

Cindy, my youngest daughter with Nancy, and her husband Albert, live in Tucson. They have no children. She is in her forties and still beautiful. She once was a gifted guitarist, but her life took an abrupt turn when in her early twenties, in graduate school in psychology at SMU, she suffered a major attack of multiple sclerosis. She copes well and is gradually improving, moving from a wheelchair to walking so well that no one knows she was once crippled.

My oldest daughter, Gail, is a gifted artist, a painter in oil. She lives in Scotland, in a small village near Fort William. Gail made three trips (1987, 1988, and 1990) with me in the Egyptian Sahara as the staff illustrator, drawing flaked stone artifacts. Her drawings grace several of my books.

My son Mike earned a PhD in archaeology at Berkeley with Desmond Clark, but soon after became interested in computers and their applications and chose not to become a full-time academic. Although Mike's career as a systems analyst keeps him busy, he has published several articles on archaeology, and has made contributions to the field of medical anthropology, analyzing the occurrence of Type II diabetes in Native American populations and Type I diabetes in Northern European populations. Mike is married to Anna, and they have two almost grown, beautiful daughters, Sarah and Laura. They live in Concord, California, a small town near Berkeley.

My oldest son, Carl, is an electrical engineer for a major electronics firm in Phoenix, Arizona. He designs the programs for the computers that control the big jets the airlines use. We talk almost every weekend. He's in his fifties now and works out every day. He has a lovely wife, Nicole, but no children.

As I look back over my life with its many adventures, honors, and awards, I find that I am proudest of my six children.

Finally, I want to acknowledge the most important person in my life, my wife and constant companion, Christy Bednar. In many ways, she supported me during the preparation of this book. She encouraged me when I was down, she advised me when I had questions, and she tolerated my behavior during those long weeks of writing when I would disappear into my study, only to come out hours later to ask, "When do we eat?" She was always there, my friend, my companion, and my love.

I have been fortunate in my friends, colleagues, and family. I've been fortunate in my experiences. I hope this book is as interesting to other readers as it was to my son Scott.

Glossary |

Acheulean: Alternative term for the Lower Paleolithic; used frequently by European prehistorians; characterized by bifacially flaked hand axes; generally dating between 1,500,000 and 300,000 years old.

Aeolian processes: Shaping of the earth's surface by wind erosion; often associated with sandy regions.

Aggradation: The deposition of sediment from a river, stream, or lake.

Alidade: A surveying instrument used to determine direction, distance, and elevation; often used to map archaeological areas and sites.

Alluviation: The deposition of sand, clay, silt, or gravel by flowing water; usually in a river valley or delta.

Anasazi: Prehistoric culture between approximately A.D. 500 and 1500 in the American Southwest; the ancestor of present-day Pueblo culture.

Arkinian: The most recent Final Paleolithic lithic industry; known from several sites along the Nile near the town of Arkin in Sudan; dating 11,000–11,500 years old; most frequent tools include straight-backed and pointed microblades and bladelets, arch-backed microblades and bladelets, and well-made endscrapers; also single platform and bipolar cores.

Assemblage: A collection of artifacts from a particular site

Aterian: A Middle Stone Age lithic industry found throughout the Sahara and in the coastal Maghreb of Northwest Africa, where some sites occur with beach deposits attributed to the Last Interglacial; three Aterian sites are also known in Egypt, one in Nile Valley, two in the Western Desert; characteristic tools include bifacially worked blades with a basal stem suitable for hafting, and medium-to-large-sized bifacially flaked foliates (leaf-shaped), both associated with numerous Middle Paleolithic points, flakes, and debris mostly produced by Levallois technology. Recent research indicates bifacial foliates were present in the Middle Paleolithic of the Eastern Sahara as early as 130,000 years ago; large, bifacial stemmed points are believed to occur in later Middle Paleolithic sites that date between 65,000 and 70,000 years ago, near the end of the Last Interglacial.

Backed microblades: Small flakes of blade proportions, less than 3.0 cm long, with abrupt, almost vertical retouch along one edge to create a steep, blunted edge.

Barchan dune: A crescent-shaped, shifting sand dune, concave on the leeward side.

Barrage: A low structure built to hold back water for later use in irrigating cultivated fields.

Bipolar cores: Cores where flakes were removed from both ends simultaneously by resting one end on a large rock and repeatedly striking the other end firmly. Sometimes referred to as "splintered cores."

Bir: Arabic term for a well or small oasis.

Black-on-white pottery: Decorative style of pottery characteristic of the northern part of the American Southwest; characteristic of the Anasazi as early as A.D. 500 until about A.D. 1350, when red and brown pottery, resulting from the introduction of a new firing technique, replaced black-on-white ceramics in most areas.

Blade: A flake twice (or more) as long in the direction of the blow as it is wide.

Bladelet: Small flake of blade proportion between 5.0 cm and 3.0 cm long.

Blowout: Landform or deflated basin hollowed out by wind.

Bodo Man: A nearly complete cranium variously dated about 600,000 years old; recovered from a site in the Middle Awash basin in Ethiopia; has clear cut marks suggesting the scalp had been removed. Usually classified as an "Archaic *Homo sapiens.*" Found on the joint Kalb/Wendorf field group in 1979.

Bryan/Antevs model: Paleoclimate model for the American Southwest in which Kirk Bryan and Ernst Antevs suggested three main paleoclimatic periods: Anathermal, from 10,000 to 7,500 years ago, in which the temperatures increased and it became more humid; Altithermal, from 7,500 to 4,000 years ago, which had warm, dry conditions; and Medithermal, from 4,000 years to the present, with fluctuations between warm, dry periods and hotter, more humid periods.

Burin: Stone tool used for engraving or shaping wood or bone where the working edge is formed by removing a flake from the edge of a thick flake to form a sharp working tip.

Caldera: Volcanic crater usually formed by a major eruption followed by the collapse of the mouth of the volcano.

Cesium magnetometer: A cesium-powered device highly sensitive to small fluctuations in the magnetic field of objects; is helpful in finding shipwrecks and other archaeological material underwater. Also used to create maps of iron or other magnetic materials buried at a surface site.

Chert: A rock composed primarily of silica with a microscopically fine-grained texture that can be chipped to create stone tools with sharp edges.

Coprolite: Fossilized excrement of animals or people.

Debitage: Discarded chips of stone created during the production of stone tools.

Deflated basin: Bowl-like landform hollowed out by wind.

Denticulate: Stone artifact with several regularly spaced "toothlike" projections; probably used as knife or saw.

Diatom analysis: Analysis of diatoms, single-celled algae sensitive to changes in the environment, to determine species present and changes in frequency through time; these data are useful indicators of changes in the environment.

Disarticulated remains: Refers to bones, either of humans or animals, disturbed intentionally or through natural causes.

Distal end: That part of the object farthest away from the center or place of attachment. In the case of artifacts, the tip of the object on the opposite end from where it was struck. With skeletal material, the part of the bone farthest from the central axis of the body.

Double-backed perforator: Tool that has been backed or otherwise worked on both lateral edges, creating steep, flat edges; thought to have been used to perforate objects such as beads, clothing, and animal hides.

Downcutting: When a river or stream erodes downward to a lower level.

Druid: A religious practitioner associated with pre-Christian Celtic polytheism found throughout Western Europe and Great Britain, a version of which is still practiced by some modern pagan groups.

Ecotone: The transitional region between two biological communities, such as the border area between grassland and forest.

El Adam pottery: Early Neolithic pottery with deeply packed exterior rocker-stamped designs; associated with the Adam cultural entity; dating between 9,500 and 8,800 years ago; known only in the Nabta Playa and Bir Kiseiba areas of the Egyptian Western Desert.

El Ghorab: Early Neolithic cultural entity known from many localities in the Egyptian Western Desert, from Kharga in the north to Nabta Playa on the south; stratigraphically later than El Adam, dating between 8,700 and 8,200 years ago.

Embayment: Recess in a coastline forming a bay.

Eocene: Geological epoch from 56.5 million to 35.4 million years ago, a time of rising temperatures and increasing populations of mammals, including the first horses, bats, and whales. Eocene sediments often have beds or cobbles of flint or chert that were widely used as raw material for stone artifacts.

Epipaleolithic: Archaeological interval dating around 10,000 years ago and lasting until around 5,000 years ago, although the exact chronology differs from region to region. In Southwest Asia it is the period when farming developed, animals such as sheep/goats were first domesticated, and pottery and microlithic tools appeared.

Ethnology: The study of modern societies.

Fauna: Animals of a particular site, habitat, region, or geological period.

Flint knapper: Craftsman who makes stone tools by flaking, using a stone hammer, a large bone, or a tool made from antler.

Fluorine analysis: Uses microchemical analyses to determine if faunal remains found in a site are of the same or different ages. Fluorine is present in almost all groundwater and is carried into buried bones, where it is locked into the chemical lattice of the bones. The longer groundwater and fluorine come into the bones, the more fluorine they contain. Bones introduced into the sediment later have lower amounts of fluorine. The technique was used to establish the antiquity of the Midland skeleton. Analyses showed the human bones and teeth had the same amount of fluorine as the extinct horse, bison, and four-horned antelope recovered in the same deposit. The bones from overlying sediments had much lower values for fluorine.

Fluted point: Projectile point primarily associated with the Clovis and Folsom Paleoindians of North America (ca. 11,200–9,000 years ago). The distinctive points were struck at the base to remove several short flakes on both sides of the base (Clovis); or a single long flake from both sides of base almost to the point (Folsom).

Folsom: Paleoindian culture found in central and western North America dating to approximately 10,500–9,000 years ago, first defined at a kill site of extinct bison near Folsom, New Mexico.

***Glycimeris* bracelets:** Bracelets made from a mollusk shell. *Glycimeris* is a genus of marine bivalve mollusks from the Pacific Coast. Jewelry made from their shells was traded as far inland as the American Southwest.

Halfa Flakes: Small stone flakes with sharp, broad distal ends; made using Levallois flaking techniques and associated with the Halfan lithic entity found at several sites in the Nile Valley from the Second Cataract near Wadi Halfa to Wadi Kubbaniya five miles north of Aswan.

Holocene: Contemporary geological period that began approximately 10,000 years ago.

Inselberg: A solitary hill or mountain that rises steeply from a plain; also called a jebel or gebel (Arabic), or mesa (Spanish).

Interglacial: Period of warmer, more temperate conditions between two glacial periods.

Interphase: Warm, wet climatic interval between two hyperarid, cold phases.

Interstadial: Brief period of warmer and wetter climatic conditions within a glacial period.

Jebel: Mountain, hill, or mountain range; term used primarily in the Middle East and North Africa (see inselberg above).

Kiva: Room or structure, often semi-subterranean, that early Puebloan peoples used for ritual performances and men's clubhouses; still used for those purposes today.

Lacustrine episodes: Periods of deposition of lake sediments.

Last Glacial Maximum (LGM): Maximum extent of the ice sheets during the last glaciation (the Würm in Europe or Wisconsin in North America), approximately 20,000–16,000 years ago.

Levallois technology: Middle Paleolithic lithic technology in which cores were carefully prepared for the removal of a wide, thin flake. In Africa, appearing as early as 200,000 years ago in the Late Acheulean.

Lithics: Stone artifacts and the debris resulting from their production.

Lucy: Nickname of an almost complete female skeleton of a fossil hominid found in Ethiopia in 1974. Approximately 3.2 million years old, belonging to the species *Australopithecus afarensis,* widely regarded as the ancestor of later Australopithecines and the earliest humans *(Homo).*

Lunates: Crescent-shaped stone tools, resembling a crescent moon.

Megafauna: Large animals, such as horse, bison, rhino, and antelope, found in some faunal assemblages.

Megalith: Large stone forming all or part of a monument.

Mesolithic: Rarely used archaeological term for the period immediately after the last ice age in northern Europe, beginning around 11,000 years ago; characterized by new elements in technology (bow and arrow; very small, microlithic tools).

Microlith: Retouched stone tool less than 3 cm long.

Mogollon: North American cultural entity first defined by Emil W. Haury; flourished in southwestern New Mexico and southeastern Arizona from approximately 2,000 years ago, distinguished by pit house architecture, and later, aboveground pueblos; by brown- and red-colored pottery; and later, by black-on-white pottery. Around 1200–1300 B.C. the Mogollon began to move northward and integrate into the Anasazi to form the modern pueblo groups still living today along the Rio Grande, as well as Laguna, Acoma, and Zuni people in western New Mexico and the Hopi villages in northern Arizona.

Mousterian: Middle Paleolithic in Europe, Southwest Asia, and North Africa; its beginning is undated, but is before the Last Interglacial and lasted to 35,000 years ago in southwest France and Spain. Associated with Neanderthals, named after the cave of Le Moustier, in southwestern France, where it was first identified.

Navaho hogan: Traditional conical dwelling constructed with forked poles and covered with branches, earth, and grass; the door always faces east. More recent hogans are often made of large sawn lumber; the doorway still faces east.

Neolithic: Period when people began to produce food by farming and/or raising domestic animals, and to make pottery, marking the emergence of a new economy that replaced the hunting and gathering of the Paleolithic. In Southwest Asia cultivation of cereals began between 11,000 to 10,000 years ago, domestic sheep/goats are known about 10,000 years ago, and pottery around 8,000 years ago. In the Western Desert of Egypt both pottery and domestic cattle are known around 9,500 years ago; sheep/goats around 7,100 years ago. Domestic plants are later still, when wheat and barley were introduced from Southwest Asia around 6,400 years ago.

Nilotic sediments: Silts, sands, and clays deposited during the annual flooding of the Nile River.

Olivella **beads:** Made from the shells of a genus of marine snails traded from the Pacific Coast to as far inland as the American Southwest.

Ouchtata bladelets: Small tools made on bladelets (less than 5 cm long) lightly retouched along one edge, common in the Maghreb and the Nile Valley. Beginning around 21,000 years ago, this type of retouch was used to form tools by shaping the edges of microblades and bladelets.

Oxygen isotope stages: Alternating warm and cold periods in the earth's climate, identified by determining the ratio of $^{18}O/^{16}O$ in the sediments and microfauna found in deep sea cores. A high ratio of ^{18}O means cold water; a high ratio of ^{16}O indicates warm water. Fluctuations in the oxygen isotopic stratigraphy can be correlated with changes in terrestrial climate. These isotopic events are called "stages" and given numbers; that is, Oxygen Isotope Stage 1 is the modern climate. Stage 2 is the most recent cold interval of the last glacial advance, and Stage 5 is the warm period of the Last Interglacial.

Paleoenvironment: Literally, "old environment"; a reconstruction of the environmental conditions in an area during the past.

Paleoindians: Earliest people who colonized the Americas, the timing of which is highly controversial, often referring to the Clovis and Folsom people and their regional variants best known for their fluted point technology (see Fluted points and Folsom above). The Paleoindian period started by at least 11,500 years ago and lasted until around 8,000 years ago.

Paleolithic: Period that began when humans first started making stone tools about 2.5 million years ago, lasting until the beginning of food-producing societies about 11,000–10,000 years ago. Is divided into Lower Paleolithic, with the first "chopping tools" and continuing through the interval of hand axes, between 1,750,000 to 300,000 years ago); followed by the Middle Paleolithic, with many tools made on flakes, around 300,000 until 45,000–35,000 years ago; then the Upper Paleolithic, with many tools made on blades, from 40,000 to 20,000 years ago; and finally, the Late Paleolithic, with many tools made on bladelets (between 5 and 3 cm long) or microblades (<3 cm), and geometrics (mostly triangles or trapezes), from 21,000–20,000 years ago to about 11,000 years ago.

Paleontologist: A scholar who studies fossil plants and animals.

Parry fracture: A break in the arm caused by warding off or blocking a blow, sometimes similar to those caused by a fall or accident.

Perched water: Where a fault or erosion leaves the water table higher than the surrounding eroded landscape, occurring when an impermeable layer of rock or sediment lies below the water table. When a perched aquifer's flow intersects the earth's surface, at a valley wall, for example, the water is discharged as a spring.

Phytogenic dunes: Formed when blowing sand covers an area of vegetation; plants hold the sand in place, forming a dune.

Piltdown fraud: A hoax in 1912 when a fossil collector used a partial human cranium and a jaw of an ape to claim he had found an early hominid fossil in a gravel quarry near Piltdown, England. For many years the fake fossil was accepted by many physical anthropologists, but fluorine analyses done in 1953 finally proved the "fossil" to be a fraud.

Pipeline right-of-way: A strip of land a gas or oil company buys or acquires the right to in order to construct a pipeline to carry petroleum products to market.

Pit house: Structure built entirely or partially below ground.

Playa: Area where rainwater forms a seasonal lake after a rain.

Pleistocene: Period between 2,000,000 and 10,000 years ago, marked by periods of cold temperatures and glacial advances, with warm temperatures during interglacial events. Some place the beginning of the Pleistocene with the first appearance of new mammals, such as the first true horses. Others use the onset of the first glacial event as the start of the Pleistocene. Some consider our present time to be part of the Pleistocene.

Points: Projectile points, hafted at the end of a spear, dart, or arrow; known colloquially as "arrowheads."

Potassium/Argon Dating (K/Ar): Method of dating sites used in areas where volcanic activity occurred. Based on known rates of radioactive decay, researchers can measure the ratio of the potassium-40 isotope with its decay product, argon-40, providing a date when the ash fall occurred.

Potsherds: Fragments of pottery.

Pottery typology: Organization of pottery varieties into a hierarchical system based on their physical attributes in order to study their relationships and chronology.

Proximal end: End closest to the center or place of attachment; with stone artifacts, the base or platform; with bones, the end closest to the central axis of the body.

Qussier member: Yellow firing clay containing shale-like platy biotite found in large patches in the basement Nubia sandstone and quartzite; used for making pottery during the Late Neolithic in the area around Nabta Playa.

Retouch: Continuously removing a series of small chips from the edge of a flake or blade to form the desired shape and strengthen the piece.

Rocker-stamped decorations: Impressed designs in pottery made by rocking a stylus or comb back and forth into still pliable clay before the pottery is fired.

Sahelian zone: Vast semiarid region of open woodlands and grasslands in North Africa, beginning at the southern edge of the Sahara and ending at the northern edge of the tropical forest, forming a transitional zone between the desert and the tropical forest.

Scalene triangles: Small stone tools that have been shaped by retouch into triangles with unequal sides. Some of these have one very long side and are identified as "elongated scalene triangles."

Scarp: Steep bank or slope; the edge of an escarpment.

Sickle sheen: Polish or gloss that forms on stone tools from the silica in grasses and cereals when used to harvest grain.

Sidescraper: Flake with semisteep retouch on one or both lateral edges, used to scrape hides, bones, or wood.

Spalls: Splinters of rock.

Stratigrapher: One who studies the sediments in a site, determines the sequence of their deposition, and relates them to the surrounding landscape.

Stratigraphic units (Strata): Layers of cultural, sediment, and geologic deposits used to study the formation of a site and to provide relative ages when each layer was deposited.

Stone Age: Refers to a period of about two million years, beginning with the first use of stone tools and ending when stone tools were no longer used.

Sufraggi: Arabic term for someone who serves people food or drink.

Tablerock: Isolated remnant of hard stone surrounded by softer sediments removed by erosion.

Tandem linear accelerator: Machine used to determine the age of small particles of charcoal, used for radiocarbon dating.

Taxa: Plural form of the term taxon; several related categories in a taxonomic classification. The group is a taxa.

Techtonic (or tectonic) trench: Formed by the movement and separation of the earth's crust.

Theodolite: Surveying instrument with a rotating telescope used for measuring horizontal and vertical angles.

Thermoluminescence dating: Technique that measures the accumulated energy in certain types of soils and ceramic artifacts; yields a date when these materials were last exposed to sunlight.

Toolkit: Variety of tools of an individual or groups.

Tumulus: Ancient burial mound or earth-covered tomb.

Vigas: Spanish word for beams used to support a ceiling.

Wadi: Arabic word for a valley or channel that is dry in all but the rainy season.

Workshop: Locality where stone tools were made, usually indicated by the debris created during their manufacture.

Bibliography

Addington, Lucile R. 1986. *Lithic Illustration: Drawing Flaked Stone Artifacts for Publication*. Chicago: University of Chicago Press.

Bagnold, Ralph. 1941. *The Physics of Wind Blown Sand*. London: Methuen.

Bagnold, Ralph, O. H. Myers, R. F. Peel, and H. Winkler. 1939. "An Expedition to Gilf Kebir and Uweinat, 1938." *Geographical Journal* 93:281–312.

Bell, Robert. 1992. *Impure Science: Fraud, Compromise, and Political Influence in Scientific Research*. New York: Wiley.

Bennett, James A. 1948. *Forts and Forays; [The Diary of] a Dragoon in New Mexico, 1850–1856*. Edited by Clinton E. Brooks and Frank Driver Reeve. Albuquerque: University of New Mexico Press.

Bunting, Bainbridge, Jean Lee Booth, and William R. Sims, Jr. 1964. *Taos Adobes: Spanish Colonial and Territorial Architecture of the Taos Valley*. Santa Fe: Museum of New Mexico Press.

Caton-Thompson, Gertrude. 1952. *Kharga Oasis in Prehistory*. London: Athlone Press.

Caton-Thompson, Gertrude, and E. W. Gardner. 1934. *The Desert Fayum*. London: Royal Anthropological Institute.

Clark, J. Desmond. 1987. "Fred Wendorf: A Critical Assessment of His Career in and Contributions to North African Prehistory." In *Prehistory of Arid North Africa: Essays in Honor of Fred Wendorf*, ed. Angela E. Close, pp. 1–11. Dallas: Southern Methodist University Press.

Colton, Harold, and Lyn Hargrave. 1937. *Handbook of Northern Arizona Pottery Wares*. Bulletin no. 11. Flagstaff: Museum of Northern Arizona.

Eddy, Frank W., and Fred Wendorf, eds. 1999. *An Archaeological Investigation of the Central Sinai, Egypt*. Boulder: University Press of Colorado.

Frazer, Robert W. 1963. *Mansfield on the Condition of the Western Forts 1853–54.* Norman: University of Oklahoma Press.

Gladwin, Harold S. 1947. *Men out of Asia.* New York: Whittlesey House.

Hanotte, O., D. G. Bradley, J. W. Ochieng, Y. Verjee, E. W. Hill, and J. E. O. Rege. 2002. "African Pastoralism: Genetic Imprints of Origins and Migrations." *Science,* no. 5566 (April 12): 336–339.

Hester, James J., and James Schoenwetter, eds. 1964. *The Reconstruction of Past Environments.* Ranches of Taos, N.Mex.: Fort Burgwin Research Center.

Huzayyin, S. A. 1941. *The Place of Egypt in Prehistory: A Correlated Study of Climates and Cultures in the Old World.* Cairo: Impr. de l'Institut Français d'Archéologie Orientale.

Kelly, Raymond C. 2000. *Warless Societies and the Origin of War.* Ann Arbor: University of Michigan Press.

Lane, Lydia Spencer. 1893. *I Married a Soldier; or, Old Days in the Old Army.* Philadelphia: J. B. Lippincott.

Malville, J. McKim, Fred Wendorf, Ali A. Mazhar, and Romuald Schild. 1998. "Megaliths and Neolithic Astronomy in Southern Egypt." *Nature* 392 (April 2): 488–491.

Mansfield, Joseph K. F. 1853. "Report of Jos. K. F. Mansfield, Colonel and Inspector General, United States Army, Regarding His Inspection of the Department of New Mexico During the Summer and Fall of the year 1853." Manuscript in the library of the Laboratory of Anthropology, Santa Fe, New Mexico.

Martin, Paul S. 1962. Review of *Paleoecology of the Llano Estacado. Ecology* 43, no. 3 (July): 578–579.

"Midland Man." 1954. *Time,* July 12.

Nelson, Kit, and Associates. 2002. *Holocene Settlement of the Egyptian Sahara.* Vol. 2, *The Pottery of Nabta Playa.* New York: Kluwer Academic/Plenum Publishers.

Sandford, K. S., and W. J. Arkell. 1929. *Paleolithic Man and the Nile-Faiyum Divide; A Study of the Region during Pliocene and Pleistocene Times.* Chicago: University of Chicago Press.

———. 1933. *Paleolithic Man and the Nile Valley in Nubia and Upper Egypt; A Study of the Region during Pliocene and Pleistocene Times.* Chicago: University of Chicago Press.

———. 1939. *Paleolithic Man and the Nile Valley in Lower Egypt, with Some Notes upon a Part of the Red Sea Littoral; A Study of the Regions during Pliocene and Pleistocene Times.* Chicago: University of Chicago Press.

Scheidt, Walter. 1948. *Das Lehrbuch der Anthropologie.* Hamburg: R. Hermes.

Schild, Romuald, and Fred Wendorf. 1977. *The Prehistory of Dakhla Oasis and Adjacent Desert.* Warsaw: Polish Academy of Sciences.

———. 1981. *The Prehistory of an Egyptian Oasis: A Report of the Combined Prehistoric Expedition to Bir Sahara, Western Desert, Egypt.* Warsaw: Polish Academy of Sciences.

————. 1989. "The Late Pleistocene Nile in Wadi Kubbaniya." In *The Prehistory of Wadi Kubbaniya*, Fred Wendorf, Romuald Schild, and Angela E. Close, vol. 2:15–100. Dallas: Southern Methodist University Press.

Sears Roebuck Foundation. 1939. *House Wiring Made Easy: A Practical Guide for the Electrician and Homeowner.* Chicago: The Company.

"20,000-Year-Old American." 1954. *Life,* July 12, pp. 35–36.

Vignard, E. 1923. "Une nouvelle industrie lithique, le Sebilien." *Bulletin de l'Institut Français d'Archéologie Orientale* 22:1–76.

Wendorf, Fred. 1948. "Early Archaeological Sites in the Petrified Forest National Monument." *Plateau* 21 (2): 29–32.

————. 1950. *A Report on the Excavation of a Small Ruin near Point of Pines, East Central Arizona.* Tucson: University of Arizona Press.

————. 1954. "A Reconstruction of Northern Rio Grande Prehistory." *American Anthropologist* 56 (2): 200–227.

————. 1956. "Some Distributions of Settlement Patterns in the Pueblo Southwest." In *Prehistoric Settlement Patterns in the New World,* ed. Gordon Wiley, pp. 18–25. Viking Fund Publications in Anthropology, No. 23. New York: Wenner-Gren Foundation for Anthropological Research.

————. 1993. Book Review of *Impure Science. American Journal of Physical Anthropology* 92:401–409.

————, ed. 1956. *Pipeline Archaeology: Reports of Salvage Operations in the Southwest on El Paso Natural Gas Company Projects, 1950–1953.* Santa Fe: Laboratory of Anthropology; Flagstaff: Museum of Northern Arizona.

————. 1961. *Paleoecology of the Llano Estacado.* Santa Fe: Museum of New Mexico Press.

————. 1965. *Contributions to the Prehistory of Nubia.* Taos, N.Mex.: Fort Burgwin Research Center; Dallas: Southern Methodist University Press.

————. 1968. *The Prehistory of Nubia.* Taos, N.Mex.: Fort Burgwin Research Center; Dallas: Southern Methodist University Press.

Wendorf, Fred, A. D. Krieger, C. C. Albritton, and T. D. Stewart. 1955. *The Midland Discovery: A Report on the Pleistocene Human Remains from Midland, Texas.* Austin: University of Texas Press.

Wendorf, Fred, and Erik K. Reed. 1955. "An Alternative Reconstruction of Northern Rio Grande Prehistory." *El Palacio* 62 (5/6): 131–173.

Wendorf, Fred, and Romuald Schild. 1976. *Prehistory of the Nile Valley.* New York: Academic Press.

————. 1981. *The Prehistory of the Eastern Sahara.* New York: Academic Press.

———. 2001. "Conclusions." In *Holocene Settlement of the Egyptian Sahara*, vol. 1, *The Archaeology of Nabta Playa*, Fred Wendorf, Romuald Schild and Associate, pp. 648-675. New York: Kluwer Academic/Plenum Publishers.

———. 2005. "Brothers in Archaeology." *Before Farming* 2005/1 article 9:1–26.

Wendorf, Fred, Romuald Schild, Polydura Baker, Achilles Gautier, Laura Longo, and Amal Mohamad. 1997. *A Late Paleolithic Kill-Butchery-Camp in Upper Egypt.* Dallas: Department of Anthropology and Institute for the Study of Earth and Man, Southern Methodist University; Warsaw: Institute of Archaeology and Ethnology, Polish Academy of Sciences.

Wendorf, Fred, Romuald Schild, and Angela E. Close, eds.. 1980. *Loaves and Fishes: The Prehistory of Wadi Kubbaniya.* Dallas: Department of Anthropology, Institute for the Study of Earth and Man, Southern Methodist University.

———. 1984. *Cattle Keepers of the Eastern Sahara: The Neolithic of Bir Kiseiba.* Dallas: Department of Anthropology and Institute for the Study of Earth and Man, Southern Methodist University.

———. 1986. *The Prehistory of Wadi Kubbaniya.* Vol. 1, *The Wadi Kubbaniya Skeleton: A Late Paleolithic Burial from Southern Egypt.* Dallas: Southern Methodist University Press.

———. 1989. *The Prehistory of Wadi Kubbaniya.* Vol. 2, *Stratigraphy, Paleoeconomy, and Environment.* Dallas: Southern Methodist University Press.

———. 1989. *The Prehistory of Wadi Kubbaniya.* Vol. 3, *Late Paleolithic Archaeology.* Dallas: Southern Methodist University Press.

———. 1993. *Egypt during the Last Interglacial: The Middle Paleolithic of Bir Tarfawi and Bir Sahara East.* New York: Plenum Press.

Wendorf, Fred, Romuald Schild, Nabil El Hadidi, Angela E. Close, Michael Kobusiewicz, Hanna Wieckowska, Bahay Issawi, and Herbert Haas. 1979. "Use of Barley in the Egyptian Late Paleolithic." *Science* 205 (September 28): 1341–1347.

Index |

The initials, FW, indicate Fred Wendorf.

About the Author |

F RED WENDORF, HENDERSON-MORRISON PROFESSOR OF PREHISTORY EMERITUS, Southern Methodist University, grew up in Terrell, Texas, was wounded as a lieutenant serving in Italy during World War II, received his Ph.D. from Harvard, and spent more than sixty years as a field archaeologist in this country and in Africa. In 1987 he was elected to the National Academy of Sciences.